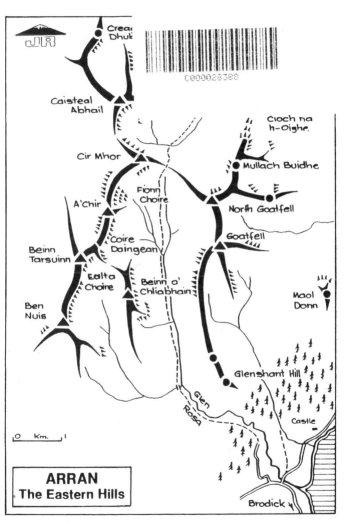

Richard Print.

ARRAN
The Eastern Hills

This guidebook is compiled from the most recent information and experience provided by members of the Scottish Mountaineering Club and other contributors. The book is published by the Scottish Mountaineering Trust, which is a charitable trust.

Revenue from the sale of books published by the Trust is used for the continuation of its publishing programme and for charitable purposes associated with Scottish mountains and mountaineering.

Arran, Arrochar

and the
Southern Highlands
Rock and Ice Climbs

*Graham Little, Tom Prentice
and Ken Crocket*

Edited by Roger Everett

'We began to understand,
a little less darkly,
what it may mean to inherit the Earth.'
W.H.Murray (1913-1996)
Mountaineering in Scotland

SCOTTISH MOUNTAINEERING CLUB
CLIMBERS' GUIDE

Published in Great Britain by the Scottish Mountaineering Trust,
1997

British Library Cataloguing in Publication Data
ISBN 0 907521-49-5

A catalogue record of this book is available from
The British Library

Diagrams by Davy Gardner
Maps by Jim Renny
Production by Scottish Mountaineering Trust (Publications) Ltd
Typeset by Elliot Robertson, Westec, North Connel
Printed by St Edmundsbury Press, Bury St Edmunds and
GNP-Booth, Clydebank
Bound by Hammond Bindery Ltd, Wakefield

Distributed by Cordee, 3a DeMontfort Street, Leicester LE1 7HD

Contents

Knapdale and Kintyre
by Graham Little

Loch Goil to Loch Fyne
by Tom Prentice

Arrochar
by Tom Prentice

The Bridge of Orchy Hills
by Ken Crocket

Other Hills and Crags in the Southern Highlands
by Ken Crocket

List of Illustrations

List of Diagrams and Maps

The Climber and the Mountain Environment

With increasing numbers of walkers and climbers going to the Scottish hills, it is important that all of us who do so should recognise our responsibilities to the mountain environment in which we find our pleasure and recreation, to our fellow climbers, and to those who live and work on the land.

The Scottish Mountaineering Club and Trust, who jointly produce this and other guidebooks, wish to point out to all who avail themselves of the information in these books that it is in everyone's interest that good relations are maintained between visitors and landowners, particularly when there might be conflicts of interest, for example during the stalking season. The description of a climbing, walking or skiing route in any of these books does not imply that a right of way exists, and it is the responsibility of all climbers to ascertain the position before setting out. In cases of doubt it is best to enquire locally.

During stalking and shooting seasons in particular, much harm can be done in deer forests and on grouse moors by people walking through them. Normally the deer stalking season is from 1st July to 20th October, when stag shooting ends. Hinds may continue to be culled until 15th February. The grouse shooting season is from 12th August until 10th December. These activities are important for the economy of many Highland estates. During these seasons, therefore, especial care should be taken to consult the local landowner, factor or keeper before taking to the hills.

Climbers and hill walkers are recommended to consult the book HEADING FOR THE SCOTTISH HILLS, published by the Scottish Mountaineering Trust on behalf of the Mountaineering Council of Scotland and the Scottish Landowners Federation, which gives the names and addresses of factors and keepers who may be contacted for information regarding access to the hills.

It is important not to disturb sheep, particularly during the lambing season between March and May. Dogs should not be taken onto the hills at this time, and at all times should be kept under close control.

Always try to follow a path or track through cultivated land and forests, and avoid causing damage to fences, dykes and gates by climbing over them carelessly. Do not leave litter anywhere, but take it down from the hill in your rucksack.

The number of walkers and climbers on the hills is leading to increased, and in some cases very unsightly erosion of footpaths and hillsides. Some of the revenue from the sale of this and other SMC guidebooks is used by the Trust to assist financially the work being carried out to repair and maintain hill paths in Scotland. However, it is important for all of us to recognise our responsibility to minimise the erosive effect of our passage over the hills so that the enjoyment of future climbers shall not be spoiled by damage caused by ourselves.

As a general rule, where a path exists walkers should follow it and even where it is wet and muddy should avoid walking along its edges, the effect of which is to extend erosion sideways. Do not take short-cuts at the corners of zigzag paths. Remember that the worst effects of erosion are likely to be caused during or soon after prolonged wet weather when the ground is soft and waterlogged. A route on stony or rocky hillside is likely to cause less erosion than on a grassy one at such times.

Although the use of bicycles can often be very helpful for reaching remote crags and hills, the erosion damage that can be caused by them when used 'off road' on soft footpaths and open hillsides is such that their use on such terrain must cause concern. It is the editorial policy of the Scottish Mountaineering Club that the use of bicycles in hill country may be recommended on hard tracks such as forest roads or private roads following rights of way, but it is not recommended on footpaths or open hillsides where the environmental damage that they cause may be considerable. Readers are asked to bear these points in mind, particularly when the ground is wet and soft after rain.

The proliferation of cairns on hills detracts from the feeling of wildness, and may be confusing rather than helpful as regards route-finding. The indiscriminate building of cairns on the hills is therefore to be discouraged.

Climbers are reminded that they should not drive along private estate roads without permission, and when parking their cars should avoid blocking access to private roads and land, and should avoid causing any hazard to other road users.

Finally, the Scottish Mountaineering Club and the Scottish Mountaineering Trust can accept no liability for damage to property nor for personal injury resulting from the use of in their publications.

The Mountaineering Council of Scotland is the representative body for climbers and walkers in Scotland. One of its primary concerns is the continued free access to the hills and crags that we now enjoy. Information about bird restrictions, stalking and general access issues can be obtained from the Access and Conservation Officer of the MCofS at 4a St Catherines's Road, Perth PH1 5SE (tel: 01738 638 227).

Acknowledgements

This guidebook could not have been produced without the extensive help of a large number of people in various capacities, including providing information, checking routes, commenting on the text, submitting photographs, proof reading and helping the authors do some on-site research. We thank them all:

Arran:
Bill Skidmore, Kevin Howett, Gary Latter, Andrew Fraser, Calum Smith, Richard Gatehouse, Robin McAllister, Jim Perrin, Bruce Goodlad, Bob Carchrie, Simon Berry, Alastair Matthewson and Neil Stevenson.

Cara, Kintyre and Knapdale:
Bob Reid, Kevin Howett, Bill Skidmore and Ian Taylor

Arrochar:
Rab Anderson, Toby Archer, Rick Campbell, Dave Cuthbertson, Grant Farquhar, Andrew Fraser, Mark Garthwaite, Bruce Goodlad, Gary Latter, Robin McAllister, Dave McGimpsey, Alec Keith, Nick Kempe, Stuart Mearns, Pat Mitchell, Colin Moody, Andrew Ogilvie, Bob Reid, Simon Richardson, Klaus Schwartz, Alan Shand, Nick Smith, Neil Stevenson, Ian Taylor and Paul Thorburn. Particular thanks are due to Rab Anderson, Gary Latter and Simon Richardson for detailed comments on the text.

The Southern Highlands:
Simon Richardson, Andy Nisbet, Brian Dullea, Alastair Matthewson, Andrew Fraser, Ian Taylor, Neil Stevenson, Dave McGimpsey, Andrew Ogilvie, Nick Smith, Erik Brunskill, Alec Keith, Pat Mitchell, Alastair Walker and Toby Archer.

In addition, this guide has been enhanced by the new series of diagrams specially drawn by Davy Gardner and by Jim Renny's maps. Donald Bennet as usual did an excellent job during the production of the book, and Roger Everett pulled together all our individual efforts in his role as Series Editor.

Introduction

To attempt a comprehensive climbers' guide which encompasses an area extending from Stob Ghabhar in the Blackmount in the north, to the near-tropical crags of the Mull of Kintyre in the south, may have been a daunting task for its three authors. It is one however which was gladly accepted. The range and style of climbing to be found in this area never fails to engage interest, whether in summer or winter. On rock you may be handling rough granite, wrinkly schist, smooth quartzite, perfect granodiorite; in winter you could be on the steepest water ice or wending your way up a mixed buttress of frozen turf and snow, at any angle.

The Isle of Arran, truly a jewel in the crown for any country, lies smack in the Firth of Clyde, a few short hours from Central Scotland's conurbations. Protected by the minor inconvenience of ferry time-tables, it remains a relatively quiet backwater, despite some of the best rock climbing in Scotland. While conditions are admittedly more difficult to predict than usual, there remain on Arran scores of superb winter lines for the taking.

The Arrochar Alps, as they have long been fondly named, remain popular in summer, with The Cobbler in particular seeing several recent ascents at the very highest levels of commitment and technical difficulty. Thankfully, the classic mid-grade rock climbs remain high on climbers' agendas.

Perhaps the greatest significant shift since the previous edition of 1989 has been the emergence of The Cobbler and Arrochar, and the maturation of the Southern Highlands, as winter climbing areas. No longer does the winter expert have to continue northwards to Glen Coe and Ben Nevis to find testing winter routes. The development of winter climbing in these areas has been dynamic, and there are now well over forty routes of Grade V and harder, including VII and VIII. These routes make higher technical demands of the climber; few of them providing long stretches of straightforward ice. Rather, you may have to work hard at finding protection, rests and pick placements. When properly frozen, Southern Highland turf is arguably one of the best climbing materials in the world. Long looked on as being useful for a day's outing when time was short, the Southern Highlands have now come of age, while Arrochar is only just beginning to have its true winter significance realised. With the greater ease of travel, the corries of the Southern Highlands are now ringing to a wider range of accents, many of them on day trips from the North of England.

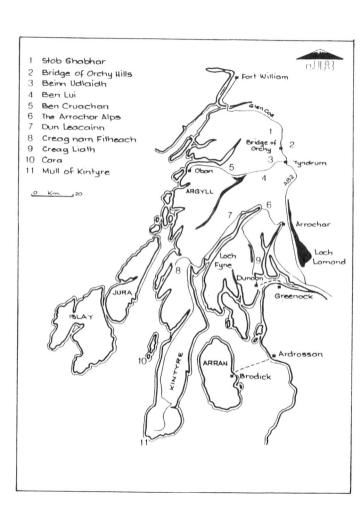

1 Stob Ghabhar
2 Bridge of Orchy Hills
3 Beinn Udlaidh
4 Ben Lui
5 Ben Cruachan
6 The Arrochar Alps
7 Dun Leacainn
8 Creag nam Fitheach
9 Creag Liath
10 Cora
11 Mull of Kintyre

New to this climbers' guide are several hills and indeed ranges, such as Ben Lawers and the Tarmachans. These can provide a good variety of middle grade climbs, which are especially useful early in the season given snow and a freeze. For the first time in a modern guide, the climbs on the surprisingly remote corries of Ben Lomond have been included, as are several other scattered classic peaks. And lastly, to gladden the hearts of the crag rat, the secrets of the Mull of Kintyre have been unlocked, with its multitude of short and exciting crags. As always, the present authors have leant for support on the guidebooks by earlier writers. These include: Jim Johnstone, Bill Wallace, Jock Nimlin, Ben Humble, Jimmy Houston and Alastair Walker. Each, in their own way, remains a part of this guide.

Ken Crocket, Graham Little, Tom Prentice
March 1997.

Geology

The area covered by this guide is very rich in geological structures and history. The island of Arran alone has been the subject of much study and several books. Accordingly this note must be a very cursory one. Generally speaking, the further north one goes within the area of this guide, the older the rocks, for the most part beautifully folded metamorphic rocks known as schists. Belonging to the Dalradian succession, these metamorphic rocks are mainly of late-Precambrian and Cambrian age, which makes some of them over 570 million years old. They lie north of the Highland Boundary Fault, which runs north-east to south-west across Scotland from Stonehaven to Arran and on even to Northern Ireland. This fault, which helped preserve younger rocks in the Midland Valley, threw up the rocks to the north, so that later erosion revealed the older rocks below. These Dalradian rocks, whose total thickness may be over 16km, were probably deposited in a shallow sea. As this marine basin continued to sink, erosion on the surrounding land fed more material, building up layer upon layer of sedimentary rocks – grits, conglomerates, muds and greywackes. We may imagine huge deltas, muddy lagoons, shallow seas with islands. Unfortunately, the fossil record is poor. Deposition of sediments could vary from day to day, with slow gentle deposition giving fine layers, and a flood or marine slide forming a conglomerate. Layers formed could be maintained through later changes, so today we see the layered rocks of Arrochar, with scalloped holds perhaps formed by the slightly different rates of weathering between the layers.

Eventually, massive crustal movements heaved this area upwards, building mountains comparable to the present-day Alps. At depth, great heat and pressure, increasing to the north, transformed the soft sedimentary rocks to harder, more resistant metamorphics – mica-schists, schists, quartzites. This graded metamorphism is seen when comparing the more altered and compact rocks of the Bridge of Orchy hills with the softer schists of the Arrochar area. The elevation and metamorphism was around 400 million years ago, with associated and very complicated folding, the unravelling of which delights professional geologists. Erosion then stripped away younger rocks, revealing the more resistant rocks familiar to climbers in the Highlands.

Some schists contain the dark red gemstone garnet, visibly projecting out of boulders in, for example, some of the Bridge of Orchy hills. Truly huge examples – almost 2cm square – have been seen in the rocks of the Tarmachans. Look for dull, rusty-looking projections. Large crystals of the dark mica, biotite, may be found on The Cobbler, while varieties of quartz crystals have been described in the gullies of Beinn Dubh. Many rock climbs on schist have thin veins of white quartz; these should be treated with caution, as they are often brittle and can snap under weight. Anyone who has dossed in the various howffs in the Arrochar area can hardly have failed to notice afterwards their equipment sparkling with minute crystals of white mica, muscovite, another silicate mineral commonly found in these metamorphic rocks.

Dalradian rocks are found on Arran too, in the north of the island. Younger rocks are also present; Old Red Sandstone, Permian, Carboniferous, with a limestone at Corrie. Landing at Brodick, one will be struck by the handsome red of the Permian, laid down as breccias and dune-sandstones when the environment must have been desert. But the rock of interest to climbers forms the magnificent hills on the northern half of the island, a coarse granite intruded during the Tertiary age – along with the classic mountains of the Black Cuillin of Skye, Rum, Mull, Ardnamurchan and St Kilda. The Tertiary age began about 65 million years ago. The sequence of volcanic events in Arran probably followed a well known pattern, with a volcano pouring out lavas then a deep-seated, dome-shaped intrusion of biotite-granite. The coarse granite is about 13km in diameter, circular in outline, and stretches from Beinn Nuis to Goatfell, forming the jagged outlines and spectacular ridges popular with climbers and walkers. A younger inner granite, finer-grained, lies mostly west of Glen Iorsa, giving rounder and lower hills. The granite is coarse due to slow cooling at depth allowing longer crystal growth.

The circular granite complex is bounded by a fault on part of the eastern side; on both sides the surrounding country rock has been pushed up by the granite. The granite weathers to form rounded edges and massive Cyclopean blocks, so that the climbing may switch between the easy and the desperate in a few moves. Other intrusive rocks make their presence known by crumbling gullies and chimneys, formed by the erosion of dykes of various ages. Arran has a very dense swarm of these dykes, mostly in a north-north-west to south-south-east direction, linking Islay and Jura with the Girvan area. Most of them are formed of quartz dolerite. The Witch's Step, or Ceum na Caillich, was formed by the erosion of just such a vertical dyke. The cliff at Drumadoon Point is another intrusion, this time in the form of a sill, or flat sheet. Other igneous rocks are to be found in this guide, including

Dun Leacainn and Creag nam Fitheach. Look for the columnar structure on the left-hand pillar of the former, formed while cooling, and the rough gabbro-like rock of the latter, squeezed through the surrounding Dalradian rocks and finally exposed by millions of years' erosion.

The great igneous activity of the Tertiary, then forming lava flows and intrusions, dramatically manifested itself in a line of volcanoes where the Inner Hebrides now lie. Further west, a second major rift in the huge land mass that included the future Greenland and part of North America began to form, slowly breaking apart the land. The Atlantic Ocean was born, and with it Scotland, waltzing away from what would become Newfoundland. The land was higher then, and most rivers in this new country flowed east. The River Clyde was a tributary of the Forth. Several rivers flowed east across what would become Loch Long, just south of Arrochar, one taking a route through Glen Douglas. Gradually, with a widening Atlantic and fast erosion, short west-flowing rivers cut back into the hinterland, pushing the watershed further east. This took place for a period of over 60 million years, interrupted only by the coming of the ice.

Global warming, evidence for which began to mount in the 1980s, has become an accepted fact. Pollution, causing a reduction in the protective ozone layer high in the atmosphere, has been blamed. One million years ago however, before man began polluting the planet, there was a major climatic shift to a colder period, cause unknown. Winters became longer, snow began to lie through the year, flowing downhill as glaciers. The Ice Age had begun. It was to last, with many retreats and advances, until about 10,000 years ago, a mere cosmic blink. The moving ice sculpted the landscape, forming and reforming the shapes of the mountains, to leave them substantially as they are today. Some cliffs were, and still are, changed by rockfall, the expansion of freezing water in cracks and other physical forces acting with sometimes dramatic effect. Beinn an Lochain is more unstable than most crags, something to be remembered during a thaw. In essence, that particular crag is slowly peeling away from the hillside. In general though, compared to our short life-spans, the rocks remain true and constant friends.

History

ARRAN

It was the splendid ridges that first promoted Arran as a climbing centre and a number of early Scottish Mountaineering Club meets were held there in the 1890s and early 1900s. The A'Chir Ridge (Moderate) resisted a number of strong attempts before the first traverse was completed by a large party in January 1892 (the ridge was not in winter conditions at the time).

When all the ridges had been fully explored, climbers turned their attention to Arran's many, though not particularly attractive, gullies. Much tweed and damp granite contact was made with the highlight of this era being the first ascent of the Gully 3 on Beinn Nuis, more commonly known as the Nuis Chimney, in August 1901. It has since been regarded as the best gully-chimney climb on the island (no particular distinction!). The first ascent team of Messrs Baker, Oppenheimer and Puttrell used combined tactics to surmount the first pitch, then made a number of excursions onto the adjacent walls to outflank seemingly impossible pitches in the chimney. This route, the first to be graded VS on the island, went unrepeated for many years. A handful of open face routes were also climbed on the great North-East Face of Cir Mhor during this period, including the thrutchy Bell's Groove (Very Difficult) by Bell and Green and Pinnacle Ridge (Difficult) by MacLay and Naismith in 1894. Most significantly, the exposed and serious B2C Rib (Very Difficult) was climbed by Bell, Boyd, Green and Napier in July 1895, a route years ahead of its time. The infamous ledges of Cioch na h'Oighe were also climbed in 1894. To quote from a comprehensive article on Arran climbing by Harry MacRobert in the 1908 Scottish Mountaineering Club Journal, there was 'much scrambling in curious places'.

Early winter exploration is not well documented, although a futuristic attempt on April Arete in February 1892 by Lawson, MacLay and Raeburn is recorded, and Ednie, Goodeve and McIntyre made an ascent of Pinnacle Ridge in December 1906 (although it is doubtful whether it was in full winter condition at the time). Perhaps the first confirmed winter ascent on Arran was MacRobert's solo ascent of Gully 4 (Grade III) on Beinn Nuis in the winter of 1907 under deep snow.

Over thirty years elapsed before further exploration took place, perhaps due to a reputation the island had gained for poor and vegetated

The Three Tier Chimney, Rosa Pinnacle

rock. However, South Ridge, Original Route (VS) by J. A.Ramsay and party in 1936 and Easter Route (HVS) by K.Barber and A.S.Pigott in 1938 confounded this reputation and signalled the potential of the South Face of Cir Mhor. This latter route, originally undergraded at Severe, was considered the hardest climb on the island at the time. In September 1941, J.F.Hamilton and D.Paterson made the first ascent of South Ridge Direct (VS), now regarded as one of Scotland's great classic rock climbs, which heralded a thorough investigation of Arran's rock climbing potential.

The next wave of exploration was by a small group of climbers based at the Admiralty Anti-Submarine Depot at Fairlie with Geoffrey Curtis, Ken Moneypenny and Gordon Townend being the main activists. After repeating South Ridge Direct they went on to develop the South Face of Cir Mhor and many other of the island's best cliffs over a period of four years. Considering the very basic climbing equipment used (initially only a natural fibre yachting rope and no karabiners), their achievements were notable; opening up the Coire Daingean cliffs, venturing onto the Meadow Face and the East Face of Beinn Nuis, and discovering the buttresses of Coire na h'Uaimh and Torr Nead an Eoin. Their catalogue of first ascents is impressive, with Caliban's Creep (Very Difficult), Sou'wester Slabs (Very Difficult), Labyrinth (Very Difficult), Prospero's Peril (Severe), Pagoda Ridge (Severe) and Midnight Ridge Direct (VS) being the best. The myth that Arran climbs were all loose and vegetated was now well and truly dismissed.

In 1946 Nuis Chimney received a second and complete ascent, the leader, 'Bim' Dowman, using the shoulders and head of Paddy Buckley to surmount the crux, Buckley employing the handy wing spar of an Allied bomber (called Skipper and the Kids) to follow. Later that year a jammed inflatable life raft was removed on abseil by the Fell and Rock Club!

Between 1947 and 1957 little of importance was discovered, although a few minor routes were climbed by J.M.Johnstone and friends during research for the first Arran rock climbing guide which was published in 1958. This slim and now very collectable guide included some superb diagrams. A notable exception was the ascent of The Sickle in November 1957 by J.H.Ashford and D.Burke which appeared fairly well down the graded list in the 1958 guide, yet was probably the hardest climb on Arran at the time; even with modern protection it is still regarded as a serious HVS route. In 1958 Davy McKelvie and Dick Sim climbed the formidable Minotaur on the Rosa

Bill Skidmore on the first winter ascent of the Nuis Chimney

Pinnacle by mistake whilst looking for Labyrinth. At a meaty HVS (now E1) it was some mistake! Bill Wallace, often with Hugh Stirling, also started to record routes at about this time and he was to go on to develop an intimate knowledge of the Arran hills.

In the 1960s harder new routes started to be produced although they often relied on aid sections or on the odd pull or rest on gear whilst gardening. 1960 saw the further development of the Lower West Face of the Rosa Pinnacle with the fine routes Hammer by Donny Cameron and Sim and Anvil by McKelvie and Bob Richardson being climbed on the same day. Although only Severe in grade, the ascent of Tidemark on Coich na h-Oighe in 1960 was very significant, initiating Andrew Maxfield's productive association with Arran and sowing the seeds for the hard routes of the late 1960s and 1970s. Bill Skidmore also entered the scene at this time and in 1962, accompanied by Bob Richardson, climbed The Rake (E2) on the Meadow Face, the first of the big routes on this complex face. They also attempted the crack lines that were later to become Brachistochrone and Bogle, but they failed on the crux pitches due to a lack of suitable pegs. The highlight of 1963 was the ascent of West Flank Route, which takes a splendid natural line up the great sweep of slabs on the Lower West Face of Rosa Pinnacle. Skidmore and Richardson were joined by Jim Crawford and John Madden for this climb. In recognition of the serious and sustained nature of the introductory chimneys this route has been upgraded to E1 in this guide. In 1965 Bill Wallace and Hugh Stirling greatly improved Slapstick Wall (Severe) on the Lower Slabs of Coire na h-Uaimh by adding the shelf variation to the J-pitch, still probably the best pitch of its grade on Arran.

The Squirrels from Edinburgh began climbing on Arran in the mid-1960s, exploring the South Slabs and other areas. Their best contribution, however, was undoubtedly Brachistochrone (E1) on the Meadow Face, finally climbed in 1966, by Mike Galbraith and 'Bugs' McKeith, using bongs to surmount the overhangs. The companion route Bogle (E2) was climbed by Ian Rowe and Ian Dundas in 1967, again using aid to overcome the crux. Over on The Bastion of Cioch na h-Oighe, Andrew Maxfield and Bob Wilde struggled up the big corner-groove line to create Klepht (E2), confirming Maxfield's eye for a good line and an appropriate name (a Greek mountain brigand). Although a significant amount of undeclared aid was used, this was a major achievement, vying only with Bogle as the hardest climb on Arran at that time. In 1968 Maxfield discovered the striking wall of Cuithe Mheadhonach and established a number of routes including the characterful Fuocco (VS). Tragically, he died soloing on the Aberdeen sea-cliffs, but he left a great legacy of Arran climbs and a vision of future direction.

1968 turned out to be a vintage year with the superb Mosque (VS) on the Coire Daingean Face of A'Chir from Ian Fulton and J.Shaw, Pothole Slab (HVS) on Cir Mhor from Skidmore and John Gillespie, and the steep Bluff (E2) on the Rosa Pinnacle by Hugh Donohoe and E.McLelland. Ian Rowe together with Sandy Trees and Mike Watson indulged in a two-day horticultural debauch to produce the mighty Silo (ungradeable!), tackling the full height of the messy North-East Face of Cir Mhor and developing Rowe's addiction to vegetated granite. The following year Rab Carrington, climbing with Ian Fulton, made his mark on the island with the ascent of The Curver (E1) on the Meadow Face and the harder Insertion (E3) on the Rosa Pinnacle. Both are serious slab climbs, the latter being a significant step forward in commitment and difficulty. Graham Little, accompanied by J.Dykes, also put up his first Arran new route in 1969, the obscure Voodoo Chile (originally HVS) on the Full Meed Tower which has matured with age and aid elimination into one of Arran's least known gems.

Early in 1970 Bill Wallace completed a new edition of the Arran Guide, producing a very readable book. February 1970 also saw the first of the modern winter routes on the island with Skidmore and Crawford's ascent of the Nuis Chimney (V,6) in 'solid state'. Large quantities of ice were present together with war time debris from a plane crash. Added to the technical difficulties of this fine route was the danger of striking live ammunition! Later that year Rowe, climbing with Blyth Wright, beat Carrington and Higgins to the dubious prize of Right On, taking a fairly central line (using much aid) up the East Face of Beinn Nuis and described in his classic article 'MacFaustus'.

The 1970s saw renewed activity on the Meadow Face with Skidmore and Crawford struggling with their consciences and a very steep corner to produce The Blinder (E1). In 1973 Skidmore and Gillespie, on the trail of Maxfield, put up Stoic (HVS) on Cuithe Mheadhonach. In 1975 Ian Duckworth, J.Fraser and G.Smith climbed the great edge to the right of The Blinder, consolidating on the earlier efforts of Rowe's indirect ascent, and a direct start was added by Geoff Cohen. The name Brobdingnag (E2), after the land of the giants in Gulliver's Travels, was very appropriate and continued the alliterative theme on the cliff. In 1976 Jim Perrin and partner freed the aid from a number of routes on the Meadow Face, most notably Bogle.

The hot summer of 1977 heralded renewed activity on the Bastion which was to result in the highest concentration of hard, high quality routes on Arran. That year saw the ascent of the slabby Gazebo (E1) by Skidmore and Walker but much more importantly Armadillo (E3), the spectacular roofed groove to the right of Klepht, by Skidmore and Richardson, fulfilling Maxfield's vision of the previous decade. In May 1979 Skidmore joined forces with Graham and Rob Little to climb the Black Cave Pillar (HVS) in the south of the island. Skidmore then introduced Graham Little to the Bastion, initiating a third wave of compulsive development. Little's first route, climbed solo using a back rope, was Rhino (E2) followed in 1980 by the stunning although much more controversial Abraxas (E4), climbed with his brother Rob and employing twelve points of aid and bolt belays (considered excessive, if not unprecedented, even by Arran standards!). This route, however involved sustained technical difficulty and a degree of exposure not hitherto experienced on Arran. In 1981 Little made a second and direct ascent of Klepht with Colin Ritchie and climbed Digitalis (E2) with Skidmore on the fine pillar to the left of Klepht (named after the bunch of foxgloves at its base). Over on the Rosa Pinnacle, Little and Ritchie made an on sight ascent of Skydiver (E3), enjoying a few falls and the best pitch on Arran. This ascent used some aid, but in 1984 Andy Nisbet and Colin MacLean made the first free ascent and added a more logical finish, to complete a route of outstanding quality, comparable with the best in Britain. In 1979 a revised edition of the Arran guide was published with a supplement by Bill Skidmore which included the HVS grade for the first time! This (sadly) was to be the last climbing guide book solely dedicated to Arran.

In 1979 and the early 1980s a series of good winters saw an unprecedented amount of new routing, with Calum Smith and Graham Little being the prime movers. Smith, with a variety of partners, and Little climbing solo, bagged most of the gullies and ice smears on Cir Mhor, with Gully C (V,5) and Pan's Pipe (IV,3) being their best routes respectively. In February 1983 an Aberdonian raiding party paid a visit, making the first winter ascent of Labyrinth (IV,5) and North-East Face Route (IV,4) on Cir Mhor, both of high quality, the latter an uninspired name but a significant progression onto a big complex face.

In 1982 Little turned his attention to Cuithe Mheadhonach in Coire nan Ceum climbing the fine Ulysses (E2) with Skidmore. This was to be Skidmore's last new route on the island. In April 1984 Little provoked further controversy with his route Achilles (originally E3) on the 'blank' wall to the right of Ulysses. On the unseconded first ascent he used two shallow drilled brass rivets (normally used to mark survey stations on road kerbs!) to pass a short holdless section but after the

Graham Little on the first ascent of Abraxas, Cioch na h-Oighe

ascent he roped down and replaced them with one bolt. The bolt hanger was later removed by another party but a number of attempts to free the route were unsuccessful. More traditionally, Craig Macadam and Simon Steer climbed the bold One Eyed Jacks (E3) the following month. Two different styles of new routing had now developed on Arran, one involving pre-cleaning on abseil, the other more traditional, involving on sight ascents but with rests on gear to clean critical sections.

The mid-1980s saw a determined attempt to free Arran routes of their aid, with Craig Macadam foremost in this movement. In 1985 he freed Armadillo and Abraxas accompanied by Simon Steer and Derek Austin respectively, then added his own bold routes Beyond the Pale (E2) and Vanishing Point (E4) on Cir Mhor, both with Simon Steer. Frustrated at being pipped at the post for the first free ascent of Abraxas by one day, Dave Cuthbertson and Kevin Howett put up Token Gesture, the first E5 on Arran, but sharing some common ground with its close neighbour Rhino. This route had been cleaned and attempted only two days earlier by Macadam, Steer and Andy Tibbs!

Winter climbing interest now concentrated on the more tenuous lines on Arran's open faces. In 1985 Little and Smith teamed up to climb the classic Pinnacle Ridge (III,4) on Cir Mhor and the technical Riddle (V,6) on the headwall of Coire Daingean. The following year Little, this time climbing with Dave Saddler, picked the plumb with the ascent of Once in a Lifetime (VII,6) on the vast North-East face of Cir Mhor. This long committing route, probably the best and certainly the hardest winter route on Arran, followed the approximate line of Rowe's Silo, realising the dream of a number of Arran enthusiasts. In 1987 the same pair made the first winter ascent of April Arete (IV,5), 94 years after the first attempt! A number of easier winter routes were also produced in the late 1980s in a variety of different locations by Alastair Walker and Fraser McKie (often climbing solo).

In 1986 Mark Charlton and Kevin Howett straightened out Insertion at E5 and added their own route West Point (E4) to the Rosa Pinnacle. The late 1980s saw the thorough development of the lichenous cliff at Drumadoon Point by a variety of activists and the addition of a very good direct start to The Rake (E1) on the Meadow Face by George McEwan and Alastair Walker. 1989 heralded the publication of a new guide book with Arran lumped in with part of mainland Scotland. It received mixed reviews!

The early 1990s saw remarkably little new route activity. Little soloed a handful of winter routes in 1991, the best being Hellfire Crack

Graham Little on the first ascent of Ulysses, Cuithe Mheadhonach

(IV,4) on Caisteal Abhail. George Szuca climbed a couple of routes including the surprisingly good Crystal (VS) on the North-East Face of Cir Mhor and a number of variations (including the excellent edge variation (VS) to the J-pitch on Slapstick Wall). He also opened up some rather esoteric minor outcrops. In 1993 and 1994 Andrew Fraser and friends put up a few routes around the Full Meed Tower, including the splendidly named All Along the Watchtower (HVS) by Fraser, Robin McAllister and Mike Reed, while McAllister freed the last few aid points on Voodoo Chile (E2). In 1994, whilst checking out route descriptions for this guide, Little plugged the obvious gap on the Lower Slabs producing The Key (HVS) – an exciting solo!

During the superb summer of 1995 activity hotted up and the mountain crags saw some serious action when Howett and Little climbed the desperate Icarus (E5) on Cuithe Mheadhonach. Only two weeks later Howett and Little brought the saga of Achilles to a happy conclusion when they free climbed the problematic bypass to the original aided section, producing an outstanding and sustained route (E5). That same weekend they made an on sight ascent of Blundecral (E3), plugging the obvious gap on the Meadow Face. Two weeks later the same pair added a couple of routes to the South Slabs, including the excellent Blankist (HVS). Only four weeks after the first ascent of Blundecral, Fraser and McAllister made the unwitting second ascent of its first three pitches, then added their own Blunderbuss Finish (HVS). They returned to the Meadow Face at the tail end of the summer, climbing from right to left across the face and linking a selection of routes, to produce the long awaited Gulliver's Travels (E2), the longest extreme on the island.

The very cold pre-Christmas week of 1995 saw a number of parties active on the East Face of Ben Nuis. At the end of March 1996 Little and Scott Muir climbed four short routes on the flanks of Western Stoneshoot – the coldest place on Arran!

The cool spring of 1996 saw Little and Howett back into action with a number of new routes in traditional places, including the brilliant Squids and Elephants (E1) on the Lower East Face of Cir Mhor (worth three stars for the name alone!). In July, accompanied by Lawrence Hughes, they eventually climbed the bold and desperate The Brigand (E6) on The Bastion of Cioch na h' Oighe after a spring attempt had been foiled by a snowstorm! In hot August weather Robin McAllister and Dave McGimpsey completed the logical and bold Blundecral True Finish (E5).

KNAPDALE AND KINTYRE

The relatively recently climbing development of the Mull of Kintyre reflects its isolated position. The rock climbing potential was only first appreciated in 1991 by Bill Skidmore who has since adopted the role of local guru and has participated in a number of the first ascents. The first route of any consequence was the splendid Rites of Passage (HVS) by Graham Little, Bill Skidmore and Bob Reid in August 1992, confirming the quality of the rock and initiating Little's sustained affair with the area.

In the early stages of development many of the routes were led on sight, but as action transferred onto more difficult lines and onto crags composed of softer rock, pre-cleaning became the standard approach. This led to the creation of the fine two pitch lines on Signal Wall, commencing with the excellent Hornblower (E2) from Reid and Little in September 1992.

In early 1993, Little introduced Kevin Howett to the delights of the Mull and another addict was born. This partnership, with the addition of the occasional guest, went on to produce a series of fine routes. They opened up the higher crags as well as adding harder lines to those already under development. These included such gems as Caulking Wall (E2) in 1992, The Children of the Open Sea (E2) in 1993 and Kissing the Gunners Daughter (E4) and Wall of the Winds (E2) in 1994. In 1995 and 1996 more routes were added with Creag na Lice, in particular, providing routes of surprising quality. These included Sixth Sense (E1) from Scott Muir and others (a magnificent line, inexplicably missed by the earlier pioneers) and the mighty Continuous Air Play (E5) from Howett and Lawrence Hughes.

Considerable scope for exploratory rock climbing remains, especially on the coastal crags, for those prepared to make the long drive to this otherwise obscure backwater.

The climbing in Knapdale has a rather longer history. Alex Small visited Creag nam Fitheach in the 1940s, appreciating its potential and probably making the first ascent of the route later to be called Moby Dick (Very Difficult). In the late 1970s, D.Hayter and friends reported having climbed on the crag, although no routes were properly recorded. Graham Little rediscovered the crag in 1981, and together with Colin Ritchie and Peter Linning climbed most of the obvious lines. Dave Griffiths plugged the gaps in the late 1980s and added the excellent sustained test-piece of Crystal Vision (E5). In 1990, belay bolts were sadly and unjustifiably placed along the top of the crag by a local outdoor centre.

ARROCHAR

In the early development of mountaineering in this area of Scotland, two factors were predominant: the great industrial city of Glasgow with its large and energetic population, and the presence of Professor George Ramsay at the University of Glasgow. Ramsay was an experienced Alpinist by the 1860s. In 1866 he founded the Cobbler Club, an informal group who were probably the earliest climbing, as opposed to walking group, in this region.

The choice of The Cobbler for the Club name was no accident. That visually striking peak above the head of Loch Long was also within striking distance of Glasgow, at a time when communication through such rough country was exceedingly difficult and slow. For a long time the easiest way to reach Arrochar, at the top of Loch Long, was by steamer, and there are hilarious stories of climbing parties trying to accommodate a day on the hill with the timetable strictures of hotels, steamers and trains, for the railway line, that great opener of countries, had reached Tyndrum by 1880. By 1895, indeed, Ernest Maylard, an active Glasgow climber, apologised for describing The Cobbler, as it was by then familiar to so many.

In 1872, as Willie Naismith later recorded, Ramsay gave his junior latin class a lecture on Alpine climbing, a seminal event for both Naismith and Scottish Mountaineering, for Naismith went on to become a founder member of the Scottish Mountaineering Club with Ramsay as its first President, in 1889. Until that point, Ramsay later wrote, he had never, with the exception of Professor Veitch, 'met with a single Scotsman who cared seriously to practise the art of mountaineering.' Naismith, whose first ascent list included the North-East Buttress on Ben Nevis in winter, was also resident in Glasgow. Writing to the *Glasgow Herald* in January 1889 to suggest the formation of a 'Scottish Alpine Club', Naismith would become known as the 'Father of the Club'.

In July, 1889, with the SMC only a few months old, Naismith and Gilbert Thomson recorded The Arete on The Cobbler, a pleasant and exposed Difficult leading to the summit of the Centre Peak. In October of the same year, Thomson and friends climbed the classic South-East Ridge on The Cobbler's South Peak. Though only of Moderate grade, this fine mountain route has several good, exposed situations, and can be linked with The Arete to gain the highest point on the mountain. It was to be the seed crystal for other routes climbed during this first, 'classic' period.

1894 was a year for successful ascents on The Cobbler, Naismith and Thomson climbing the South Peak by the shorter Original Route. This section of the South Peak was then explored further, leading to a fine ascent of North-West Crack in September 1898, with James Rennie. Climbed on awkwardly placed holds, this VS 4c indicates the high technical ability of Naismith. Two years earlier, Naismith and MacGregor climbed Right-Angled Gully, Very Difficult, an excellent route on the North Peak. If you think the Doorway Route to the summit of Centre Peak, with its window and exposed traverse is a doddle, try MacGregor's Ledge, climbed in 1895.

In October 1896, a pair of hard men from the East visited The Cobbler—Willie Tough (pronounced tooch) and Harold Raeburn. They attempted what was to become Ramshead Gully, failing due to ice. A traverse right across the Halfway Terrace then led to The Fold, the crux pitch of Recess Route, which they declined to attempt, reversing their steps. Instead, they made the second ascent of Right-Angled Gully, typically attempting the Direct Finish and getting to within 5m of the top. Raeburn admitted that it was 'clearly impossible, a snow cornice several feet thick overhanging its outlet.' Hard men indeed! Instead, they 'escaped to the right by a most convenient grass ledge, and gained the summit by a steep fifteen-foot rock wall'. With the snow line lying at about 1,000 feet, this was probably the route's first winter ascent. As a reminder of Raeburn's renowned determination, he returned in October 1904 and climbed The Fold, in the company of several ladies.

At the end of 1896, Raeburn joined the SMC. Living in Edinburgh, the long journey across the country was not impossible, but made day outings very difficult. He left his mark in the Arrochar district however, with the Cave Route on The Cobbler's Centre Peak Buttress in 1898, climbed with Rennie, as well as the crux pitch of Recess Route.

Another raiding party from Edinburgh was that of the Inglis Clark family. William, a successful chemist, visited The Brack in July 1895 with his daughter Mabel and son Charles. They climbed the Moderate Arete which bears their name. Charles, who died in the Great War, would inspire the CIC Hut on Ben Nevis, which was built in his memory. Also on The Brack, the Difficult Elephant Gully, named because its lush vegetation was 'sufficient to feed a herd of elephants', was climbed in 1906 by McLaren and the Shadbolts, gully and chimney experts all. In the same period they climbed the Very Difficult McLaren's Chimney on Creag Tharsuinn. This latter crag had been opened up by Maclay, who had climbed his eponymous Gully in April 1900.

This busy time of exploration, lasting from about 1894 to 1906, was the first of three recognisable periods of activity in the area. It must have been a great time, with every climb either a first, or a second ascent. As it turned out, it was the Golden Age. Scottish mountaineering then went through its Middle Ages, plunging even deeper into the mirk with the Great War. Nothing was done, or could be done, as all energy went into that horrendous conflict.

We have to jump to 1921, with Garrick's Route on Creag Tharsuinn. Very Difficult in summer, it bridged that long gap between the classic age and the new age just about to begin, with an awakening awareness of the great outdoors and new blood keen to leave the cities. This lonely ascent echoes that of Raeburn's in 1920 – the winter ascent of Observatory Ridge on Ben Nevis. The next age was slowly dawning. In 1927 a variation to Bell's Route on The Cobbler's South Peak was recorded by Rutherford and Hutchison, two of the founders of the Junior Mountaineering Club of Scotland – the JMCS. Refreshingly new, they were one of more than half a dozen clubs formed between 1920 and 1933, including the Ptarmigan Club (1929), the Creagh Dhu Club (1930), and the Lomond Club (1933). Between them, these clubs would be responsible for the majority of climbs in the Arrochar Alps. Though it is normally unfair to single out any one climber when looking at the history of an area, an exception can be happily made with Jock Nimlin, who with eleven routes on The Cobbler alone, including the Direct Finish to Right-Angled Gully (1930), Nimlin's Direct Route (1933) and the complete Recess Route (1935), to mention a few, can be singled out as one of the major players. Climbers remember his superb first guide to the Arrochar area (co-authored with another unique person – Benny Humble) with great respect.

The Creagh Dhu, that almost legendary crew from the shipyards of the Clyde, polished off what lines Nimlin had left, taking over after the Second World War. Bill Smith arrived in 1945 to begin the stream of hard and excellent routes which would continue through the 1950s. Several climbs are, however, emboldened, and we must mention Cunningham and Smith's S-Crack (1948), Punster's Crack (1949) and Smith's Gladiator's Groove (1952). Hamish MacInnes took some time away from his hammer and pegs over on the South Peak, (Porcupine Wall, 1951 and Ithuriel's Groove, 1952), to record one of the finest VS routes in the area, Whither Wether (1952), with Tommy Paul.

Mention must be made of Club Crack (E2) put up by Pat Walsh in 1957 and for many years climbed only by members of the Creagh Dhu. It remains a demanding lead and was for years a shibboleth for that club. Even more impressive is the overhanging wide crack above Punster's Crack, of which the story goes that on attempts by the Creagh Dhu table legs were sawn to order, but to no avail. The crack finally fell to Rick Campbell and Paul Thorburn in 1994.

Back on the South Peak, on the sunny South Face, Taylor and Crawford's Dicer's Groove (1956) was at E2 a hard and serious lead for the time. A curious visit by a very young Robin Smith in June 1957 resulted in Glueless Groove (E2), with a typically bold wall section. Things quietened down somewhat after this, as transport made Glen Coe more accessible.

Elsewhere in the Arrochar area, Pat Mitchell from the Greenock M.C. was quietly nibbling away at other crags. His Great Central Groove on The Brack (1958) with Jimmy Morrison is probably his biggest find, while Capricorn, Difficult, next to The Upper Couloir on Stob Ghabhar and soloed in 1982, indicates a life-long devotion to the Southern Highlands.

Mitchell wrote an interesting account of their struggle up Great Central Groove in the 1959 SMCJ. Ben Humble, as he did so often, had pointed them towards the route, and on a Saturday in June, with one day's leave from their families, they excavated and muscled their way up a very wet climb. In summer, the climb has been described as a grand struggle, if the muck is ignored. Ten years later Bill Skidmore and Bob Richardson (also, as it happened, from the Greenock M.C.), made the first winter ascent to give the area its first Grade V.

Skidmore, Richardson, and 'Black' Jim Crawford, were the core of a group who climbed actively in Arrochar and the Southern Highlands in summer and winter. They recognised the intrinsic value of the less spectacular crags and hills of the region and recorded routes for over 20 years. In particular, The Brack came under their focus in the 1960s, with an aided ascent of Mammoth (1967), taking the fine crack in the wall left of Great Central Groove. This epic route was climbed over the summer and early autumn of that year. On one occasion a round table leg was just the right size for one section of the crack, while on another day Black Jim was despatched to Tiso's Emporium through in Edinburgh, to buy up the available stock of pegs. Time was obviously more spare in these days (and petrol cheaper). Mammoth was freed in 1978, by Dougie Mullin, at E3.

Another sterling story from the Greenock boys involved Richardson in 1968. Stripping gear from Sideline, another aid route on The Brack, he arrived at the classic situation of hanging from the last peg on a roof, above the vast overhanging wall left of Elephant Gully. Somewhat akin to sawing off the branch on which one sits, he departed company from the rock holding the peg, to find himself well out from the wall. Another late night. In July of that year, Skidmore and Crawford climbed the fine Mainline, aid being confined to a short section up an overhanging corner.

We are not sure when Dun Leacainn was developed; it was done on the sly, mainly by teams from Outdoor Centres and kept out of the Journal, resulting in some confusion regarding first ascents. Its granodiorite provides a welcome respite from lichenous mica schist and there is even a Robin Smith route here, the fine and natural central line of Pluvial, climbed with Bill Rowney of the Creagh Dhu. They had easy access to the crag, probably in the late 1960s, as the evils of easy profit trees had not then been planted. Creag Liath was also developed about the same time but not as secretly, as it is not as good.

Also around this time, instructors from the Benmore Outdoor Centre near Dunoon were developing the winter corries of Beinn Mhor. Rustie Baillie was the prime mover, with Klaus Schwartz continuing the impetus through the late 1970s and into the 1980s. Some thirty-five routes in the corrie are described in this guide for the first time.

Creag Tharsuinn, somewhat neglected due to its proximity to The Cobbler, had several excellent rock climbs recorded in the 1970s, all creations of Bill Skidmore. The Tingler (1974), Terminal Wall (1975), and Trilogy (1976), are all worth doing. In 1963, Skidmore had climbed one of the harder winter routes in the corrie with an ascent of the excellent McLaren's Chimney (IV).

But attention soon shifted back to the unclimbed walls high on The Cobbler. In 1979, Dave 'Cubby' Cuthbertson succeeded after several falls on the futuristic Wild Country (E6), the overhanging scooped wall left of Punster's Crack. Lichen and dirt stopped an on sight attempt, so Cuthbertson cleaned the route from above and tapped in a Stopper 5 before making the successful ascent with Rob Kerr. The route has been repeated twice, but it still awaits an on sight lead, both subsequent leaders inspecting the top crack and pre-placing a runner.

The following year, this time climbing with Ken Johnstone, Cuthbertson added Rest and be Thankful (E5) to the impending wall left of Club Crack. Again attempted on sight, both climbers got above the crux and reversed from it, before the route was finally climbed after a 'quick clean'. Also in 1980, Lakeland activist Pete Whillance slipped in to record Edge of Extinction (E6) on The Brack. The climb remains one of the very finest mountain routes at the grade in Scotland. Unfortunately, it is often quite dirty, making repeats rare and on sight repeats even rarer.

Trends in the mid to late 1980s, which had always pointed to shorter, lower, and harder rock climbs, manifested themselves with activity on the crags of Glen Croe. These had been useful alternatives to the higher crags in poor weather for many years, with both free and aid climbing, as well as a teaching ground for the Arrochar Outdoor Centre staff, but now the crag rats arrived, with Gary Latter, Dave Griffiths and friends. Climbing at a high technical standard, they freed old aid climbs and pioneered new routes. In 1989, Griffiths took his technical cragging skills up the hillside to record the superb Osiris (E4) on the clean slabby rock of the South Face of The Cobbler's South Peak.

Also of note around the mid 1980s were the handful of Extremes climbed at Sub-Station Crag, near Loch Sloy by Jim Divall. Of these, Charge of The Light Brigade (E3) is particularly noteworthy, and in 1988 Colin Moody and Ian Taylor added the excellent White Meter (E4).

The Cobbler had never been a popular winter venue. The obvious gullies and routes like Recess Route had been climbed and the slopes were popular with walkers. However, despite notable ascents such as Norrie Muir and Arthur Paul's superb North Wall Groove (V,6) in 1977 and the earlier North Wall Traverse, (IV,5) by Skidmore and McKenzie, in 1961, the mountain was generally ignored as a winter venue. North Wall Groove more than any route pointed to the future – it is now regarded as one of the best Grade V routes in this guide – but more than twenty years passed before the potential was realised. But by 1990, the winter blitzkrieg recently unleashed on the Northern Corries of Cairn Gorm and Aonach Mor was steadily advancing.

In the vanguard was Rab Anderson, ably supported by Rob Milne and sometimes by Chris Anderson and Tom Prentice. First off, Anderson and Milne climbed Deadman's Groove (VII,7), following it up with the excellent Gibber Crack (VI,7). In the following six years some twenty-two winter routes were added, some winter ascents of existing rock routes, others completely new lines. Some of these additions deserve particular mention. The winter ascent of Punster's Crack (VII,8), by Andy Clarke and Mark Garthwaite in 1993 produced an impressive, if controversial, technical route. In 1996 Garthwaite also added the most out-there winter route on the mountain so far, Viva Glasvegas, (VIII,7). Robin McAllister's ascent of the very technical Direct Direct (VII,9) with Dave McGimpsey in 1995 should also be noted – not least for the route's HVS 5a grade in summer.

Of the other winter routes, particularly good are: 1990 – Ramshead Ridge and Right-angled Chimney Direct (V,6), climbed by Chris Cartwright and Simon Richardson; 1994 – Chimney Route (V,7) from

Prentice and Peter Beaumont, Right-Angled Chimney (IV,5) from Bruce Goodlad and Andy Forsyth, North Rib Route (V,7) from Rab and Chris Anderson, Duncan McCallum and Milne; 1995 – Aeonoclast (VI,6) from Colin Stewart and Prentice and in 1996 – Megabyte (VI,6) from McAllister, Milne and McGimpsey. However, The Cobbler also offers a wide selection of excellent routes around Grade III and IV.

It wasn't only winter climbers who were paying The Cobbler more attention. In 1991 Gary Latter completed Horus (E6) on the sunny South Face of the South Peak – the first in a clutch of hard routes to be added on this side of the mountain. Latter followed this in 1993 with Wild at Heart (E6) up the wall just left of Wild Country, climbing the top pitch red point style. The main summer success of 1994 was Rick Campbell and Paul Thorburn's ascent of the impressive overhanging off-width in the headwall above Punster's Crack to give Wide Country, (E5). With a new guide in the offing the pace hotted up in the summer of 1995 with Latter and Thorburn climbing Geb (E4) and Ra (E4) to the Osiris slab on the sunny side of the South Peak, while Thorburn and Campbell added Ethereal (E6) and Thorburn and Iain Pitcairn climbed Sleeping Gas (E6) on the sparsely protected wall right of Dicer's Groove. Also worth mentioning is the obscure gem A Crack in the Clouds (E3) added by Thorburn and Latter to the retaining wall of Chockstone Gully. However, the big event of the summer was Latter's Dalriada (E8) up the soaring prow right of Right-Angled Groove on the North Peak. Undoubtedly one of the finest technical lines in this guidebook, attempts were spread over a total of seven days, and the climb was red pointed. The grade remains speculative until the first on sight ascent.

With winter conditions not always reliable on some of The Cobbler's south faces, climbers looked afresh at other north-facing Arrochar crags. Simon Richardson, Chris Cartwright and Roger Everett had already begun looking further afield, adding the excellent and massively overhanging Flakewalk (VI,8) on Beinn Donich in 1990. Despite its low altitude and southerly aspect, Creag Tharsuinn received considerable attention; Pulpit Grooves (V,7, 1994) and Anonymous Gully (IV,6, 1994) filling obvious gaps. However, pride of place was Mark Garthwaite and George Szuca's 1991 ascent of the steep ice route on Terminal Wall – Terminator (VI,6).

A visit to Beinn Ime by Anderson, Milne and Prentice in early 1995 led to confirmation of the quality of Ben's Fault (IV,5) climbed by Skidmore, and Bob Richardson in 1963, and later to Default Mode (V,5) from Simon Richardson, Charles French and Prentice, and Headfault (VII,7) from Anderson and Milne.

A visit to Beinn an Lochain by Prentice and McGimpsey in 1993 confirmed the quality and relative solidity of John Mackenzie's tremendous Monolith Grooves (IV,5) climbed in 1977. McGimpsey, McAllister, Andrew Fraser and Stuart Mearns returned the same year to add the pleasant Megalith (IV,4). The unclimbed rock on the mountain was also proving of interest. Julian Lines, Thorburn and Campbell investigated the lower Kinglas Crag and added AWOL In Thailand (E4) in 1996, quickly followed by Swimming With The Tide (E5) from Thorburn and Appoggiatura (E6) from Campbell. The impressive walls of the Monolith in the higher corrie finally got their first free rock route courtesy of Campbell and Thorburn – Pious Ejaculation (E4) on the lower buttress. The overhanging upper buttress awaits attention.

Also in 1996 some eleven routes up to E1, mostly the work of Nick Smith, were added to Binnein an Fhidhleir, the crag above Abyssinia first recorded by John Mackenzie in the 1970s. Mackenzie's routes, and a further nine added in the late 1980s and early 1990s make the crag a worthwhile day out.

With the new guide about to go to press Prentice, Anderson and Milne added the atmospheric Purple Blaze (VI,6) to the upper buttress, climbing the grooves and slab right of the final pitch of Monolith Grooves. A few days before this ascent McAllister, McGimpsey and Fraser climbed the fine Resolution (VI,7) up the slabby arete right of Great Central Groove on The Brack, finishing up the groove right of the groove's Right-hand Finish.

Although many of the most obvious lines have been climbed in summer and winter, there is no doubt that the Arrochar area still has considerable potential. The crags and corries are generally quiet, the climbing technically demanding, and patience and careful planning pay dividends all year round.

THE SOUTHERN HIGHLANDS

For the earliest recorded route outwith The Cobbler, we have to go further north to Stob Ghabhar. We describe this route in what may seem unnecessary detail, to highlight technical details and climbing styles of the time. The West Highland Railway Line to Fort William was opened in the autumn of 1894. Until then, the nearest station to the fine mountains around Bridge of Orchy was at Tyndrum. From Tyndrum the primitive road ran west along the south shore of Loch Tulla, passing the small Inn at Inveroran before bending north to Glen Coe. Tantalising the early pioneers and highly visible from the old road across the

Blackmount was the Upper Couloir of Stob Ghabhar, a deep gully slicing through the summit rocks, with a classic finish at the summit. Maylard, along with Ramsay, Joseph Coats and Naismith, attempted the gully in April 1892, from a Club Meet at the Inn. It may be worth mentioning, as an indication of the general levels of fitness, that at 8.30 p.m. on the Friday night, Naismith and Gilbert Thomson arrived at the Inn, having walked from Dalwhinnie *via* Ben Alder, a distance of 41 miles (65 km) in just over 18 hours. The next day Naismith led the hard middle section of the Couloir. Unfortunately, the ice pitch in the Couloir, normally the crux, was voted impracticable, and Naismith took to the rock buttress on the right for some way before regaining the Couloir proper. This ascent was therefore disallowed! The climbing was probably technically as hard as the ice pitch, but steep ice with long axes was rarely a feasible proposition. A second attempt, in March 1894, was defeated by poor conditions. The third, and successful attempt, was on the 1st May 1897, and was notable for the composition of the party, two being ladies. So Maylard, Professor and Mrs Adamson, and Miss Weiss (a sister of a member) approached the crux icefall. They carried, naturally, those long ice axes so desperately clumsy-looking to modern climbers – all of 44 inches (112 cm) long. The four were on a 60-foot rope, giving some logistical problems. These were circumvented by Miss Weiss standing unroped at the foot of the ice pitch while Mrs Adamson seconded it on the rope. Just below the summit cornice, they were caught in a raging but fortunately short-lived whirlwind and blizzard.

The winter development of Beinn an Dothaidh began in 1894, on the same Easter Meet of the SMC at Inveroran Inn attended by Collie (who moved on to climb Tower Ridge in winter condition). Following that 1894 discovery, with ascents of several easy gullies including West Gully, no other route was recorded until the 1969 ascent of Taxus (III) by an Edinburgh team. It is hard to believe that no climbing was done here between these two dates. Rumours of this cliff began to circulate by the mid 1970s, though not before Skidmore and Black Jim had mistakenly re-ascended Haar (III). In 1976, a good winter saw ascents of the Icefall Finish to Taxus (IV), West Buttress (III), The Skraeling (IV), and in December, Clonus (IV). These routes were climbed either by the Greenock regulars or by various rag-tag Glaswegians. Over the next few years several more lines at III, IV, and V or harder were to be climbed, consolidating this cliff as a worthy alternative venue to Glen Coe. One such was Valhalla (IV), the corner right of Haar, climbed by Schwartz in 1984 but not recorded until 1996, thereby causing much confusion and irritation to climbers unaware of its earlier ascent.

Also in 1976 (we said it was a good winter), the other cliff of Beinn an Dothaidh was unveiled. This was Creag Coire an Dothaidh, facing directly down to the hotel bar at Bridge of Orchy, and therefore more often talked about or overlooked than climbed on. Salamander Gully (III) and Fahrenheit 451 (IV,3) stand out, though we should not overlook B.O. Buttress (III), if only as a foretaste to Beelzebub (VI,6), recorded in 1994 by Roger Everett and Simon Richardson and currently the hardest line on the crag. Catch an early freeze and climb the ice of Fahrenheit or Salamander. A few years later, the action had moved down the road to Beinn Udlaidh (known to some climbers as Ben Ugly, due to the somewhat drab backdrop of the corrie). It's difficult to explain why this corrie should have remained neglected for so long, but then the highly visible Fahrenheit 451 was driven past until 1976, so the well-hidden Coire Daimh, down a minor road, has some excuses. Edinburgh-based climbers found it, and they kept very quiet about it. Steep ice early in the season separates the men from the boys. Perhaps one outing to be praised is the two routes in one day by Bob Duncan, Organpipe Wall and The Smirk (both V,5), the latter named from 'that irritating twitch of Bob Duncan's observed when he was recounting the details of his ascent to a thrice-failed Ian Duckworth and Alan Pettit, at the end of the day'. Dave Cuthbertson arrived in January 1980, to produce Captain Hook (VI,6). All of these routes are formed from frozen springs. Activity since the major exploratory period has been confined to the recording of intermediate routes, mainly on the mixed climbing of the buttress walls.

Graham Little opened the second wave of exploration on Beinn an Dothaidh when with Dave Saddler he climbed the striking steep corner to the left of Clonus in February 1986, giving Menage à Trois (V,6). Only three days later they returned to climb Pas de Deux (V,6), taking the barrel-fronted buttress skirted by Slow March. With Carte Blanche and Splitting the Difference (IV,4) in March 1989, Little declared the crag worked out, which, as is so often the case, meant that there were several fine and indeed outstanding eliminate lines still to do. These began to be attacked in 1993, with Coup de Grace (V,7), the fine technical line just left of Menage à Trois, by Robertson and Richardson in February. In 1995 Brunskill and companions climbed two pleasant Grade IV routes on the buttress left of West Gully, Circean and Femme Fatale, whisking the routes from under the very nose of Little.

Simon Richardson and partners effectively tied up this wave of exploration with several fine ascents in 1996, including Bete Noire (V,7) in February with Roger Everett. This takes in the unlikely headwall between Cirrus and Carte Blanche. A few weeks later, Everett and Richardson climbed The Screaming (VIII,8), a gravity-defying mixed route whose outstanding feature is the crack line cutting up the final tower on the Pas de Deux buttress. The unrelenting overhanging angle enforced the use of axe rests to find protection. With a crucial runner in place from an attempted repeat, Mark Garthwaite was able to force a free ascent in December 1996, a very fine achievement.

On Beinn Dorain is Creag an Socach, the steep crag seen in profile from Bridge of Orchy. This had several routes recorded on it up to 1980. The harder lines were finally broken, with Little recording The Promised Land (VI,6) in 1987, and Messiah (VII,7) in January 1988. Bob Duncan led the crux pitch of The Glass Bead Game (V,6) in December 1987. Serious climbing on this cliff, with the line of Messiah in particular one which had been looked at for many years. A major series of climbs saw Howett and Little record The Sting (V,6) and The Prophet (VI,7) in January 1991, while Everett and Richardson continued the trend of hard routes here with Antichrist (VI,7) in March 1992. All these routes have two stars and, with the cleaning of a little turf from rock features, perhaps a bit more protection.

This is Southern Highland winter climbing at its current apogee, with the routes on Beinn an Dothaidh and Beinn Dorain indicative of the healthy state of Scottish winter climbing. Other fine collections of routes are to be found in this area, especially for those prepared to walk further, with the routes recorded on Ben Cruachan's corries being one such example. Much pleasant climbing can also be found on Ben Lawers and the Tarmachans, described here for the first time. The new Millenium looks to continue to provide good climbing.

Notes on the Use of the Guide

CLASSIFICATION OF ROUTES

Summer

For summer rock climbs the following grades have been used: Easy, Moderate, Difficult, Very Difficult, Severe, Hard Severe, Very Severe (VS), Hard Very Severe (HVS), Extremely Severe. The Extremely Severe grade has been subdivided into E1, E2, E3, E4, E5, E6, E7 and E8 in keeping with the rest of Britain.

Technical grades are given for routes of VS and above where known. Much effort has been made to elicit information from active climbers about routes, some of which will have all the relevant pitches graded while others will have only the crux pitch so described. The normal range for technical grades expected on routes of the given overall grade are as follows; VS – 4b, 4c, 5a; HVS – 4c, 5a, 5b; E1 – 5a, 5b, 5c; E2 – 5b, 5c, 6a; E3 – 5c, 6a; E4 – 5c, 6a, 6b; E5 – 6a, 6b. Routes with technical grade at the lower end of the range will be sustained or poorly protected, while those with grades at the upper end of the expected range will most likely have a shorter and generally well protected crux.

Although the British system is thought second to none by those familiar with it, it is known to confuse visitors from abroad. For their benefit, it can be assumed that 5a, 5b, 5c and 6a correspond to the American grades of 5.9, 5.10a/b, 5.10c/d and 5.11a/b respectively. Eurocraggers should note that there is little or no fixed protection on these routes and if they are used to cruising bolted French 6c, they may suffer some distress while attempting the corresponding 6a pitches here, with their sometimes spaced and fiddly protection. Grading information is in some cases scanty or even lacking, particularly in some of the older or more obscure route; climbers should therefore be even more circumspect in their approach to such routes. Further information about any routes is always welcome.

Winter

Winter climbs have been graded using the two-tier system in which the Roman numeral indicates the overall difficulty of the climb and the accompanying Arabic numeral represents the technical difficulty of the hardest sections of climbing. This is built on the old Grades of I to V, which was previously used, but it is only for climbs of Grade IV and above (occasionally grade III) that the two-tier system has been applied. Both parts of the grading system are open-ended.

Grade I – Uncomplicated, average-angled snow climbs normally having no pitches. They may, however, have cornice difficulties or dangerous run-outs.

Grade II – Gullies which contain either individual or minor pitches, or high-angled snow with difficult cornice exits. The easiest buttresses under winter conditions.

Grade III – Gullies which contain ice in quantity. There will normally be at least one substantial pitch and possibly several lesser ones. Sustained buttress climbs, but only technical in short sections.

Grade IV – Steeper and more technical with vertical sections found on ice climbs. Buttress routes will require a good repertoire of techniques.

Grade V – Climbs which are difficult, sustained and serious. If on ice, long sustained ice pitches are to be expected; buttress routes will require a degree of rock climbing ability and the use of axe torquing and hooking and similar winter techniques.

Grade VI – Thin and tenuous ice routes or those with long vertical sections. Buttress routes will include all that has gone before but more of it.

Grade VII – Usually rock routes which are very sustained or technically extreme. Also sustained routes on thin or vertical ice.

Grade VIII – The very hardest buttress routes.

The technical grades which are shown by the Arabic numbers, are based on the technical difficulty of classic winter routes of Grade III, IV and V. This is used as a basis for assessing the technical difficulty of the route, while the Roman numeral gives an indication of the overall seriousness of the climb, in a very similar way to which the E grades and the numerical grades are used in summer. In this way a V,4 is normally a serious ice route, V,5 would be a classic ice route with adequate protection, V,6 would be a classic buttress route and V,7 would indicate a technically difficult but well protected buttress route. Each route is of the same overall difficulty (V) but with differing degrees of seriousness and technical difficulty.

Equipment and Style

It is assumed that a good range of modern nuts and camming devices will be carried for the harder climbs, both in summer and winter. The summer climbs described in this guide are graded assuming the presence and stability of any of the *in situ* pegs that are mentioned. If pegs are essential on new routes, it is hoped that they will be kept to a minimum and left in place; please keep to the Scottish tradition of bold climbs with leader-placed protection. Please make every attempt to find a safe alternative to pegs before resorting to them. Unfortunately pegs are still necessary on some winter routes to make them acceptably safe. This tends to be more often the case on the harder gully climbs than on the better rock of the buttress routes.

Many of the hardest rock climbs that are described in this book will have been cleaned or otherwise inspected prior to the first ascent, but most routes of E2 and many of E3 were climbed on sight. Although every attempt has been made to grade them for an on sight lead, this should be borne in mind. Many of the difficult winter routes were also initially climbed with prior knowledge; sometimes unintentionally gained by a summer ascent of the route, some through previous failure and sometimes by deliberate inspection prior to a winter ascent. Again, every attempt has been made to grade for an on sight ascent.

Damage to rock and vegetation

Many of the winter climbs described in this book rely on frozen turf and rock rather than on ice and snow. The increasing popularity of such routes, excellent though they are, raises a thorny environmental question for inevitably both the rock and the vegetation can be irrevocably damaged by the passage of climbers. The scars caused by crampons on the soft schists of Arrochar are clearly evident after only a handful of winter ascents, and they will occur however skilled the climber's precision footwork. It is not many decades ago that the use of nailed boots for rock climbing became frowned apon, not only because better alternatives were available, but mainly because it was realised that nail scratches were rapidly destroying the climbs. Similarly, the tell-tale sign of a winter buttress team in action is a steady stream of moss and turf descending from the line of the climb. In time, the turf may be removed to such an extent from a popular climb that it becomes much harder. Therefore, to ensure the longevity of our winter sport and the continuing pleasure of summer ascents of classic summer rock climbs, it is common sense that we all take account of these potential problems. Damage to turf can be minimised by avoiding such routes when they are poorly frozen – unfrozen turf strips easily from the underlying rock, often with climber attached. A covering of snow and verglas protects both the turf and the rock, so avoid routes which are totally bare (anyway, that's not playing the game!). Finally, whatever the temptation, please avoid making winter ascents of classic summer rock climbs which have little or no turf; why should a handful of winter climbers jeopardise the enjoyment of the summer hordes when there are plenty of opportunities for excellent new winter climbs at all levels of difficulty on ground which would be unsuitable for good summer rock climbing.

Left and Right
The terms left and right refer to a climber facing the direction being described, i.e. facing the cliff for route descriptions, facing downhill in descent.

Pitch Lengths
Pitch lengths are in metres, rounded to the nearest 5m, and they should be used only as a guide as they have been estimated rather than measured. Where lengths greater than 50m are given this does not indicate moving together, merely belay where required or desired.

Recommended Routes
No list of recommended routes has been given, instead a star grading system for quality has been used. Stars have been given as a selection guide for occasional visitors and consequently have been allocated somewhat sparingly and spread throughout the grades, although vegetation and poor rock limits the number of stars below VS. Many of the routes without stars are still very good. Higher grade routes tend to be more sustained and on better rock but somewhat higher standards have therefore been applied. Equally, starred routes on different cliffs may vary slightly according to the quality of the cliff, but it is necessary to apply stars as a route selection aid. Winter stars are a problem because quality will vary with conditions, so stars, like the grade, is applied for average conditions which may not exist at the time.
*** An outstanding route of the highest quality, combining superb climbing with line, character, situation and other features which make a route great. Could compare with any route in the country.
** As above, but lacking one of the features while having similar quality of climbing.
* Good climbing, but the route may lack line, situation or balance.

First Ascents
The year of the first ascent is given in the text. Further details are listed cliff by cliff in chronological order at the back of the guide. The original aid has been listed when this is known, usually with the first free

ascent. Details of variations are given under the parent route. Whether the route was ascended in summer or winter conditions is indicated by an S or W at the left end of each line. Winter ascents are listed separately from their corresponding summer route.

Litter and Vandalism
Litter is a continuing problem at popular camping sites and crags, despite a slow improvement in recent years. All litter, including spare and unwanted food, should be taken out of the mountains. The justifications for leaving food that is bio-degradable is spurious in these areas, as the breakdown of material in such a cold environment takes years. Likewise, leaving food for birds and animals is misguided as this only attracts scavengers into the area where they prey on the residents. If you take it in, take it out again; this includes finger tape and chalk wrappers, litter that climbers cannot blame anyone else for. Another problem is rings of stones used round tents; if you must use them, return the boulders where they came from. In the end, justified complaints by landowners can lead to access problems. Please co-operate by not leaving any traces behind you.

Mountain Rescue
In case of an accident requiring rescue or medical attention, telephone 999 (police).

AVALANCHES

Every year avalanches occur in these mountains, sometimes with tragic results. Climbers venturing onto the hills in winter should aquaint themselves with the principles of snow structure and avalanche prediction. There are a number of suitable books on the subject. A knowledge of what to do if involved in an avalanche, either as a victim or an observer, may help to save lives. A knowledge of first aid and artificial resuscitation is an obvious necessity.

Avalanches most often occur following heavy snow fall or during periods of strong thawing conditions, when slopes between 22 and 60 degrees are suspect, with the main danger area being between 30 and 45 degrees. Any danger will last longer in colder conditions when the snow pack takes longer to stabilise. The main danger is windslab avalanche, which occurs when snow is re-deposited by the wind. This snow bonds poorly with underlying layers and in these conditions lee slopes are the main danger areas, but pockets of windslab can be found in any sheltered location. Knowledge of the preceding weather, especially wind direction, is of great importance in predicting which slopes and climbs are avalanche prone and this must always be borne in mind.

Climbers and walkers, however, should be able to make their own predictions by studying the pattern of snow deposition from the past and present weather conditions. Being able to dig a snow pit, study the snow profile and assess the relative strengths of the various snow layers and draw sensible conclusions from a profile is an important skill for those venturing on the hills in winter. The sheer test and the Rutchblock test can be very useful tools in assessing avalanche risk, although their application requires some knowledge and experience. A simple indication of severe avalanche risk is when the snow splits easily into slabs with defined boundaries when walked on; these small slabs indicate that much bigger ones may be waiting to peel off. Along with the means to make a realistic risk assessment it is also necessary to understand the principles of movement in avalanche terrain to minimise any risk.

If avalanched, try either to jump free or anchor yourself for as long are possible. If swept down, protect your access to oxygen by 'swimming' to stay on the surface, by keeping your mouth closed and by preserving an air space in front of your face if buried. Wet snow avalanches harden rapidly on settling, so try and break free if possible at this point. If trapped, try to stay calm to reduce oxygen demand.

If a witness to an avalanche, it is VITAL to start a search immediately, given that it is safe to do so. Victims will often be alive at first but their chances lessen quickly if buried. Unless severely injured, some 80% may live if found immediately but this drops rapidly to about 30% after one hour and 10% after 3 hours. Mark the burial site if known, the site when last seen and the position of anything else found and search until help arrives. Again, a working knowledge of first aid may safe a life, as many victims may have stopped breathing. Remember IMMEDIATE SEARCHING CAN SAVE LIVES.

The ability to make your own assessment of risk is vital to anyone venturing into this area; avalanche predictions produced by the Scottish Avalanche Information Service are readily available during the winter, but they do not cover Arrochar and the Southern Highlands. However, the forecast prepared for Glen Coe may be helpful as a rough guide. This information is also available on local radio and in the local and national press and from the Police SAIS Avalanche Information Service on 01463 713191. For the computer-literate to get a report on e-mail, simply send an empty message to:

avalanches@dcs.gla.ac.uk

On World Wide Web, the URL for the avalanche service is:

http://www.dcs.gla.ac.uk/other/avalanche/

Maps and other sources of information

The meaning and pronunciation of local place names can be found in *Scottish Hill and Mountain Names* by Peter Drummond, published by the SMT (1991). Much useful information about the hills and the area as a whole can be found in the SMC District Guides *The Southern Highlands* by Donald Bennet, and *The Islands of Scotland including Skye* (various authors), published by the SMT. Additionally, the growing use of the Internet is producing some sites useful for climbers and walkers. While it is dangerous to provide addresses in such a rapidly-changing medium, one such site is that of the SMC, which includes links to other sites. Its address is:

http://www.smc.org.uk/smc/

Club Huts within the area of this guide

Ochils Hut, Ochils Mountaineering Club:
Crianlarich (Map Ref 392 250)

Clashgour, Glasgow University Mountaineering Club:
Below Stob Ghabhar, Loch Tulla (Map Ref 257 425)

MacDougall's Cottage, Clachaig Mountaineering Club:
Below Beinn Dorain on the West Highland Way (Map Ref 312 373)

Full details of the above, including a booking contact, are contained in *Scottish Clubs' Huts*, an annual MCofS publication.

Arran

Arran, 32 kilometres long and 15 kilometres wide, is cradled in the Firth of Clyde and sheltered by the long peninsula of Kintyre to the west. Despite its popularity and relative proximity to most of Scotland's population, Arran manages to retain an air of unspoilt rugged grandeur and to exhibit a certain Hebridean charm. It lies on the Highland Boundary Fault and boasts a varied geology and a splendid concentration of granite peaks in the north of the island, rising to a height of 874m at Goatfell, with another ten peaks over 700m. Two great glens, Rosa and Sannox, cut into the heart of this massif and provide a spectacular through walk and access to many of the best rock climbing areas. The Arran peaks are frequently compared to the Skye Cuillin but there is no real comparison, both mountain groups having there own distinctive character and ardent enthusiasts. Arran, as well as being a rock climber's playground, offers many fringe attractions such as golf, water sports, fishing and pony trekking, making it a good venue for a combination holiday. As with many of Scotland's islands, the most favourable months to visit tend to be May and June, although good weather can be enjoyed in mid-summer and autumn.

Perhaps more has been written about Arran rock climbing than any other area in Scotland. Although granite is found in many other parts of Scotland, there is something undeniably unique about the Arran variety. At best it is clean and solid with superb friction, at worst, crumbling and vegetated with lingering dampness. The cliffs and ridges display a striking architecture, the great 'Cyclopean' block walls and vast bare boilerplate slabs so characteristic of granite erosion, whereas the deep gullies and gashes are the result of heavily eroded basalt dykes As a rule, open face routes dry quickly after rain and are little affected by it, whereas routes following fault and corner lines require three to four days of dry weather before a pleasurable ascent can be enjoyed.

The climbing exhibits a certain perversity, with apparently easy sections proving anything but, whilst reasonable routes may be found on the most improbable of walls. As Bill Skidmore put it in his definitive article in the 1978 Scottish Mountaineering Club Journal: 'holds usually materialise where least and vanish where most expected'. The through-route, a feature of a number of Arran climbs, is an esoteric pleasure not to be missed! Arran granite is full of contradictions, it both attracts and repels, yet once you've savoured its rough texture and grand design there is no escape from ultimate addiction!

Many of the minor climbing areas provide contrasting rock types (sandstone, conglomerate, dolerite, schist etc.) and often enjoy better weather and are therefore suitable for an off-day or as a break from the rigours of Arran granite.

Many of Arran's harder routes were initially climbed using varying amounts of aid, often admitted, sometimes not. Over a period of time virtually all this aid has been eliminated. Any exceptions are noted in the text. In the history section the grades given with the first ascents are as a rule the current grades, but take account of any remaining aid. Where known, technical grades are given for pitches of 4b and over. The true grades (both overall and pitch) of a number of routes are still shrouded in mystery. Proceed with care!

Winter climbing on Arran is an even more esoteric experience, transient in nature yet at its best of incomparable quality. Barring the small matters of low altitude, proximity to the sea and the inconvenience of the winter ferry timetable, the Arran peaks, with their great dank vegetated faces and dirty gullies offer unparalleled poten- tial. All the characteristics of Arran granite that detract from the rock climbing enhance the winter climbing experience. As a general rule the poorest quality rock routes prove to be the best winter ones. It is strongly urged that winter ascents are not made of high quality rock routes, there are plenty of alternatives! Although good conditions can develop rapidly, with as little as four days of frost preparing the ground, they tend to be short-lived, calling for a quick response. Snow build-up is not critical, although it does create the right atmosphere! During prolonged cold spells huge ice cascades (many still unclimbed) form in certain locations offering the quick and the bold a very special challenge.

In addition to a summer rack, plenty of drive-in/screw-out ice pegs should be taken as they provide excellent protection when placed in well frozen turf — the winter climber's greatest ally.

Access

Caledonian MacBrayne operate a regular passenger and vehicle ferry service from Ardrossan to Brodick (crossing time 55 minutes); telephone Ardrossan (01294) 463470 or Brodick (01770) 302166. During holiday periods, bookings for vehicles should be made well in advance. A bus service, which is synchronised with the ferry timetable, provides a round island service, although on Sundays there is a dearth of transport in the north of the island. Taxis are usually available, at a reasonable cost, for swift access from Brodick to Glen Rosa.

Another ferry service (frequent in summer, two days per week in winter) runs between Lochranza on Arran and Claonaig in Kintyre

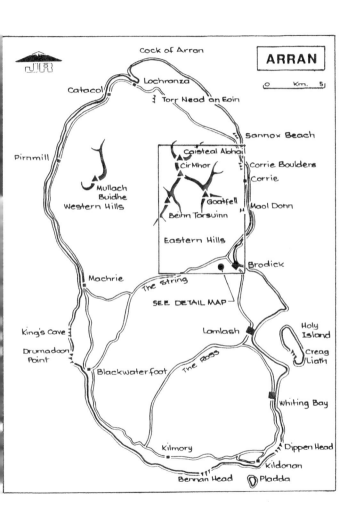

(crossing time 30 minutes) which is rather convenient if a combined Arran and Kintyre or Knapdale climbing trip is planned. A third and rather limited ferry service (summer only) runs between Brodick and Rothesay on Bute (crossing time 1 hour 30 minutes).

Maps
Ordnance Survey 1:50,000 Sheet 69
Ordnance Survey 1:25,000 Outdoor Leisure Sheet 37
Harvey Mountain Map 1:40,000 The Isle of Arran

Accommodation
Being a popular holiday island, Arran has plenty of guest houses and hotels at all the main centres, the best bases for a rock climbing holiday being Brodick, Corrie or Lochranza (which also has a Youth Hostel). Details are available and bookings can be made through the Tourist Information Centre, telephone Brodick (01770) 302140. There is a conveniently situated private bunkhouse at High Corrie (called North High Corrie Croft) run by Arran Estates Trust; telephone (01770) 302203 for details and booking. Camping provides a more flexible option with an 'official' campsite in lower Glen Rosa and delightful, less ordered camping, at a nominal charge, in lower Glen Sannox (please respect this privilege). For a really lightweight approach there are a number of natural howfs (shelters) under some of the enormous granite boulders that litter the corries.

BEINN NUIS

792m   (Map Ref 955 399)

The East Face of Beinn Nuis dominates the view from Lower Glen Rosa, promising some fine rock climbing. However this grand face, although steep, is quite vegetated and has so far failed to produce anything of real quality. In winter conditions it is a different story, with

---

KEY TO MAP OPPOSITE

1 Beinn Nuis, East Face	6 Cioch na h-Oighe, East Face
2 Beinn Tarsuinn, Meadow Face	7 Cir Mhor, North-East Face
3 A'Chir, Coire Daingean Face	8 Coire na h-Uaimh, Lower Slabs
4 Cir Mhor, South Face	9 Caisteal Abhail, Upper Rocks
5 Goatfell, Rosa Slabs	10 Cuithe Mheadhonach

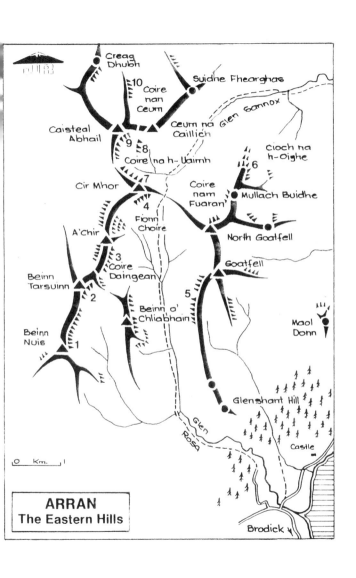

ARRAN
The Eastern Hills

the normally messy gullies giving good sport and the slabby open faces offering great potential for harder lines.

The main face is split by five gullies, the much celebrated Gully 3 being the most distinctive. To the left of the main face is a 'Cyclopean' wall with a diagonal rake running up from right to left below it. This provides a descent route but care is required. Below this rake lies an area of slabby rock (holding Anvil Gully).

Leave the main Glen Rosa track just beyond the bridge over the Garbh Allt. Follow the path up the side of the burn to reach level ground. Cross the burn, then head for the crag either *via* the path up the East Ridge or by cutting across country (no path) from further up Coire a' Bhradhain. Allow about one and a half hours from the Glen Rosa road head.

1 Anvil Gully 50m Difficult * (1946)
This short chimney/gully lies in an area of slabby rock below the 'Cyclopean' wall. It is an atmospheric climb, packing a lot into its short length, but is impossible for the stout! The initial thin chimney can be climbed or avoided by a ramp on the right. Thereafter surmount two jammed boulders to reach a gravel-filled gully stoppered by a jumble of huge blocks. Climb up behind the blockage, then crawl back outwards into a cave. An improbable through-route on the left (facing out) gives a testing finish – take off sack, harness and excess clothing!
Winter: III,3 * (1995)
Follow the summer line, but the through-route can prove even more demanding when choked with snow!

2 Gully 1 95m III,3 (1995)
After ascending the initial open groove, with one constriction, take the gully flanking the 'Cyclopean' wall on the left. At its top, step down onto a boulder jumble. Scramble over this to reach a bay below the final wall. Climb this by a thin chimney on the extreme left, exiting by a tight through route. It is an unpleasant Difficult in summer (1897).

3 Gully 2 95m II,3 (1995)
Climb the easy shallow gully to a point where a left traverse into Gully 1 is possible. Instead, move right over a chockstone, then climb the thin gully to reach a boulder jumble. Squirm through this (several through-routes) to reach a bay below the final wall. The gully continuation is blocked, so take a groove and ledge to its left, then go up to finish. Again, it is an unpleasant Difficult in summer (1897).

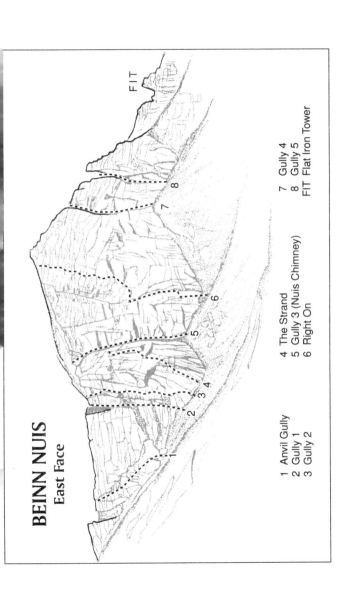

BEINN NUIS
East Face

FIT

1 Anvil Gully
2 Gully 1
3 Gully 2

4 The Strand
5 Gully 3 (Nuis Chimney)
6 Right On

7 Gully 4
8 Gully 5
FIT Flat Iron Tower

4   The Strand   175m   V.6 **   (1995)

This fine, exposed climb follows a prominent ramp running across the lower part of the slabby buttress between Gully 2 and the Nuis Chimney. Start on the left about 30m above the toe of the buttress.

1. 50m   Follow the most prominent of a number of ramps that run across the face, with a thin slab and hard move round a block just beyond a corner.

2. 50m   Continue by a rising right traverse line, aiming for the far right edge of the buttress just above a prominent overhung niche (close to Nuis Chimney). This pitch involves a difficult corner and some thin moves across a slab to reach the edge by a large block.

3. 45m   Climb directly upwards to reach an obvious ledge system below the steep headwall. Follow this rightwards towards the upper reaches of Nuis Chimney.

4. 30m   Finish as for the last pitch of Nuis Chimney.

5   Gully 3 (Nuis Chimney)   130m   VS *   (1901)

This is the obvious deep chimney bounding the left-hand side of the main face. It has the somewhat dubious distinction of being regarded as the finest chimney/gully on Arran! A route for the serious body contact enthusiast.

1. 20m 4c   Ascend a scoop of damp disintegrating rock, then climb a shallow groove on the right-hand side to a platform and thread belay higher up on the right.

2. 15m 4b   Climb up *via* a through-route to a large jammed block.

3. 30m 4b   Continue up the gully bed until another through-route under a mass of blocks leads to a large stance.

4. 10m 4b   Climb grass and moss to an overhanging block, above which a narrow chimney leads to a stance and belay.

5. 15m 4c   The chimney now widens and is divided by a rib. Take the deeply cut left branch to a jammed block.

6. 20m 4b   Continue until the chimney narrows again. Reach a little cave, then climb its right wall to pull over onto more open ground.

7. 20m   Grass and a final through-route finish the climb.

Winter: V.6 ***   (1970)

This superb expedition requires a variety of skills and comes into condition as quickly as any winter route on Arran. Follow the summer route throughout. Pitch 5 is normally the crux.

6   Right On   185m   VS (aid)   (1970)
The upper left side of the main face presents a massive bulge of clean rock. Directly below it a long corner/groove runs up the steep vege – Difficult (1895).

7   Gully 4   125m   iii,3 *   (1907)
The deep gully flanking the right-hand side of the main face gives an interesting climb in magnificent scenery, with caves and chockstones to overcome.

The awful **Sucker Slabs**, VS (1943), takes the line of least resistance immediately to the left and traverses in and out of Gully 4.

8   Gully 5   100m   iii, 3 *   (1987)
Another worthwhile gully with a short technical start and a final through-route. Again, the scenery is magnificent. It is unpleasant in summer – Difficult (1895).

FLAT IRON TOWER   *(Map Ref 955 401)*

This large tor of sound rock is the northerly of a group of three that lie just to the south of the Nuis-Tarsuinn col. There are a number of routes up to about 35m, mostly in the lower grades.

BEINN TARSUINN

826m   *(Map Ref 959 412)*

This long mountain ridge has two tops. All the rock climbing is on the east flank of the peak facing Coire a' Bhradhain and Ealta Choire.

FULL MEED TOWER   *(Map Ref 956 404)*

This striking tower-like buttress of good rock lies just to the north of the Nuis-Tarsuinn col. It rises above a belt of slabs, and is very obvious when approached from Coire a' Bhradhain.

1   Baron Samedi   50m   HVS   (1994)
This route tackles the straight off-width crack in the slabs immediately below Full Meed Tower.
1. 25m 5a   Climb the off-width crack to a niche.

2   Full Meed Chimney   60m   Severe *   (1947)
The south face of the tower is split by a steep chimney. This is the line of the route, which is quite strenuous.
1. 20m   Climb the chimney to chockstones.
2. 15m   Go left along a ledge, climb a short chimney to a platform, then climb the right-angled corner above.
3. 25m   Finish up a nose on the right.

3   Voodoo Chile   90m   E2 **   (1969)
A fine climb, with excellent situations, taking the front face of the tower. Start at the top end of a heather rake, which slants up from right to left above steep slabs, just to the right of the edge of the tower.
1. 30m 5c   Climb a corner, on poor rock, to surmount a small roof and reach a grassy triangle. Continue up a crack, then move left to a splendid platform on the very edge of the tower.
2. 15m 5a   Climb a leaning block to two roofs. Move right above the lower roof, then continue rightwards to step into a sentry box belay.
3. 10m 5a   Exit left and follow a crack to an inset block. Move right into a chimney/corner, then climb a jammed block overhang to a ledge.
4. 35m   Climb a corner crack and chimney to rock ledges. Scramble to the top.

4   All Along the Watchtower   85m   HVS *   (1993)
A route of some character, climbing steep chimneys on the east face of the tower. Start 10 metres right of Voodoo Chile at a deep chimney.
1. 25m 5a   Scramble unpleasantly to the back of the chimney, then back and knee over a chockstone (crux). Continue up flakes to belay on a small grass ledge.
2. 15m 5a   Continue up the chimney, then easy grass to a spike belay.
3. 35m 5a   Traverse shelves leftwards to gain and climb the fine upper chimney.
4. 10m   Scramble to the top of the tower.

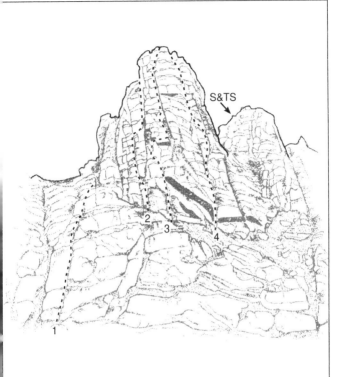

FULL MEED TOWER

1 Baron Samedi
2 Full Meed Chimney
3 Voodoo Chimney
4 All Along the Watchtower
S&TS Solpadeine and Tight Squeeze

The following two short routes are accessed from the top of the tower by descending a gully immediately to the north. About 100m down this gully on its left (in descent) are three aretes.

Solpadeine   30m   VS 4c   (1993)
Climb the cracks in the rightmost (lowest) of the three aretes.

Tight Squeeze   30m   VS 4c   (1993)
The middle arete, climbed by cracks.

MEADOW FACE   (Map Ref 962 412)

This massive crag rises at the head of Coire a' Bhradhain (Ealta Choire) to a height of over 250 metres. It is named after a distinctive patch of turf at its base. Facing south and east it enjoys a sunny aspect and despite holding its fair share of turf, it dries out quite quickly after rain. The most prominent features of the face are a great edge (dividing the long slabby south-east face from the narrow south face) and two parallel crack lines to the right, splitting the face from bottom to top. To the right of the parallel cracks, the south-east face comprises a fan of great curving, overlapping slabs, expanding from right to left. On the extreme right the face is more broken and vegetated and holds three prominent grooves. Left of the great edge, on the south face, is a big corner crack (The Blinder) and further left a prominent gully and chimney high on the face. A wide, grassy shelf, known as The Terrace, extends in from the right demarking the top of the steepest part of the crag. Above The Terrace lies a long belt of slabs and big overlaps.

The rock on the face is generally good, but as may be expected on a cliff this size, the odd section of poor rock will be encountered. The main climbs on this relatively remote face are long and serious undertakings and although not of the very highest quality, they offer grand mountaineering experiences.

Follow the Garbh Allt path from Glen Rosa, then branch off right to follow the Beinn a' Chliabhain path over the first hillock. From the slight col beyond this, contour down into Coire a' Bhradain, then follow the burn into Ealta Choire to the base of the face. Allow about two hours from the Glen Rosa road head.

1   Hanging Gully   75m   Very Difficult   (1944)
High up on the narrow south face (round the left side of the crag) is a deep gully which narrows to a crack in its lower section. Only the upper

section is climbed, gained from the left *via* an overhung corner and a grass ledge. Once in the great square recess, take the leftmost chimney.

2   The Blinder   140m   E1 **   (1971)

This entertaining climb follows a superb line up the striking corner crack immediately left of the great edge.

1. 35m 5b   Gain the crack from a small ledge and climb it directly until it is possible to traverse left to a grass ledge and belay.

2. 20m 5a   Regain the main corner and surmount a small roof. Continue to a belay in a small recess.

3. 30m 5a   Climb the groove to a messy section and follow this to an undercut bulge which leads to a good stance in a deep chimney.

4. 25m 4c   Step left and climb the wall on the left of the chimney *via* flakes to gain the great square recess of Hanging Gully (the original line climbed the repulsive chimney direct).

5. 30m 4c   Enter a slot in the right-hand corner of the recess and climb it to reach a boulder bulge. Surmount this, moving onto the left wall for finishing holds. Continue left up an easier groove to the top.

3   Brobdingnag   205m   E2 **   (1975)

A spectacular route taking a line just to the right of the great edge and parallel to it. Start at a sloping grass ledge to the right of the corner of Blinder.

1. 30m 4b   Traverse right into a small corner, climb it and continue straight up to a large grass ledge.

2. 20m 5b   Climb a grassy groove to an overhang (often wet), then turn it on the left to reach a belay below twin cracks.

3. 20m 5a   Climb the cracks to an overhang, then step right to a shelf below a shallow chimney. Climb the chimney to a belay below a thin crack in a wall.

4. 45m 5b   Climb the crack and swing left to a ramp. Move right then left on good holds, then follow the corner to belay on chockstones below a small cave.

5. 10m   Climb easily up left through a remarkable rock arch to belay in a deep hole.

6. 20m 5a   Climb a loose slab to a ledge. From the ledge climb directly up a good jamming crack and exit right onto a large stance.

7. 15m 5a   Follow the left-hand crack, then transfer to the right-hand crack to pull over a jammed block.

8. 45m 4c   Climb the corner and slabs to the top.

4   Blundecral   115m   E3 **   (1995)

This varied and interesting route, destined to become a classic, climbs a line on the wall between Brobdingnag and Brachistochrone, taking the obvious break through the band of overhangs at the end of the long roof running left from Brachistochrone. Start on a vegetated ledge at a bay to the left of the first chimney of Brachistochrone (gaining this point by scrambling up the groove to below the chimney, then traversing left).

1. 25m 4c   Climb a flake, then move right to an obvious groove (which runs parallel to the Brachistochrone chimney). Ascend the groove, then move left to belay at a pointed turf ledge.

2. 25m 5c   Follow the line of a thin diagonal crack up and left to a left-trending ramp which leads to the base of a right-facing corner. Climb this, then step left to grasp a huge (detached!) block/flake. From its top make a difficult step right to gain a ramp and belay.

3. 15m 5c   Climb the diagonal undercling to reach a hidden left-trending groove. Ascend this for 3m, then traverse back right across the wall to gain the obvious thin rock ramp. Move right to belay at a small turf ledge. A spectacular pitch.

4. 25m 5c   Climb the fine diagonal ramp above to step left onto a continuation ramp. Go up this to a knobbly vein on the wall above. Pull up onto a shelf and move left up this to gain the obvious flake crack which leads to a ledge above. Belay on the right. A bold pitch.

5. 25m 4c   Graded for the jump! Walk right along the ledge until a 'mauvais pas' is reached. Jump down onto a grass ledge and grab an enormous flake. Ascend this, then climb over blocks to a belay on Brachistochrone (at the end of the difficult climbing on this route). Scramble up a grassy groove, then traverse right off the crag.

5   Blundecral True Finish   30m   E5 6a   (1996)

An alternative and direct finish, significantly raising the overall grade of the route. It is bold and poorly protected on the crux traverse. From the belay at the top of pitch 4, move left and ascend a steep slab on tiny holds to a wide horizontal break. Move left along this break until a hard step up onto a narrow sloping ramp can be made. Move left again (joining the Blunderbuss Finish) to reach and climb a flake crack leading to a narrow chimney. Ascend the chimney, taking either fork, to reach a wide ledge. Belay on a big spike well back (joining Meadow Slabs). Traverse right to quit the crag or continue up the Blunderbuss Finish.

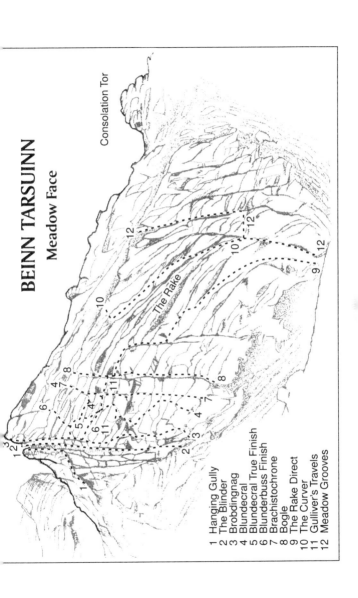

BEINN TARSUINN

Meadow Face

Consolation Tor

The Rake

1 Hanging Gully
2 The Blinder
3 Brobdingnag
4 Blundecral
5 Blundecral True Finish
6 Blunderbuss Finish
7 Brachistochrone
8 Bogle
9 The Rake Direct
10 The Curver
11 Gulliver's Travels
12 Meadow Grooves

6   Blunderbuss Finish   150m   HVS   (1995)
This long finish extends Blundecral to the very top of the crag and misses out its crux section of the original route (on Pitch 4). The Blundecral-Blunderbuss combination is therefore 215m, E2 **. Start from the small turf ledge at the top of pitch 3 on Blundecral.
4. 25m 5a   Climb the fine diagonal rock ramp, as for Blundecral, step left onto a continuation ramp and follow it for 7m to a spectacularly situated belay on the ramp.
5. 25m 4b   Continue up the ramp for 3m, then move up to a higher ramp. Follow this leftwards until it leads to a wide grassy fault on Brobdingnag. Ascend this for 7m to a cave belay under a rock arch.
6. 25m 5a   Quit Brobdingnag by jumping onto a grass ledge to the right of the belay. Follow this rightwards and down to its end. Above this is a flake crack leading up to a narrow chimney. Climb these, taking either fork of the chimney to reach a wide ledge.
7. 50m 4c   Climb a slab at the extreme left of the upper face to its apex, move right, then continue to and climb left-trending flake cracks above.
8. 25m   Pleasant climbing up walls and cracks leads to the top.

7   Brachistochrone   230m   E1 *   (1966)
A fine line following the left-hand of two long parallel cracks that split the front face of the cliff. Although wet and vegetated in places, the situations are good particularly in the lower half. Scramble up a groove to start at the foot of chimney.
1. 45m 4c   Climb the chimney (often wet), then a flake overhang to twin cracks (again often wet) leading to a belay on a ledge below a huge roof.
2. 15m 5a   Climb the strenuous twin overhanging cracks through the roof to a block belay in a chimney.
3. 45m 5a   Traverse left up a layback shelf, then go back right to a grass ledge and a crack. Follow the crack over a smooth (often wet) bulge to the next roof. Climb the overhanging crack to a wet recess in the roof (peg in situ), swing down left onto a steep slab, then go straight up to a grass ledge and belay.
4, 5 and 6. 80m   Continue up the same general line by grassy grooves, slabs and flakes, taking belays as required, to reach the continuation crack in the upper slabs.
7. 45m 4b   Climb the crack over three overlaps, turning the middle one on the right.

8   Bogle   220m   E2 *   (1967)

An impressive partner line to Brachistochrone, taking the right-hand of the two long parallel cracks that split the front face of the cliff. The climb is somewhat unbalanced, having one disproportionately difficult crux pitch. Scramble up to a belay at the foot of the crack.

1 and 2. 60m 4c   Climb the crack, with a few minor deviations, for two pitches, to a slab below the large overhang.

3. 15m 5c   Move up onto a pedestal, then climb the bulging crack (bypassing the overhang) for 6m. Move 3 metres right, then climb a parallel crack to belay on the ledge above. Vicious jamming!

4. 25m 4b   Continue up the crack to below a cave.

5. 15m 4c   Climb up into the slimy cave, quit it by a contortionate through-route, then move left up a slab to belay. (A recent report suggests that this through-route is blocked by turf and rubble. It can be bypassed by a stomach traverse left along a shallow wet sloping shelf).

6. 30m   Scramble up to the foot of the upper slabs.

7. 50m 4b   Climb the continuation crack to a large block overlap.

8. 25m 4c   The crack now divides. Climb the left-hand crack system to finish.

9   The Rake Direct   210m   E2 *   (1962/1988)

The original line was by a long grassy ramp running left from the top of the first pitch of Meadow Grooves. The direct start is of much higher quality and now supersedes the original line. At the bottom right-hand corner of the main face is a huge clean slab bounded on its right by a big groove. Start at the foot of this slab.

1 and 2. 90m 4b   Climb straight up the middle of the slab, in two pitches, to belay on a large grass ledge below a slabby corner containing two small overlaps.

3. 35m 5a   Climb up and left over bulges, then traverse left to another slabby corner. Climb this, then traverse left to a belay on a huge flake.

4. 15m 5b   Gain and climb the overhanging crack above to belay below a corner.

5. 30m 5c   Move up then around right into a corner. Climb this (crux) to gain an obvious bay on the right. Follow a crack in the slab on the left, then go over rock ledges to a grass ledge and belay.

6. 10m 4b   Climb the corner above to a grass ledge and belay in an overhanging cave.

7. 15m 4c   Exit the slimy cave by a contortionate through-route, then move left up a sloping slab to a belay 6m above.

8. 15m   Scramble up to The Terrace.

10   The Curver   130m   E1 **   (1969)
This good route, which is slow to dry, follows a series of grooves up and through the curving overlaps above and roughly parallel to The Rake. The climbing is no harder than 5b but is fairly sustained. Start near to the end of the first pitch of Meadow Grooves near two overlapping steps.
1. 25m   Climb a slab and groove to belay above a damp corner.
2. 25m   Climb the groove on the right for 10m, gain a higher slab on the right, then follow the slab corner for 10m. Move out right to reach a small stance and belay.
3. 40m   Move leftwards to gain the foot of a narrow slab gangway, then continue to a deep flake crack. Climb either the crack or the layback shelf on the right to a large ledge.
4. 40m   Pull round the edge on the right on quartz holds, then follow a line of holds across slabs to a corner. Finish up the corner.

11   Gulliver's Travels   300m   E2 *   (1995)
A logical combination of routes, with interesting links, effecting a natural rising traverse encouraged by the leftward trend and ledged nature of the cliff. The first 5 pitches are as for The Rake Direct.
6. 30m 5a   Move up to a ledge on the left, then follow it leftwards to the crack line of Brachistochrone. Descend this for 3m, past a chockstone, then follow a ramp up and left past an awkward break (crossing Blundecral) to take a spectacularly situated belay on the ramp 7m beyond the break.
7. 30m 4b   Continue up the ramp for 3m, then move onto a higher ramp. Follow this leftwards until it leads to a wide grassy fault on Brobdingnag. Ascend this for 7m to a cave beneath an arch, then traverse left to a block belay overlooking The Blinder.
8. 40m 5c   A sensational and intimidating traverse leads into The Blinder (a rope looped over the top of the arch gives some reassurance). Continue to a chimney and climb this over a chockstone to exit onto the floor of a great square recess (Hanging Gully).
9. 30m 4c   Finish as for the last pitch of The Blinder.

12   Meadow Grooves   Severe   (1944)
Three prominent grooves seam the extreme right-hand side of the face. This route starts in the leftmost groove, then transfers into the middle groove higher up. A messy vegetated route; not recommended.

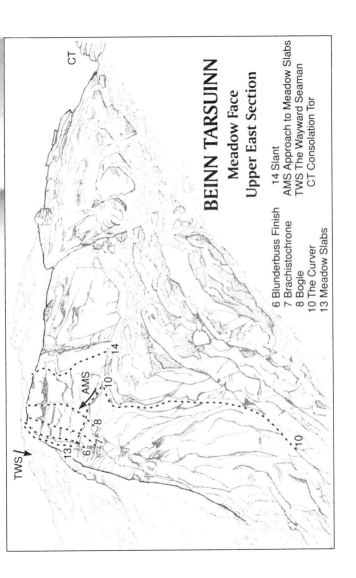

BEINN TARSUINN
Meadow Face
Upper East Section

6 Blunderbuss Finish
7 Brachistochrone
8 Bogle
10 The Curver
13 Meadow Slabs

14 Slant
AMS Approach to Meadow Slabs
TWS The Wayward Seaman
CT Consolation Tor

13 Meadow Slabs 60m Difficult (1944)
This pleasant route climbs the left edge of the upper slabs. At the left end of The Terrace a chockstoned crack is formed by a slab and the wall above. Climb the crack, then descend turf ledges towards the foot of the blunt skyline ridge. Cross a slab beyond which forms the foot of a 3m chimney that marks the start of the climb proper.
1. 10m Climb the little chimney which narrows to a crack and leads to the crest.
2. 20m Climb a short undercut chimney on the left, then take easier ground to a belay.
3. 15m Move slightly right, then slant left up a grassy crack to reach a branching chimney.
4. 15m Climb the left branch, then the wall above by a slanting crack. Gain a short arete to finish.
Winter: III,3 (1994)
Follow the summer line.

14 Slant 100m Severe (1962)
Starting on The Terrace above the finish of Meadow Grooves, this route follows a series of grooves which run up the slabs through a line of overlaps.
1. 30m Climb up and left by grassy grooves, over a bulge, then go left until a crack leads to a grass ledge.
2. 20m Move left to a slab, ascend it, then move left to loose blocks and belay.
3. 30m Follow turfy ledges to a slab below a crack in an overlap. Climb the crack to a belay.
4. 20m Move right, bear left up a small slab, then follow a chimney crack through an overlap, surmounting chockstones, and thence up to the top.

The area of slabs to the right of Slant can form into a huge easy-angled ice sheet in a good winter. It is climbable almost anywhere at about Grade II.

SOUTH OF SUMMIT BUTTRESS
(Map Ref 959 411)

This vegetated buttress lies to the left of the Meadow Face and south of the summit of the mountain.

The Wayward Seaman   85m   IV,5   (1996)
Start below and left of a prominent rectangular roof at the lowest point of the buttress.
1. 15m   Climb an easy vegetated ramp and belay on the right of an iced corner.
2. 45m   Climb the corner and ice-glazed wall to a ledge. Climb a second ice groove through an ice umbrella to gain an easy turf ramp leading to a thread belay.
3. 25m   Climb the chimney above, passing beneath a chockstone, to finish on the summit ridge.

CONSOLATION TOR   (Map Ref 962 413)

This small flat-topped mass of fine rock lies on the north-east ridge of Beinn Tarsuinn and provides some good bouldering. It can be easily accessed from The Meadow. Below Consolation Tor a steep 'Cyclopean' wall faces into Coire Daingean. Footpaths skirt both the top and the base of this wall. It is split by two deeply cut chimneys, both of which provide routes.

Tarsuinn No.1 Chimney   40m   VS 4c   (1947)
This is the leftmost, well defined, chimney.

Tarsuinn No.2 Chimney   40m   VS 5a   (1941)
This is the rightmost chimney (complex). The first five metres is the crux, thereafter the climbing is much easier.

Woolpack   40m   Difficult   (1933)
Ascend the wall to the right of No.2 chimney. Some variation is possible.

BEINN A' CHLIABHAIN

675m   (Map Ref 970 406)

This fine mountain separates Coire a' Bhradain from Glen Rosa. It holds only two climbs, one on the Glen Rosa flank and one on the Coire Daingean flank.

The Big Slab   45m   Very Difficult   (1960)
This is the large, smooth slab halfway up the flank of Glen Rosa between the twin tops of the mountain. Climb it by a central line.

Haakon's Highway   80m   Very Difficult *   (1945)
This route is on the largest of the buttresses which lie on the Coire Daingean slopes of the mountain. The easiest approach is from the ridge, descending to the foot of the climb. Start just to the right of the foot of the buttress.
1. 15m   Climb to a large ledge.
2. 30m   Continue up the right flank.
3. 15m   Gain the left flank of the buttress by a wide gap, then climb cracks and grooves to the base of a chimney.
4. 20m   Climb the strenuous chimney past a rotating chockstone and a through-route.

A'CHIR

745m   (Map Ref 966 421)

The peak of A'Chir lies on the narrow rocky ridge between Beinn Tarsuinn and Cir Mhor. The rock climbing is concentrated in Coire Daingean, on the east flank of the ridge to the south of the peak. The west face of the ridge consists of extensive although largely vegetated areas of slabby rock with limited climbing. The actual summit of A'Chir is a massive block, climbable in a number of ways (all requiring some ingenuity!).

A'Chir Ridge Traverse   1.5km   Moderate ***   (1892)
This fine ridge, one of the best in Scotland outside Skye, gives a splendid outing. Much variation is possible and the grade given is for the easiest line traversing from south to north. The most problematic section of the traverse is at the Mauvais Pas about 300 metres to the

north of the summit. After a steep step in the ridge, turned on the west flank, a narrow gap is reached which can be stepped across without difficulty. Beyond this lies a short level section terminating in a vertical rock wall dropping to a little col. The correct route is to descend the right (east) side of the ridge, roughly midway between the gap and the termination, initially by a steep wall with good holds, then by a grassy ledge, becoming a rock trench, across an exposed wall. At the end of the trench a short chimney gives access to the col (in reverse this short polished chimney becomes the crux of the route—at least Very Difficult). The section to the north of the col is particularly enjoyable and the ridge continues with decreasing difficulty towards the Cir Mhor col.

Winter: III,3 ***
A superb and challenging experience with the slabby nature of the rock adding to the difficulties. The grade assumes that the easiest line along the ridge will be taken but route finding is far from straightforward, especially in poor visibility. The crux is normally as for summer at the Mauvais Pas.

COIRE DAINGEAN

The cliffs of Coire Daingean lie in two distinct sections, The Headwall at the back of the corrie and a series of slabby buttresses on the east side of the A' Chir Ridge. The latter area, traditionally known as the Coire Daingean Face, comprises seven buttresses and six main gullies/chimneys. The Coire Daingean Face is separated from The Headwall by the wide Boundary Gully, a fairly easy ascent/descent line.

Access to both these cliffs is *via* the main Glen Rosa path to where the Coire Daingean burn meets the Rosa Water. Follow the burn, initially on its north bank (no path) up into the corrie. Allow about two hours from the Glen Rosa road head into the base of the corrie.

THE HEADWALL

At the back of the corrie this is a largely steep, wet and vegetated crag providing ideal winter climbing potential. The most obvious feature is a big vertical curving fault, as yet unclimbed.

The Shelf   180m   II   (1985)
On the left-hand side of the headwall a vegetated ramp cuts up from right to left, ending on the ridge just above the Beinn a' Chliabhain col. This is the line of the route giving an exposed snow climb.

The Riddle   110m   V,6 ***   (1985)
A superb climb with considerable exposure. Start 45 metres left of the
obvious vertical curving fault.
1. 45m   Climb steepening ice to a ledge, then traverse left onto a
projecting rock pedestal.
2. 25m   Continue leftwards up a ramp until below an open chimney
splitting a vertical wall. Step down, move left, then move up to below a
second well defined chimney.
3. 20m   Climb the chimney with difficulty to a ledge which is traversed
left until it fades.
4. 20m   Ascend a steep wall by flakes, then traverse left and go up a
groove to finish.

Cascade   85m   III,3 *   (1981)
An obvious icefall forms some distance down and right of the vertical
curving fault. Climb this line directly.

   Lower down on the right-hand section of The Headwall, close to the
main Coire Daingain Face, is a short steep slabby area. There are two
single pitch routes.

Lower Left Chimney   45m   Very Difficult   (1933)
Climb the left-hand of the two flake chimneys.

Lower Right Chimney   50m   Severe   (1977)
Climb the right-hand chimney.

COIRE DAINGEAN FACE

The buttresses are steep and slabby, giving good middle grade
climbing, but they are unfortunately traversed by many grass and
heather ledges which detract from some of the climbs. This vegetation
results in all but a handful of routes being slow to dry after rain. The
gullies/chimneys, numbered from 3 to 8 from the left, are best avoided
in summer but are more attractive in good winter conditions. The
mystery of the two missing gullies/chimneys is solved if Tarsuinn No.1
and No.2 Chimneys are included at the start of the sequence.

1   Boundary Ridge   115m   Difficult *   (1943)
An entertaining climb with some good situations, generally following
the left edge of the buttress. Start at a notch on the crest some 15m up
from the lowest rocks.

1. 20m   Climb a slab to a block on the crest. Swing left onto a grassy shelf leading to a block belay.
2. 20m   Follow a wide crack to a spike set against the wall on the right.
3. 20m   Climb the wall above and enter another crack leading to the foot of a steep arete.
4. 20m   Climb the arete to a ledge, traverse a few metres right, then climb a steep slab and broken ground to a platform with a jumble of blocks overlooking Boundary Gully.
5. 35m   Follow a horizontal ledge rightwards past a pool of water and climb the slab above. Slant up left to a wall with a Y-shaped crack and climb this to a rock shelf and the final short wall.

Variation I: Severe   (1943)
Behind the jumble of blocks at the top of pitch 4 is a steep open corner. Climb this, then move right to join the parent route just below the Y-shaped crack.

Variation II: Severe *   (1994)
From the jumble of blocks at the top of pitch 4 follow a ledge leftwards across the face overlooking the gully. The ledge ends in a slightly overhanging flake. Ascend the flake to a small platform, then finish up the wall on the right to a shelf above, joining the last few metres of the parent route.

Winter: III,3 *   (1986)
Follow the summer route, apart from pitch 4 where a left traverse from the top of pitch 3 leads to a strenuous chimney which is climbed to join the normal route at the platform with the jumble of blocks.

2   Sesame Street   105m   Severe   (1987)
This route follows a line up cracks, grooves and slabs in the centre of the buttress to the right of Boundary Ridge.

3   Gully 3   135m   Difficult   (1911)
This is the most prominent gully on the face. The lower section is not co-linear with the upper section. Climb a turfy groove to the right of the lower gully for about 45m until a left traverse into the upper gully can be effected. Not recommended.

Winter: III,4 *   (1984)
The natural winter line takes the true gully in the lower section which leads to a cave formed by an enormous chockstone. Difficult moves on the right give access into the well defined upper gully. Follow this past two short pitches. If the summer line is followed throughout, the grade is III, 3.

4   Crack Climb   135m   Difficult   (1908)
Climb the summer start to Gully 3 (the turfy groove), then continue up
the continuation groove and wide crack above.
Winter: III,3   (1987)
Follow the summer line throughout.

5   Minaret   180m   HVS (aid)   (1968)
A route on the big slabby buttress between Crack Climb and Imposter
Crack. A striking overhanging vein crosses the face at a height of about
60m. The initial pitches are slow to dry. Start at the lowest slabs.
1. 20m   Climb diagonally left, then right to a grassy ledge and belay.
2. 35m 4c   Continue up the slabs to an overlap. Traverse left, then
climb up to reach a grassy ledge below the main overhang.
3. 30m 5a   Surmount the overhanging vein, using one point of aid,
then climb a crack in the slabs above to a grassy ledge.
4 to 6. 95m   Continue up slabs in three pitches to the top.

6   Imposter Crack   100m   Difficult   (1943)
A poor route that is more of a shallow gully than a crack, filled with
grass and gravel, apart from one short pitch at about mid-height.
Winter: II,3   (1985)
Steep snow leads to the short pitch (a cave in a rock barrier). Surmount
this (crux) to gain the straightforward upper gully.

7   Intruder   155m   HVS   (1947)
A fairly sustained line on the narrow buttress left of Gully 4. The route
has some fine situations but is somewhat messy in places. Start near
the foot of Gully 4.
1. 30m 4c   Climb a corner and slab to traverse left and cross an
overlap at its central point. Ascend a slab to a flake belay in the middle
of the buttress.
2. 35m 5a   Move right and climb a curving crack in a steep slab to a
small ledge. Trend left up the slabs to a line of roofs girdling the
buttress. Traverse right under these to obvious cracks leading to a
belay.
3. 20m 4b   Climb a slab and traverse right below an overlap to a small
niche and thread belay.
4. 30m 4c   Climb a crack and slab, then traverse right below overlaps
to a flake crack leading to a heather stance with belays on the right.
5. 40m 5a   Surmount a double overlap and climb a slab above to the
left edge. Ascend the edge to an overhang, move right and cross the
overhang (strenuous) to finish up steep slabs.

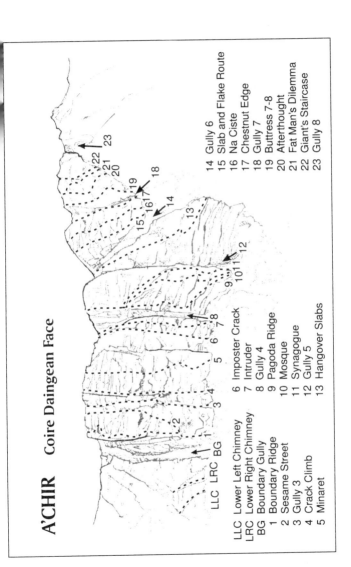

A'CHIR   Coire Daingean Face

LLC Lower Left Chimney
LRC Lower Right Chimney
BG   Boundary Gully
1 Boundary Ridge
2 Sesame Street
3 Gully 3
4 Crack Climb
5 Minaret

6 Imposter Crack
7 Intruder
8 Gully 4
9 Pagoda Ridge
10 Mosque
11 Synagogue
12 Gully 5
13 Hangover Slabs

14 Gully 6
15 Slab and Flake Route
16 Na Ciste
17 Chestnut Edge
18 Gully 7
19 Buttress 7-8
20 Afterthought
21 Fat Man's Dilemma
22 Giant's Staircase
23 Gully 8

8   Gully 4   100m   Moderate   (1907)

This deep gully contains much loose vegetation and shattered rock and is best avoided in summer.

Winter: I *

When banked out with snow this gully offers an easy descent from the ridge.

9   Pagoda Ridge   220m   Severe **   (1943)

A classic and popular climb, generally following the left edge of Buttress 4-5 overlooking Gully 4. It may be started from what is in fact the third pitch but the lower two pitches should not be missed. Start at the toe of the buttress, just left of the lowest slab (arrow and scratched letters PR).

1. 25m   Climb a heathery crack ending in a sharp flake. Traverse left, climb to a heather patch, then cross a slab to a stance below an overlap.

2. 25m   Move up onto a sloping shelf above (delicate), then go left to the edge. Climb the edge for 10m to a side belay.

3. 20m   Follow the edge with one short dogleg, then move right to a pile of blocks below a heather ledge.

4. 20m   Climb a short steep wall above the heather to reach a good stance behind a large block overlooking Gully 4.

5. 10m   Traverse right to a little corner with a spike belay.

6. 25m   Using the spike, swing round the corner on the right and traverse across the slab until the wall above can be climbed from left to right. Now traverse back left to the edge and a jammed block belay overlooking Gully 4. An excellent pitch. An alternative is to climb the spikes directly, mantelshelf onto the slab above, then move left to the edge. This is as good as the original line, but shorter.)

7. 35m   Climb the short crack above and follow the edge to a steep wall. Climb this to belay between large boulders.

8 and 9. 60m   Finish up the edge overlooking the gully in two pitches of easier but pleasant climbing.

10   Mosque   230m   VS **   (1968)

This long and quite sustained climb provides excellent climbing up to its junction with Pagoda Ridge. Start just left of the slabby toe of the buttress. The letters PR and the name Mosque are scratched on the rock.

1. 40m 4c   Pad up the widening slab (ignoring the heathery crack of Pagoda Ridge) to an overlap. Traverse left to a bulb-shaped

protuberance. Cross the overlap, then go up to the next overlap. Move down and right to belay at an old peg. Quite a bold pitch.
2. 30m 4c   Climb the slab above, then move right to a flake on the edge of the next overlap. Cross this, then continue to another and awkward overlap. Surmount it and climb a slab to a ledge with a flake belay above.
3. 25m 4b   Climb a bulging wall to the right of the belay, then ascend a slab and some heather to a hollow flake belay below an overlap.
4. 20m 4b   Cross the overlap just left of the belay, then move left to a good hidden thread runner. Follow a line of pockets rightwards over an edge to belay in a small recess on the right. An excellent pitch.
5. 40m 4b   Climb the recess, ascend a short slab, then traverse right to a crack in the overlap. Climb the crack and the slabs above (next to a turfy crack) to a belay.
6 and 7. 75m   Traverse left over slabs, then follow the line of least resistance up the edge overlooking the gully (as for Pagoda Ridge) in two long pitches.

11   Synagogue   225m   VS   (1981)
This route follows a line to the right of Mosque, but it is not of the same quality as its celebrated neighbour. Start at the very toe of the slabs.
1. 45m 4c   Climb directly up the slab to an overlap. Traverse left to surmount it on good holds. Trend left using undercuts, then climb directly over another overlap to a grass ledge. Trend rightwards up a slab to a short wall.
2. 40m 4b   Negotiate the wall on the right by an obvious groove, then continue by a slab and short overlap to a ledge.
3. 40m   Climb rightwards up the slab, then directly by a line of pocks to a heather ledge (to the right of the small recess on Mosque).
4. 40m   Trend rightwards up the slab by an undercut flake, then traverse left to join Pagoda Ridge.
5 and 6. 60m   Finish up the edge in two pitches as for Pagoda Ridge.

12   Gully 5
This ill-defined turfy gully between Buttresses 4-5 and 5-6 contains a few short pitches — not recommended.

13   Hangover Slabs   190m   VS   (1961)
A more enjoyable climb than appearances would suggest, but it is slow to dry. A walk-off at about half-height into either Gully 5 or 6 is possible. Start about 20 metres to the left of the foot of Gully 6.

1 . 45m 4b   Climb a clean slab over a detached block, then a slight bulge to a vegetated corner. Ascend this or slabs on the right, then trend left to a block belay below an overlap.

2 to 5. 115m 4b   Cross the overlap, then climb slabs in four pitches to a stance below a short wall.

6. 35m 4c   Ascend the short awkward wall, then traverse right to turn an overhang. Finish up easy slabs to large blocks.

14   Gully 6

This wide grassy gully provides an easy ascent or descent route.

15   Slab and Flake Route   110m   Severe *   (1943)

Despite its rather grassy upper section, this is an enjoyable route on the left side of Buttress 6-7. Hard for its grade. Start at the bottom left corner of the buttress.

1 . 25m 4b   Climb the slab edge for 15m, traverse diagonally right, then go back left again to the edge and a large flake belay.

2. 10m   Climb the flake by either edge, then cross a heather ledge to a block belay.

3. 15m 4b   Climb a cleft slanting right behind a flake containing a chockstone. From the top of this flake step across to gain a steep wall opposite and so reach a ledge above. Move right past a thin crack to a ladder of pock holds leading to a ledge above and an eyehole belay.

4. 25m   Follow the rising grass rake on the right to a rock shelf. Follow the shelf leftwards to another shelf, then move right up a slab to a flake belay.

5. 20m   Climb a corner to a bouldery terrace and a spike on the wall behind. Climb the spur behind and a slab above, then move back right to a block belay.

6. 15m   A wall and crack lead to a grass terrace at the top of the buttress.

16   Na Ciste   135m   VS   (1977)

This route takes a fairly central line on Buttress 6-7 to the right of Slab and Flake Route. The climbing is no harder than 4c and belays can be taken as required. Start at the lowest slabs, below and to the right of a the vertical turfy crack. Climb a slab to the top of a short heather corner on the right. Move right and go up to belay on flakes. Move back left onto the slab and climb it to a terrace. Continue up leftwards behind a large flake onto a slab, traverse this rightwards and go up to the next terrace. Move right and climb up rightwards on flake holds until it is possible to reach another terrace. Climb a wall by a flake crack on the left. Directly above is a fault formed by detached blocks; climb this to a small platform. Traverse right, then go up leftwards by a short layback crack. Move left and pull over a final bulge on good holds.

17   Chestnut Edge   95m   VS *   (1974)
This is the seemingly continuous right edge of Buttress 6-7. The prominent crack is 4c, the rest of the climb easier. Belay as required. Start at a shelf. Climb mossy rock to a clean slab and niche on the right. Climb up and left across a steep slab to a prominent crack. Ascend the crack (crux) to a ledge and large spike. Gain a slab and ledge overlooking Gully 7. Climb a steep cracked pinnacle to a ledge, then walk to the top.

18   Gully 7   90m   Difficult   (1944)
Unpleasant, loose and vegetated – not a good descent!
Winter: II *   (1987)
From the foot of the gully follow a shelf up and along the left-hand wall, followed by a chimney above. Easy snow then leads to the top.

19   Buttress 7-8   80m   Difficult   (1944)
A vegetatious route, even by Coire Daingean standards, starting at the foot of Gully 7 and following the line of least resistance. Not recommended.

20   Afterthought   90m   Severe *   (1961)
This route takes a line near the centre of Buttress 7-8. Start 6 metres to the left of the fault line of Giant's Staircase.
1. 20m   Climb straight up slabs to a grass ledge. Continue up the wall above by cracks, then mantelshelf onto a detached flake. Take a block belay on the left.
2. 30m   Climb a short slab, then traverse left around a bulge. Layback up to a heather ledge.
3. 40m   Climb a flake to an overhang, then move right to blocks. Trend right to crawl into a restricted through-route behind a huge boulder and thence to the top. Alternatively, from the belay traverse delicately right along a sloping ledge to a triangular flake with a hole at its apex. Climb this flake, then go straight up to join the original line at the through-route.

21   Fat Man's Dilemma   85m   VS   (1995)

Start at the very lowest point of a thin chimney below the corner line of Giant's Staircase on the right side of the buttress.

1. 20m 4b   Scramble up to the base of the chimney, move left to an obvious flake, step up, then climb to a vegetated ledge. Move right around an edge to find a belay.

2. 25m 4c   Move back left and climb to a big flake (not visible from below). Step up and left to move behind a semi-detached flake. Climb heathery rock to a juniper ledge.

3. 20m 4c   Traverse up and right on flakes until a step right across a groove onto a slab allows a heather ledge above to be gained. Scramble up and to the right to gain and climb a deep crack which separates an enormous block from the crag. Belay on the flat top of this block.

4. 20m 4b   On the left is a distinctive horizontal spike. Pull up to this, move left then back right to crawl into a restricted through-route behind a huge boulder (in common with Afterthought) and thence to the top.

22   Giant's Staircase   75m   Severe   (1943)

A corner/fault line defines the right edge of the main section of Buttress 7-8 (to the right of this fault lies a short section of vegetated cliff before Gully 8 is reached). This route follows the fault *via* a series of short chimneys with ledges in between. All the chimneys should be climbed direct, giving strenuous climbing.

23   Gully 8   50m   Moderate   (1907)

The final gully of the face, with the summit buttress beyond, contains two short pitches.

Winter: II

The gully can bank out to reduce the grade to I.

COIRE BUIDHE FACE

This corrie is formed by the main ridge running north from the summit of A' Chir and a lateral ridge jutting out into Glen Rosa. It holds a number of very steep Cyclopean walls, separated by short gravelly gullies, on the east flank of the main ridge. No climbing has been recorded on them so far. One prominent little buttress just to the south of the A' Chir – Cir Mhor col does however hold two routes.

Leaning Block Chimney   30m   Very Difficult   (1958)

This route lies on the left half of the little buttress and follows the chimney with a conspicuous leaning block near its foot.

Birthday Chimney   30m   Very Difficult   (1947)
Climb the prominent chimney up the centre of the face with a large
projecting block at about one-third height.

GLEN IORSA FACE

From the little col at the Mauvais Pas an easy gravelly gully leads down
on the west side of the ridge. Immediately south of this there is a 20m
high wall buttressing an expanse of slabs just below the crest of the
ridge. This is the Glen Iorsa Face; two routes have been recorded.

November Chimney   55m   Very Difficult *   (1958)
The wall is breached by a steep curving chimney holding a
chockstone. Climb the narrow chimney (strenuous), belaying about
5m beyond its top. Move slightly right to the foot of the slabs, then climb
these by cracks and grooves. Finish up slabs to gain the ridge crest.

Cairn's Cream Corner   55m   Severe *   (1978)
Start at a chimney crack 6m right of November Chimney. Climb this,
then follow an obvious slab corner to a belay. Move up and left to a flake
crack with a pointed top. Surmount this, exiting left at the top.

CIR MHOR

799m   (Map Ref 972 431)

This magnificent peak, the finest on Arran and one of the most striking
in Scotland, sits at the heart of the main massif. It presents two
contrasting rock faces, the vast dank and gloomy North-East Face
(described later in the Glen Sannox section) and delightful South Face
with its impeccable granite slabs.

SOUTH FACE

This splendid face is best viewed from afar from where its distinctive
topography can be well appreciated. The Rosa Pinnacle, the main
buttress dropping from the summit of the mountain, dominates the
face. To its right lies Sub Rosa Gully, beyond that the Prospero Buttress;
to its left, beyond the sea of slabs comprising its west face, lies Green
Gully flanked on the left by Caliban's Buttress. Further left again lies the
more broken buttress of Cubic Ridge. The South Face holds a selection
of the finest routes on Arran with quality at almost every grade.

Access is *via* the main Glen Rosa path to take the left fork at Map Ref 978 414 which leads up into Fionn Choire. Allow about two and a half hours from the Glen Rosa road head to the base of the cliffs.

1   Cubic Ridge   100m   Difficult   (1944)
This buttress has a very steep east face and a more broken slabby west face with a shark's fin-shaped rock on the ridge at about half-height. Start just left of the foot of the buttress and climb a series of cracks and short walls to the shark's fin. An easy walk off is available at this point. Keeping to the right, the upper buttress offers easy but pleasant climbing to the (avoidable) final wall.
Winter: III,3 *   (1988)
An enjoyable climb with the lower buttress providing the difficulties.

CALIBAN'S BUTTRESS

This buttress lies immediately west of the Rosa Pinnacle. It has a slabby west face and a vertical east face (forming the left retaining wall of Green Gully).

2   Caliban's Creep   150m   Very Difficult **   (1943)
This route has over the years sandbagged a good number of climbers and has been dubbed the hardest Difficult in the world. It is no longer so! It is a very characterful route with some splendid situations. Start on the right of the toe of the buttress which forms a square-cut overhang.
1. 25m   Climb slabs diagonally leftwards to belay in a pile of boulders under an overhang and left of a shattered-looking wall. This pitch can be avoided by entry from the left.
2. 25m   Traverse across the wall on good holds, move down and round the edge and gain an easy chimney which leads to an area of slabs.
3. 15m   Cross the slabs to below a vertical wall and belay at its right-hand edge.
4. 20m   Crawl through a narrow rock tunnel (the Creep), then cross a narrow exposed ledge on the east face to reach a deep chimney. Climb this into the floor of a great fissure and belay.
5 and 6. 65m   Escape from the fissure, then climb slabs near the right edge for two pitches to the top.

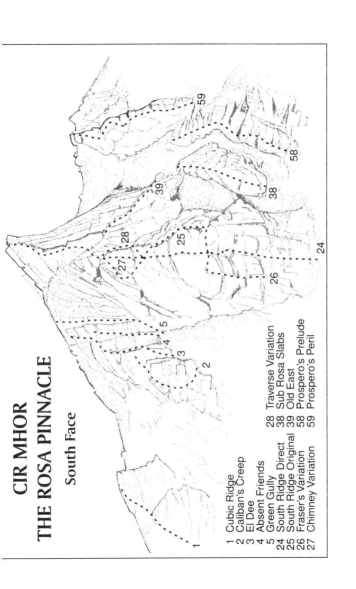

CIR MHOR
THE ROSA PINNACLE
South Face

1 Cubic Ridge
2 Caliban's Creep
3 El Dee
4 Absent Friends
5 Green Gully
24 South Ridge Direct
25 South Ridge Original
26 Fraser's Variation
27 Chimney Variation
28 Traverse Variation
38 Sub Rosa Slabs
39 Old East
58 Prospero's Prelude
59 Prospero's Peril

3   El Dee   30m   HVS 5a   (1979)
This can be used as a hard direct start to Caliban's Creep. Start to the
right of that route. Climb up slabs to gain a ramp sloping up from right to
left beneath an inverted triangular block. Climb a small crack on the left
of the block over bulges to a small ledge. Traverse hard left to avoid a
loose flake, climb over small ledges, then go up a groove to belay.

4   Absent Friends   30m   E2 5c (aid)   (1985)
This is the prominent crack high on the right wall of the buttress,
starting about 10m above the ground. Start up an offwidth crack to the
left of the upper crack (two points of aid), then traverse right into the
upper crack and climb it.

5   Green Gully   90m   Very Difficult   (1897)
This aptly-named climb lies between Caliban's Buttress and the Rosa
Pinnacle. It is best avoided in summer.
Winter: II,3 *   (1979)
A worthwhile route with one ice pitch in the lower gully, a through-route
in the left-hand finish and steep mixed ground above.

ROSA PINNACLE

This great ridge-like buttress of excellent rock is the best advert for
Arran rock climbing! It holds some of the finest routes and despite the
relatively long walk in, it is the most popular climbing venue on the
island. The Pinnacle is divided into two sections by The Terrace on the
west flank and the break line of Old East on the east. The Lower West
Face comprises an area of huge slabs whilst both the Lower and
Upper East Faces are much steeper. A girdle of the Pinnacle has been
made.

LOWER WEST FACE

This is the wide area of immaculate slabs on the west flank of the Rosa
Pinnacle below The Terrace. Most of the routes are quick to dry and the
rock is superb.

6   Fourth Wall   125m   Severe *   (1945)
Only the last pitch is Severe; the easier lower section of this climb is
shared by a number of routes. Start at the foot of a long slanting
groove, level with the foot of the vertical wall on Caliban's Buttress.
1 and 2. 50m   Follow the groove to a point level with the foot of an

open chimney/corner on the slabs to the right (this is the point where Sou'wester Slabs traverses right).
3 and 4. 50m   Continue in the same general line to reach the top of a huge plinth below a steep narrow chimney.
5. 25m 4b   Climb the chimney for a short distance, then using a small ledge, traverse right, descending slightly, for 6m across the face until it is possible to climb the wall above. A final awkward step right into an easy groove leads to the finish on The Terrace. A fine pitch. Two alternative finishes to this pitch are available at about the same grade:
Variation A: 20m   (1945)
Climb the chimney direct.
Variation B: 35m   (1959)
From the base of the huge plinth, traverse 5 metres right and downwards to a sloping grass ledge. Traverse diagonally right across slabs until it is possible to climb directly up a shallow groove to a belay. Climb the broken slab above to a small roof, then exit right to reach the ridge crest. A rather wandering line.

7   **The Ozone Layer**   190m   IV,4 **   (1989)
This natural winter line in the vicinity of Fourth Wall has continuous interest. Start below an open turfy groove just uphill from the common start of Fourth Wall and Sou'wester Slabs.
1. 15m   Gain and climb the groove to belay just beneath a short chimney.
2. 35m   Move right and climb turfy cracks and grooves to a belay 3m below a small overhang.
3. 30m   Move down and left round an edge into a short corner. Climb this to a traverse left on flakes into a groove which is followed to a belay.
4. 45m   Climb the grooves trending leftwards (common to Fourth Wall) to belay on top of the Plinth.
5. 40m   Descend left for 6m onto a wide grassy shelf. Follow it over steep steps to a belay 5m below the steep wall holding the final corner.
6. 25m   Climb the groove and corner to reach The Terrace.

8   **Arctic Way**   65m   VS **   (1982)
Below and to the right of the huge plinth on Fourth Wall an obvious left-facing corner crack runs up the slabs. Start at the foot of this corner (reached by climbing the lower section of Fourth Wall). A fine and sustained climb.
1. 40m 4c   Climb the corner to its top, then follow the continuation crack over a bulge to another bulge which is climbed directly, then ascend the slab above to belay under an overlap.
2. 25m 4c   Move left to a crack through the overlap and go left again

to a bulge above an old peg. Climb over the bulge, then trend left up the slab for a metre or so. Traverse right to below a thin crack, climb it, then trend left to a block belay at the top.

9 Arctic Way Variation 85m VS (1987)
Not as good as the original route, but worth climbing.
1. 40m 4c From below the improbable-looking bulge above the initial corner, traverse right into a small corner. Gain the slab on the right of this and climb to a belay overlooking West Flank Route.
2. 45m 4b Traverse hard left across the slab to a grass patch and an edge beyond. Climb the edge to the old peg on the parent route. Climb the fine left-trending crack to The Terrace.

10 Lawyer's Leap 80m E1 * (1983)
This route follows the big distinctive corner line that lies between Fourth Wall and Sou'wester Slabs. Start two pitches up Fourth Wall at the point where Sou'wester Slabs traverses right.
1. 40m 5b Climb directly up the slabs by a series of thin layback cracks to reach the corner proper. Climb to the top of the corner and pull onto the overhanging wall before making committing moves out leftwards onto the slab above. Continue up the slab to a belay.
2. 40m 4b Ascend to the junction with West Flank Route 6m above. Traverse 10 metres right onto a large expanse of clean slab and climb this to join South Ridge Direct.

11 Ne Parl Pas 40m E1 5b * (1989)
A good single pitch linking Sou'wester Slabs to West Flank Route. Start just to the right of the point where Fourth Wall and Sou'wester Slabs diverge. Ascend a line of pockets to reach a thin ledge. Continue up and right on more pockets to gain a shallow left-slanting groove. Follow this to reach an obvious slim right-facing corner. Climb it to belay on the left traverse under the roof taken by West Flank Route.

12 Sou'wester Slabs 110m Very Difficult *** (1944)
A much celebrated route and the finest of its grade on Arran. A real classic.
1 and 2. 50m Climb the slanting groove of Fourth Wall for two pitches until level with the foot of an open chimney/corner on the slabs to the right.
3. 20m Traverse easily right to the foot of the chimney/corner, then climb it to a spike belay below prominent twin parallel cracks.

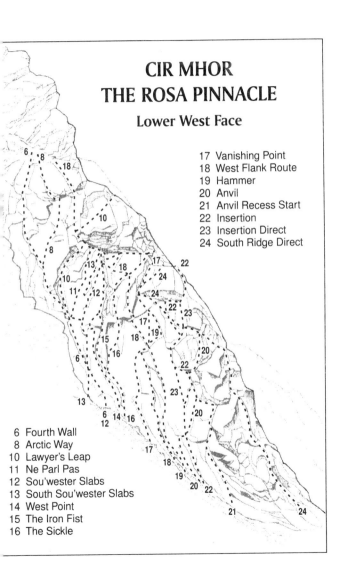

CIR MHOR
THE ROSA PINNACLE

Lower West Face

17 Vanishing Point
18 West Flank Route
19 Hammer
20 Anvil
21 Anvil Recess Start
22 Insertion
23 Insertion Direct
24 South Ridge Direct

6 Fourth Wall
8 Arctic Way
10 Lawyer's Leap
11 Ne Parl Pas
12 Sou'wester Slabs
13 South Sou'wester Slabs
14 West Point
15 The Iron Fist
16 The Sickle

4. 30m   Climb the parallel cracks to the right edge of the slab, drop down onto the lower slab on the right, then climb a right-trending groove to belay under the great overhang.

5. 10m   Traverse easily right under the roof (joining South Ridge Direct under the Three-Tier Chimney). From this point, South Ridge Direct can be ascended (Very Difficult), providing contrasting climbing to The Terrace. Alternatively, traverse further right and move up on grassy ledges (one exposed step) to allow a descent to the top of Old East, which gives a Moderate descent into Sub Rosa Gully.

A winter ascent of Sou'wester Slabs has been claimed (V,5) in 1994, but given its high quality status as a rock climb and the total absence of turf or ice, repeat ascents are not recommended.

13   South Sou'wester Slabs   90m   Severe *   (1981)
This good direct line shares some common ground with its more famous neighbour. Hard for its grade. Start 6 metres uphill from the start of Fourth Wall's groove, below a part vegetated groove running up to an obvious triangular roof.

1. 40m 4b   Cross the line of Fourth Wall, then climb the groove to below the triangular roof. Turn the roof on the left (crux), then continue up to belay below the open chimney/corner of Sou'wester Slabs.

2. 45m   Climb the chimney/corner, then move left to gain and climb the excellent flake crack (running parallel to the twin flake cracks on Sou'wester Slabs) to a small ledge below the slab rib on West Flank Route. Drop down on the right, cross a delicate slab, then move up to belay under the great overhang.

3. 5m   Traverse easily right as for Sou'wester Slabs. Continue as for the Sou'wester Slabs alternatives.

14   West Point   90m   E4 *   (1986)
This bold route presents poorly protected slab climbing, following a line to the left of the twin chimneys taken by The Iron Fist and The Sickle respectively. Start 3 metres left of the common start of these two routes, and 6 metres right of the groove of Fourth Wall.

1. 10m 4c   Climb directly up the slab to belay on a ledge just left of the chimney of Sickle.

2. 35m 5c   Ascend the edge of the left-hand chimney, palming its left arete, until it veers right. Make committing moves left to a thin crack which is climbed to a roof. Move left again into a corner, then go over the roof to a belay.

3. 45m 5b   Follow a quartz intrusion rightwards to a rib and follow this to belay below the great overhang. The upper part of West Flank Route can now be climbed, or traverse off to the right as for Sou'wester Slabs.

15   The Iron Fist   75m   HVS *   (1978)

This route follows the left-hand of the twin chimneys defining the left edge of the great central slab, the right-hand one being taken by The Sickle. It is at the upper end of its grade. Start about 10m down from the groove of Fourth Wall, to the left of the start of West Flank Route.

1. 30m 4c   Follow the obvious fault slanting up left to a belay on a sloping ledge just below the chimneys.

2. 45m 5b   Climb the left-hand chimney, then pull over a bulge into a notch on the rib. Climb the rib and cracks to belay on Sou'wester Slabs below the great overhang.

16   The Sickle   75m   HVS **   (1957)

Start as for The Iron Fist. The middle section is slow to dry, and the route is at the upper end of its grade.

1. 30m 4c   As for The Iron Fist.

2. 25m 5a   Gain and climb the right-hand chimney for 5m, then traverse up and right across a steep bare slab to reach a good flake edge (bold). Follow the flake to below the overlap. Move right and cross the overlap *via* a deep narrow groove which leads to a bollard belay.

3. 20m 4c   Continue up the groove in the slab above, then traverse diagonally rightwards using veins of microgranite to reach the big platform at the finish of Sou'wester Slabs. It is also possible to avoid the traverse and climb straight up to below the great overhang. Continue *via* West Flank Route or Sou'wester Slabs.

17   Vanishing Point   100m   E4 ***   (1985)

An excellent and very bold route starting up the crack system to the left of the chimney line of West Flank Route, just left of the bottomless flake crack in the slab above.

1. 30m 6a   Climb the crack system, then traverse right to gain the obvious flake crack and follow it to belay on the edge above the second chimney of West Flank Route.

2. 45m 4c   Step right onto the slab, then follow a direct line to belay below the layback crack on South Ridge Direct.

3. 25m 5c   Climb the layback crack for 3m, then break out left to gain a sandwiched slab and groove. Climb this, then go up the headwall above to finish at the top of Sou'wester Slabs.

18 West Flank Route 155m E1 *** (1963)

A truly classic route following a natural line of chimneys and cracks running diagonally leftwards across the huge central slab. Although at the lower end of its grade, the initial chimneys will provide even the most stylish performer with moments of doubt and a deeper insight into the joys of Arran climbing!

1. 20m 5a Climb the first chimney to a belay.

2. 15m 5a Climb the second chimney to a ledge below a small overlap in the slab.

3. 25m 4b Follow the long diagonal crack in the slab above to a big overlap. Move right around the corner into a niche.

4. 30m 5b Step up and left from the niche round an edge into a groove and crack. Follow these to reach a small spike and flake by a rounded layback. The crack now branches. Take the right-hand crack for a metre or so until a move can be made across the slab. Climb to a horizontal crack, then traverse left across the slab (crux) and up to gain a thread belay on Sou'wester Slabs (at the top of a groove). The crux traverse can be avoided by descending to the left from the horizontal crack to the base of a groove which leads to the belay.

5. 35m 4c Climb the corner above the belay, then step left onto a small ledge on a slabby rib. Ascend the rib to the great overhang, then traverse left to gain a wall and continue left around a bulge. Climb up to easier ground and belay.

6. 30m Ascend broken slabs above to a short wall and climb through a recess, moving up a crack to finish on The Terrace.

19 Hammer 85m VS ** (1960)

A good route starting at a tapering slab just right of West Flank Route.

1. 25m 4b Climb up onto the slab, then go left to a crack. Follow the crack which becomes a small groove to belay above the first chimney of West Flank Route.

2. 20m 4c Descend a short distance until it is possible to traverse right a metre or so into a good crack containing a few tufts of grass. Climb the crack to belay on a large ledge.

3. 40m 4b Climb the crack in the slab above to reach a microgranite vein 5m from its end. Follow the vein rightwards (delicate in places) to a crack, then climb up to belay on South Ridge Direct.

The next route is more a complex of pitches than a single distinct line. The best route is the combination of the Recess Start and the Variation Finish, although the original route does have its moments.

20 Anvil 55m HVS ** (1960)

Start a short distance right of Hammer at a broad crack.

1. 30m 5a Climb the crack to a point just left of the corner of a small overlap. Descend, then traverse right across a steep slab to gain holds on the slab edge leading up through the overlap to a sloping platform. Climb a thin groove to a grass ledge.

2. 15m 4b Climb up leftwards by awkward grassy grooves into a cave.

3. 10m 5a Break out right from the cave and follow an easy shelf to reach South Ridge Direct.

Variation Finish: 25m VS 4c ** (1965)

From the cave, traverse left under the big overhang and climb a bulging rounded groove to beneath an overhang. Move right up a slab, then climb a groove and more slabs to finish on South Ridge Direct.

21 Anvil Recess Start 40m HVS *** (1964)

Start at a corner crack directly below the huge inverted-V recess on the front face of the ridge. It is really too good to be called a variation!

1. 15m 4b Climb the corner crack to its finish.

2. 25m 5a Pull round left onto the slab and climb up until it is possible to move right to gain a large flake lodged under the right wall of the recess. Climb the flake, then step left to the opposite wall and gain the slab above by a strenuous pull-up. It is also possible to gain the pull-up *via* the left-hand corner of the recess, but this is often wet. Continue more easily by a crack on the right, then move left to reach the top of the second pitch of the original route.

22 Insertion 105m E3 ** (1969)

A hard slab climb. Start about a metre to the right of Anvil.

1. 45m 5c Climb straight up a steep slab to an overlap. Surmount this, continue up another steep slab, then trend right to belay a little way below the cave on Anvil.

2. 30m 4c Traverse up and left under the big overhang and climb the bulging rounded groove of Anvil Variation Finish to beneath the overhang. Move out right up a slab, then climb a groove to below a roof. Pull out right onto a slab and move easily left, crossing South Ridge Direct, to belay below a steep slab.

3. 30m 4c Move up left, then traverse horizontally right below an overhanging wall. Continue round an edge to a crack which is climbed to the big platform below the Three-Tier Chimney on South Ridge Direct.

23 Insertion Direct 95m E5 ** (1986)

A very bold first pitch, requiring continuous motion (upwards!). Start as for Insertion.

1. 50m 5c Climb a steep slab to an overlap. Surmount this, then climb straight up into a scoop in the centre of the slab. Ascend this, then teeter rightwards to take a hanging belay under the big overhang at the base of the bulging rounded groove of Anvil Variation Finish.

2. 25m 4c Gain and climb the groove to below a roof. Move out right up a slab to belay at its top below a bulging wall with a large pocket.

3. 20m 5c Pull past the pocket and smaller ones above. Swing round the edge, then climb to reach easier ground on South Ridge Direct.

24 South Ridge Direct 395m VS *** (1941)

This splendid long and varied climb, one of the most popular on the island, has achieved classic status. Although by no means sustained, it has some testing pitches and route-finding skills are undoubtedly required. Being south-facing it dries quickly and catches all the available sunshine. The standard route is described first, followed by a number of variations. From Fionn Choire the ridge rises as a steep nose out of a jumble of vegetated slabs. A distinctive elongated S-shaped crack splits the face of the nose and is the first main pitch of the route.

1 to 4. 130m Climb the vegetated slabs, by the line of least resistance (at most Very Difficult), to the base of the S-Crack and a large flake belay on the left.

5. 15m 4c Climb the S-Crack to a wide shelf with a large block belay.

6. 10m 5a Climb the strenuous, overhanging Y-Cracks (crux) to belay just above. A meaty little pitch nudging 5b.

7. 45m Move up to a block-strewn terrace, step around a rib on the left, then make an easy ascending diagonal traverse across the top of the great western slabs to take an awkward belay in the far corner below the Layback Crack.

8. 20m 4b Climb the Layback Crack until a vein runs out to the right. Follow it across the slab (good hand holds above) to reach a large platform via a short corner. A very fine pitch.

9. 30m Above the platform, on the left side of the ridge crest, lies an obvious chimney in three sections, the Three-Tier Chimney. Climb it to gain the ridge crest.

10 and 11. 55m Two easy pitches along the crest lead to The Terrace below the Upper Pinnacle. The Upper Pinnacle can be avoided by walking off The Terrace, but it gives good quality climbing at about Very Difficult standard and should not be omitted.

12. 40m   Start on the left and climb a short steep wall, *via* two undercut flakes, to gain a slab. Climb straight up this, near the ridge crest, to gain a fault coming in from the right. Follow this, then climb a chimney to a grass ledge.

13. 35m   Move left across the grass ledge to a little chimney. Climb the slab on its right to the ridge crest. Move round right onto the east face, then make an exposed traverse right to a corner. Climb the corner to a crevasse belay.

14. 15m   Climb a corner and short slab to the top of the Upper Pinnacle. A short descent leads to a path traversing westward to join the descent path of Cir Mhor's South-West Ridge. However, if time and energy allow, an ascent of The Rosetta Stone *en route* to the summit of Cir Mhor provides a fitting climax to a splendid climb.

25   South Ridge Original   60m   VS **   (1935)

Although easier than the Direct, the Original variation provides a good alternative for climbers who find themselves queuing below the S-Crack. The main corner pitch of the Original route is in fact just as intimidating as any on South Ridge Direct.

1. 30m   From the foot of the S-Crack, traverse right below the steep wall, then move up into a turfy recess below a big undercut corner.

2. 30m 4b   Climb out of the recess (problematic) into the corner above. Ascend it until cracks running up the steep left wall can be climbed to the block-strewn terrace above. Alternatively, follow the corner all the way to the terrace – a bit grassy. The corner can also be accessed from Sub Rosa Gully up steep vegetated ground and can therefore provide a start to South Ridge independent of the initial messy slabs of the normal route.

26   Fraser's Variation   40m   Severe 4b *

An alternative and more satisfying approach to the S-Crack from the foot of Anvil Recess Start. Climb the initial corner of that route for 6m, then break out right up a groove. From the top of the groove head right to the foot of an obvious flake chimney. Climb it, then traverse right to the foot of the S-Crack.

27   Chimney Variation   30m   HVS 5a **

From the block-strewn terrace above and to the right of the Y-Cracks there is a narrow and slightly overhanging chimney on the true ridge line. Climb it and slabs above to the big platform above the Layback Crack.

28   Traverse Variation   35m   VS 4b *   (1944)
From the block-strewn terrace above the Y-Cracks follow a right-slanting fault line out onto the east face to reach a turfy chimney crack. Climb this to the big platform above the Layback Crack.

29   Lovat's Variation   10m   VS 4b **
This climbs the Layback Crack in its entirety, avoiding the right traverse of the normal route. Awkward and strenuous.

30   Fault Variation   15m   VS 4c
An alternative start to the Upper Pinnacle. From The Terrace follow a sloping shelf round the corner to a steep fault. Climb it to join the normal route.

LOWER EAST FACE

This is the east flank of South Ridge, bounded at its lower end by the big corner of South Ridge Original and at its upper end by Old East. It has traditionally been described as an 'area of wet and vegetatious slabs'. This, however, does it an injustice, as there is much clean rock and all the routes have some interest, including one the best 5b pitches on the island (Squids and Elephants). The base of the face is gained *via* an ascent or descent of Sub Rosa Gully.

31   The Crack   45m   HVS *   (1973)
This route climbs the impressive flake crack forming a slim right-facing groove to the right of the corner pitch of South Ridge Original. Start in Sub Rosa Gully at two parallel cracks in a proud buttress of poor rock beneath the flake crack.
1. 15m 5a   Climb the parallel cracks (crumbly rock) and a groove to reach a grass ledge and belay.
2. 30m 5a   Climb a groove on the left until level with the flake crack. Traverse left to gain the flake crack which provides very good climbing and leads to the block-strewn terrace on South Ridge Direct.

32   Squids and Elephants   45m   E1 5b ***   (1996)
Despite the initial messy scramble this is a really excellent pitch, at the upper limit of its grade. It gains and follows flakes and cracks up the striking edge (flanked on its right by a massive slab), to the left of Lower East Chimney. A climb for the party animal! Start at a messy bay just

Pitch 1 of Insertion on the Rosa Pinnacle (Climber, Martin Donnelly)

right of the proud crumbly buttress taken by The Crack. Scramble up the bay, then move left to a ledge. Ascend a tricky little wall, then pull right into the flake crack system. Climb this, then take a remarkable thin crack seaming the very edge, to chill out on a rock ledge above. Ascend a slab past large pockets to belay at a horizontal fault. A short descent to the left, down a rock ramp, leads to the block-strewn terrace on South Ridge Direct. Alternatively, the Chimney Variation or the Traverse Variation provide a logical continuation.

33   Lower East Chimney   50m   Very Difficult   (1946)
This is the wide vegetated open corner (not really a chimney), rising out of Sub Rosa Gully, well right of the corner pitch of South Ridge Original. It is best avoided.

34   Flakes and Foreigners   70m   HVS *   (1996)
A worthwhile route with a fantastic thin fingery flake on the first pitch. Start at a large tablet of rock resting against the face, just left of the big groove holding a strange pinnacle high up.
1. 45m 5a   Climb the tablet, then trend left to reach a detached slab. Move left to the base of a cracked groove. Climb it, using knobbles on the left wall, to reach huge flakes. Step right onto these, then climb a thin fingery flake crack (crux), followed by curious tramlines to belay on a rock ledge.
2. 25m 5a   Ascend a left-slanting slot capped by a big projecting block. From the block move slightly down and left, then climb an open groove (the top of Lower East Chimney) to reach South Ridge at a large platform below the Three-Tier Chimney.

35   The Eyrie   65m   VS   (1975)
This is not to be confused with a feature of the same name on Labyrinth. Start in Sub Rosa Gully to the right of Lower East Chimney where a large tablet of rock rests against the face, below a big groove holding a strange pinnacle about 30m up.
1. 35m   Climb the tablet, then move right into a corner. Climb this until it is possible to move left onto the arete. Ascend this, then move up and left to belay at the pinnacle.
2. 30m   Climb the groove directly behind the belay and continue up a steep chimney to reach South Ridge at a large platform below the Three-Tier Chimney.

Arctic Way on the West Face of the Rosa Pinnacle
(Climbers, Alastair Walker and partner)

36   The Engie   65m   VS   (1975)
Start in Sub Rosa Gully about 40 metres above Lower East Chimney,
some 4 metres right of a large block leaning against the crag.
1. 35m   Climb up for a couple of metres until it is possible to traverse
awkwardly left across a slab to a grass strip. Climb the good crack
above directly to an awkward finish. Take a belay on the right.
2. 10m   Traverse left to belay on a grass ledge beneath the start of a
fine left-trending crack that splits the upper wall.
3. 20m   Follow the crack to finish at the large platform below the
Three-Tier Chimney.

37   The Geordie   90m   VS   (1975)
Start as for The Engie.
1. 30m   Climb the obvious chimney-crack to an awkward exit.
2. 35m   Step down and left and climb a dirty chimney. Move left and
belay beneath a V-shaped break in the centre of the overhangs.
3. 25m   Climb the overhanging crack to the large overhang. Move left
beneath this, then continue more easily to join South Ridge Direct.

38   Sub Rosa Slabs   50m   Difficult   (1946)
Start at a grassy neck that projects from Sub Rosa Gully near the
bottom right-hand corner of the face. Climb up three tiers of slabs to
reach Old East.

39   Old East   60m   Moderate   (1946)
This route conveniently links The Terrace with Sub Rosa Gully. It
follows an obvious line of weakness curving up and leftwards from Sub
Rosa Gully below the base of the steep Upper Pinnacle. It gives
access to the routes on the Upper East Wall and is also useful as a
descent route.

UPPER EAST FACE

This fine steep face rises above the upper reaches of Sub Rosa Gully.
It is bounded on the left by the break line of Old East, above which rises
a very steep cracked wall, and on the right and upper side by Pinnacle
Gully. The Sub Rosa Gully face forms a monolithic wall low down and is
seamed by a number of chimney and crack lines to the right of this.
Sweeping down from the summit is the slightly overhung edge known
as The Prow.

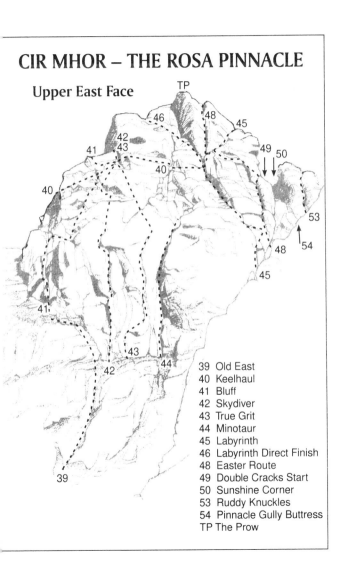

CIR MHOR – THE ROSA PINNACLE

Upper East Face

39 Old East
40 Keelhaul
41 Bluff
42 Skydiver
43 True Grit
44 Minotaur
45 Labyrinth
46 Labyrinth Direct Finish
48 Easter Route
49 Double Cracks Start
50 Sunshine Corner
53 Ruddy Knuckles
54 Pinnacle Gully Buttress
TP The Prow

40 Keelhaul 75m Severe * (1968)
Start on The Terrace just to the right of the line taken by South Ridge
Direct on the Upper Pinnacle.
1. 40m Easily gain a shelf sloping rightwards to a corner. Move round
the corner onto the east face, following grooves slanting slightly
upwards to reach the big corner at the end of Bluff's third pitch.
2. 15m Ascend 3m on the left of the corner, then move easily right to
a stance and block belay.
3. 20m Step down, then traverse right across a wall to reach a grassy
fault. Descend this to The Eyrie on Labyrinth. Continue by either of the
Labyrinth variations.

41 Bluff 75m E2 * (1968)
A good climb, low in the grade, but slow to dry. Start on The Terrace at
the top of Old East where the wall is criss-crossed by vertical and
horizontal cracks below a grass platform on the wall above.
1. 20m 5a Climb the crack to a bulge and continue to gain an edge
leading to a spike in a corner. Climb the corner to the grass platform.
Climb the continuation corner to another grass platform.
2. 10m 5b Move right across a steep wall below an overlap to a
down-sloping ledge. Descend this to a belay.
3. 25m 5b Climb a scoop above to a corner, then move right onto a
steep slab. Traverse round the corner of the overlap, then move right to
a crack on a slab edge. Traverse up and right into a big corner.
4. 20m Move left from the belay and climb a groove above to join the
final pitch of South Ridge Direct.

42 Skydiver 80m E3 *** (1981/1984)
A brilliant route on excellent rock. The first pitch lays claim to being the
best on Arran and the route is as good as any of its grade in Scotland.
Start at the foot of an arete, below a big lug of rock high up.
1. 30m 5b Climb the left side of the arete *via* a corner and pull right
onto the edge. Enter a superb twin-cracked corner and climb it to a
sloping stance below a roof. A magnificent pitch.
2. 10m 6a Make a contorted move left below the roof to enter a
groove behind the lug. Follow the groove to a small stance beside a
detached flake (good nut placements in a crack on its right).
3. 40m 5a Stand on the detached flake, then climb a crack to a
horizontal break. Move right to reach a flake. Climb this and the twin
roofs above to enter a recess. Pull out right and move up slabs to reach
a good ledge. Finish up an overhanging corner.

43 True Grit 85m E1 (1984)

Just to the left of Minotaur there is a prominent line of flakes on the wall.
An obvious line, but as the name suggests the rock is rather crumbly.
Start below and left of the flake line.

1. 40m 5a Climb a grassy corner until a traverse right across a slab
and a short crack lead to the base of the flake line. Climb a decaying
flake, then go up the main flake to its top.

2. 35m 4c Move slightly right, ascend thin flakes, then move left to a
grass tongue directly above the ground belay. Trend left to a good
ledge and belay.

3. 10m A slab and a short overhanging corner lead to the Pinnacle
crest.

44 Minotour 55m E1 (1958)

This route follows the frequently damp curving crack line to the left of
the monolithic wall that flanks Sub Rosa Gully. It has been described
as 'that acme of awfulness' – truly a climb for the connoisseur! From
the gully scramble up to the foot of the corner where the crack makes a
narrow beginning.

1. 10m 4c Climb the crack to a grassy patch in a corner.

2. 15m 5a Climb the widening overhanging crack for about 6m, then
gain the rib on the left. Move up, then enter the wider chimney and
belay. A desperate pitch!

3. 30m Carry on up the chimney, then leave it to the right of a large
boulder. A short distance further leads to the junction with Labyrinth.

45 Labyrinth 120m Very Difficult * (1943)

A varied and interesting route following the general line of the central
chimney-crack. Start at a short rock alleyway just below the bottom
right-hand corner of the monolithic wall.

1. 20m Enter the alleyway, moving behind an enormous jammed
block. Exit left and continue up to a grass platform abutting the
monolithic wall.

2. 10m Ascend a right-slanting groove to a sloping grass patch (the
crack of Easter Route lies just to the right).

3. 15m A horizontal ledge runs across the wall on the left. Traverse
across to reach a little undercut corner. Belay in the groove above.

4. 30m Climb the chimney line above, initially grassy, then holding
two groups of chockstones above a grass platform (optional belay), to
belay in a rocky recess (The Eyrie) situated under the base of The
Prow.

5. 35m   Traverse rightwards and slightly up, passing below a steep curving crack (on Easter Route) to reach an easy right-slanting grass rake. Continue to a cluster of blocks.
6. 10m   Drop behind the blocks to a recess overlooking Pinnacle Gully, then climb a short steep chimney and a slab to finish.
Winter: IV,5 ***   (1983)
Follow the summer line throughout *via* excellent and sustained climbing.

46   Labyrinth Direct Finish   40m   VS 4b **   (1951)
Also known as the Stewart Orr Finish, this provides a better finish to the route than the original final pitches. Start from The Eyrie. Climb straight up a big corner for about 5m to reach two horizontal faults running out left. Traverse these (crux) moving round a corner to join the final pitch of South Ridge Direct.

47   The Sword of Theseus   100m   HVS 5a *   (1979)
This is basically a direct version of Labyrinth climbing the chimney-crack line directly. Finish by the Stewart Orr variation.

48   Easter Route   95m   HVS **   (1938)
A good climb following the chimney line to the right of Labyrinth. The final pitch can (but shouldn't) be avoided!
1. 15m   Scramble up to a block below the first chimney.
2. 20m   Climb the chimney to a grass ledge with blocks.
3. 10m   Continue up to a grass patch below a steeper chimney.
4. 12m 4c   Climb the steep chimney until a move right can be made onto a turf-capped ledge.
5. 10m 4c   Two shallow horizontal faults about a metre apart cross the steep wall above. Using these move left to the edge of the wall, then climb straight up to a grass ledge on the left.
6. 8m   Traverse left to the base of a steep curving crack on the right side of The Prow.
7. 20m 5a   Climb the crack to a ledge (crux), then continue up the final chimney-crack to the top.

49   Double Cracks Start   10m   Severe   (1958)
On the Pinnacle Gully flank of the face there is a prominent right-angled corner. Its walls are split by steep cracks. Climb these to reach the turf-capped ledge at the top of the fourth pitch of Easter Route.

PINNACLE GULLY AREA

Pinnacle Gully bounds the upper side of the Upper East Face.

50   Sunshine Corner   45m   VS 5a *   (1971)
Immediately right of the Double Cracks start to Easter Route is a large corner enclosing twin cracks. Climb the corner to finish up the short final chimney of Labyrinth.

51   Keyhole Crack   35m   Very Difficult   (1946)
This climb follows a vertical chimney splitting the centre of the steep north face of the Rosa Pinnacle. The start is problematic. Finish by tunnelling through boulders.

52   The Rosetta Stone   15m   VS 5a **   (1955)
This huge block lies on the west side of the Pinnacle summit, near the top of Pinnacle Gully. It is climbable on its west side — an exercise in pure friction! Descend by the same line on all fives.

Beyond Upper East Face and Pinnacle Gully is Pinnacle Gully Buttress.

53   Ruddy Knuckles   35m   Severe   (1947)
Opposite Keyhole Crack, a well defined corner runs up the vertical south wall of Pinnacle Gully Buttress. A large square block forms a platform below it. From the top of the block climb the corner. Near the top either finish up the left wall or more sportingly via a through-route.

54   Pinnacle Gully Buttress   50m   Difficult   (1958)
The route climbs the east face by the line of least resistance — loose rock may be encountered.
Winter: III,4 *   (1983)
Follow the summer line with an interesting finish up the final wall.

55   Brodick Chimney   45m   Difficult   (1947)
This route follows the most prominent and continuous of the chimneys scarring the south face of the summit tor.

56   Sub Rosa Gully
This is the broad grassy and gravelly gully which separates the Rosa Pinnacle from Prospero Buttress. In its lower half it is divided into two branches by a tongue of slabs. Neither branch is particularly attractive for ascent or descent, being rather loose and slimy, with the left branch containing a jammed boulder pitch. (In winter both tend to bank out).

57   Gully Slabs   60m   Difficult
The tongue of slabs that divides the lower reaches of Sub Rosa Gully
gives pleasant climbing.

PROSPERO BUTTRESS

This is the long discontinuous rib of rock defining the right-hand side of
Sub Rosa Gully. The lower half is easy-angled and slabby whilst the
upper half is steeper and well defined.

58   Prospero's Prelude   120m   Moderate *   (1943)
Start near the watercourse draining the east branch of Sub Rosa Gully.
Gain and climb the crest which gives pleasant climbing up slabby
grooves following the line of least resistance. This provides a enjoyable
approach to Prospero's Peril and to the climbs on the Upper East Face.

59   Prospero's Peril   125m   Severe *   (1943)
An interesting route giving varied climbing on mostly excellent rock.
Start to the right of the toe of the upper buttress, above the lower end of
the short gully dividing it from the lower slabby buttress of Prospero's
Prelude.
1. 20m 4b   Move up slightly right to gain a slab, then traverse left to a
ledge on the crest. Climb a short groove to the foot of a concave slab.
Climb up leftwards to the left edge of the slab, then go straight up to a
big ledge beside an open corner.
2. 30m   Move round the corner on the right, then climb an undercut
chimney. Easier ground leads to a boulder-strewn ledge.
3. 20m   Climb a scoop on the left until a short right traverse can be
made to the foot of a curving flake crack. Gain the crest of the ridge,
then take to the right wall for a metre or so and ascend to a niche.
Follow a ledge left to a stance under a little overhang.
4. 10m   Traverse 3 metres left to enter a narrow groove. Climb it, then
go up a slab to belay below a right-angled corner.
5. 30m   Traverse left up a steep narrowing slab to footholds on the
wall of the gully. Two delicate steps right lead to easier slabs above.
Continue up to a grass ledge and belay.
6. 15m   Climb a little chimney splitting the final short wall to the top of
the buttress.

NORTH GOATFELL

818m   (Map Ref 990 422)

A prominent belt of slabs, overlapping from left to right, lies high up on the south-west slopes of the mountain, breaking up a short distance below the summit. A series of divergent grooves, all starting relatively near each other near the left side of the base, curve up rightwards. Well to the right, near the North Goat Fell — Goat Fell col lies a prominent diamond-shaped slab. A terrace, invisible from below, slants down from left to right separating these two areas of slabs.

Whit Fur   100m   Difficult   (1968)
Start at the first groove near the left edge of the area. Climb this for about 30m, then climb diagonally up and right to a grass ledge. Finish straight up the slabs above. Belay as required.

Whit Wey   100m   Severe *   (1968)
Start below the second groove from the left edge of the slabs.
1. 30m   Climb a slab to the foot of the groove and follow it. Continue up to a prominent flake jutting out right, then move up and right to the foot of another groove.
2. 20m   Climb the groove to belay in a crack below and to the right of the main upper slab.
3. 35m   Traverse hard right to the slab edge, then climb diagonally right to belay 10m below and to the right of a jutting block.
4. 15m   Climb the slab to an overlap, then move left to finish up a crack to the right of the jutting block.

Diamond Slab   45m   Very Difficult *   (1960)
A short but enjoyable route starting at the lower left angle of the diamond. Traverse diagonally up and across to the extreme right edge, then finish up the edge.

GOATFELL

874m   (Map Ref 991 415)

The highest mountain on the island is devoid of the steep walls that flank almost every other peak, but it does hold extensive areas of slabs. From the summit , Goatfell throws out a well defined blunt ridge running south towards lower Glen Rosa. There are several tors on this ridge, the most prominent, Forgotten Tor, being about 200 metres from the summit. It is well defined with a short east side and a longer slabby west side which gives pleasant climbing at about Difficult standard. The east flank of the ridge is steep and slabby but appears to offer no continuous rock. Closer inspection, however, reveals that the south end of the flank has a tilted U-shaped belt of slabs about 60m high. The main features are a long clean slab on the right and a series of small overlaps on the left curving from left to right. Two pleasant routes are recorded that can be used to enliven a day out on Goatfell.

Introduction   75m   Difficult   (1974)
1. 40m   Climb up the middle of the long clean slab on the right to a belay.
2. 35m   Continue more or less straight up by slabs and corners to the top.

Encore   60m   Very Difficult   (1974)
Start 8 metres left and slightly higher than the previous route.
1. 35m   Climb a smooth slab to a right-curving groove. Follow this, cross an overlap, then climb straight up to a spike belay.
2. 25m   Climb straight up to a bigger overlap, move around the corner on the right to surmount it, then finish straight up.

ROSA SLABS   (Map Ref 986 415)

This is the great expanse of slabs which plates the western flank of the mountain. From the Glen Rosa path the slabs are much foreshortened, their actual height being some 220m. There are two grass rakes, known as the First and Second Terraces, which run up from left to right, splitting the slabs into three sections. The upper left and bottom right sections give the best climbing. The routes tend to cross each other and therefore a number of combinations can be created and in fact the slabs can be climbed almost anywhere at a reasonable grade.

   The slabs are best reached by toiling up the heather-covered hillside from the Glen Rosa path. Allow about 2 hours from the road to the base of the slabs.

1   Zigzag   120m   Severe *   (1958)
The original route took an illogical and indeterminate left-trending line from the lowest point of the slabs to gain the left edge and better

climbing. The direct start is now the accepted way, although the route name is now somewhat inappropriate! Start below and to the left of a prominent waterslide at a little rib.

1. 45m   Climb the rib and carry on straight up to belay on the gully edge.

2 and 3. 75m   Follow the edge in two pitches, which give good climbing all the way.

2   Airlift   210m   E1 *   (1973)

Start at a long clean slab to the right of the start of the Second Terrace.

1. 35m 4b   Climb a slab, then trend right *via* quartz holds to another slab and a scoop leading left.

2. 15m   Go left to a rib and climb it to the Second Terrace.

3. 30m   Walk up the terrace to below an overhung corner with a turfy cracked slab on the left.

4. 25m 5a   Follow the turfy crack over an overlap, climb the slab above to a small overlap, then move left and climb a mossy slab. Surmount an overlap on the left and climb a flake to surmount yet another overlap. Belay by an overhung corner on the left.

5. 30m 5b   Climb the left wall of the corner *via* a crack and ascend the slab beyond. Avoid the grass on the left by a delightful slab to reach a horizontal ledge. Move left along this ledge and climb the fine thin crack on the left, then go up to belay on Zigzag.

6 and 7. 75m   Finish up Zigzag, taking the top overlap direct.

3   Gwynserthni   70m   E2   (1991)

About 40m above and left of the lowest slabs is an obvious white water streak. This is the start.

1. 30m 5b   Climb up the obvious white water streak, passing a horizontal crack at 5m, to a scoop at 15m. Move up into the groove just right of the streak and follow it to a ledge.

2. 40m 5b   Climb a slab to a scoop about 3 metres to the right of the gully. Continue up on cusps and pockets to climb the double overlaps via the obvious pocket and just left of the pebble on the second overlap. Climb to a ledge and a poor spike belay just below the First Terrace.

4   Extraction   75m   HVS   (1982)

This route takes the clean slab 30m above and left of the lowest slabs, continuing directly through the triple overlaps above to finish on the First Terrace. There are two pitches (5a, 4c).

5 Evening Traverse 245m Very Difficult (1955)

This is a worthwhile route despite having a rather scrambly and ill-defined middle section. It tackles the full height of the slabs. Start at the lowest slab, a huge undercut specimen, which lies left of the watercourse draining the right-hand side of the slabs.

1. 30m Traverse left across the top of the undercut slab and make for a crescent-shaped overlap on the left.

2. 25m Climb to the right of the crescent, then move left above it into a shallow scoop bounded on the left by a steep slab.

3. 40m From a ledge below the slab, climb a groove a short distance from its right edge. When the groove ends continue up on small holds, then move obliquely left to a rounded spur of rock. Follow a scoop to the First Terrace.

4. 25m Well above the terrace a projecting boss of rock will be seen on the left. Climb slabs to its right to a grass ledge aligned towards it. Traverse left across steep slabs, then climb up to a large block belay.

5. 35m Easy ground leads to an overhanging edge slanting up rightwards. Climb a crack in the overhang and continue up to a spike belay.

6. 10m Easy ground leads to the Second Terrace.

7. 40m Follow cracks and grooves above to a small platform with a flake shaped like a gravestone. Climb the groove above to reach a pile of blocks below the edge of the huge slab on the left.

8. 20m Twin corners, one set below the other, lie above. Climb the right-hand one until the corner crack gives out. A little wall with a slab above leads to a good spike belay.

9. 20m Cross two short overlaps above the belay and finish up slabs. A broken ridge and easy ground lead to the summit ridge.

6 Angel's Pavement 80m Severe ** (1960)

An excellent clean route at the bottom right of the slabs. Start at the highest point of the grassy rake which runs above the first slab of Evening Traverse.

1. 20m Climb slabs to the right-hand of two cracks splitting the overlap above. Climb the crack to a small stance and spike belay.

2. 25m 4b Follow an obvious line diagonally left, then a prominent chain of pitted holds leading right. The holds give out 3m below a rounded ledge which must be gained. Traverse easily left to a small belay.

3. 35m Climb straight up the slab over two small overlaps to finish on the upper reaches of the First Terrace.

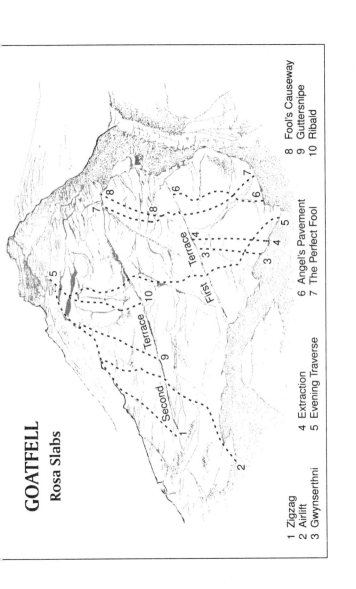

GOATFELL
Rosa Slabs

1 Zigzag
2 Airlift
3 Gwynserthni
4 Extraction
5 Evening Traverse
6 Angel's Pavement
7 The Perfect Fool
8 Fool's Causeway
9 Guttersnipe
10 Ribald

7   The Perfect Fool   170m   HVS *   (1981)
Described as the best non-line on the slabs, it tackles the blankest and steepest section. Start about 10 metres right of Angel's Pavement. The climbing is no harder than 4c. Climb diagonally leftwards across the clean slab, crossing a small overlap, until it is possible to climb straight up to the First Terrace at the foot of Fool's Causeway. Climb the first 7m of that route, then climb straight up the slab to an overlap. Surmount this and continue straight up, keeping to the rock. Protection is scarce and belays should be taken as available.

8   Fool's Causeway   90m   HVS *   (1960)
This route starts on the First Terrace and finishes on the Second Terrace. Either of the previous two routes can be used as access. Start lower down the First Terrace from the top of Angel's Pavement, below a smooth water-streaked slab, where two blocks form a thread belay. The climb is slow to dry.
1. 25m 4c   Traverse left and up onto the slab. A metre or so higher, follow a very thin grassy crack slanting rightwards. From its finish, move up a short distance to a rock pocket. Poor belay.
2. 35m 4c   Pad up right to a line of pockets leading to a tiny groove. This develops into a layback crack curving left to a small overlap. An easier groove and a slab now lead to a ledge.
3. 30m   Easier slabs lead to the top of the Second Terrace.

9   Guttersnipe   130m   VS *   (1964)
A fairly good route on the slabs above and to the left of the Second Terrace. Start about 90m up from the foot of the Second Terrace where the overlaps look more amenable to attack.
1. 20m 4c   Climb a slab and an overlap at 6m, then move up left into a mossy corner. Climb another overlap above to a small stance.
2. 30m   Climb diagonally right across a mossy slab to a crack, then go straight up to a heather ledge.
3. 40m   Climb up for 25 metres, traverse horizontally right above an overlap, then move up to a heather terrace. Ascend a quartz band diagonally up across a grassy corner to an eye-hole belay on a steep edge.
4. 15m   Continue straight up to a belay below the break in the overhang on Zigzag.
5. 25m   Move left below the overlap, at 15m cross it, then climb leftwards to finish.

10   Ribald   110m   VS   (1985)
This climb lies above the Second Terrace on the huge slab mentioned
in the description of Evening Traverse.
1. 20m   From the terrace climb to gain a flake belay in a heathery
corner at the bottom left of the large clean slab which lies to the left of
Evening Traverse.
2. 35m 4c   Cross the slab and climb it close to its well defined right
edge to a thread belay.
3. 45m   Continue more easily up the right edge and over a small
overlap to meet Evening Traverse.
4. 10m   A corner leads through a short wall to easy ground.

MID SLABS   (Map Ref 986 412)

An extensive but very broken area of slabs outcrop on the hillside
between Rosa Slabs and South Slabs. Only one route has been
recorded.

Staravation   90m   Very Difficult   (1967)
This route lies just to the right of the watercourse closer to the South
Slabs than the Rosa Slabs. It is a pleasant enough climb once gained
by a fairly arduous toil up the flank of the glen. Start at the lowest slab.
1. 35m   Climb straight up to a grassy ledge 5m below the left end of
an overlap.
2. 40m   Climb right past the right end of the overlap, then follow a line
of pockets upwards to an obvious groove. Climb the groove over a
small overlap, then move up and right to a belay.
3. 15m   Go leftwards up a smooth slab to finish.

SOUTH SLABS   (Map Ref 986 409)

This prominent area of slabs lies some 400 metres south of the main
Rosa Slabs and over 300m above the Glen Rosa path. The rock is
excellent and in general cleaner and more continuous than the main
slabs. Although these slabs are climbable almost anywhere, the routes
described provide some of the best middle grade slab climbing on the
island. However, as they tend to criss cross each other, it is possible to
create your very own pitch combinations! Protection is sparse on most
routes. Near the centre at the bottom of the slabs an obvious vegetated
fault runs up diagonally left. This is the line of Route 1, the original

route on the slabs, and it provides a good reference point for locating the start of other routes.

From the main Glen Rosa path cross the burn, then head straight up the hillside – a lot further than it appears! Access from the road takes about 1 hour 40 minutes. In misty weather a good guide to locating the slabs is to go straight up the hillside from just south of an enormous boulder on the lower east flank of the glen.

1   Trundle   130m   Severe *   (1964)
Start 12 metres to the left of the start of Route I.
1. 30m   Climb up into a scoop, step right, then climb to the foot of narrow grooves. Follow these up left to a prominent flake.
2. 30m   Move up a little, then traverse right to a thread runner on an edge. Continue up, bearing slightly left by a thin fading layback crack, then climb over bulges and slabs to a heather ledge.
3. 35m   Make an ascending traverse right (crossing Route 1) to a mossy corner. Ascend this, then move right onto the slab and climb a crack to a block belay.
4. 35m   Traverse right on ledges for 5 metres, then climb up rightwards past a large knob to the top.

2   Pochmahone   120m   VS *   (1966)
This rather contrived route has some enjoyable sections. It is worth HVS if two harder variations are taken. Start 2 metres left of Route 1.
1. 10m 4c   Climb straight up a steep slab, cross Route 1, then take a belay on a big spike just above.
2. 35m 4b   Continue up slabs, crossing a small overlap, to reach a heather ledge and block belay.
3. 30m 4c/5a   Climb the wall above the belay (or the rib on the right – being the left side of the scoop on Blank). Climb directly up the steep slab, cross an overlap, then continue to a quartz band. Move left along this to a spike belay at the foot of a corner.
4. 45m 4b   Traverse back right a little, then ascend slabs just right of the corner, continuing on up slabs to the top. Alternatively, this pitch can be started by climbing the corner direct at 5a.

3   Route 1   80m   Difficult   (1957)
This is the original and easiest route on the slabs taking the line of the left-trending broken fault. It is a useful descent for competent parties.
1. 50m   Follow the fault to the horizontal vein of the Girdle line.
2. 30m   Traverse 3 metres left, then finish straight up.

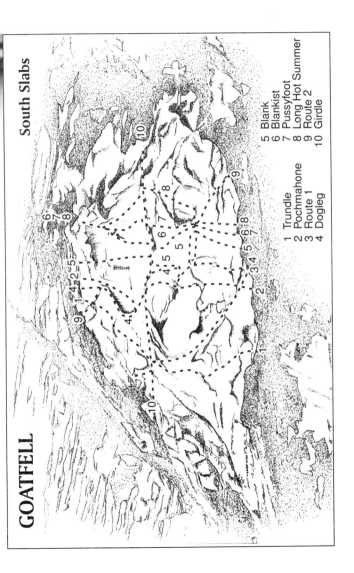

GOATFELL

South Slabs

1 Trundle
2 Pochmahone
3 Route 1
4 Dogleg

5 Blank
6 Blankist
7 Pussyfoot
8 Long Hot Summer
9 Route 2
10 Girdle

4   Dogleg   125m   VS **   (1964)
A fine bold route, as good as its neighbour Blank. Start at the foot of
Route I.
1. 40m 4b   Ascend the slab to a break in a thin overlap at 6m. Cross
this, then climb a flake edge. Trend slightly right up undulating slabs to
reach a short flake groove (common to Blank's lower traverse option).
Climb this, then traverse left to a heather groove and go up to belay on
a big detached block.
2. 45m 4b   Move back down and around into a scoop. Ascend the
groove with a flake crack on the left of the scoop, then traverse left until
a line of pockets leads straight up to a small spike in a corner.
3. 40m 4b   Climb the rib on the left of the corner to reach and climb
the easier upper slabs.

5   Blank   130m   VS **   (1963)
A fine route, easy in its grade if the lower traverse on pitch two is taken.
Start at an exposed area of rock, 5 metres right of Route 1.
1. 30m 4b   Climb boldly up the slab to gain a line of scoops and
flakes, trending slightly right to belay on a small gravelly ledge in a
heather groove.
2. 30m 4b   Step left, move up, then follow a wide vein running left
across the slab to gain a heather groove. Scramble up this to belay at a
big detached block. An easier alternative (4a) is to step down and
traverse left along a lower vein to reach a short flake groove on Dogleg.
Climb this to join the upper vein.
3. 35m 4b   Move back down and right around a rib into a steepening
scoop. At the top of the scoop traverse 3 metres right (along the Girdle
line), surmount an overlap, then follow a line of pockets straight up to a
stance and belay.
4. 35m 4b   Climb directly up slabs to the top.

The next three routes have a common finish.

6   Blankist   110m   HVS ***   (1995)
A memorable experience and the best route on the slabs, taking a direct
line up the centre on perfect rock. Start 10 metres right of Route 1.
1. 30m 4c   Climb straight up the holdless slab, immediately right of a
black streak, to reach flakes. Ascend these to belay on a small gravelly
ledge in a heather groove (this pitch shares the same line as
Pussyfoot).

2. 25m 4b Step left and climb straight up a line of perfect pockets, moving left to gain an obvious long thin down-facing flake. Thin moves above the flake lead to a fine flake belay on the Girdle line.

3. 45m 4b Climb straight up a bare slab to gain and follow an obvious rib (overlooking a long corner to the right), then go up on easier-angled slabs to a small rock ledge at the base of a short banana-shaped groove.

4. 10m Easier climbing up broken slabs leads to the top.

7 Pussyfoot 110m HVS * (1964)

A direct route with a rather messy middle section. Start as for Blankist, 10 metres to the right of Route 1.

1. 45m 4c Climb straight up a holdless slab, immediately right of a black streak, to reach flakes. Ascend these, then continue straight up skirting a heather groove on its left.

2. 15m 4b Continue up and cross an overlap to reach a flake belay on a small ledge below a long corner (in common with Route 2).

3. 50m 4b Traverse 3 metres right, then ascend a slanting groove. Climb slabs trending slightly right, then go back left to a short banana-shaped groove. Climb this and broken slabs to finish.

8 Long Hot Summer 115m HVS * (1995)

Start 13 metres to the right of Route 1 at a vague rib.

1. 30m 5a Climb boldly up the vague rib, then continue up easier slabs and flakes to belay on a small gravelly ledge in a heather groove.

2. 45m Traverse right, then climb a brown slab, cross an overlap and continue up slabs to reach a belay on a ledge on the right.

3. 30m 4c Move slightly left, climb a short tricky rib, then follow slabs leftwards to belay on a small rock ledge at the base of a short banana-shaped groove.

4. 10m Easier climbing up broken slabs leads to the top.

9 Route 2 95m Severe (1961)

An unsatisfactory route, taking the line of least resistance from the bottom right to the top left of the slabs. Start at the bottom right-hand corner.

1. 20m Slant up leftwards *via* slabs and grooves to a grassy depression.

2. 30m Continue, first up grass, then *via* a steep slab, slanting left to a narrow grass band below a small overlap. Cross this to a ledge and flake belay below a long corner.

3. 35m   Climb the corner for 5m, then traverse left to a small rock ledge. Climb diagonally up and left to reach a thin corner crack. Follow this to a nook on the left.
4. 10m   Scramble up and left to finish.

10   Girdle   75m   Severe *   (1965)
A natural line following the obvious horizontal vein cutting across the slabs at just over half-height. As good as girdles get! Start on the left-hand side of the slabs.
1. 25m   Follow the vein to belay on Route I.
2. 25m   Cross the slab, go round a corner, then cross the top of the scoop of Blank to an obvious flake belay (shared with Blankist).
3. 25m   Continue by the same general line to quit the slabs.

COIRE LAN   (Map Ref 995 420)

This large corrie lies between the east ridge of Goatfell and Am Binnein, and is drained by the Corrie Burn which enters the sea about 1km south of Corrie. A number of small buttresses fall from the Stacach ridge at the head of the corrie. The largest of these is split by a steep gully. Three routes have been recorded on this buttress.

Left-Hand Route   60m   Very Difficult   (1949)
This inspirationally-named route climbs the well defined rib to the left of the gully. The final short undercut wall is turned on the right.

Stacach Gully   75m   II   (1960s)
The steep gully splitting the buttress usually holds one short ice pitch.

Right-Hand Route   100m   Moderate   (1949)
A poor vegetated route but worth climbing for the name alone!

COIRE NAN LARACH   (Map Ref 005 428)

This corrie is enclosed by Mullach Buidhe to the north and Am Binnein to the south. A prominent belt of slabs about 90m high lie below Am Binnein. A shallow broken gully and its draining watercourse divide the area into two. On the left the slabs are broken and vegetatious but on the right they are more continuous and cleaner. They form a tilted triangle with a slightly curving undercut base. Above and to the right of the centre of this area is a smooth slab crossed by a diagonal vein.

Diagonal   85m   Very Difficult   (1969)
Start at the left side of the undercut base.
1. 30m   Climb diagonally up and right over short overlaps to belay below an obvious wide vein.
2. 25m   Continue up right for 12m, then climb up onto the vein to a small grass ledge.
3. 30m   Follow the line up and right to a rock ledge. Finish by the same line and broken ground above.

Hedonist   120m   Severe   (1981)
Start at the extreme bottom left-hand corner of the slabs. Follow a right-trending narrow slab to where it joins the main body of the slabs, then take a zigzaging line up the centre of the face. Belay as required.

Changeling   80m   Severe *   (1981)
A hard start leads to easier climbing above. Start near the right end of the undercut base at a bay jammed with flakes.
1. 10m 4c   Climb the flakes and the steep rock above to a ledge.
2. and 3. 70m   Follow the cleanest line to the top.

CIOCH NA H-OIGHE

661m   (Map Ref 999 439)

The grandeur of Cioch na h-Oighe can be well appreciated from lower Glen Sannox. For all its modest height it presents one of the most spectacular mountain views on Arran. Coire na Ciche, also known as The Devil's Punchbowl, is the classic miniature corrie to the east of this excellent little mountain. Although all sides of the mountain are rocky, it is the Coire na Ciche flank that is its true pride, a long cliff rising over 200 metres from the corrie floor to the summit ridge, containing the very best and the very worst that Arran rock has to offer. The Bastion, the great clean wall in the centre of the face, holds a concentration of high standard climbs, some of the best on the island and comparable with the best in Scotland. All have a serious mountaineering feel about them. Unless otherwise indicated, the routes dry quickly after rain, although seepage may affect some routes, especially in spring..

Five roughly parallel rakes run diagonally upward across the face from left to right. Numbered 1 to 5 from the right, these infamous ledges consist of crumbly rock and unstable vegetation and are best avoided other than Ledge 3 which gives access to the base of The Bastion and the upper part of Ledge 4 which provides access to the summit ridge. Great care should be exercised when ascending or descending Ledge 3 as it involves exposed moves on dubious combinations of heather and crumbling rock.

The main features of The Bastion are the great parallel grooves of Klepht and Armadillo on the left and the striking horn-like flake of Rhino on the right. A rock shelf cuts across this great wall at two-thirds height (the line of Tidemark). Another enormous flake sits below this shelf on the left, forming the reversed image of the Rhino flake which in combination resemble the pincers of a giant crabs claw. A tenuous line running up the blank wall to nearly reach the left-hand pincer presents Arran's 'last great problem' and a major challenge for the 21st century.

Access to the corrie is up the main Glen Sannox track to the ford over the Allt a' Chapuill. A path follows the side of this burn leading into the floor of Coire na Ciche in about 40 minutes from the main road.

1   Pinnacle Gully   150m   I *
The obvious gully at the back of the corrie gives a straightforward snow climb (in summer it is a loose scramble over grass and scree).

2   Outrider   90m   II   (1983)
Climb the obvious icefall about 35 metres to the right of Pinnacle Gully.

3   Gazebo   110m   E1   (1977)
A huge block-roofed cave high on the slabs to the left of the main wall of The Bastion is the most distinctive feature of this climb, which is the first route of any value encountered when ascending Ledge 3 from the corrie. Two other routes, **1986 Route** (Difficult) and **Galaway Slabs** (Severe) to the left of Gazebo have been recorded but they are of poor quality and are best avoided. Gazebo is very slow to dry and is a good grade harder in anything other than bone-dry conditions. Start a short distance downhill from a diagonal overlap.
1. 30m 5b   Climb a short groove and slab to the overlap. Either continue up the slab or take to the narrow raised slab above the overlap until it is possible to move up and right to a grass ledge. Quite bold.
2. 40m 5a   Follow the obvious partly grassy corner with a hard section near the top into the cave. It is also possible halfway up the corner to hand traverse a ledge on the right wall and climb directly up to the cave.
3. 40m 5a   Drop down left onto the slab. Move slightly left, then climb delicately to the overhang. Step left round a corner which leads to a crumbly groove and heather and thence to Ledge 4.

CIOCH NA H-OIGHE

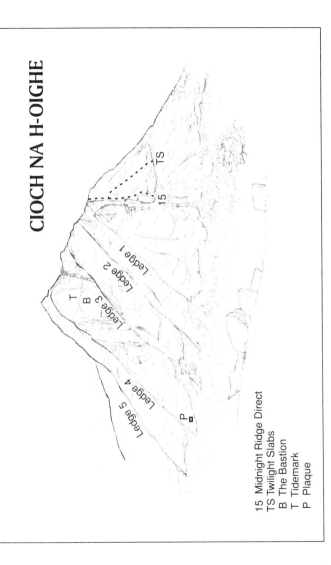

15 Midnight Ridge Direct
TS Twilight Slabs
B The Bastion
T Tidemark
P Plaque

4   Ziggurat   60m   HVS   (1969)

A poor route with an overabundance of turf. Start to the left of the initial corner of Klepht where a narrow turf gangway runs up left.

1. 20m   Gain and follow the exposed turf gangway to its termination at a corner (there is scope for a hard direct entry to this point).

2. 20m 5a   Climb the strenuous corner crack to the top of a pinnacle. Move up onto a ledge on the left, then climb up to reach a spike belay at another ledge on the left.

3. 20m 5a   Climb by the line of least resistance over rock steps and turf ledges to reach Ledge 4.

5   Digitalis   70m   E2 **   (1981)

A fine exposed route tackling the roofed pillar to the left of the big groove of Klepht.

1. 20m 5c   Climb the corner as for Klepht for 12m to a small ledge. Traverse left across a bare slab to gain a small hold. Move round an edge to a bolt belay in a grass niche.

2. 30m 5b   Climb the corner above a detached pillar to below a roof. Turn the roof on the right and climb cracks trending left to a small ledge (possible belay). Ascend an awkward corner, then go directly up to a small ledge between twin roofs. An excellent pitch.

3. 20m 5c   Climb the overhang between the twin roofs (crux) to gain a groove. Move left and go up easier rock to a heather ledge. Climb a slabby groove trending right to a terrace and thread belay. The twin roofs can be outflanked on the right (the left wall of Klepht) at 5b, reducing the overall grade of the route to E1. Walk, then scramble off left to gain Ledge 4.

6   Klepht   65m   E2 *   (1967/1981)

A fine if daunting line, with slightly disappointing climbing, up the great groove on the left side of the Bastion. The original line avoided part of the lower groove *via* a grassy traverse on the right. The direct line is now the accepted way.

1. 30m 5c   Climb the corner, then pull left and up to gain a small ledge. Move right and climb the groove directly to reach a bolt belay at a turf ledge.

2. 35m 5c   Follow the main crack past a crumbly recess until a narrower crack on the left wall allows the final groove to be climbed to a terrace and thread belay. Walk, then scramble off left to gain Ledge 4.

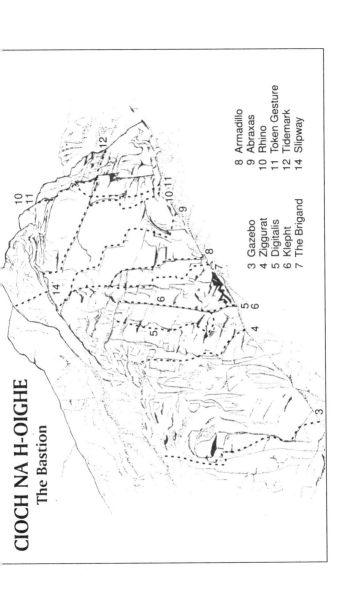

CIOCH NA H-OIGHE
The Bastion

3 Gazebo
4 Ziggurat
5 Digitalis
6 Klepht
7 The Brigand

8 Armadillo
9 Abraxas
10 Rhino
11 Token Gesture
12 Tidemark
14 Slipway

7   The Brigand   60m   E6 *   (1996)
A seriously 'out there' route, climbing the pillar between the great
grooves of Klepht and Armadillo and finishing at the bolt belay at the
top of the second pitch of the latter. Sadly, a band of disintegrating rock
on the second pitch mars what is otherwise excellent and sustained
climbing. Start below a slim double roofed corner immediately left of
the Armadillo groove.
1. 20m 6a   Enter and climb the slim corner to below the capping roof.
Move left across the wall, with difficulty, then step up onto a rock ledge.
Move left to belay. A fine pitch.
2. 40m 6b   Climb a crack above the belay to a band of disintegrating
granite. Gain a thin hanging flake groove in this band. Struggle up this
to reach some pockets and a step right onto better rock. Climb up to a
diagonal flake corner. Mantelshelf onto its top, then climb pockets in
the wall above. Beyond the top pocket is a narrow sloping ledge. Palm
left to gain a small flake which leads to a naughty exit onto a sloping
rock ledge on the edge of the pillar. Climb the short open corner above
the ledge, pulling out left at the top. A short slab and flake groove lead
to a grassy ledge and the bolt belay on Armadillo. Either finish by the
last pitch of Armadillo, drop down left and traverse clear of the face as
for Klepht, or abseil off the bolt back down to Ledge 3.

8   Armadillo   100m   E3 ***   (1977)
This brilliant route gives excellent climbing up the prominent roofed
groove to the right of Klepht. It is worth its three stars, despite a rather
messy top pitch.
1. 25m 6a   Climb the groove until hard under the second roof.
Desperate but well protected moves lead left around this to a ledge
and belay under the third and biggest roof.
2. 35m 5b   Re-enter the groove and climb it to near the top where a
hard traverse left gains a ledge. Climb an awkward slab wall to reach a
grass rake and bolt belay. Alternatively (and more logically), instead of
taking the left traverse, continue straight on up into a slabby groove to
gain the grass rake. Although it is possible to drop down and traverse
off left above Klepht at this point, the character building pleasures of
the final pitch should not be missed!
3. 40m 5b   Climb a hard scoop, then take the short overhung corner
above to gain a grass ledge. Traverse left, move up, then step back
right to gain an easy turfy groove leading left to a flake belay on
Ledge 4.

9   Abraxas   105m   E4 ***   (1980)
A stunning route in a magnificent situation, one of Scotland's finest, taking a sensational line across the bare central section of The Bastion. Start directly below the right-hand end of a prominent arched overhang.
1. 30m 6a   Traverse leftwards and slightly up to the left end of the arch. Move left around the edge to the base of a yellow roof-capped corner. Climb this, then pull right onto the wall. Move slightly left at a horizontal break, then move up to gain a hidden finger pocket. Climb up from this to gain a hand traverse line leading right to a belay on a small rock ledge just above.
2. 35m 6a   Climb a diagonal finger crack to a narrow sloping shelf. Gain this awkwardly, then undercling left to reach a vertical waterworn groove. At the top of this groove, step left onto a sloping rock ledge (two bolts *in situ* just above). Cross the thin ledge (initially rock, then turf) with some difficulty (often wet) to gain a niche and bolt belay. This pitch can be split by taking a bolt belay on the ledge at the start of the final traverse.
3. 40m 5b   Climb a crack on decomposing rock to an undercut flake. Pull left on good holds to reach a crack which leads to a heather ledge. Follow a narrowing slab ramp leftwards to join the easy turfy groove on the final pitch of Armadillo and climb this to Ledge 4.

10   Rhino   85m   E2 **   (1979)
This fine line climbs the crack defining the left side of the great horn-like flake on the right side of the wall. Start directly below the flake.
1. 25m 5b   Gain and climb a short left-facing flake. Mantelshelf up, go straight up to a bulge, then pull left to reach a small ledge. Climb up to a curious hole, then ascend the left-hand of the twin grooves above (the right-hand one contains an old peg and is slightly harder). Traverse right to reach a grass ledge and belay below the horn.
2. 20m 5b   Climb straight up on good flakes, then by a crack to enter the widening flake crack which leads to an exit around a chockstone at the top. Belay on the ledge of Tidemark.
3. 40m 5b   Walk right and climb the corner above a big block (often wet). Make a slight detour on the left wall, then continue up the corner to a large grass ledge (optional belay). Climb a short overhanging corner to a ledge and belay. An alternative, harder and better start (5c) to this pitch is to climb the slabby pocketed wall directly above the horn to gain some small flakes and a right-trending ramp which leads back to the original line; bold! Ledge 4 can be reached *via* a short scramble.

11 Token Gesture 85m E5 ** (1985)
A spectacular route that climbs the exceedingly steep wall to the right of Rhino (i.e. the face of the horn), joining Rhino at the Tidemark ledge. Start just to the right of the initial flake of Rhino.
1. 25m 6b Pull up the bulging wall using a hanging flake. Stand on the flake, then move slightly right to some flakes leading up and left to a large hold. Move back right to further flakes and cracks leading to a bulge (level with the grass ledge below the horn of Rhino). Move left on pockets to the ledge.
2. 20m 6b Move back right to regain the line and the foot of a slim hanging groove in the edge of the Rhino flake. Climb this to a right traverse for a couple of moves along the lip of the wall until a hard pull onto the slab above can be made and the Tidemark ledge gained.
3. 40m 5c Climb the top pitch of Rhino *via* the left-hand start.

12 Tidemark 75m Severe ** (1960)
A delightful and exposed girdle following the striking curving rock shelf that divides the lower two-thirds from the upper third of The Bastion's main wall. The shelf can be clearly seen from the main Corrie to Sannox road. The situations are tremendous and when used as a link between Midnight Ridge Direct and Slipway the route provides a great mountaineering expedition. Start near the upper end of and well above Ledge 3 at a rounded flake belay close to the obvious start of the line. If only Tidemark is to be climbed, this point can be reached by ascending Ledge 3 below The Bastion, then scrambling across to the start).
1. 30m Cross two slabs (often wet) to reach a grassy corner and a split block. Climb over the block, then follow the grass ledge to take an eyehole belay a short distance up the clean rock gangway.
2. 30m Follow the exposed gangway to its end and belay on a small ledge just left of an overhang. A splendid pitch!
3. 15m 4b Climb an awkward flake crack, then traverse left into a heather groove to finish on Ledge 4.

13 Coxon's Route
A scrappy climb linking the lower end of Ledge 2 to Ledge 3 below Klepht – not recommended.

14 Slipway 45m HVS * (1975)
A steep little buttress lies above Ledge 4, almost immediately above the finish of Tidemark. Slipway lies on this buttress and offers a good continuation to almost any of The Bastion routes.

1. 15m 4c   Start at an open corner. Climb the right wall *via* a blocky flake, then follow a left-trending ramp over a block to a small turf ledge.
2. 30m 5b   From the belay, gain the ramp above (crux). Follow it for a metre or so, step down, then traverse left to gain cracks. Go up to a square-cut recess and exit left to a large chockstone. Scramble to Ledge 5.

15   Midnight Ridge Direct   85m   VS **   (1944)

This climb follows a ridge formed by the junction of the main south-east face and the east face of the mountain and lies directly below the top of Ledge 1 as seen from the corrie. It is a surprisingly good route with a serious air. From a prominent gravely grass patch on the right of the corrie lip, climb up to the foot of the ridge *via* awkward vegetated grooves. Start at a little recess.
1. 15m 5a   Climb the short strenuous overhanging scoop to a sloping ledge (crux), then go up a short wall to a platform. From the left end of the platform gain the undercut slab above. This leads to a turf ledge with a spike belay.
2. 25m 4b   To the left of the belay is a vertical wall. Climb this on good holds, then go up a little corner to a grass ledge. Ascend a vertical crack on the right, then trend left up broken rocks to a platform. Climb a scoop to gain the ridge crest. An alternative and harder start (5a) can be made to this pitch by traversing left around the edge from the belay, then climbing a steep corner to the top of the vertical wall, rejoining the parent route. This variation increases the overall grade to HVS.
3. 45m   Finish up the narrow ridge by easier but enjoyable climbing.

The poor route **Twilight Slabs** (Severe, 1944) gains the final easy section of Midnight Ridge Direct *via* slabs, starting well to the right.

CREAG DHUBH

This crag, or rather cluster of crags, lies on the east flank of the north-west ridge of Caisteal Abhail about 1.5km from the summit. The walls and buttresses have so far revealed only one minor route, but there is scope for more.

15 Minute Ridge   70m   Difficult   (1945)

This route climbs the shortest and most continuous of the buttresses, just to the right of the biggest scree gully.

MULLACH BUIDHE

829m   (Map Ref 993 427)

This twin-topped mountain has little recorded climbing. The Glen Sannox and Coire nam Fuaran flanks are steep and hold areas of slabs and a number of small buttresses. Two routes have been recorded, but there is some scope for more.

Bonus   75m   Moderate
A clean easy-angled buttress drops from the northern top of the mountain. It gives pleasant climbing by the line of least resistance.

Anticlimax   180m   Severe   (1968)
About 100m more or less below the start of Bonus a prominent gully runs down the slope for about 200m. Its lower end is marked by a triangular belt of pale waterworn slabs. The retaining wall of the gully is well defined where it abuts a converging fan of slabs. The climb follows this edge, starting at the top of the pale slabs.

CIR MHOR

799m   (Map Ref 972 431)

The Glen Rosa side of Cir Mhor has already been described in an earlier section. The cliffs of the north-east face are most readily approached from Glen Sannox, and being close to Cioch na h-Oighe, the climbs are described here for convenience.

NORTH-EAST FACE

This huge and complex face, nearly 300m in height, dominates the head of Glen Sannox. From a distance its great triangular bulk prom- ises much good rock climbing, but in reality there is limited clean rock, the majority of the face being vegetated and normally damp. The few worthwhile rock routes that have been recorded require a good week of dry warm weather to be enjoyable. Some obvious rock climbing challenges remain for those willing to invest the time and energy.

   The paucity of good rock routes is compensated by the excellent winter climbing, probably the best concentration on the island, with face and gully routes to suit all abilities. Its altitude and aspect favour good winter conditions as frequently as anywhere on Arran.

The vast face is divided in the middle by a large tapering wedge of grass, known as The Wedge, narrowing from a shoulder east of the summit ridge down rightwards to the base of the cliff. It provides a quick means of descent from the top of the crag in both summer and winter, although care must be taken, particularly in the lower part. To the west of The Wedge (referred to as the Lower North-East Face), the roughly triangular face comprises massive, high-angled slabs cut by filthy gullies, whilst to the east (referred to as the Upper North-East Face), lies the summit buttress complex bounded by the deep gully of Western Stoneshoot. Beyond this lies the steep but heavily vegetated Stoneshoot Buttress.

The face is best approached *via* the Glen Sannox path (either side of the burn, but the north is marginally drier) which becomes a bit messy in the upper glen until an ill-defined path on the south side of the burn leads up into Coire na h-Uaimh. Allow about two hours from the road.

LOWER NORTH-EAST FACE

This huge face dominates upper Glen Sannox and is split by a number of messy gullies.

1   Nor-Easter Slabs   135m   VS 4c   (1961)
A typical Arran 'mixed' route, with much turf. The climb lies on the slabby face below and left of the foot of Gully A, starting about 20 metres to the right of the right-hand end of the overhanging base of the wall. Climb by grooves and slabs, following the easiest line, to gain the foot of Gully A. Not recommended!

2   Crystal   140m   VS *   (1992)
This route lies on a belt of slabs below the start of Gully A. Start below a clean pale slab at a deep pocket, left of a distinctive area of turf that breaks through the surrounding heather. Good climbing but poor belays.
1. 30m 4c   Climb straight up the slab *via* a line of flakes to a grass ledge.
2. 15m   Move down the ledge for 15m.
3. 35m 4b   Climb a slab to belay at a circular depression.
4. 35m 4c   Traverse 10 metres right to an overlap, pull through this on pockets, then continue up and right through a couple of small overlaps to belay at a block.
5. 25m   Climb straight up *via* some thin cracks to finish at a grassy recess.

3   April Arete   120m   Severe   (1959)
This route effectively follows the left edge of Gully A, with belays taken as required.
Winter: IV,5 **   (1987)
Three pitches involving short, hard, but well protected sections lead to a narrow ramp on the right of the arete which gives access to Gully A above the second barrier. The edge can be regained above or the easy gully followed to finish.

Gully A is the distinctive but unclimbed gully, which appears easy apart from two nasty-looking overhanging cave pitches.

4   When the Going Gets Turf   130m   III,3   (1991)
This route follows a line of turfy grooves just to the right of and parallel to Gully A. Although exposed, the line is a lot easier than it appears. Start on the grassy ramp leading into Gully A, about 10m below the toe of April Arete. Move up turfy slabs on the right, with one short difficult section, to gain a diagonal turfy groove. Climb the groove in a couple of pitches to the top.

5   Eastern Ridge   90m   Difficult   (1961)
This route starts at the low left edge of the vertical wall above the finish of Gully A. Climb a crack, then follow the ridge, keeping as near to the right as possible.

6   Silo   370m   E1 (aid)   (1968)
A formidable climb calling for a wide variety of traditional skills and a high tolerance of slime, loose turf and disintegrating granite. In short, a real adventure! It takes the obvious line of a chimney-fault splitting the great face between Gully A and Gully B1. At about mid-height the fault splits to enclose a huge triangular nose of clean rock. The right fork is taken to finish up the crest of the nose. For a full description see SMCJ 1971.

7   Once in a Lifetime   350m   VII,6 ***   (1986)
This is the natural winter line up the great face in the vicinity of Silo and has its middle pitches in common with that route. When in condition, it is a superb and committing excursion and the hardest winter route on Arran to date. Climb broken ground to reach an ice scoop which falls

The S-Crack on the South Ridge of the Rosa Pinnacle (Climber, Ken Clarke)

from a narrow chimney (parallel and to the right of the initial chimney of Silo). Climb the scoop and go up into the chimney-groove system. Pass under a chockstone and 15m above it (below a steepening) traverse down and left, passing a steep groove, to reach a vertical chimney-crack. Climb this and a second shorter chimney-crack above (common to Silo). Mixed ground now leads to a shallow right-trending iced groove (in the right-hand fork of the fault, right of the triangular nose). Climb this with increasing difficulty, passing a big flake on its left at half-height, to make a desperate exit on very thin ice then continue up to a ledge above. Move up and right on complicated ground, then break back left and thence to the top of the face.

8   Gully B1   130m   III,4 *   (1979)
This is the gully bounding the right-hand side of the great face. Steep snow leads to an ice pitch divided by a rock rib. Take the left runnel and easy snow above to a steep funnel-shaped ice pitch (crux). A through-route leads to the final easy-angled pitch. The climb is unpleasant in summer (Very Difficult, 1942).

The rib on the left of Gully B1 has been climbed and named **Ribbish** (180m, Severe). It is appalling!

9   Gully B2   135m   III,4   (1981)
A steepening ice pitch leads to the easier-angled upper gully which contains huge jammed blocks. Turn these on the right wall. An alternative start is *via* a thin right-slanting gully, starting a pitch up Gully B1 and linking it to Gully B2. This link includes an interesting cave with a hole in its roof – the Bottle Dungeon Cave – which should provide some amusement. It is another unpleasant Very Difficult in summer (1892).

10   B2C Rib   70m   Very Difficult   (1895)
Start near the bottom right-hand corner of the rib between Gully B2 and Gully C.
1. 40m   Climb a series of co-linear grooves near the right edge to reach a large grassy ledge.
2. 30m   From the left end of the ledge, move up a short distance, then climb a thin groove to a niche just left of a little overhang. Move slightly right, then climb the overhang on good holds to finish in Gully B2.

Blankist, South Slabs, Goatfell (Climber, Graham Little)

Variation A:
About 30m up the original route traverse to the left edge of the rib and climb up on good holds to reach the niche on the parent route.
Variation B:
From the top of the first pitch on the original route traverse right to the edge and finish up that.

11   Gully C   180m   V,5 **   (1979)
Easy snow leads to a big cave pitch, turned on the right. Continue up the gully, narrowing to a groove with several tricky pitches, to a chock-stone constriction. Pass under this, then go up easier snow to belay in a recess. Take a left traverse *via* a flake to gain the final snow slope.

12   Beyond the Pale   125m   E2 **   (1985)
A fine and intimidating route which climbs the great tapering slab between Gully C and Gully D. It is slow to dry and dry conditions are highly desirable! Start to the left of the pothole at the base of the slab (left of Pothole Slab).
1. 25m 4c   Climb a direct line up the slab to the left end of an obvious ledge.
2. 45m 5c   Move right a few metres, then ascend directly to an undercut flake. Climb out left from this, ascend to a short gangway, then climb right to cracks. Ascend up and left across a wall to an easing in the angle. Move up and right to a ledge.
3. 40m 5b   Move right from the ledge and climb up and left to a crack which leads to a line of roofs. Trend up and right, following this line for about 20m, to a ledge and belay.
4. 15m 4c   Climb trending left and follow a pocketed slab to the top.

13   Pothole Slab   115m   HVS *   (1968)
The pioneering route up these slabs is slightly spoiled by a rather messy middle section. Start just left of the prominent pothole at the base of the clean sweep of slabs.
1. 25m 4c   Pad straight up the slab until it is possible to step left onto a small ledge.
2. 35m 4b   Traverse rightwards along a thin vein, past a groove, then climb straight up to a ledge and belay.
3. 30m   Climb up messy broken ground to belay in a wet corner.
4. 25m 5a   Move right up a short crack, then step left into a corner. Climb the strenuous flake crack curving left to a groove (crux) which finishes abruptly on open ground.

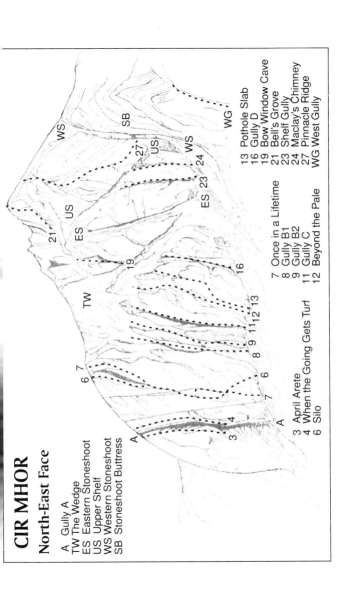

CIR MHOR
North-East Face

A Gully A
TW The Wedge
ES Eastern Stoneshoot
US Upper Shelf
WS Western Stoneshoot
SB Stoneshoot Buttress

3 April Arete
4 When the Going Gets Turf
6 Silo

7 Once in a Lifetime
8 Gully B1
9 Gully B2
11 Gully C
12 Beyond the Pale

13 Pothole Slab
16 Gully D
19 Bow Window Cave
21 Bell's Grove
23 Shelf Gully
24 Maclay's Chimney
27 Pinnacle Ridge
WG West Gully

14   Pan's Pipe   90m   IV,3 **   (1981)
This is probably the best pure ice climb on the island. It takes the obvious thin smear up the slabs to the left of Gully D in two long pitches on reasonably-angled ice, but with no protection.

15   Pan's Pillar   95m   HVS *   (1979)
This route tackles the cigar-shaped pillar lying against the slabs just to the left of Gully D.
1. 45m 5a   Gain the pillar and follow the right edge with difficulty to a small thread runner at 30m. Continue straight up for a short way, then trend left onto a delicate slab leading to the top of the pillar.
2. 50m 4c   Move right up a short slab to a ledge and continue up waterworn slabs to a thin crack. Trend right to the bottom of a narrow grassy strip and follow this to the top. If dry, the thin crack gives a better finish.

16   Gully D   85m   II
This short gully, also known as Trap Dyke Climb, lies to the right of the main slabs. It is an unpleasant Moderate in summer (1891).

UPPER NORTH-EAST FACE

This is the complex area of the face dropping from the summit of Cir Mhor, bounded on the left by The Wedge and on the right by Western Stoneshoot.

17   Stoneshoot Ridge   120m   Difficult   (1891)
This ill-defined vegetated ridge lies to the immediately right of The Wedge and forms the left retaining wall of Eastern Stoneshoot. A thoroughly disgusting and dangerous climb!

18   Eastern Stoneshoot   120m   II   (1979)
This is the obvious gully immediately right of The Wedge with an ice pitch to start. Not surprisingly, it is unclimbed in summer.

19   Bow Window Cave   Moderate   (1894)
This experience perhaps gave rise to the expression 'much scrambling in curious places'. A journey up through this large cave, formed of jammed boulders, can be enjoyed from near the top and left of Stoneshoot Ridge or by ascending directly from The Wedge.

20 Summit Chimney   30m   Moderate   (1891)
Above the finish of Stoneshoot Ridge, steep gravelly slopes lead up to
a grassy neck near the east ridge of the mountain. To the right of this, a
prominent chimney splits the steep east side of the mountain. Climb
the chimney.

21 Bell's Groove   60m   Very Difficult *   (1894)
An interesting route finishing at the top of the mountain. Start about
30m below Summit Chimney. Scramble up into a grassy bay on the
right, then climb a short chimney at the back to gain a recess behind a
huge block. Continue up to a grass platform, behind which a narrow
chimney slants up. This is the 'Groove' and its ascent requires some
good, old fashioned thrutching, with the start proving especially
repellent. Beyond the 'Groove', climb straight up to the summit.

22 Naismith/Haskett-Smith Route   60m   Moderate (1896)
This route follows the obvious rising traverse across the summit gable,
parallel to the approach to the 'Groove' on Bell's Groove, but a little
below it. Poor climbing but fine situations.

23 Shelf Gully   90m   II   (1983)
This gully is the first breach to the right of Eastern Stoneshoot. It
normally gives two short pitches. It is repulsive in summer (Very
Difficult, 1896).

24 Maclay's Chimney   75m   II   (1983)
This lies just to the left of the wide start of Western Stoneshoot. It
normally holds one ice pitch in the narrow upper section. Again, a
repulsive Very Difficult in summer (1896).

25 North-East Face Route   245m   IV,5 **   (1983)
A fine route, sustained in its upper reaches. Start by climbing either
Shelf Gully or Maclay's Chimney to gain the Upper Shelf. Follow it to its
termination above the Eastern Stoneshoot, traversing below and
beyond the prominent plinth of rock. Reach a small snowy bay
immediately to the right of a large slabby buttress with a short narrow
chimney on the right (holding a large chockstone). Climb a groove to the
left of the chimney, then trend left and go up steep grooves to a large
snowy ramp abutting steep slabs above. Negotiate the slabs by climbing
a steep narrow ramp to reach a further snowy ramp and a cave. Exit right
from the cave and trend left up steep mixed ground to gain the upper

groove of Bell's Groove. Climb up immediately right of this groove, then follow another groove diagonally up left over slabs and go back right to finish on the summit.

26   First Pinnacle Chimney   45m   Very Difficult   (1958)
A series of chimneys seam the eastern flank of Pinnacle Ridge. This climb follows the one between the first and second pinnacles and is reached from the Upper Shelf.

27   Pinnacle Ridge   140m   Difficult   (1894)
This ridge, holding four pinnacles, runs from the top of the great plinth above the Upper Shelf towards the main western ridge of the mountain. Although not seen from the corrie, it comes into view from the foot of the Western Stoneshoot. The best approach to the ridge proper is from this point *via* vegetated rock ramps. The ridge is well defined and in places narrow. Follow the crest to the gap before the last pinnacle, where a short right traverse is necessary to avoid an overhang. The ridge ends at a little col separating it from the mountain's main west ridge. From the col, either gain the west ridge by climbing straight up or follow a subterranean passage leftwards to reach the ridge nearer the summit.
Winter: III,4 ***   (1985)
When in full conditions, this is a classic climb with superb situations. Start below the pitch in Western Stoneshoot. Traverse up and left to the edge and follow the true ridge by the line of least resistance.

28   Bypass Route   210m   II **   (1983)
Start on the left at the base of Western Stoneshoot. Follow a succession of grooves, each slightly right of the other, on the right of Pinnacle Ridge to the final col. Finish straight up.

29   Western Stoneshoot   140m   Moderate   (1893)
This wide deep cut gully divides the Upper North-East Face from Stoneshoot Buttress. It is largely filled with unstable rubble with one short pitch at about mid-height. It forks some distance above the pitch, the left fork being the main gully.
Winter: II *
An atmospheric route with one ice pitch about mid-height. In heavy snow conditions this can bank out reducing the grade to I, when it provides a useful descent route.

30   Right Fork/Right Branch   65m   III,4 **   (1996)
A fine dramatic climb with a very tight squeeze through route at the top
– not for the overweight! Start at the junction with the main gully.
1. 20m   Ascend easy snow from the fork to reach a second fork.
2. 25m   Take the very thin right-hand branch which leads to a belay
below a huge cluster of jammed blocks (the left-hand branch links back
into the main gully *via* a short pitch and a ledge – Grade II).
3. 20m   Climb up under the blocks to the back of the chimney. Force
your body up through an improbable constriction to gain freedom and
the ridge above.

31   Mixed Emotions   120m   V,5 *   (1996)
An enjoyable and varied route taking the obvious wide-based tapering
slabby rib that rises on the left-hand side of Western Stoneshoot at its
fork. This rib is bounded on the left by a wide shelf and on the right by
an open vegetated groove. The middle section of this route coincides
with Garrick's Route.
1. 25m   Climb a short chimney-groove on the right of a big rock bulge.
Continue up to an overlap. Traverse left to belay on the edge.
2. 35m   Move back right, then climb a superb right-angled slabby
corner holding a thin ribbon of turf to reach the apex of the rib and
easier ground. Ascend this to belay at the next steepening.
3. 35m   Climb a short wide crack on the right, then continue up to join
the right flanking groove just below its top. Ascend this to belay on a big
block at a tiny col beneath the headwall. This col is separated from the
final col on Pinnacle Ridge by a stretch of easy ground.
4. 25m   Gain the narrow chimney directly above the belay, pass
under a chockstone, then make exposed moves up and left to gain the
ridge. A meaty pitch!

32   Garrick's Route   75m   Difficult   (1920)
Start at the base of an open vegetated groove to the right of the
tapering slabby rib of Mixed Emotions. Climb the messy groove for
about 12m, then traverse leftwards across the slab to the edge (joining
Mixed Emotions). Finish up the rib to reach a little col. From this point a
walk leftwards leads to the col on Pinnacle Ridge.

The route recorded as Book In in previous editions of this guide
takes an identical line to Garrick's Route.

33   Manners   75m   Severe   (1975)
Start to the right of the open groove taken by Garrick's Route and climb an easy rib, right of a subsidiary gully, to a through-route behind a massive chockstone. From the top of the boulders above, move left across a 3m slab, then climb straight up by slabs and grooves to finish.

34   Un Petite Voyage   65m   IV,5   (1996)
Start at an icefall issuing from a shallow chimney on the right wall of Western Stoneshoot a short distance below the gully fork.
1. 30m   Climb the icefall (usually on very thin ice), then take the shallow chimney capped by a chockstone. Belay on the slope above.
2. 35m   An easy snow slope leads to the ridge.

35   Generation Gap   70m   V,6 **   (1996)
This short but rather fine route tackles the vertical dyke chimney line on the right wall of Western Stoneshoot, just above its pitch. The initial chimney packs a real punch!
1. 25m   Climb the iced chimney – excellent.
2. 45m   Take the easier-angled groove on the left which leads to the short chimney continuation. Climb this to the ridge.

STONESHOOT BUTTRESS

This impressive feature forms the relatively clean flanking wall of Western Stoneshoot and presents a heavily vegetated front face, bounded on the right by West Gully.

Original Route   185m   III, 3   (1983)
This route takes the easiest line on the buttress, starting centrally and linking two snow patches on the front face. The second snow patch slants right towards the top. The turf must be thoroughly frozen for an enjoyable and safe ascent.

West Gully   60m   Very Difficult   (1958)
This short rubbishy gully to the west of Stoneshoot Buttress contains one nasty little pitch of friable granite. Not recommended!
Winter: II   (1984)
When banked out, the grade reduces to I.

CAISTEAL ABHAIL
834m   (Map Ref 968 443)

This peak, commonly known as The Castles, has a cluster of five buttresses outcropping high on its south-eastern slopes (collectively known as the Upper Rocks). Some distance below these, in Coire na h-Uaimh, lies Portcullis Buttress.

Most of the routes are fairly short and of a modest grade. Opinion is divided as to their contribution to the wealth of Arran climbing! Access is as for the North-East Face of Cir Mhor, adding at least another 20 minutes for the final ascent.

PORTCULLIS BUTTRESS

1   Donjon   65m   Severe   (1969)
On the left of the buttress is a ill-defined shallow gravelly gully. Start about 30m up the gully at a little cave.
1. 30m   Climb clean slabs rightwards to reach a crest and follow this left to a ledge.
2. 10m   Climb a short steep layback crack above (often wet and slimy) to a grass tuft. Enter a groove on the right and climb up to a ledge with a thread belay.
3. 25m   Climb the obvious stepped layback crack above to a ledge, finishing up the slab above.

2   Lee Climb   60m   Very Difficult *   (1950)
An enjoyable climb on good rock. Start 6m below Donjon.
1. 15m   Climb a short wall on to the top of a semi-bollard and follow a groove above to reach a chimney coming up from the right. The chimney bifurcates 3m higher up. Climb to the top of its right fork.
2. 15m   Semi-layback round the corner on the left into a groove, then go up steep grass to a corner.
3. 10m   Move slightly left, climb over a large split block and traverse left past the foot of a steep slab (crossing Donjon) to a good stance round a corner.
4. 20m   Climb a short narrow chimney, then another wider chimney in the same line. Move left up a slab, then finish up another short chimney.

3 Portcullis 90m Very Difficult (1945)
The foot of the buttress overhangs and the climb starts in a little gully about 15m from its foot.
1. 20m Climb the wall *via* a short tilted, part grassy crack, then cross the slabs to a grass patch.
2. 25m Walk up grass to a corner and climb a short crack. Gain the crest below a vertical step.
3. 10m Traverse out onto the right wall of the buttress, then climb the slab above by a thin left-slanting groove. Move up to a pile of boulders below an overhang.
4. 35m Climb the overhang direct, or the wall on its left. Scrambling, then a little wall finish the climb.

4 Avalanche Gully 60m Difficult (1945)
A very scrappy climb containing much grass and loose rubble. Start at the overhang base of the buttress and follow a grassy shelf rightwards to reach the gully which is climbed with a diversion up a chimney on the right.

5 V Gully 110m Very Difficult (1945)
To the right of Avalanche gully is a prominent V formed by two chimney lines. It has a short left limb (co-linear with the gully section of Avalanche Gully) and a long right limb, which is broken at mid-height; this is the line of this climb. The short left limb is a steep mossy chimney and is unclimbed.
Winter: III,3 * (1985)
Follow the summer route, the upper section often providing thin ice climbing when not banked out.

THE UPPER ROCKS

BUTTRESS 1

This is the most prominent buttress above Portcullis Buttress.

6 The Rift 115m II, 3 (1991)
This is the prominent deep cleft splitting the buttress from top to bottom. The lower part is easy, virtually a walk, but as height is gained it becomes progressively more interesting with the final 30m providing a bit of a tussle! It provides a poor route in summer (Difficult, 1945).

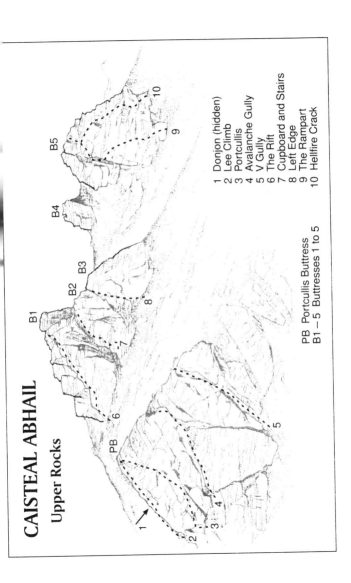

CAISTEAL ABHAIL
Upper Rocks

1 Donjon (hidden)
2 Lee Climb
3 Portcullis
4 Avalanche Gully
5 V Gully
6 The Rift
7 Cupboard and Stairs
8 Left Edge
9 The Rampart
10 Hellfire Crack

PB Portcullis Buttress
B1 – 5 Buttresses 1 to 5

BUTTRESS 2

This sits immediately below and to the right of Buttress 1.

7   Cupboard and Stairs   50m   Difficult *   (1945)
A good entertaining route, almost worth the long approach. Start about 15m up on the left from the toe of the buttress, below a big roof. It is also possible to start from a slightly lower point but this increases the grade to Severe. Climb to the left end of a shelf, then step up onto the slab above. Traverse right below an overhang with a curious pothole, and gain the edge of the buttress. Follow the crest to a 3m wall which leads to the summit of the buttress. Descend into a gap to finish.

BUTTRESS 3

This is down and right of Buttress 2.

8   Left Edge   65m   Difficult   (1962)
Seen from below, this slabby little buttress is pyramidal in shape, with a steep lower half. It is divided from Buttress 2 by a gully. Gain a rib to the right of this gully and climb by the line of least resistance to the top.

BUTTRESS 4

The summit buttress gives a number of short routes of various grades.

BUTTRESS 5

This is the largest buttress of the group with a broad, slabby south face.

9   The Rampart   140m   Difficult   (1945)
1. 20m   At the foot of the buttress is a clean wall. Climb the wall and slab above to a recess.
2. 25m   Continue up slabs to a grass terrace below a steep step. Climb the step, then go up another little wall. More slabs lead to a big grass platform.
3. 30m   Easy climbing leads to a steep wall.
4. 25m   Skirt the wall on the left and traverse into a leaning chimney ahead. Climb the chimney to the second jammed block, then climb up to a cleft at the top of a pitted slab.
5. 10m   Step up onto a sloping shelf on the corner above the cleft and gain the crest from the left.
6. 30m   Easy climbing to finish.

10   Hellfire Crack   135m   Very Difficult   (1945)
This route ascends the right flank of the buttress to join The Rampart at
the pitted slab. The name derives from one of the pioneering party,
placing a lighted pipe in his pocket! Start 30m up from the toe of the
buttress on the right flank. A short wall leads to an easy chimney which
in turn ends on a grassy terrace. Beyond the top right corner of the
terrace enter a thin gully which leads to a recess. Ascend a steep
V-chimney on the left wall of the recess and a scoop above to reach the
pitted slab on The Rampart. Finish by that route. An escape to the right
from below the V-chimney is possible.
Winter: IV,4 *   (1991)
An interesting and varied route taking the summer line. The V-chimney
is the crux.

COIRE NA H-UAIMH LOWER SLABS
(Map Ref 974 437)

An extensive belt of slabs, known as Lower Slabs, forms the lip of Coire
na h-Uaimh and separates it from Glen Sannox. A path skirting the
southern extremity of these slabs gives access to and from the corrie
and provides the safest descent route after a climb. The slabs are most
continuous on the right, whereas in the centre they are divided at half-
height by a heather terrace running in from more broken ground on the
left. A very distinctive raised slab tongue drops from the heather
terrace to the base of the slabs. The slabs provide pleasant climbing in
the middle grades although limited protection on some routes calls for
a confident approach. Access is *via* the path up Glen Sannox.

1   Socket Slabs   155m   Severe *   (1996)
To the left of the raised slab tongue is a smaller tongue at the base of
the slabs. Start to the left of this at a distinctive line of big pockets.
1. 45m   Climb straight up easy-angled slabs to a slight overlap. Pull
over this and climb a steeper slab next to a distinctive turf-filled crack.
Continue up a raised section of slab to belay on the left.
2. 25m   Continue up to the heather terrace, then walk left to belay
below a prominent white streak on the upper tier.
3. 45m   Climb boldly onto the white streak (crux), then continue
straight up, passing a pair of sockets, to gain a big flake edge. Brilliant
climbing with a single runner low down.
4. 40m   Climb up the slab to the right of the flake edge, then go on up
to cross a short wall and thence to the top.

2 Mystic 150m Severe * (1971)

Start at the base of the raised slab tongue at a regular cluster of pockets.

1. 35m Climb the twin cracks on the left side of the tongue to an overlap and belay in a corner above.

2. 30m Step right and climb slabs trending left to a block belay.

3. 45m Cross the heather terrace and climb pleasant slabs to the left end of an overhanging wall.

4. 40m Climb the wall by sloping shelves and continue up slabs to the top.

3 Central Grooves 125m Very Difficult (1962)

Start as for Mystic at the base of the raised slab tongue at a regular cluster of pockets.

1. 30m Climb a steep little slab to gain the left edge of the prominent groove. Follow the edge to a small stance and spike belay.

2. 20m Continue up in the same line to a huge block on the lower edge of the heather terrace.

3. 45m A little above and to the right, across the heather terrace, is another large block at the base of the upper slabs. From this block gain the slab above. Move slightly left, then move right to gain an obvious groove. Ascend the groove for a short distance to a small stance.

4. 30m Follow the groove to the top.

4 Hode On 125m Severe * (1971)

Start 10 metres right of the raised slab tongue at a pock marked slab, just left of a large pointed block beneath the slabs.

1. 25m Climb the slab to an overlap and belay.

2. 30m Surmount the overlap at its lowest point, then continue straight up to the heather terrace.

3. 35m Follow a thin crack to the bottom of a steep wide crack.

4. 35m Climb the wide crack to the top.

5 The Key 115m HVS * (1994)

Start at an elongated pocket to the right of a large pointed block beneath the slabs.

1. 45m 4c Climb straight up a clean slab to below the overlap. Step right onto a projecting block. On the slab above a thin flake crack runs out left. Ignore this and climb straight up a slight rib on small pockets and dimples to a wide heather ledge.

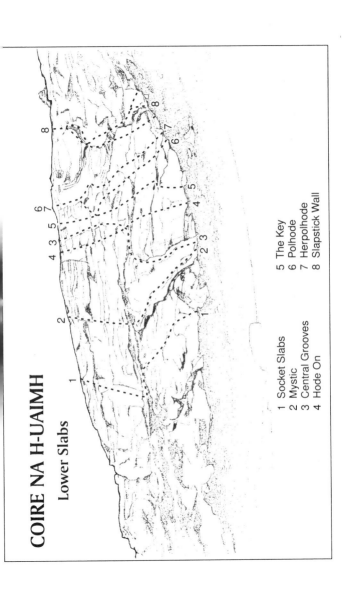

COIRE NA H-UAIMH

Lower Slabs

1 Socket Slabs
2 Mystic
3 Central Grooves
4 Hode On
5 The Key
6 Polhode
7 Herpolhode
8 Slapstick Wall

2. 30m 5a   Climb a clean slab in two steps (a perched block lies to the left) to a small turf patch left of a small corner. An incipient crack runs out left. Follow it for 3 metres, then climb boldly up a steep slab on minimal holds to gain a keyhole thread belay just above a big crumbly flake.

3. 40m   Ascend the pocketed slab above the belay, then cross an overlap to gain a thin rock crevasse (joining Polhode). Move slightly right, then climb straight up the centre of a narrow slab to finish.

6   Polhode   120m   Severe *   (1966)
Start about 40 metres right of the raised slab tongue, beyond a diamond-shaped hanging slab.

1. 25m   Climb up slabs to a grass ledge about 10m below distinctive short twin cracks (the left one holding grass tufts, the right one being incipient).

2. 25m   Climb up to the twin cracks *via* a short slab and groove, then go up the cracks and slab above to reach a grassy ledge.

3. 30m   Move up left *via* a pocketed slab to gain a thin rock crevasse. Step above this, then traverse back hard right to reach a poor belay at pointed flakes below a clean slab (this point is above and just to the right of a striking inverted V-overlap).

4. 40m   Finish straight up the impeccable undulating slabs above.

7   Herpolhode   115m   HVS 4c *   (1966/1996)
The precise line of this route has always been in some doubt, appearing in different positions on various guidebook diagrams. However, the following line, incorporating a short thin section, gives the best value. Start just right of Polhode beyond the diamond-shaped hanging slab.

1. 40m 4b   Climb straight up undulating slabs to reach a poised block below a short wide right-facing corner crack.

2. 15m   Ascend the short corner crack, then trend left up messy ground to belay at a flake.

3. 20m 5a   Climb the slab directly above the belay to the base of a clean slab topped by an overlap (narrowing to the right). This is to the right of the striking inverted V-overlap. Step up boldly onto the clean slab (crux), then move right on shallow pockets until the overlap can be crossed and a short left traverse made to gain the poor pointed flake belay on Polhode.

4. 40m   Finish up the impeccable undulating slabs above as for Polhode.

8   Slapstick Wall   115m   Severe **   (1959/1965)
This route, superseding the much less attractive original line, is probably the best on the slabs. It climbs to and follows the distinctive J-shaped overlap high up. A number of variations have been climbed. This description gives the best combination of pitches at Severe with a number of worthwhile but harder variations listed after it. Start at an obvious long, rather vegetated groove that bounds the right side of the main lower slab (a steep little slab lies just beyond it forming the right wall of the groove).

1. 30m   Climb into the right-hand of the two short corners at the start of the groove. Ascend this until it is possible to move right onto slabs. Ascend the slabs to belay a short distance below a short open corner.

2. 20m   Climb up to the short corner, ascend it, then move left to make a delicate step up onto the slab above which abuts the base of the J-shaped overlap.

3. 30m   Follow the curve of the J *via* the obvious narrow shelf caught between the two overlaps. At the top of the upright make an awkward move left onto the upper slab (crux). Ascend the slab passing pockets and a minimalist thread to gain a flake. A very fine pitch.

4. 35m   Climb straight up easier-angled slabs to the top.

Variation I: 25m   4c *   (1992)
The initial section of the groove on pitch 1 can be avoided altogether by moving in from the right to climb, near the left edge, the steep little slab forming the right wall of the groove. The thin cracks above join the normal route.

Variation II: 35m   4c *   (1983)
This is another variation to pitch 1. To the left of the groove is a clean sweep of bare slab. Climb this, then traverse right along a break to belay as for the normal route.

Variation to pitch 2:   20m   4c *   (1983)
Instead of making the traverse right on Pitch 1 Variation II belay at the break, then climb straight up the clean slab to belay at the base of the J.

Variation to pitch 3:   25m   4c **   (1993)
Pull over the bulge above the belay, then follow the edge overlooking the shelf of the J-shaped overlap to join the normal route at the move left. Excellent climbing.

CEUM NA CAILLICH
727m   (Map Ref 976 443)

From a distance this striking cleft appears as two towers of solid rock. However, actual rock climbing potential is fairly limited.

Witch's Step   45m   Difficult *   (1889)
This is the north side of the gap which is ascended (or descended) during the ridge traverse. It is now well polished and rather hard for its grade, especially when wet. In ascent, from the gap climb a little diagonal chimney leading leftwards to an awkward slab. Beyond the slab climb straight up an obvious grassy fault and enter a cleft on the right splitting the enormous summit block. Climb the cleft to the top.

Carlin's Rib   60m   Very Difficult   (1965)
High on the west side of the debris-filled gully, dropping into Glen Sannox from the gap, is a steep slabby rib. This is the line of the route.

Broomstick Ridge   150m   Difficult   (1944)
This is the ridge on the east side of the debris-filled gully dropping into Glen Sannox from the gap. Much variation is possible but the best climbing can be obtained by staying close to the edge overlooking the gully. Finish on the summit. Belay as required.
Winter: III,3 *   (1988)
Pleasant climbing keeping close to the gully edge.

Geison   60m   VS *   (1969)
Some 60 metres to the right of Broomstick Ridge, not far below the crest of the main ridge, is a roughly pear-shaped mass of rock about 45m high. A prominent thin gully, starting left of centre of the base, slants up leftwards. Start at the bottom left corner of the slab area.
1. 30m   Climb straight up the middle of the slabs left of the thin gully.
2. 30m 4c   Traverse right, cross the top of the thin gully, then move slightly down to the corner of the main slab mass. An obvious ledge will be seen running round the upper part of the main slab. Gain this ledge and follow it to its finish.

White Magic Groove   170m   III,4 *   (1984)
Immediately to the west of the Witch's Step a broad slabby buttress falls to the north into Coire nan Ceum. An open groove splits the centre of this buttress and is the line of the route. Climb the groove and the continuation gully with several short pitches.

CUITHE MHEADHONACH
(Map Ref 970 451)

This striking slabby wall, some 75 metres high, lies on the east flank of the north ridge of Caisteal Abhail facing into Coire nan Ceum. Cuithe Mheadhonach means Central Stronghold, a very appropriate name. Although the crag holds some crumbly rock, it also has some excellent climbing, mainly in the higher grades.

The best approach to this cliff is by way of North Glen Sannox in about 1 hour 15 minutes. A fairly wet path runs from the bridge carpark (Map Ref 993 467) along the south side of the burn. The walk is rather uninspiring until the cliff comes into sight before quitting the forestry plantation. The side of a picturesque small gorge then leads to the burn junction. Cross the burn just above this junction, then head straight up to the crag. The pale wall on the left dries quickly, whilst the rest of the crag is prone to seepage and requires several days to dry out after heavy rain. The routes are described from left to right.

1 Pegasus   40m   HVS 5a *   (1983)
This route follows the obvious line of weakness near the left edge of the face. Start below the base of the messy gully bounding the left side of the main face (this has been recorded as **Ardito**, HVS, but is really not worth climbing). Traverse horizontally right to blocks. Ascend directly up to surmount a block roof at its narrowest point. Move slightly right, then climb a crack line to a grass ledge. Step right and climb a short rib and thence to the top.

2 One Eyed Jacks   45m   E3 *   (1984)
Start 2 metres left of the vegetated crack near the left side of the main face. Bold for its grade.
1. 20m 5c   Climb the wall moving slightly right, then go back left to gain an obvious flake crack. Climb this, then cross the left end of the long roof to reach a ledge and the bolt belay of Ulysses. A very serious pitch with minimal protection.
2. 25m 5b   Follow a left-trending line to the edge of the crag, then climb this to the top (in common with Pegasus).

3 Ulysses   50m   E2 **   (1982)
This route takes a left of centre line up the pale wall on the left side of the crag. A fine climb despite the presence of some crumbly rock. Purists wishing to dispense with the bolt belay can regard the route as

E3! Start on a vegetated terrace (accessed by scrambling in from the left) 6 metres right of the obvious vegetated crack.
1. 25m 5c   Trend right, bypassing the right end of a thin roof, to gain a slight right-facing scoop. Move up, then take a left-trending line to reach the right end of the long roof. Move left under the roof to a good thread runner. Surmount the roof directly, then climb the short wall above (crux) until a short left traverse can be made to a small ledge and bolt belay.
2. 25m 5c   Traverse right to reach crumbling flakes. Climb these and the crack above to reach a small flake. Traverse right to shallow corner cracks which lead to a traverse left for 3 metres under bulging rock. Strenuous moves over the bulge and short rock steps lead to the top.

4   Icarus   55m   E5 **   (1995)
A sustained line on the wall between Ulysses and Achilles. Moving left to the belay of the former, the route then tackles the headwall to the left of Ulysses. Start, as for Ulysses, 6 metres right of the vegetated crack.
1. 30m 6b   Trend right, bypassing the right end of a thin roof, to gain a slight right-facing scoop and small ledge above (Ulysses goes up and left from here). Traverse hard right to gain big flat holds. From the top of these traverse slightly left, then move up *via* a finger pocket to reach an undercling. Move left to an incipient flake, climb this, then make precarious moves over a bulge and go up to reach a deep horizontal break. Traverse left strenuously to below twin flakes (Friend 0). Pull up to stand in the break, then teeter left to reach the left traverse leading to the bolt belay of Ulysses. Very sustained climbing.
2. 25m 6b   Climb up the flakes and cracks of Ulysses to a jug where that route traverses right. Traverse left to a big flake. Pull up, then ascend a line of small pockets in the wall above with desperation to a horizontal break. Finish straight up.

5   Achilles   50m   E5 ***   (1984/1995)
A spectacular and excellent climb taking a fairly central line on the pale wall on the left side of the crag. The crux sequence is probably the hardest on Arran. This description is for the free variation of the route, superseding the original line (which employed two points of aid). With careful rope management, the route can be led as a single pitch, but a double set of small Friends is required to protect it adequately. Start about 10 metres right of Ulysses at the highest point of the vegetated terrace.

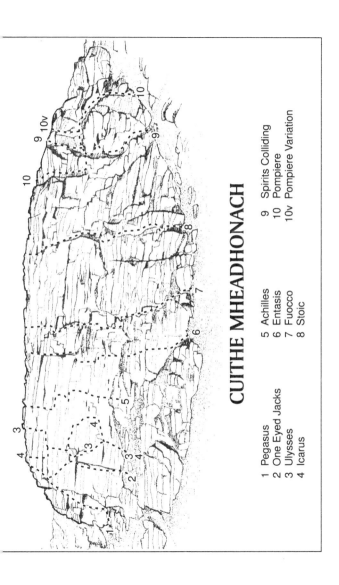

CUITHE MHEADHONACH

1 Pegasus
2 One Eyed Jacks
3 Ulysses
4 Icarus

5 Achilles
6 Entasis
7 Fuocco
8 Stoic

9 Spirits Colliding
10 Pompiere
10v Pompiere Variation

1. 20m 5c   Climb the slabby wall to reach an easy left-facing flake system. From the top of this a second and fragile flake is gained by difficult moves on the left. A long stretch allows a step up onto the top of the fragile flake, from where a bombproof Rock 9 belay can be placed in a short deep vertical crack.

2. 30m 6c   The belay crack curves left to become a horizontal break. Hand traverse this break until a step up can be made onto a higher break. Move right, then make desperate moves to gain a fat left-facing flake (crux). Pull over this to reach a horizontal break, then reach left to gain another flake edge. A horizontal crack, becoming a rail, runs out left. Follow it to reach the obvious vertical crack and flake system which leads strenuously but more easily to the top.

6   Entasis   65m   E1 *   (1969/1975)

The direct version of this route is described as it effectively supersedes the original one. It is characterised by a distinctive thin chimney in its upper half and lies near the right-hand side of the pale wall on the left side of the crag. Start as for Fuocco, the obvious vegetated chimney-fault that divides the crag into two sections.

1. 40m 4c   Move up left on heather to reach the start of a flake crack system in line with the obvious thin chimney above. Climb this to reach grass ledges. Climb straight up to a ledge below a thin crack. Traverse hard left to reach a flake edge which is climbed to reach a turf ledge below the thin chimney.

2. 25m 5a   Climb the chimney (which contains a hanging garden and is often wet and repulsive) the last few metres closing to a crack. A right traverse into Fuocco is possible from the belay ledge giving an alternative finish (5a) and reducing the overall grade to HVS.

7   Fuocco   75m   VS   (1968)

A route of some character, following the chimney-fault that divides the crag into two sections. Despite a lot of turf it is worth an ascent for the excitement of the upper chimney. Start directly below a chimney.

1. 35m 4b   Climb a short chimney slanting slightly right, then continue up over several short walls and ledges to belay under a long overhanging nose.

2. 15m 4b/c   Climb up to a ledge (two possible lines), then follow a wall up and right to belay at the foot of a chimney.

3. 25m 5a   Ascend the chimney (or wall on the left) to adopt a contorted pose below twin rock noses. Emerge strenuously and rather dramatically between these onto a grass ledge on the right. Easier rock steps lead to the top.

8 Stoic 80m HVS * (1973)

This route climbs the highest part of the crag some 30 metres to the right of Fuocco. Start at the base of a short corner, the central and best defined of three similar features.

1. 25m 5a Climb the short awkward corner, exit left, then traverse right until it is possible to climb up and left to a stance and a small spike under a short crack.

2. 15m Ascend the crack and soon traverse left to a grass terrace. Belay up and round a corner on the right.

3. 15m 5a Climb a wall on the left and gain a ramp. Follow the ramp up left, then step up onto a grass moustache. Thread belay.

4. 25m Climb a stepped wall, traverse left, surmount a cracked bulge and finish up short walls.

9 Spirits Colliding 60m HVS * (1995)

Well to the right of Stoic, as the crag bends round and reduces in height, there is a short chimney holding a loose chockstone. This is the start of the route.

1. 10m 4c Climb the deceptive little chimney, then scramble up grass to take a belay at the base of an open flake-groove in the wall above.

2. 20m 5a Climb the flake-groove, passing two clumps of grass to reach a huge, hollow, right-pointing flake. Traverse right to its point, move up to an undercling, then pull left onto a small rock ledge. Move slightly up and right to belay at the start of a grass ledge (this ledge is traversed by Pompiere).

3. 30m 5a Move slightly right along the ledge, then traverse back left to enter a slim groove on the right flank of an obvious rib. Climb this until it becomes a crack, then make a difficult left exit onto a small rock ledge. Climb straight up to finish.

10 Pompiere 90m VS (1968)

Near the right-hand side of the crag in its upper half there is a prominent right-facing right-angled corner. This route takes a long left traverse in from the upper right-hand edge of the crag to climb the corner. Start at the base of a right-facing fault at the upper right edge of the crag.

1. 30m 4c Climb the slim wall (effectively the right wall of the fault) to a block-covered platform.

2. 10m Traverse left onto the face and go left again to gain a grass ledge and block belay.

3. 20m 4c   Walk left to the end of the ledge, drop down, then traverse left across a wall to a rock ledge below the foot of the prominent corner.
4. 30m 4c   Climb the corner crack to reach easier ground and thence the top.
Variation: Severe
Starting from the block belay at the end of pitch 2, take a gangway and climb the crack above.

OUTLYING AREAS AND SEA-CLIFFS

TORR NEAD AN EOIN   *(Map Ref 949 493)*

This geologically interesting crag lies on the west face of a rounded hill about 2.5km south-east of Lochranza. The cleanest section of crag, roughly pyramidal in shape, is composed of schist and is about 75m in height. It is bounded by broken ground on the left and by a messy gully on the right (Verdant Gully). Immediately left of this gully is a tower-like mass of rock, teeming with overhangs, which is separated from the main face by a part grassy rake, hidden from below. The rock is mostly sound with the odd shaky hold, the exposure considerable and the views rather fine. It is probably the most interesting of the outlying crags and provides a pleasant contrast to Arran granite.

1   First Footing   75m   VS *   (1967)
This climb lies on the left side of the main face and starts 4 metres left of a line of black overhangs.
1. 20m 4c   Climb a wall and trend left and up until a move right can be made at 12m (the rock requires care). Move right and up to the grass terrace to belay beside a small tree.
2. 20m 4b   Climb the steep wall behind the tree, then move up and right to a belay beside a detached flake.
3. 35m   Finish straight up on good rock.

2   Schist Buttress   65m   Severe   (1947)
This is the original route on the face, following the shallow diagonal groove starting near the base and finishing near the top on the left. A better finish is to step right on the grass terrace and climb straight up to join Aquila.

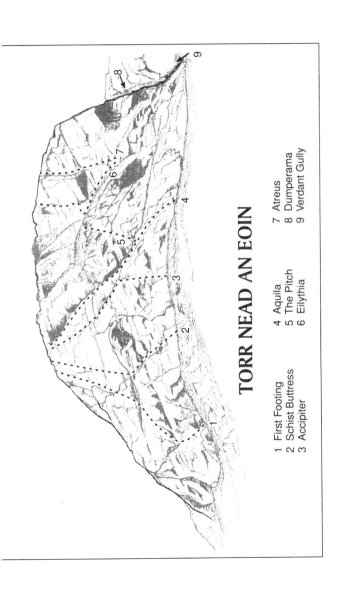

TORR NEAD AN EOIN

1 First Footing
2 Schist Buttress
3 Accipiter
4 Aquila
5 The Pitch
6 Eilythia
7 Atreus
8 Dumperama
9 Verdant Gully

3 Accipiter 65m VS   (1991)
Start at an open crack between Schist Buttress and Aquila.
1. 10m   Climb straight up the crack, bypassing a large fragile flake on the left. Belay at the far right end of a terrace.
2. 25m   Climb a short steep wall, then veer left and climb to the right of a shallow ramp.
3. 30m   Continue straight up to the top on small holds, finishing just left of Aquila.

4 Aquila 90m Very Difficult *   (1950)
A good climb up the best natural line on the face, following the prominent deep diagonal groove.
1. 20m   Climb the groove to a stance below a steepening slab. The right wall is deeply undercut here.
2. 25m   Climb a steep little wall on small holds and continue up past a ledge to a second ledge and belay.
3. 25m   Continue up to a good stance in a recess.
4. 20m   Finish more or less straight up. The wall behind gives a final scramble to the top.

5 The Pitch 25m HVS 5a   (1968)
Climb the first pitch of Aquila until left of a prominent roof. Climb the wall and break through overhangs to finish on the terrace.

6 Eilythia 65m Severe   (1967)
This route is on the upper tower, starting some 12m up the rake separating it from the main face, at a crack with some small trees growing at its base. A small gangway slants up the left side of the tower.
1. 30m   Climb the gangway to a belay.
2. 30m   The upper part of the gangway becomes grassy. Move right and climb a steep wall on good holds to a block.
3. 5m   Move right again to reach a corner and climb it to easy ground.

7 Atreus 45m HVS 5a   (1969)
Start 6m below Eilythia. The rock requires some care. Climb onto the slabs on the right and follow these for about 12m to a crack. Climb the crack to the overhang, then follow a V-shaped groove above the overhang to the top of the tower.

8   Dumperama   45m   HVS   (1979)
A loose but challenging line up the left wall of Verdant Gully. Start at the
bottom of Verdant Gully below a black lichen-covered wall on the left
wall of the gully. Climb the wall for 5m, move left into a green groove,
then climb it past a loosely wedged block and move up left to a small
heather ledge. Climb the loose wall above to an overhanging nose,
then go past this on the left to reach a broken wall and so the top.

9   Verdant Gully   60m   Very Difficult   (1946)
The messy gully to the right of the tower. The rock, where it appears, is
not to be trusted.

A girdle traverse of the cliff has been made, starting on the left-hand
side of the face at about half-height. It is a poor climb, about VS,
becoming easier as one progresses.

BEINN BHARRAIN 721m (Map Ref 901 427)

The highest of the western hills lies to the south-east of Pirnmill. The
north-west ridge of the mountain gives a rough scramble for about
150m and is rather fine in winter. Rock climbing is limited to the north-
east flank of this ridge. There are three buttresses, the left-hand one
holding two routes and the central one holding one. None are of any
great quality.

Route 1   55m   Severe   (1960)
A prominent grassy and gravelly gully runs up near the centre of the
left-hand buttress. Start left of this, at a narrow left-slanting groove.
1. 25m   Climb the groove which is greasy in damp conditions.
2. 30m   Traverse left for 6 metres, climb a steep 3m high wall, then
finish easily up grass. An alternative top pitch (20m) is to continue in
the same line of the initial groove with a through-route to finish.

Route 2   55m   Severe   (1960)
Some 12 metres left of the start of Route 1 is a corner crack, an
obvious line of weakness.
1. 25m   Climb the corner crack until a difficult move left leads to the
slabs above.
2. 10m   Traverse easily left until under the upper part of the crag.
3. 20m   Climb an undulating wall to the top.

Grimly Fiendish   65m   VS   (1992)
Start five metres to the right of the toe of the central buttress.
1. 35m 4c   Climb three short walls directly to a steeper wall, then
climb this with difficulty on the left to a grass ledge. Follow the ledge
leftwards, then climb a crack to further ledges, which lead rightwards
to a belay on a large moss ledge beneath a detached block adjacent to
the prominent upper corner of the crag.
2. 30m 4b   Move right into the corner and climb it for 4m to a ledge.
Move left along the ledge, climb a layback crack, then continue up
short walls to the top.

KING'S CAVE   (Map Ref 884 308)

A series of sandstone crags lie either side of the spectacular
prehistoric dwelling known as King's Cave. Access is either from
Blackwaterfoot along the coast below the Drumadoon cliffs or more
directly from the A841 *via* a forest walk. The rock is fairly soft with a
sandy surface and the top of the crags comprise a jungle of
overhanging vegetation. Although two routes have been recorded
here, it is better suited to bouldering or general tourism.

DRUMADOON POINT   (Map Ref 885 293)

This columnar sill lies just to the north-west of the village of
Blackwaterfoot. The west-facing cliff line, rising to a maximum height of
40m, is about half a kilometre in length and displays a succession of
cracks, grooves, aretes and pillars. Although this cliff looks good from
afar and the rock is of reasonable quality, close inspection reveals
copious drapes of hairy lichen and a number of nesting birds. Given
the cliff's status as an Site of Special Scientific Interest, over-
enthusiastic cleaning is strongly discouraged either on existing routes
or new ones. An additional deterrent is the bramble jungle guarding the
foot of a number of routes. This is a primitive crag – both the grades
and star ratings should be viewed with a healthy scepticism!
    Due to the repetitive nature of the cliff's topography, locating the
existing routes in not easy. The following overview description may
help. About halfway along the cliff (below its highest point) the path
passes below a large boulder. About 7 metres to its left is a semi-
detached pillar with a narrow chimney on its right (Warp Drive), and on
its left a chimney which narrows at half-height (Electric Chair). Twin

parallel cracks, capped by a roof, are found 5 metres left of the pillar
(First Shock). After another 15 metres lies an easy open gully-chimney.
Another 10 metres left of the gully is an open wall with a groove-crack
system on either side of a roof at the top (How's Your Teslas). About 30
metres left of this is a chimney ending in an overhang at half-height.
Twin parallel cracks run up from this (Tellingbone). About halfway
between this and the end of the cliff is a chimney which starts at half-
height. There is a large loose roof at mid-height and a very loose wall
below caused by the collapse of the lower columns (Do Androids
Dream of Electric Sheep). Some 50 metres from the end of the cliff lies
a left-facing groove with a prominent right-slanting crack at its top
(Electro-Therapy).

From Blackwaterfoot village take the road to the Golf Club House,
then follow the main track beyond until the cliff is reached in about
fifteen minutes (alternatively walk along the beach). The routes are
described from right to left.

Ohm   25m   VS 4c   (1986)
Climb the groove and crack 5 metres right of the old fence. Near the top
it is possible to step right onto a ledge. Make a few moves up, then
traverse left into an easier groove to gain the top.

Electrocak   25m   HVS 4c   (1986)
Climb the second crack left of Ohm, 2 metres right of the old fence. It is
a wide crack with a ledge on the left 5m from the top. The rock above
the ledge is loose.

Wind Generator   25m   HVS 5a *   (1986)
Climb the groove immediately behind the old fence; it becomes more
sustained near the top.

Dodgy Transformer   25m   E1 5b **   (1986)
A sloping overhang halfway up the cliff lies 30 metres left of the old
fence (the path almost touches the cliff at this point). Start up a crack to
a ledge at 10m. Follow the crack at the back of the ledge until stopped
by the sloping overhang. Swing left onto good holds on the face and
continue to the top.

Repeater   25m   HVS 5a **   (1986)
Two metres left of Dodgy Transformer is a wide right-facing groove
leading to a ledge at 7m. Start up this and before reaching the ledge

move into a V-groove on the right. Follow this to another ledge, then go up to the overhang and move right to surmount it, gaining a ledge just below the top.

Circuit Board   30m   Hard Severe 4b   (1986)
Climb the wide groove of Repeater to the ledge at 7m. Climb the wide crack at the left end to a smaller ledge. Shuffle along this, then ascend a crack to stand on a pedestal below a roof of loose blocks. Traverse under the roof until it is possible to exit on loose blocks.

Alternative Medicine   30m   E5 6a ***   (1988)
Two-thirds way between the old fence and the vegetated chimney-gully is an obvious V-groove starting at ground level and running out at half-height. Follow the groove to a good foothold below its end, then move out right to a large hold. Trend up leftwards to the obvious flake which leads to the top.

Electric Avenue   30m   VS 4c **   (1985)
Some 50 metres left of the old fence (10 metres right of the recess) is a right-facing groove with a prominent flake at the top. The flake comes down to produce a small roof above a niche. Climb the groove, then go up the crack to the niche. Take the flake on its right side and follow it to the top.

Endangered Species   30m   E6 6a ***   (1988)
Immediately right of the brambly recess is a slender pillar projecting slightly beyond the rest of the crag. In the front face of the pillar a bottomless groove terminates at half-height. Gain the base of the groove proper and follow it until a good ledge can be gained on the left. Climb the wall above to a niche below a small roof and continue more easily to the top.

Fork Lightning   30m   VS 4b *   (1985)
To the left of the brambly recess is an S-shaped crack. Climb the right-hand of the two cracks and step left onto a ledge when the crack ends. Follow the left-hand crack to the top.

Shock Treatment   30m   E4 6a ***   (1985)
To the left of the Fork Lightning is an open groove which peters out at half-height. The start is a projecting sandstone band with a small overhang above. Climb the overhang, moving slightly rightwards, then

go back left to the ledge at the bottom of the groove. Climb the groove until it peters out, then move up the wall on small holds to a ledge. A small flake leads to a larger ledge and so to the top. A high side runner was used to protect the start on the first ascent.

Quark Jive 30m VS 4c * (1986)
Some 3 metres to the left of Shock Treatment is a large flake, right of a recess, starting halfway up the cliff. From the sandstone ledge at the bottom, follow the crack to the flake, then climb this to a ledge near the top and finish straight up.

The Groove of Distinction 30m E5 6b *** (1988)
About 15 metres left of Shock Treatment and 8 metres right of a small pinnacle, is a big open left-facing groove terminating at half-height in a roof. Gain the top of the small pillar at the base of the groove, then follow the groove to the roof. Move out leftwards to a series of small hanging grooves which lead to a good ledge 3m below the top. A crack finishes the route.

Hertz Crack 30m VS 4c (1985)
Just to the right of the large boulder on the path is a left-facing groove with a ledge on the right 3m below the top. Follow the groove until stopped by a blocky overhang near the top. Step right onto the ledge, then climb to the top.

Warp Drive 30m VS 4b (1986)
Climb the groove, then take the chimney on the right side of the semi-detached pillar running the full height of the cliff.

Electric Chair 30m VS 4b (1985)
This route takes the chimney on the left side of the pinnacle with a horrendous thrutch at half-height.

Are Friends Electric 30m VS 4c (1986)
Climbs the overgrown groove-crack 2 metres left of the pinnacle and 3 metres right of First Shock. Turn the roof near the top on the left to reach the ledge of First Shock. Finish by that route.

First Shock 30m VS 4c * (1985)
Climb twin cracks 15 metres left of the pillar, moving right under the roof near the top onto a ledge, thence to the top.

How's Your Teslas   20m   VS 4c   (1986)
About 10 metres left of the recess is a narrow open clean wall with a
groove-crack system at either side and capped by an overhang. Climb
the wall and either crack to the roof. Move left round the roof on loose
blocks and gain the top.

Electrickery   20m   Hard Severe 4b   (1986)
Climb the groove 4 metres left of the previous route. The groove
widens and can be entered before reaching the top.

Giv'em Enough Volts   20m   VS 4c *   (1986)
Follow the wide crack 3 metres left of Electrickery. A long run out in the
middle leads to a ledge on the right and some protection. Move back
out right and climb the crack to finish.

Short Circuit   20m   VS 4c   (1986)
Climb the groove immediately right of Tellingbone to a small ledge on
the left, then go up a shallow groove to join Tellingbone and finish as for
that route.

Tellingbone   20m   VS 4b *   (1986)
About 25 metres left of Give'em Enough Volts is a chimney ending at
half-height in an overhang. Above this are twin parallel cracks. Climb
this to a ledge on the right, then climb a crack just right again to an
overhang block which provides a finish on good holds.

Do Androids Dream of Electric Sheep   20m   VS 4c * (1986)
A large section of the bottom half of the columns has fallen away,
leaving a roof at half-height and a wide chimney-crack to finish. The
bottom wall up to the roof is very loose. From its top, make difficult
moves left under the roof to become established in the crack. Several
finishes are possible.

Electro-Therapy   25m   VS 4b   (1985)
This route takes the groove and the right-sloping crack at the top, 50
metres from the left end of the cliff.

BENNAN HEAD   *(Map Ref 993 200)*

This headland is the most southerly point on Arran. It provides one
good, long route which is well worth a visit as a contrast to the granite

in the north or when the mountain crags are wet. From a small quarry, visible from the main road, follow the farm track past Craigdhu, taking the right-hand branch to its end. Walk over the fields southwards to the highest point of the cliff where a path zigzags down the slope. Follow the path to the beach, then go along to the Black Cave (a prehistoric dwelling).

Black Cave Pillar   65m   HVS *   (1979)
An enjoyable route taking the striking pillar to the right of the Black Cave. It is best climbed early in the year before the cliff's plentiful vegetation takes control. The final belay is on stakes driven into the turf on the flat top of the crag; before tackling the climb it would be wise to confirm that they are still in place!
1. 25m 4b   Start centrally and climb trending left to a groove which leads to a right traverse and a way up to ledges and a belay below the overhangs.
2. 20m 5a   Move right to blocks and gain the wall above with difficulty. Step left and climb the wall until it is possible to traverse right into a small recess under twin cracks. Follow the cracks to a ledge and belay.
3. 20m 4c   Traverse 3 metres left and start up a short slabby wall to gain a small ledge left of a little shattered pillar under an overhang. Swing right around the pillar to gain the main corner, pull over a detached flake, then climb to the final corner which leads to the top. A sustained pitch with some dubious rock.

DIPPEN HEAD   (Map Ref 050 221)

This coastal cliff stretches for over 1.5km below the village of Dippen in the south-east of the island. Steep and rising to a height of about 30m it is composed of variable quality rock. A number of routes have been climbed but not recorded. Pigs may interfere with climbing activity!

HOLY ISLE

This steep and rocky island plugs the mouth of Lamlash Bay. It is now used as a retreat by the Buddhist Samye Ling Community. There are a number of crags, the vertical Creag Liath (Map Ref 062 293) being the best. A number of routes have been climbed but not recorded. An energetic swim from Kingscross Point is fine preparation for a spot of cragging or meditation!

CREAG ROSA   (Map Ref 992 387)

These small schist crags lie high above Glen Rosa on the southern spur of Glenshant Hill. They are of limited interest. A prominent split pinnacle lies to the west of these crags. It was first climbed in 1907.

MAOL DONN   (Map Ref 018 409)

This interesting sandstone crag takes it name from its parent hill which lies about 3km south of the village of Corrie and about 1km from the coast road. It faces due north and the cleanest rock lies nearest to the sea. Elsewhere the rock is fairly heavily vegetated. The recorded climbs are interesting and worth doing, although direct access to the crag can only be described as horrendous; the original heather, boulders and bracken being supplemented by a nasty coniferous plantation! The best route is to take the Goatfell path past High Corrie and to contour south once above the trees. The most obvious feature on the crag is a deep-cut chimney (The Chimney). The other routes are described in relation to it.

The Chimney   30m   Severe 4b *   (1907)
Follow the prominent deep-cut chimney near the east end of the crag. The start is hard and strenuous. A little classic.

Donn Corner   35m   VS   (1966)
Start about 8 metres right of The Chimney at a buttress with a wide-angled corner on its left. Follow the corner to the top of the crag.

Spelunca   35m   VS 4c *   (1966)
Some 5 metres left of The Chimney is a small cave. Climb its back and move out right by a crack. Follow the crack, then finish more easily.

The Cannon   65m   Severe   (1966)
1. 15m   Start about 35m below and left of The Chimney. Climb a crack to a grass ledge, taking a belay in a small cave under the main face.
2. 50m   Climb out along a spike of rock on the left of the cave to reach the upper face, then follow the buttress to the top of the cliff.

Oread   35m   Very Difficult   (1966)
This route lies on an isolated tower about 100 metres further up the hill. Climb a right-angled buttress on the left of the tower to a good ledge. Move left up a slab to a crack which leads to the top.

CORRIE BOULDERS

In time-honoured tradition, these granite boulders have been included in this guide. With the exception of Clach a' Chait, they are of limited interest. Clach a' Chait (Map Ref 020 445), sitting tight in against the road over 1km north of Corrie, has so far survived a number of threats to dynamite it. It provides a variety of challenging routes in the upper grades. Beware of passing cars! The other boulders are:

Clach Mhor – The largest (said to weigh 620 tons) lies 90 metres west of the road just south of the Corrie Burn.

Clach an Fhionn (Hero's Stone) – Lies 120m north of the Corrie Schoolhouse on the shore side of the road.

Rocking Stone – Lies on the shore side of a bend in the road just before the first house in Sannox. A deep cave nearby is worth exploring.

CONGLOMERATE CRAG (Map Ref 017 459)

An impressive 30m high streaked wall of vertical conglomerate, topped by an overhanging lip, lies to the north of Sannox Bay backing a raised beach. It currently holds one route but has scope for further development in the higher grades. However, there is almost no natural protection. To the left of the main crag some steep, shorter, friendlieRef 003 485)

On the right-hand side of the Fallen Rocks is an obvious orange sandstone buttress. A number of short routes of around VS have been climbed.

Stranger than Fiction   25m   E3 5b   (1990)
This route tales the slabby right-hand side of the main wall with in situ runners (including a bicycle spanner!). Start below a red runner. Move up to clip it, then traverse left to a peg just before the large protruding boulder. Move up to a ring peg, then climb the wall trending slightly right to belay on a ring peg below the lip. Abseil off.

FALLEN ROCKS   (Map Ref 003 485)

On the right-hand side of the Fallen Rocks is an obvious orange sandstone buttress. A number of short routes of around VS have been climbed.

Knapdale and Kintyre

These two districts form a long peninsula to the south of Argyll and immediately west of Arran. Although some way from the main centres of population, there is some excellent rock climbing in splendid locations which are unlikely to be crowded. Cara is a small island lying off the west coast of the peninsula, and the climbing here is even less likely to over-run with visitors.

KNAPDALE

Knapdale lies at the very root of the Kintyre peninsula, the Crinan Canal defining its northern extent. It is a relatively low-lying, fairly rugged area with extensive commercial afforestation. The west coast is deeply indented by sea-lochs which together with the many inland lochs and hill topography exhibit a striking north-east to south-west orientation. In addition to attractive scenery there is much of historical and archaeological interest. Knapdale contains many small crags although, to date, only two hold recorded routes. The rock, similar in texture to gabbro, is epidiorite giving positive climbing and distinctive rock architecture. Scope for exploratory rock climbing on small crags abounds.

Access
From Lochgilphead follow the A816 towards Oban for 3km, then turn left onto the B841 which runs alongside the Crinan Canal. Turn left at Bellanoch onto the B8025 (towards Tayvallich). Continue along this road for An Garadh, but for Creag nam Fitheach turn left at the first junction onto a minor single track road leading to Achnamara (and eventually to Kilmory *via* Castlesween).

Maps
Ordnance Survey 1:50,000 Sheet 55

Accommodation
There are hotels and guest houses at Crinan, Tayvallich and Cairnbaan and caravan/camping sites at Castlesween and Tayvallich. Wild camping opportunities are plentiful.

CREAG NAM FITHEACH (Map Ref 782 848)

This superb crag, without doubt Knapdale's finest, faces due south and rises from a boulder jumble to a height of over 30m. It holds an exceptional concentration of high quality routes and dries quickly after rain. The crag is approached on foot in about 20 minutes from the tiny settlement of Kilmichael of Inverlussa, to the south of Achnamara, *via* a private road on the north side of the Lussa Water. The routes are described from left to right.

1   Moby Dick   45m   Very Difficult   (1940s)
Climb the slabby face on the left-hand side of the obvious arete.

2   Captain Ahab   50m   HVS 5a   (1980s)
A difficult slabby corner leads to the arete which is followed to the top.

The next three routes lie on the vertical right flank of the arete. The heights quoted are to the arete and not to the top of the crag.

3   Maneater   10m   E4 6a **   (1988)
Climb the obvious off-width crack which is strenuous and sustained.

4   Temptation   12m   E3 6a **   (1988)
Start behind the rowan tree, just to the right of Maneater. Climb the slim groove and the flake above.

5   Crucifixion Crack   15m   E2 5c ***   (1982)
Start immediately right of the rowan tree. Climb a steep ramp and the groove above to gain a triangular niche. Pull over the roof, then hand traverse the diagonal crack to the arete.

6   Pocket Wall   20m   E1 5b **   (1982)
Climb the centre of the second buttress on obvious pocket holds, trending left to finish.

7   The Razor's Edge   25m   VS 5a ***   (1981)
Start at the base of the third buttress holding a huge flake on its right flank (Africa Flake). Ascend the rib to a ledge. Gain a fine sharp-edged flake crack (crux), then climb it and the short corner above. A splendid route.

8 Trundle Crack 20m Severe (1982)
Start at a pinnacle in the corner to the right of The Razor's Edge. Climb a groove and crack on the right wall.

9 The Changeling 25m E5 6a ** (1995)
Start at a crack just right of a rowan tree below the left arete of the obvious pod-shaped groove of Metamorphosis. Gain a detached block, then climb directly up the arete to a semi rest on a large foothold. Climb a slabby wall to gain a hanging crack, ascend it, then move left to a ledge and finish up a ramp.

10 Metamorphosis 25m E2 5c * (1982)
Climb the obvious pod-shaped groove between the fourth and fifth buttresses to reach a large hanging flake. Move left to gain good holds and thence to the top.

11 America 30m VS 4c ** (1982)
Start in a groove right of the pod-shaped groove of Metamorphosis. Climb to the top of a large flake on the left. Climb directly up for 3m, then move right into a crack and follow it to the top.

12 The Trial 30m E2 5c ** (1982)
Start to the left of the enormous leaning block. Climb a rib to a small bush. Surmount the overhang to gain a roofed niche, pull out of the niche, then climb directly up the wall above.

13 The Castle 25m Very Difficult (1980s)
Climb the right side of the enormous leaning block, follow the ramp, then climb the left side of a rib to the top.

14 Czechmate 20m VS 4c * (1980s)
This route takes the recessed corner to the left of the distinctive jutting rib of The Prow.

15 The Prow 35m E1 5b ** (1982)
This outstanding route tackles the distinctive jutting rib. Using a flake on the left, gain and climb a finger crack running parallel to the edge. Climb the exposed arete and the short difficult wall above (crux).

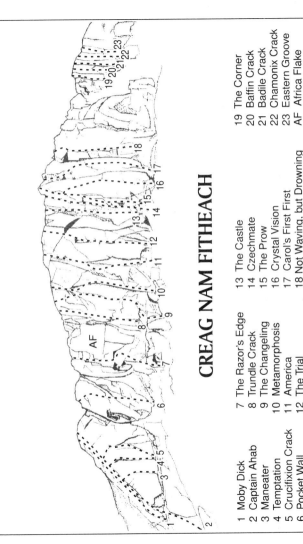

CREAG NAM FITHEACH

1 Moby Dick
2 Captain Ahab
3 Maneater
4 Temptation
5 Crucifixion Crack
6 Pocket Wall

7 The Razor's Edge
8 Trundle Crack
9 The Changeling
10 Metamorphosis
11 America
12 The Trial

13 The Castle
14 Czechmate
15 The Prow
16 Crystal Vision
17 Carol's First First
18 Not Waving, but Drowning

19 The Corner
20 Baffin Crack
21 Badile Crack
22 Chamonix Crack
23 Eastern Groove
AF Africa Flake

16   Crystal Vision   35m   E5 6b ***   (1988)
A superb sustained pitch, taking the thin crack on the right wall of The Prow. Start at the lowest point of the wall and climb up and left to gain good slots. Hard moves rightwards give access to the crack and this is followed with difficulty to a good rest ledge. Continue up a groove, exiting out left through a gap, to finish up the crux wall of The Prow.

17   Carol's First First   30m   VS 4c   (1980s)
Scramble up the gully to the right of The Prow. Climb a wall on the left to reach an obvious corner line which leads to the top.

18   Not Waving, but Drowning   30m   E6 6b **   (1990s)
A very serious route, taking the striking vertical edge to the right of The Prow, with minimal protection on the crux arete. Climb to a small roof at 5m, then follow the edge above (bold and sustained) to a triangular roof. Move right, then climb the wall back left to the top.

The next five routes lie close together on the rightmost buttress.

19   The Corner   10m   VS 4b   (1982)
Climb the obvious corner bounding the left side of the rightmost buttress.

20   Baffin Crack   10m   Severe   (1982)
Climb a clean rib past a tiny sapling, then go up the crack above.

21   Badile Crack   10m   Severe 4b   (1982)
Ascend heathery rock and the clean vertical crack above.

22   Chamonix Crack   10m   VS 4c *   (1982)
Ascend a short wall and the fine diagonal jamming crack above.

23   Eastern Groove   10m   Severe   (1982)
Climb a flake on the right of the rightmost buttress and the right-trending groove above.

AN GARADH   (Map Ref 760 902)

This south-east facing crag lies 1km west of the B8025, 4km north of Tayvallich. It looks promising from a distance but is somewhat disappointing on closer acquaintance. However, there is scope for more routes. Access is steep and partly afforested (30 mins).

Flakeaway   20m   Very Difficult   (1985)
Climb the sharp-edged flake and the crack above on the upper leftmost slab.

Steerpike   25m   HVS 5a   (1985)
A worthwhile route on the clean wall at the lowest point of the crag. Climb flakes, then go up the converging crack lines above.

CARA

Cara is the tiny island to the south of Gigha lying off the west coast of Kintyre, 5km south-west of Tayinloan. It is normally uninhabited, although there is a house near the north end. Boat hire from Tayinloan or from Gigha is possible. The best landing point is the beach at the northern tip of the island. The appropriate map is OS sheet 62.

CARRAIG MHOR   (Map Ref 638 433)

This fine epidiorite cliff lies at the southern tip of the island, rising to a height of 40 metres above a boulder jumble, it forms the abrupt termination of the Mull of Cara. The main section of the crag faces due south and is largely steep and clean with few nesting birds. Scars and debris from several relatively recent rockfalls are evident although the cliff now appears stable. The main face is bounded on its east side by a sheer wall above a deeply-eroded dipping band of sandy rock and on its west side by a dwindling slabby face. The base can be approached from either the east or west. Only seven routes have been climbed to date but there is potential for more. The climbs are described from left to right.

Carapace   20m   E4 6a ***   (1995)
On the far left-hand side of the crag lies a short immaculate slab. Start below this. Pull up, move left, then climb a thin crack to a ledge. Step right onto the slab, then follow an incipient crack with increasing difficulty to gain a good hold at its top. Crab left to finish.

Caraway   40m   VS 5a *   (1995)
Start at a proud shield of rock between two obvious diverging groove lines seaming the slabby face on the west side of the crag. Move up to gain a diagonal crack sporting tufts of campion. Follow this, then climb a guano-splattered slab and go over a bulge to finish.

Rubha Rib   45m   VS 5a *   (1990)
This route takes a clean line up the slabby face and rib on the west side
of the crag. A kite-shaped recess, just above ground level (just left of a
black overhanging corner) marks the start of the route. Climb into the
recess, then continue directly above to smoother rock (strenuous). Pull
right, then climb to the top of a large flake. Ascend the clean slab wall
above, just left of a groove, then step right onto the rib. Climb the rib
and the left-trending groove above.

Carachameleon   30m   E2 5b **   (1995)
This route tackles the obvious corner, with a subsidiary crack on its left
wall, to the right of the slabby face. Squiggle up the corner with
continuous interest to exit onto a slab, then go over blocks to finish. An
intriguing route, calling for some traditional skills.

Caracontortion   40m   E2 **   (1995)
Start at the base of a sharp arete near the centre of the crag. An
athletic route on sharp rock!
1. 30m 5c   Follow a fine groove on the immediate left of the arete to
pull right onto a block ledge on the very edge. Pull back left into a crack
and climb it to belay on the guano slab above.
2. 10m 4a   Climb the easy slab, then go up a short corner to finish.

Thomas Traverse   40m   E1 5b **   (1990)
An obvious corner divides the main face from the sheer undercut wall
on the right. Start at the bottom of the prominent crack (unclimbed)
splitting the face to the left of the corner. Traverse hard left to gain a
grass patch under a dark roof. Move left to gain a foothold (crux), then
layback up a flake edge into a groove. Gain a foothold on the left-
bounding rib of the groove, then climb up to below a small overhang.
Pull over this, then climb short walls to reach a good ledge below the
final corner. Climb this strenuously in two steps to the top. An excellent
and varied route.

Cara Corner   30m   E2 5b **   (1990)
This route gives spectacular climbing with some friable rock, and
tackles the obvious corner dividing the main face from the sheer
undercut wall on the right. Protection is just adequate although difficult
to place. Scramble to the base of the corner. Climb it past a grass tuft
and a slim groove on the left wall to gain a semi-detached flat-topped
flake on the left. Ascend the left wall to another small ledge. Move back
right to a rock pedestal, then climb the corner to finish.

MULL OF KINTYRE

The rugged headland of the Mull of Kintyre lies at the southern termination of the Kintyre peninsula, further south than the north of England and only 22km from the coast of Northern Ireland – Fair Head is clearly visible. The Mull is blessed with a favourable climate, often being dry and clear when the rest of the mainland is wet and cloudy. However, it is prone to fog and the fog horn at Map Ref 590 072 when in operation can prove a serious distraction to the climbers concentration!

The sea to the south of the Mull, the North Channel, displays dramatic turbulence under certain tidal conditions and the sight of small yachts making heavy progress is common. The Mull is a natural habitat for birdwatchers. Happily, the birds, lurking twitchers and dedicated crag rats enjoy a comfortable co-existence. Seals, otters and adders are also frequently seen.

Rock Climbing

The coastline of the Mull is very rocky with many crags both immediately above the sea and on the backing hillsides. The rock is predominantly schist and it varies in quality from clean and sound to loose and vegetated. Fortunately there is much of the former in evidence, making the Mull a rock climbing playground of some importance. Many bizarrely eroded, often fragile sections and projecting quartz holds add interest and spice to the climbing. As a general rule, the crags are steeper and the routes harder than they initially appear.

Most of the climbing to date has been on crags to the south of the lighthouse. All are south- or west-facing and dry quickly after rain. Most routes, with the exception of those on the main face of Signal Wall, are single pitch but they pack a lot in to their relatively short lengths. Although the crags are scattered around the headland, they all have distinctive characteristics making them reasonably easy to identify using the topo and individual crag descriptions.

Protection is generally good, if awkward to place, with small Friends often providing critical placements. No pegs or bolts have been used on any routes to date and this precedent should be respected.

Access

From Campbeltown, well down the Kintyre peninsula, take the A83 to a road junction at Stewarton, then turn left onto the B842. Follow this to a point a couple of kilometres short of Southend, then take a right turn after a war memorial onto a minor road. Turn right again at the second junction. This road is signposted to the Mull Lighthouse and it winds its way to a car park at the termination of the public road (Map Ref 597 081). Beyond the car park a spectacular private road drops nearly 300m *via* a series of hairpin bends to the lighthouse. It is wise to leave cars parked in the public car park at the top as parking lower down is neither practicable nor permitted (unless occupying the cottage – see below). The distance from Glasgow to the Mull by road is around 250km, involving a four hour drive.

Maps
Ordnance Survey 1:50,000 Sheet 68
Ordnance Survey 1:25,000 Sheet 489 (NR 50/60/70)

Accommodation
The rugged coastline of the Mull lends itself to wild camping, but a discreet minimum impact approach is advisable. The cottage of Ballinamoill may be available for rent from the Estate (contact Mrs Souden, Carskiey Lodge, Map Ref 657 081, telephone 0586 830672); this is a useful option in midge active months. The village of Southend, about 14km from the Mull, has accommodation, a pub, a shop and some sandy beaches.

BALMAVICAR CRAG   (Map Ref 594 095)

This steep crag lies 250 metres south-east of the ancient settlement of Balmavicar and is a good half-hour walk to the north from Ballinamoill Cottage. It is split into two parts by a deep straight crack running the full height of the crag. The rock to the right of the crack is clean and compact, that to the left broken by vegetated ledges.

The Slice   25m   E1 5b *   (1994)
Climb the obvious straight crack with a ledge at half height; a fine line and harder than it looks. Size 5 Friends would be useful!

Cakewalk   25m   VS 4c   (1994)
Start 2 metres left of the vertical crack. Move up and across a slabby wall to gain a jungle-filled niche. Fight through this, then ascend broken rock leftwards to step back right into a steep bent groove. Climb this on good holds.

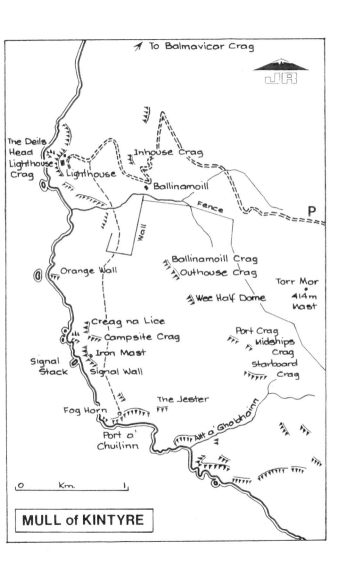

INHOUSE CRAG   (Map Ref 591 084)

This hidden craglet lies a short distance to the north of Ballinamoill Cottage. About 90 metres down the road from the cottage a slight path runs off to the right. It leads in a short distance to the crag. A roofed groove is the dominant feature.

Hooded Groove   7m   VS 4c *   (1994)
Climb the obvious roofed groove, moving left at the top.

LIGHTHOUSE CRAG   (Map Ref 587 084)

This crag lies directly below the lighthouse and can be accessed *via* a well defined but grassy path that zigzags down steep terrain starting at the south corner of the lighthouse enclosure. The crag is initially broken, but as one scrambles northwards over a coastal boulder jumble the formidable main section of the cliff comes into view. This 60m high wall is severely undercut, an enormous roof barring access onto the overhanging wall above.

A deep, dank recess demarks the right-hand side of the wall whereas the left side swings round above a grassy bay. The left side of this bay is bounded by a tall triangular slab. Further left again is a vegetated but striking twin-horned stack called The Deil's Head. The main section of Lighthouse Crag offers scope for new routing for the very bold (in the high E grades). The only routes to date lie on the friendly triangular slab.

White Water Slab   65m   Very Difficult   (1994)
1. 45m   Climb the centre of the triangular slab to meet the arete at a ledge.
2. 20m   Scramble up steep heather and rock to the top.

White Water Arete   65m   Severe   (1994)
1. 45m   Climb the arete bounding the left side of the triangular slab to a ledge.
2. 20m   Scramble up steep heather and rock to the top.

ORANGE WALL   (Map Ref 586 078)

This short distinctive coastal crag lies at South Point, to the south of the lighthouse, and rises above a jumble of enormous boulders. A well built cairn lies close to the top.

The Christening   20m   VS 4b *   (1995)
A wide crack starts to the right of the central arch (caused by a fallen block) and snakes right before cutting the final orange wall to finish just right of the cairn. This is the line of the route.

BALLINAMOILL OR COTTAGE CRAG (Map Ref 592 079)

This bold steep 30m high crag lies 400 metres south-south-east of the estate cottage of Ballinamoill. It is characterised by a severely undercut vertical arete with two parallel grooves to its immediate right.

Amino Flacid   25m   E4 5c *   (1993)
This very pumpy route, with some fragile rock and poor protection, climbs the wildly overhanging left wall of the obvious hanging arete. Start at a big projecting ledge in the centre of the wall. Pull onto the ledge, then move up to a fragile-looking dinner-plate flake. Bypass this on the left, then move right above it and climb the centre of the wall to a short groove at the right end of a small overlap. Climb the groove, then go up easier rock above, trending slightly right to finish.

Cresting the Wave   30m   HVS 5b **   (1993)
An impressive route taking the left-hand of the two parallel grooves. Ascend to below the roof, move left (crux), then go up to gain the groove. At the top of the groove hand traverse left below the big overhang to reach a niche on the arete, then climb to the top.

Rites of Passage   25m   HVS 5a **   (1992)
A fine partner route to Cresting the Wave, taking the right-hand groove. Ascend the excellent flake crack to a ledge below the big roof. Climb directly up the vertical wall on good holds (crux) to the left edge of the roof. Step right above it and move up to gain easier slabby rock. Belay at a big boulder on the left.

The Hoot   30m   Severe   (1992)
Immediately right of the right-hand groove is a narrow slabby wall
leading to a prominent short crack high above a patch of grass. Climb
this line, moving left over dubious blocks to finish. Thread belay to the
left.

Black Crack   20m   HVS 4c *   (1994)
This route climbs an obvious dark crack in the narrow wall which
divides the higher left from the lower right parts of the crag. Ascend the
vertical crack on big holds to a juniper ledge. Climb the short wall
above. Belay well back.

Olive Oyl   20m   VS 4c *   (1993)
Start a short distance right of Black Crack. Climb the obvious diagonal
flake crack up right to a detached block at a horizontal fault. Climb
straight up past a small heather ledge, stepping right to gain and climb
the final corner and crack just right of a wet weep. Belay well back.

The Spinach Trail   20m   E3 6a *   (1994)
An eliminate technical climb between Olive Oyl and Bluto. Start as for
Bluto at the pointed block. Climb the wall to the horizontal fault. Pull
over at the centre and make delicate moves to better holds. Pull over
the centre of the overlap above and exit up and right into a scoop to
finish.

Bluto   20m   E2 5c *   (1993)
Start at a pointed block on the ground between two recesses in the wall
on the right-hand side of the crag. Climb the wall to a horizontal fault.
Traverse right to good holds at the top of a recess, then go straight up
to gain a short diagonal crack. Ascend this, reach up and left to a
quartz knobble, then move left to a thin horizontal fault below bulging
rock. Strenuous moves lead up through a slight break in the bulge
(spike runner), then go up the layaway crack to the top. Spike belay well
back. A deceptive little route!

Popeye   20m   VS 4c   (1993)
This climb takes the attractive light grey rib near the right end of the
crag, starting at its lowest point. Climb straight up to a horizontal fault
below a short bent groove. Ascend the awkward groove and swing
round left (strenuous) to good holds at a short crack. Go straight up to
finish by a heather corner.

Old Dog   15m   Severe   (1994)
This short route lies on the apparent pinnacle 100 metres to the left and slightly lower than Ballinamoill Crag. Climb the frontal edge to a halfway ledge, then finish up the arete.

OUTHOUSE CRAG   (Map Ref 593 078)

This is the small but seriously overhanging wall immediately right of Ballinamoill Crag.

Cold Scuttle   20m   E3 6b *   (1994)
The diagonal ramp that splits the main overhanging face. Start at the first point of weakness right of centre. A short steep slab appears to offer access onto the diagonal ramp but it does not. The strenuous overhanging crack on its immediate right provides the route. Make desperate moves through the roof crack into a slim hanging groove to reach jugs in the break above. A couple of tenuous moves left gains the ramp which leads to a finish up the quartz-rich wall above.

Canopy Crack   12m   E1 5b   (1996)
This is the discontinuous crack on the right side of Outhouse Crag, opposite an enormous block. Climb the crack, then traverse left to pull over at projecting flakes. Belay well back. A tricky wee route!

WEE HALF DOME   (Map Ref 593 077)

This is a small, compact, convex dome of wrinkled schist. The left side is defined by an obvious depression, the centre by a shallow cracked groove and the right by a small overlap low down. All routes share a common finishing belay on the left.

Flak   10m   Severe   (1994)
Climb the prominent flake crack on the left side of the crag.

Brain Dead   15m   Severe 4b   (1994)
The obvious depression on the left side of the crag.

Big Chief Skidding More   20m   E1 5a *   (1993)
Start 5 metres left of the central groove. Climb directly up the wall past two obvious blotches of quartz with some tricky moves to reach easier ground.

Ripple Groove   20m   HVS 4c *   (1993)
Climb the central groove by cracks and the small hanging corner
above.

The Pretender   20m   E1 5b *   (1993)
Start 3 metres right of the central groove. Climb up and slightly right to
ascend a pocketed wall, finishing at a small diagonal groove.

Brass in Pocket   20m   HVS 5a *   (1993)
Start at the right side of the crag under a small overlap. Move up and
pull over the overlap on the left to gain a crack. Climb up and right to
ascend a pocketed wall and finishing bulge.

CAMPSITE CRAG   (Map Ref 589 075)

This fine edge lies just north of the iron mast and small stream (neither
are shown on Ordnance Survey mapping). The left side of the crag
sports a band of overhangs broken by diagonal faults, the centre a
clean wall between two cracks and the right a recessed corner.

Black Dog   15m   HVS 5a *   (1996)
This route tackles the short orange side wall before it becomes more
broken to the left. Scramble up to the base of the wall. Climb steeply to
a horizontal break, traverse 2 metres right and follow a short groove to
the top.

Barking Rock Shrimp   15m   E3 5c *   (1993)
The line of this climb follows the left edge of the crag over a small roof
(below and to the left of the main band of overhangs). Climb a juggy
wall to a dubious block below the small roof. Pull over the roof into a
shallow scoop, then climb up to gain a finishing crack cutting through
an overlap.

Rusty But Still Working   20m   E2 5b **   (1993)
A fine route, pulling through the roof above the rusty wall. Start below
the widest point of the roof. Go up and right to a crack, then move up to
under the roof. Traverse left across the bare, rusty wall, then pull
through the roof. Follow the groove above, then take a right-slanting
groove to finish.

Pulling Through   20m   E2 5b *   (1993)
This follows the left-hand of the two diagonal faults breaking the band
of overhangs. Ascend to the notch in the roof (the left-hand side of the
notch is formed by a huge, hanging wedge of rock with no visible
means of support!). Pull through with difficulty, then climb a diagonal
slabby groove to finish.

The Tablet   25m   HVS 5a **   (1992)
An excellent climb following the right-hand of the two diagonal faults
breaking the band of overhangs. Climb a short detached slab, then go
up the wall to below the roof. Traverse right below the roof to the base
of a hanging groove holding a slim tablet of rock of doubtful security.
Gain the groove, then pull out left at the tablet to finish at the same
point as Pulling Through.

Campion Crack   10m   Severe   (1992)
Climb the left-hand of the two vertical cracks with a distinctive pad of
campion (avoidable) part-way up.

Straight Reaching   10m   VS 4c **   (1992)
Ascend the centre of the clean wall between the two vertical cracks on
perfect incuts, moving left to finish.

Bramble Crack   10m   Severe   (1995)
Climb the right-hand of the two vertical cracks with a bramble bush at
its base.

In the Lee   10m   E1 5a   (1995)
At the base of the centre of the steep wall to the right of Bramble Crack
is a projecting nose. Climb the short corner on the left of this, then go
directly up *via* a thin crack on the left of the break. Pull over the bulge
above on big holds.

The Cleat   10m   E1 5b *   (1995)
Ascend the right side of the projecting nose and continue up to a deep
break. Pull through the overlap and climb the wall with a thin move to
the top.

Close Hauled   15m   VS 4c *   (1992)
Climb the obvious recessed corner near the right end of the crag,
passing a dubious flake to finish up a delightful slab.

Arms Beat   10m   E1 5b **   (1993)
A good route on the short wall to the right of the recessed corner of
Close Hauled. Start just right of centre. Climb up to the left end of the
overlap. Pull over and step right to climb the centre of the wall to the
top.

Grattons Galore   10m   HVS 5a *   (1994)
Climb the thin crack near the right edge of the short wall taken by Arms
Beat.

CREAG NA LICE   (Map Ref 588 076)

This largely hidden west-facing crag lies immediately north of
Campsite Crag, just round the corner from Black Dog. It is broken into
three sections by deep vertical faults. The left-hand section has the
appearance of a large, pale slab but in fact it is a lot steeper than first
impressions would suggest. The centre section is a cracked concave
wall (radically overhanging in its upper half) with a ledge at half-height.
The right-hand section, initially a projecting square-cut pillar, swings
round to present a narrow south-facing slabby wall which abuts the
easy slab and broken ground before the start of Campsite Crag. The
rock on Creag na Lice looks suspect but it is actually largely clean and
solid. The routes are described from right to left as approached by a
scramble from the west end of Campsite Crag.

RIGHT-HAND SECTION

To the left of the easy scramble and slab lies the section of crag which
increases in height as the ground drops away to the left. The south-
facing base of the wall is split by three distinctive cracks and above
these lie an arete and mid-way ledges. Above these again is an area of
steep white rock which looks sandy and loose, the most prominent
feature being a roof crack. All the routes are much better than they
appear.

Slow Pup   20m   Severe   (1996)
Climb the corner formed between the buttress and the slab to reach a
small vertical corner near the top. Finish up this.

Stairway to Heaven   20m   VS 4c **   (1996)
Climb the slabby corner as for Slow Pup until below a diagonal shallow
groove left of that route. Climb this with continuous interest to the top.

Sixth Sense 20m E1 5b *** (1996)
Start at the base of the prominent flake crack that cuts vertically
up the wall to the right of Horatio. Climb the flake until moves
right gain a shallow scoop below the upper bulge. Pull through
directly and finish in a fine position up the wall above on
surprising holds.

Horatio 25m HVS 5a * (1992)
Climb the right-hand pair of cracks to the arete, then follow this for 3m
until a move right allows the centre of the wall to be climbed to
overhanging rock above. Move up and left on rock of a biscuit-like
quality to gain a ledge and thence the top.

The Female of the Species 30m E4 (1996)
1. 15m 4a Climb the left-hand of the three distinctive cracks, then go
up to a spike belay below the centre of the upper wall.
2. 15m 6a Climb up to below the roof crack. Follow the crack on good
holds in a wild position.

Realm of the Senses 30m E2 (1996)
This route climbs the hanging corner to the left of the roof at the top of
the crag. Start 4m down left of the left-hand of the three distinctive
cracks.
1. 15m 5a Climb the wall to the spike belay below the upper wall,
shared with the previous route.
2. 15m 5b Climb the wall into the hanging corner and exit wildly
through this to reach a walk-off right.

CENTRAL SECTION

This is the cracked concave wall between the two deep recesses.

Continuous Air Play 40m E5 *** (1996)
Start at the prominent right-hand crack in the vertical lower wall.
1. 20m 5b Climb the crack to a sandy ledge. Take a slim corner to
gain the halfway ledge below the impending upper wall. Large thread
belay.
2. 20m 6b Climb the quartz wall trending left to gain the base of a
large flake. Follow this leftwards, then climb directly up the wall from its
end. A stunning and very strenuous pitch!

LEFT-HAND SECTION

This is the large pale slabby wall.

Honeysuckle Wall   25m   E2 5c **   (1994)
This route lies on the right-hand side of the wall. Start below a big
sandy flake down and left from the deep recess. Climb up to the flake,
then move right and up to gain a little rock ledge. Ascend directly to
below the obvious overlap. Move left to a flange-like hold. Pull onto the
quartz-studded wall above, then move up to reach a diagonal flake
crack. Move right into the groove and follow this to the top. Belay at the
big block.

Second Thoughts   25m   E1 5b *   (1995)
Start just above the section of the base of the wall that drops away
steeply. Easy ground trending slightly left allows moves back right to
enter a prominent short groove. Climb this to an overhung ledge.
Traverse the steep wall rightwards to gain another overhung ledge.
Move left and exit through a large recess in the roof above.

SIGNAL WALL   (*Map Ref 588 074*)

This 50m high hidden wall lies directly below the iron mast and ruined
lookout post. The wall is essentially divided into two parts. On the left,
at full height, is the main face, its right edge defined by a series of roofs
and grooves. On the right above a vegetated ledge lies the upper tier,
reducing in height to the south. The lower part of the main face has a
distinctive right-facing banana-shaped corner at its bottom right and a
left-facing hanging corner right of centre. To the left of this corner the
rock is heavily eroded and covered with a toothpaste-like film of gunge
– no routes. The upper part of the main face is split by two parallel
slabby grooves.
   The base of the wall can be reached by descending broken terrain
overlooking Signal Stack to the south of the crag. Start the descent at a
slight col on the cliff top, south of the ruined lookout post. It is sensible
to pre-arrange a belay rope on the iron mast prior to tackling routes on
the main face.

1   Silver Darlings   55m   E4 **   (1993)
A demanding route and by far the hardest of the collection of fine
climbs on the front of the main face.

1. 30m 6a   Start at the toe of a slight pillar 5 metres left of the banana-shaped corner, at the lower left end of a huge flattened boulder that sits at the base of the crag. Step onto a ledge and pull over a bulge onto the wall. Move up, then take a diagonal traverse left on good quartz holds to gain a ramp-ledge leading to the obvious left-facing hanging corner. Climb the corner with difficulty to a wild swing out right at the top. Traverse left over the lip of the corner to a vertical crack. Climb this to a horizontal break and Friend belay.
2. 25m 5b   Pass the first roof on the left and gain the left side of the second roof. Traverse rightwards between the roofs and pull over onto the wall above at the first break. Step right into a shallow groove which leads to a heather ledge. Climb the short final wall.

2   Hornblower   55m   E2 *   (1992)
An excellent line which although not sustained contains some steep and committing climbing. Start at the base of the obvious banana-shaped corner at the right side of the lower main face.
1. 20m 5b   Ascend the corner for a short distance until a horizontal fault leads out left to the edge. From the edge move left across a vertical wall until a good hold allows a move onto a narrow ramp. Pull out left again until blind moves lead onto a wider ramp, leading to a small stance above.
2. 35m 5c   Traverse left to another small ledge. Move up and right to a short wide crack. Climb vertical rock on quartz holds immediately right of the crack until a horizontal fault is reached. Move up and left on slabby rock to below an obvious small overlap barring access to a big slabby groove (this is the left-hand of the two slabby grooves well seen from below). Cross the overlap (crux), climb a slabby wall to bulging rock, move left, then go up to a heather ledge. A short wall leads to the top.

3   Captain Pugwash   55m   E2 *   (1993)
This route shares a common start with Hornblower.
1. 15m 5b   Climb the banana-shaped corner passing the first horizontal fault (taken by Hornblower) to the second. Traverse left below the overhang to the edge, then move up to a small stance.
2. 40m 5b   Move slightly right up a ramp to a flake, then ascend the impending quartz-studded wall on flakes to easier ground. Continue directly up the right-hand of the two slabby grooves and follow it to its end. Traverse left under an overlap, then go up to the final roof. Pull over this, then climb the wall to the top.

4   The Captain and the Kid   55m   E2 *   (1996)
Start as for Hornblower and Captain Pugwash.
1. 25m 5c   Climb the banana-shaped corner to the roof. Undercling rightwards and turn the roof to gain the wall above. Climb this past a thin vertical crack to belay directly below the large open corner to the right of the start of Walking the Plank.
2. 30m 5c   Ascend the corner, passing a large ledge to gain the roof. Pull through leftwards on large holds to gain the slab of Walking the Plank. Traverse out left under the roof above *via* the obvious horizontal crack to gain the arete. Follow this, then climb directly to the top.

The following routes start from the grassy ledge under the upper tier which is gained from the right.

5   Walking the Plank   30m   VS 4c *   (1993)
An atmospheric and exposed route following the high curving slab between the obvious long arching roof and the big block roof below. The route gets progressively more difficult with an exposed crux at the nose formed by the right-hand end of the arching roof. Start at the left end of the vegetated ledge. Climb a slim corner to gain the slab. Traverse out right until it is possible to step up to gain a slight arete. Climb the slabby wall just right of the nose to finish.

6   Coming up Smelling of Fish   20m   E3 5c   (1993)
An esoteric route taking a line up the right side of the big block roof. Start on the vegetated ledge below the centre of the block roof. Step off a block diagonally right to gain a diagonal crack. Pull up the quartz wall above and traverse right to a small ledge on the arete. Climb through the apex of the roof above onto a slab, then traverse right below small overlap to jugs. Ascend a slabby wall to the top.

7   Caulking Wall   25m   E2 5c ***   (1993)
To the right of the large roofs is an obvious brown/black-streaked wall of compact rock which weeps water after rain. This characterful route avoids nearly all the damp sections and gives some excellent climbing. Start 5 metres left of a dirty brown corner at two parallel cracks. Follow the left-hand crack until it is possible to gain a short groove leading to an overlap. Pull over this onto a slab, then step left and go up to a ledge. Move up rightwards to gain the lip of another overlap (crux), then climb directly up the slabby wall, *via* a short groove and crack, to exit up a shallow scoop.

MULL OF KINTYRE

Signal Wall

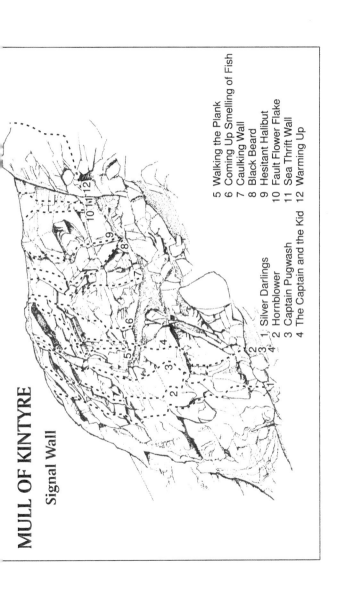

1 Silver Darlings
2 Hornblower
3 Captain Pugwash
4 The Captain and the Kid
5 Walking the Plank
6 Coming Up Smelling of Fish
7 Caulking Wall
8 Black Beard
9 Hesitant Halibut
10 Fault Flower Flake
11 Sea Thrift Wall
12 Warming Up

8   Black Beard   25m   E3 6a **   (1996)
Climb the left-facing diagonal corner to the right of Caulking Wall to
beneath a small roof. Pull over into a hanging corner-ramp above and
climb up to bulges. Pull out right above these and climb the wall directly
to the top. Immaculate rock when dry, but it is often wet.

9   Hesitant Halibut Hits Horrendous Heather   20m   E1 5a **
(1995)
A fine varied route, with a problematic finish, up cracks and flakes to
the right of the brown/black streaked wall. Start on fallen blocks below
a deep crack. Climb the crack to a ledge. Hand traverse a big sandy
flake leftwards with an awkward move into a groove. Step up and right
onto a hanging slab. Ascend this, then climb to detached blocks below
the final wall. Move slightly up and left, then make a short hand
traverse right under a small roof to good hand holds. Pull over onto the
top using heather roots or any other available means!

Near the southern (right-hand) termination of the upper tier of
Signal Wall there is a distinctive vegetated V-corner. The short slabby
wall to its left holds two routes.

10   Fault Flower Flake   12m   Severe 4b   (1993)
Start at a boulder next to the deep fault caused by the slippage of a
large block. Climb the fault to a flower ledge. Move slightly right to gain
and climb a flake and wall above.

11   Sea Thrift Wall   10m   VS 4c *   (1993)
Midway between Fault Flower Flake and the vegetated V-corner lies a
thin crack. Gain and climb this to the wall above. Move slightly right
about 3m from the top for the most sporting finish.

12   Warming Up   13m   Severe 4b   (1996)
Start at the vegetated V-corner. Follow a rock ramp out right to a crack
in a steep wall. Climb this (crux), then go up the heavily eroded rock
above to finish at a big block belay.

SIGNAL STACK   (Map Ref 588 074)

This small stack lies just above high water mark and can be accessed
down broken terrain to the south of the ruined lookout post. When

viewed from the south, its capping block can be likened to a face profile or to the head of a tomahawk. The blocky landward side of the stack can be ascended with relative ease *via* a couple of variations.

Plumbline   30m   HVS 4c **   (1993)
A route of great character on the south face of the stack, with a spectacular and exposed finish. Start at a slight corner just above high water mark. Climb this and the strangely eroded rock above until a ledge is reached below the final tower (possible belay). Pull strenuously into a groove (just right of the edge defining the junction of the south and west faces), then climb the centre of the face above on superb holds to a rock ledge and belay just below the summit block.

THE JESTER   (Map Ref 592 072)

This tall crag lies 200 metres to the east of the foghorn building. It consists of two clean walls with an area of roofs and vegetation between them. The right-hand wall is essentially a diagonal slab sandwiched between overhanging areas.

Foolish Journey   55m   E2   (1994)
Start beneath the large slabby corner on the right-hand section. An adventurous, poorly protected route with some loose rock.
1. 50m 5b   Climb the wall on the left to enter the base of the corner. Ascend it until 3m below its termination at a roof. Swing out right around the arete onto a wall, then traverse right to a hanging slab. Follow this to near its end at roofs. Pull out right past a large 'heuco' in the roof, then traverse back left in a wild position to gain a sandwiched wall under a further diagonal roof. Follow this up and right to a ledge. Pull through a roof to the belay.
2. 5m 4c   Exit up and right to escape rightwards over heather.

PORT CRAG   (Map Ref 595 075)

This south-facing crag lies at an altitude of 270m above a grassy depression containing an occasional spring and a dry stone enclosure. The most obvious feature of the crag is a crack on the right, starting at a V-shaped recess and running through the right end of a long roof at mid-height (Blood on the Cracks).

Wall of the Winds   20m   E2 5b **   (1994)
A steep quartz-veined pale wall lies at the left-hand side of the crag. It
provides a fine committing climb. Start 4 metres right of the stone dyke
that abuts the left-hand end of the crag. Climb the centre of the wall,
crossing a shallow break high up, to reach a narrow ledge and belay.
Move off left to descend.

Bella's Groove   50m   VS   (1993)
This seriously traditional route follows the long diagonal fault cutting
across the crag from bottom left to top right which is vegetated in its
middle and upper sections.
1. 25m 4c   Start 8 metres right of the short stone dyke that abuts the
left end of the crag. Climb the fault, moving right where it steepens, to
make difficult moves leading up to a ledge. Follow the fault rightwards
over a juniper at a heather ledge, then move up to a small rock ledge
below a wide slot.
2. 25m 4b   Climb into the slot, then follow the awkward groove which
becomes heathery in its upper part. Belay well back.

Coming up for Air   30m   E1 *   (1994)
Start 4 metres left of the V-shaped recess at the base of a left-trending
fault.
1. 25m 5b   Climb the fault to the left end of the long roof. Pull through
the break, then step right to climb a clean wall on small holds which
lead to the base of a heather ramp.
2. 5m 4a   Climb a short corner to finish.

Blood on the Cracks   25m   E3 5c (aid) *   (1996)
The most obvious line on the crag tackling the crack that runs up
through the right end of the long roof. Start in the V-shaped recess.
Climb the crack with increasing difficulty to the roof. Pull through the
roof with a nut for aid (dubious rock), then go up to gain and climb the
easier continuation crack. Belay on a heather terrace above.

Undertow   25m   E1 5a *   (1993)
Start at the right-hand side of the crag, 3 metres right of the V-shaped
recess. Move up left to gain a big semi-detached flake. Pull up over
bulging rock (crux), then step right to a slight crack. Ascend this and
the wall above, moving left high up *via* a flat topped flake to finish. An
exposed climb with minimal protection in its upper half.

Man Overboard   25m   E1 5b *   (1993)
Start at the extreme right edge of the crag. Pull left onto the face and
climb it staying close to the right edge until forced into the middle of the
wall. Finish directly with the last moves providing the crux. Belay well
back.

MIDSHIPS CRAG   (Map Ref 596 075)

Situated slightly higher and to the east of Port Crag, this crag has a
jumble of large blocks at its foot and an impressive, massive
appearance. A vertical fault splits the crag into two parts and the base
of the right-hand section is buttressed by a wedge of compact fine-
grained rock.

Back to Basics   30m   Severe   (1994)
Climb the obvious two and a half stepped corner on the left flank of the
crag.

Crime and Punishment   25m   E3 5c **   (1994)
Left of the central fault is a vertical wall broken by a narrow horizontal
ledge below half-height and an overlap high up. A crack runs the full
height of the wall to the overlap. Start up the crack, then using holds on
the left, climb to gain the narrow ledge (superb climbing). Continue up
the crack to a deep horizontal break below the overlap. Either finish
directly up the wall above the break or more easily by moving up and
left to gain a bay.

Guilty by Default   25m   E1 5a   (1994)
Climb the vertical fault splitting the crag in two, initially by the obvious
corner, then the wide crack line above the bulge.

Kissing the Gunner's Daughter   25m   E4 6a **   (1994)
This excellent route takes the right-hand side of the immaculate clean
wall to the right of the central fault. Start 3 metres in from the right edge.
Climb easily up a broken corner to stand on top of a huge block. Take
the flake crack above with a hard move to gain a shallow recess near
the right edge of the wall. Pull out left and climb by thin moves to the
base of a deep diagonal crack. Follow this for a short distance, then go
directly up a quartz-studded wall to exit right under the huge projecting
block.

STARBOARD CRAG   (Map Ref 596 074)

This long south-facing crag, situated due south of Midships Crag and a short distance to the north of the Allt a' Ghobhainn, rises above an extensive boulder jumble. The western end of the crag presents a high slabby triangular face dropping from a knoll, whereas the east of the crag is lower and more broken. The rock on Starboard Crag is slightly softer and therefore more fragile in nature than most, adding an extra spice to the climbing.

Covine Chimney   20m   Severe 4b   (1996)
This is the prominent chimney on the narrow left face of the main crag. Enter the chimney (crux), then climb it and the groove above to belay on the iron spike.

Lightning Crack   20m   E1 5b *   (1996)
Start at an obvious short zigzag crack on the left-hand side of the front face of the crag. Climb the fine crack to enter a triangular niche. Follow a left-trending fault to a small overhang. Cross it, then climb a shattered groove to the top. Belay on the iron spike. There is some (avoidable) loose rock.

The Dragon's Run   25m   E2 5b *   (1993)
This route climbs the obvious groove-crack system running up the highest section of the triangular face. Start below two slim parallel grooves. Climb the left-hand groove, then move slightly right into a short brown leaning corner. Above this, exit the groove line rightwards and go up a steep wall to gain the base of a prominent diagonal crack. Climb this and the wall above, trending right to finish. Belay on the iron ring.

The Children of the Open Sea   25m   E2 5b **   (1993)
A very fine route, despite its somewhat scrappy start and finish, up the centre of the compact wall that lies in the V-formation created by the main groove-crack line and a thin diagonal crack on the right. Start at a point just left of a vegetated ramp cutting up right on the right-hand side of the triangular face. Ascend a shallow, initially messy groove with increasing difficulty to a good hand hold on its right. Step left and climb the slabby wall on small holds to gain a deep pocket. Pull past the pocket and climb the wall above with decreasing difficulty. Belay on the iron ring.

Loch Goil to Loch Fyne

The following crags and mountains are situated in the area bounded by Loch Goil to the east and Loch Fyne to the west.

CREAG AN FHITHICH
(Map Ref 193 043)

This is the west-facing crag above Pole Farm, about 5km north of Lochgoilhead. It is 45m high and dries quickly. The main feature is a left-slanting overlap. One climb has been recorded, which provides a steep pitch.

Three Steps to Heaven 40m E1 (1984)
Start below the centre of the crag. Follow a layback crack to a roof, turn it on the right, then follow a left-slanting crack. Finish to the right at a rowan.

BEINN BHEULA
779m (Map Ref 155 983)

A handful of routes have been recorded on the eastern flank of Creag Sgoilte, Map Ref 158 976, which lies just to the south of Beinn Bheula, overlooking Loch Goil.

From Lettermay, beyond Lochgoilhead, a track and a path lead through the forest. Follow them until it is possible to gain the hillside below the crags. Alternatively, approach from the west *via* forestry tracks above Craigbrack, overlooking Loch Eck.

Rough Gully 90m III * (1982)
This route lies about 100 metres south of a very small corrie, just left of a prominent icefall. The line follows a slightly curved, heavily iced right-facing open-book gully. Some steeper sections on the lower half can be avoided by ledges on the right.

Head Gully 30m II (1982)
This is to the right of the top of Rough Gully, overlooking the small corrie.

Day After   110m   III **   (1987)
About 30 metres left of Rough Gully a prominent icefall on a ramp
leads right into the gully proper. Avoid its lower half by a traverse from
the right to the short chimney section above. Climb the large ice slabs
above close to the rocks on the left.

Wee Point Gully   55m   II   (1982)
This is just right of the first small corrie before the wide saddle between
Creag Sgoilte and Cnoc na Tricriche.

Chock End Gully   75m   III *   (1982)
This chockstone gully can be found just before the wide saddle
between Creag Sgoilte and Cnoc na Tricriche.

BEINN MHOR

741m   (Map Ref 108 908)

The extensive crags of Coire an t-Sith (Map Ref 120 900) overlook
Loch Eck and lie in an impressive amphitheatre enclosed by Beinn
Mhor to the north and west, and Clach Bheinn to the south. Despite the
quite low altitude, a large number of winter routes have been recorded,
mainly in the lower grades, although the close proximity of Benmore
Centre for Outdoor Education has undoubtedly helped in their
development and popularity. The few buttress routes require solid
snow cover to make them worthwhile and are in condition infrequently.
However, snow and short spells of frost are sufficient for most routes,
and for the jaded winter climber, a change of scenery may well be
worth the effort of a longer drive. Part of the corrie is well depicted in
the SMC guide *The Corbetts and Other Scottish Hills*, Beinn Mhor
being one of the latter.

The crags are described clockwise, starting with the north face of
Clach Bheinn, progressing to the north flanks of Creachan Mor,
followed by the central, east-facing crags of Creag Tharsuinn and
finally the south-east facing crags of Beinn Mhor. A few of the easier
routes have been omitted, leaving climbers to explore for themselves.

The corrie is easily accessed by following forestry tracks south from
near Bernice (Map Ref 133 961) on Loch Eck (between half and one

Rites of Passage, Ballinamoil Crag, Mull of Kintyre   (Climber, Graham Little)

hour's walk from the upper track), or from the lochside *via* the path starting at Map Ref 138 895 (not marked on the map), past the 'paper cave' (half an hour from the top hairpin bend).

CLACH BHEINN

643m (Map Ref 126 886)

BISHOP FLANK

The northern flank of Clach Bheinn is marked by a 45m pinnacle; The Bishop. The Nun, a slightly higher pinnacle, lies just hidden behind The Bishop. About 60m higher and 200 metres to the east, above a jumbled field of boulders, is yet another pinnacle, The Pawn.

Directly above the Bishop is a steep little corrie terminating in two gullies and flanked on the right by the large Horror Wall above some large boulders and on the left by an ill-defined ridge above a wall facing The Pawn.

Poit Ridge   60m   II   (1986)
This is the ill-defined crest just left of Poit Dubh Gully (a Grade I snow climb), which lies at the back of the small corrie above The Pawn.

Ungodly   90m   II   (1968)
Climb the ridge formed by the wall facing The Pawn and the small corrie above The Bishop and The Nun.

Gog   40m   III *   (1968)
The left-hand gully about 90m above The Bishop in the headwall of the little corrie. It freezes up less rapidly than Magog.

Magog   45m   III **   (1968)
The right-hand gully, right of Gog, in the little corrie's headwall. Avoid the cornice on the left.

The 15m chockstone-filled gully facing the east flank of Beinn Mhor is **Caves Gully**, Grade II. Three other short Grade I routes have been recorded between The Bishop and The Nun.

Crystal Vision, Creag nam Fitheach, Knapdale (Climber, Kevin Howett)

WESTERN FLANK

The western flank of Clach Bheinn stretches from the right-angled, and in its lower part overhanging, edge of Horror Wall to the Creachan Mor – Clach Bheinn saddle.

Thread the Needle   70m   II **   (1968)
This is the first obvious gully going rightwards from the Bishop, about 50m up and right from the base of Horror Wall.

Worm Heckle   60m   II   (1978)
Below the ridge bounding Thread The Needle on the right is a square 5m pinnacle. Climb the gully above for 25m before 'worming out' right by an interesting through-route below the steeper upper section.

Gibes   55m   II   (1987)
Start about 10 metres right of Worm Heckle. Climb a short gully finishing at a thinly iced steepening which can be avoided on the left by two awkward steps and a finish straight up, or right *via* a tree bay.

Nopitch   II   (1979)
About 30 metres to the right is an ill-defined gully, **Deity**, Grade I. Right of its foot two gullies join; Nopitch follows the left-hand gully with interest (Grade II). The right-hand gully is **Angelus**, Grade I, and the ridge between is **Idol**, Grade I. The ridge between Deity and Nopitch is **Ra**, Grade I.

The most conspicuous tributary branching off from the Allt Ruadh at Map Ref 121 893 is taken by **Coda**, Grade I.

CREACHAN MOR
571m (Map Ref 119 881)

The Allt Ruadh (Red Burn) descends from the flanks of Creachan Mor to join the Allt Coire an t-Sith. The large Red Burn Gully leads to the saddle between Creachan Mor and Clach Bheinn. Several steep watercourses lie right of the gully and there is a 60m triangular buttress high on the right at Map Ref 117 891.

Candlemas Ice Variation   115m   III **   (1978)
This is the gully branching off from Red Burn Gully on the left at the 380m contour. The frozen watercourse leads easily to a snow gully bending left.

The curving gully right of Red Burn Gully is taken by **Curves**, Grade I; the gully 60 metres left of Pats is taken by **Trees**, also Grade I.

Pats   55m   III *   (1987)
Start left of an obvious 25m rock buttress, low on the flank right of Red Burn Gully. A 5m thinly iced steep pitch leads to easier pitches.

Rabs   90m   III *   (1986)
This route climbs the watercourse branching off right from the Allt Ruadh at the 300m contour and immediately right of the obvious 25m rock buttress.

Lilac   120m   III **   (1978)
The right-hand and largest gully branching off the Allt Ruadh at the 300m contour forms quickly and is characterised by a large ice cataract on the top right.

The small gully leading left from Bang to join Lilac is Little Descent, Grade I, or Grade II by its slabby left flank.

Bang   25m   II   (1987)
The gully to the right of the top section of Lilac and left of a steep rock nose gives a pleasant short climb.

Cascade   40m   III   (1987)
This is the interesting ice cascade 10 metres left of Unfinished.

Unfinished   25m   III   (1987)
Climb the obvious chimney just left of the centre of the triangular buttress, avoiding the vertical icefall at the top by traversing left.

CREAG THARSUINN   (Map Ref 117 897)

Between the 300m contour and the Beinn Mhor plateau rim at 550m and near the centre of the corrie, are four east-facing gullies. **Slant** (Grade II) is the leftmost of the four gullies. The gully to its right is taken by **Across**, Grade I.

Oblique   90m   III   (1978)
The third gully from the left gives two steep ice pitches to a near vertical 10m pitch where the gully turns slightly left.

Obscure   105m   II   (1978)
The rightmost gully is quite narrow gully.

Fairy Snow   180m   II   (1977)
The steepest and rightmost of the four gullies in the ill-defined buttress
to the right of Obscure.

BEINN MHOR, COIRE AN T-SITH

The large crags on the eastern flank of Beinn Mhor are scarred by
several gullies which give winter routes. The best routes are found
towards the right-hand side where the crags face south-east.

GROUSE BUTTRESS

This is the smaller buttress furthest to the left, at Map Ref 114 903.
It is separated from the main crag by an easy snow slope. The
conspicuous ledge crossing the buttress is taken by **Intersection**,
Grade I.

Whelp   60m   II   (1978)
The mixed slope left of the lowest rocks leads to a narrow hidden gully
on the right in the top section.

Links   60m   III   (1978)
The mixed slope right of the lowest rocks leads to a 10m groove in the
vertical wall above.

Grouse   55m   III   (1978)
This route is on the right-hand side of Grouse Buttress. A mixed slope
leads to a 10m thinly iced right-angled groove. Climb this groove,
keeping right near the top, then continue *via* easy ramps to the
plateau.

Right of Grouse Buttress is the easy **Silent Gully**, which offers
several easy branches on either side near the very top.

Crawler Lower Right-Hand   30m   III   (1987)
Start halfway up Silent Gully where it splits into three branches. Climb
ice ramps immediately right of and above the left-hand fork, to finish
out left.

The wide shallow snow slope to the right, the Skislope, divides Silent Gully and Grouse Buttress from the main east flank crags, and offers the easiest descent route in the vicinity.

MAIN EAST FLANK

The main east-facing buttress offers the best winter climbing on Beinn Mhor.

White Falls   115m   II   (1979)
Start up left-hand side of lowest rocks left of Winalot. Steps, ridges and a left traverse gain the bay below an icicle curtain – the White Falls. Go left, then straight up to the ridge on the true left of **Hidden Gully** (Grade I). Cross the gully, ascend to a recess and a left-trending groove to finish up a narrow gully.

Winalot   140m   II *   (1968)
This is the narrow slightly twisting gully about 60 metres left of the most obvious gully, the Gangway. The large chockstone is most easily avoided high on the left. It is also possible to climb the ice between the chock and the wall on the left at the same grade, or on the right (slightly harder).

Blemish   60m   II   (1978)
Leave Winalot where it narrows for a narrow snow-ice gully on the right.

Black Fever   135m   II   (1979)
From the bottom of Gangway, go up left to climb a 15m groove-chimney. Slabby ground left of a 15m cliff leads to a tiny ridge overlooking Blemish. Climb this and the buttresses directly above.

Gangway   135m   I **
The most obvious and deepest of the gullies on the east flank of Beinn Mhor gives a scenic and interesting route.

Waiting   30m   II   (1987)
From 10m above the two-thirds point on Gangway, climb an icy groove on its left flank, immediately right of the stepped ice cascades.

Terminal   60m   III   (1979)
Terminal Buttress divides Gangway into two at the top. This route
climbs its steep right flank by a groove in its upper part. It is not often in
condition, but worthwhile when it is.

Mark   60m   III *   (1978)
Climb the right-hand branch of Gangway.
Variation: Pound   55m   II   (1978)
Follow the ice slope 10m right of and parallel to Mark.
Variation: Pence   55m   II   (1978)
Start between Mark and Pound and traverse up and right *via* an initially
steep shelf to cross Back Up above its groove.

Back Up   60m   III   (1986)
Start two-thirds up Gangway and climb ice grooves on the right wall,
trending slightly left with a narrow chimney further up.

Keystone   50m   IV **   (1979)
Just above the first narrowing in Gangway a gully leads off right
(**Passage**, Grade I). Follow it to below the main chimney line in the rock
above, passing a large chockstone near the top on the left.

Girl's Best Friend   120m   IV ***   (1979)
The hardest and best route in the corrie is also one of the longest. It
takes the thin but obvious steep chimney-gully left of Scaur. An easy
shallow gully leads to a narrow chimney section, followed by a difficult
move left round a bulging ice rib to a thinly-iced slab. Continue up a
steepening on the right to a bay at a diamond-shaped icefall, then
follow an easier-angled gully to the top.

Scaur   105m   III **   (1978)
This is the narrow easier-looking gully splitting the right side of the
buttress. Pass the small rock buttress marking the entrance to the gully
on the right (best) or the left, then continue to steeper ground above,
which is climbed trending left.

   Sore, Grade I, traverses the obvious ramp going left from Scaur
below the steepening to finish above.

Track Buttress   90m   II   (1978)
The buttress right of Scaur needs a good covering, which is rare.

The twisting gully marking the right-hand side of the main crag is **Question Mark Gully**, Grade I, with an obvious alternative to its right, Drift, Grade I. Right again is **Blackface Buttress**, Grade III, a line finishing up a short chimney.

CREAG LIATH *(Map Ref 144 873)*

This impressive little crag stands on the hillside above the south-east end of Loch Eck. The rock is a compact mica-schist, but the crag on the whole is rather vegetated and disappointing. Although some of the cleaner routes are fairly popular, most of the other climbs see few ascents and they have not been checked for this edition. The situation was complicated by the inaccurate diagram in the previous edition of the guide, and while a diagram has not been incorporated this time, hopefully the descriptions are clearer. The crag faces west-north-west and the routes are described from bottom left to top right.

Park at a small lay-by on the A815 Dunoon road, below the crag. Climb over a fence, then ascend steep slopes. The main feature of the crag is a corner crack leading to a large roof; the line of Paranoia. At the top left of the crag is a clean wall with some of the best rock and routes on the crag.

Bye Bye   10m   VS 4c   (1977)
Climb the top left-hand edge of the crag or the wall on the right, to a sloping ledge. Move right and finish up the groove.

Farewell   20m   Severe   (1962)
This is the broken left-slanting heather-filled fault at the top left end of the crag.

Aye-up Youth   20m   E2 5c **   (1987)
The obvious clean-cut crack in the convex wall right of the heather-filled fault. Climb poor flakes to the fault of Farewell, then follow crack.

Hand-Out Crack   15m   E1 5b *   (1974)
Start right of Farewell and climb a vertical crack with difficulty to a small tree at 10m, finishing up the crack.

The Pod   10m   VS 4c *   (1974)
Climb the peapod-shaped corner at the right end of the upper left wall to finish on hidden holds on the right wall.

Right of the upper left wall is a messy series of vegetated corners, then a cleaner wall with a prominent holly tree high on the face. Below and left of the tree is a flake.

H'eck   35m   HVS   (1974)
1. 10m   Climb left side of the overhanging flake crack to a ledge and belay.
2. 25m 5a   Traverse right to a ledge and go up the bulging wall above to a small tree, peg. Trend left up heather grooves to finish.

Pig Face   30m   · HVS 5a   (1982)
Start below an overhanging flake 2 metres right of H'eck. Traverse airily right, go over a bulge on good holds, then trend right to climb the obvious groove to the holly. Continue up a short awkward wall and move right to finish by a short steep wall.

Guides' Route   35m   HVS 5b   (1980)
The corner left of Paranoia. Start at a scoop in the wall, below a small overhang 4 metres left of Paranoia. Step right, climb over a bulge past an old peg and climb up and right to gain the corner.

Paranoia   35m   E2 5b   (1982)
The corner crack leading to a roof is the main feature of the crag. Unfortunately rockfall has left the lower roof in a dangerous condition. Start below a prominent overhang and climb the steep groove to below a large roof. Climb up and traverse right across a steep slab below a roof, to exit by a crack splitting the roof at its right edge.

Fall Out   40m   VS (aid)   (1967)
The thin groove right of Paranoia has been climbed on pegs.

Fall Out Wall   40m   VS 4c   (1980)
Start 2 metres left of Apex Groove. Climb up 5m to join Apex Groove at the steep rock and a curious thread runner. Quit Apex Groove after this and traverse up and left *via* a groove to join Paranoia at the right end of the prominent overhang.

Apex Groove   45m   HVS *   (1963)
Start below the edge right of Paranoia.
1. 25m   Climb to the second of two trees at the foot of the edge, with a large ledge on the right. Step left from the tree onto steep rock and

continue left past a curious thread runner. Go straight up with difficulty to a grass ledge.
2. 20m   Go up behind the ledge to a tree, move right below another tree and climb the groove above. Good holds lead to a holly and a finish out right.

Dawn Patrol   40m   E3 **   (1987)
Start as for Apex Groove.
1. 15m 4c   Follow Apex Groove to where it moves left to the curious thread runner, then move right along the terrace to the tree on Wedlock and Canaille.
2. 25m 5c   From the tree move out left to a crack in the right edge of the wall and follow it to where it terminates. Step right (thread runner *in situ*), and continue directly up the wall past a peg runner to gain a horizontal break. Climb up to reach broken ground and the top. There is a large boulder belay well back.

Canaille   40m   HVS   (1977)
1. 15m 4c   Climb the crack 2 metres right of Apex Groove to the terrace and tree belay.
2. 25m 5a   Continue by the large right-angled groove above to a ledge and finish by an easy chimney.

• **Wedlock**   45m   VS   (1963)
A poor route. Start 5m below and right of Canaille.
1. 15m 4b   Go up and right to climb a steep wall until an awkward step can be made left onto the terrace and a tree belay.
2. 30m   Climb the chimney on the right to a ledge. Climb a wall, then a hollow bulge right of the chimney to finish up a wall.
Direct Start: 15m   VS 4c
The groove right of the original start can be reached from the right. Follow this to the terrace.

Heirat   20m   Severe   (1977)
The first big groove below and right of Wedlock Direct curves up left past trees to the terrace.

Ehe   25m   Very Difficult   (1977)
Below and right of Heirat is a large leaning block, right of which are two grooves. Climb the right-hand groove to a large ledge. Move right and go up to a small gap.

Severe Slab   15m   Severe *   (1963)
The cleanest bit of rock on the whole crag, with scarce protection.
Climb the obvious slab nearest the road starting in the centre and
finishing on the left.

Stag   15m   Hard Severe   (1963)
About 15 metres right of Severe Slab is a narrow grooved wall. Follow
grooves to a flake and swing round an overhang to easier ground.

DUN LEACAINN
Map Ref 034 014)

An impressive nose of rock high on the hillside overlooking Loch Fyne,
Dun Leacainn is an unmissable sight for eagle-eyed climbers travelling
the Inveraray road. Although forestry makes the access awkward, the
rough bright granodiorite provides a welcome rest from the ubiquitous
mica-schist, and the views are tremendous. Dun Leacainn is not
popular, but it is hard to understand why as the climbing is excellent
and some of the routes are truly outstanding – a visit is highly
recommended.

   The rock is good, if a bit vegetated in places, but the south-west
outlook ensures lots of sun and quick drying after rain. However, the
closeness of the trees means the midges can be bad on a still and
cloudy summer's day. The crag is divided into two pillars by the big
central corner taken by Pluvial. The left pillar, scoured by the steep slim
groove of Dominator Direct, is particularly inspiring.

   Take the A83 road from Inveraray to Furnace. Turn left in the village
and cross the bridge over the Leacann Water. Just over the bridge on
the left is Bridge Cottage and the rough road to South Craleckan.
Follow the road to the house and park discreetly off the road just before
the cottage. Take the path which passes the cottage on its right and go
up alongside a burn to a forest track. Turn left, continue for 200 metres
to a small cairn on the right and take an intermittent path up sometimes
atrocious ground through the forest, which leads to a fire break and a
boulder at the far left of the crag. The trees extend right to the foot of the
climbs, making some bushwhacking unavoidable. The approach takes
about 30 minutes, but more if you get lost in the forest and land up
forcing a way through the jungle.

Excavator   70m   VS

Start next to a small tree on the left side of the left-hand pillar. The route follows the groove trending up and left, away from cleaner rock to the right. The first pitch is sustained and could be mildly interesting, given a good scrub.

1. 40m 4c   Climb the groove to a short corner topped by a bulge, step onto the left arete and go up to a grassy ledge and belays below a steep wall.

2. 30m   Gain the wall above, move right *via* a fine flake crack, then go back left and continue to the top.

Dominator Direct   70m   E2 ***

This superb route is both bold and committing and takes the obvious slim groove on the left side of the pillar.

1. 40m 5b   Climb to a poor peg at 10m. Continue *via* a suspended flake on the right to better pegs at 20m. Move boldly up and right to a flake crack which leads to easier ground and a belay in a grassy niche. Both the holds (hidden pockets) and protection (small wires) are far better than they appear from below.

2. 30m 4c   Continue directly by the right-hand side of the pillar.

Original Start: 40m   E1 5b *

Start at the lowest rocks. Gain and climb a steep groove up and right, then step right and go up past a bulge. Continue just right of the edge of the pillar to reach the direct route at the grassy niche.

Eliminator   40m   E2 5b **   (1991)

Climb the faint groove in the right side of the pillar, right of the more obvious groove of Dominator Direct and left of its Original Start, to join that route at the grassy niche. Finish as for Dominator Direct.

Pluvial   80m   HVS

This route provides interesting and varied but sometimes vegetated climbing up the big central corner of the crag, which is guarded by a small overhang and topped by roofs. Most of the vegetation can be by-passed. Start below the overhang.

1. 40m 4c   Climb up to and over the overhang to enter the corner and continue to belay below a shallow roof.

2. 40m 5a   A line of small holds, the higher of two such lines, leads out left to the buttress edge. Follow the edge for a short way until above the roofs, then go back right and straight up to finish.

Direct Link: 20m   HVS 5a
Climb the left-hand vertical fault above the belay below the shallow roof at the end of pitch 1.

Devil's Elbow   75m   HVS ***
An excellent route with varied climbing on clean rock. Start just right of a tree at the lowest part of the buttress, right of the big central corner.
1. 30m 5a   Climb a steep wall to gain the arete right of the big central corner and follow this to belay below a roof of jammed blocks.
2. 45m 5a   Left of the arete are two steep vertical faults. Climb the right-hand fault until it is possible to break out right. From a sloping ledge continue straight up the steep wall past a horizontal spike.

Mutation   70m   Hard Severe *
A superb first pitch on excellent rock with good protection, but the route as a whole is slightly marred by turf and vegetation above. Start 3 metres left of a shallow cave on the front of the right-hand pillar.
1. 20m 4a   Climb up and right for 6m, traverse 3m hard left to a dubious spike and go over a bulge. Trend up and right to an exposed ledge and belay.
2. 30m   Continue directly up to belay on a turf ledge.
3. 20m   Finish up increasingly turfy ledges and blocks. This pitch may be avoided by either traversing right onto vegetation, or moving left onto harder rock and a finish up Devil's Elbow.

The Rambler   85m   HVS
This is a right-to-left rising girdle of the crag. Start on the rib right of the shallow cave in the right-hand pillar. Rising up out of the cave is a fine crack line.
1. 20m 5a   Climb up, then go left to gain the crack and follow it and a wall to belay on Mutation.
2. 10m   Traverse horizontally left to the arete of Devil's Elbow, descend Pluvial and belay just above its first overhang.
3. 25m   Go left and follow the line of Dominator to the grassy niche in the left-hand pillar.
4. 30m   Keeping to the left-hand side of the pillar, finish up the prominent corner.

ARROCHAR AREA

JR

1　Eagle Falls, Inverarnan
2　Loch Sloy Crags
3　A' Chrois
4　Creag Tharsuinn
5　Beinn Narnain
6　Beinn Ime
7　The Cobbler
8　Glen Croe Crags
9　The Brack
10　Ben Donich
11　Beinn an Lochain
12　Binnein an Fhidhleir

0　Km.　2

Inverarnan

A82

Ardlui

Glen Kinglas

Loch Sloy

Ben Vorlich

• Abyssinia

12 Creag Coire
an Creagach

Binnein an
Fhidhleir

Inveruglas
Power
Station

P

Ben Vane

Sub Station

11

P
Loch Restil

Beinn Ime
6

A'Chrois

3 Creag Tharsuinn

Beinn an
Lochain

Rest & Be
Thankful

Bealach
a'Mhaim

Beinn Narnain
5

Dam

P

A83

Glen Croe

7

The Cobbler

Narnain Boulders

P

10
Ben Donich

8

P

9

P

Arrochar

A83

Tarbet

The Brack

Loch Long

Loch
Lomond

Arrochar

This chapter describes the wealth of climbing that can be found in both summer and winter in an area which is really Glasgow's back yard. Despite the ease of access, only The Cobbler is likely to crowded with climbers. However, many of the other cliffs and outcrops provide climbs that are well worth a visit and deserve greater popularity.

The crags and mountains are described in a sequence going roughly north-east to south-west.

LOCH SLOY CRAGS

These crags lie on the southern flanks of Ben Vorlich, overlooking Inveruglas Water and the electricity sub-station between Loch Sloy and Loch Sloy Power Station. The crags are of compact mica-schist, face south, dry quickly and are easily accessible. They are best viewed from beyond the sub-station where the track to Tarbet and Arrochar branches off left. The impressive slabby wall on the right is Sub-Station Crag.

The other crags rise diagonally left in three tiers. The Upper Tier has scope for new routes, although many of the buttresses turn out to be disappointing. The Middle Tier is characterised by the prominent Roof Buttress at the right end. The Lower Tier starts below Roof Buttress and ends at the small but impressive Floating Buttress.

Access
Park beyond Loch Sloy Power Station on the banks of Loch Lomond at the car park at Map Ref 323 099. Walk back along the A82 and follow the road under the railway and steeply uphill to the electricity sub-station. The first crag is just up on the right and is about 30 minutes from the road.

SUB-STATION CRAG   (Map Ref 306 094)

This is the best crag and it is also the closest to the road. It presents a compact slabby wall immediately above the sub-station, with a large flake low down and left of centre. The crag offers excellent sunny routes and deserves much more traffic. An extra rope is useful to arrange belays at the top of the crag.

The Pylon Effect   50m   E2 5c **   (1988)
Good climbing up the left arete of the crag; high in the grade. Start left
of the large flake at a short crack and follow it until a traverse leads to a
flake on the arete which leads to the top.

Charge of The Light Brigade   45m   E3 5c ***   (1985/86)
An excellent wall climb which is protected by several pegs which are
still in reasonable condition. Climb up left of the large flake, then climb
the groove left of the flake to the first peg. Move up and right to the
second peg, then traverse back left and work up past stacked pegs
and finally cunningly right past a fourth peg to reach a grass ledge.
Easier climbing leads to the top.

White Meter   30m   E4 5c ***   (1988)
Good, bold wall climbing, but lowish in the grade. From near the left
end of the large flake, move up and step right, then go up to a jutting
quartz lump. Move up left to a bulge (Friend 1.5 in the horizontal crack),
go over the bulge using a quartz hold, and continue up to tree.
Descend by abseil.

Power to the People   35m   E3 5c *   (1985/86)
Another quite bold route, a bit lichenous but not high in the grade.
Ascend the large flake on the right. From its right end, climb up boldly
past a peg to a horizontal break. Climb a small overlap and the groove
on the right. Step right to a ledge, continue up heather ledges and
continue straight up to the top on cleaner rock.

Current Affair   35m   E2 **   (1985/86)
A fine line up the parallel cracks right of the large flake. Technically a
little harder than Power to the People, but better protected.
1. 15m 5c   Gain the thin parallel cracks and follow them past a peg
runner. Go left to a flake, peg, then move right to a peg belay.
2. 20m 4c   Climb up left, pass a bulge on the right to reach a grass
ledge, then go up heather ledges and go right to finish.

Wired for Sound   35m   E1   (1985/86)
This route takes the groove and crack line left of a rib at the right end of
the crag. It has some good technical moves, but is a bit mossy.
1. 20m 5b   Climb the crack past a peg runner on the left, then go up
the wall above and move right to a ledge.
2. 10m 5a   Continue straight up to a grass ledge.

Live Coverage   50m   E1   (1985/86)
At the right end of the crag is a large rib which provides an unbalanced route with poor protection.
1. 15m 4c   Climb the left side of the rib to a break, then go up the slab above.
2. 25m 5a   Climb the slab on the right, go left to a small corner and climb the crack above.
3. 10m 5b   Finish up the overhang above, or walk off below it (which reduces the overall grade to HVS).

LOWER TIER

This starts left of and slightly above Sub-Station Crag, directly below the obvious Roof Buttress on the Middle Tier. The Lower Slabs start with a fine slab which steepens at the top and is flanked on the left by a square gully with a small tree near the top.

LOWER SLABS

Silver Soles   20m   E2 5b *   (1988)
The right side of the slab leads to a left-slanting crack line and a short groove which leads to the top; easy for the grade.

Around the corner left from Silver Soles is a series of heather-flanked slabby walls.

Molehill   10m   VS 4b *   (1989)
Climb the first small slabby buttress *via* a heather ledge at mid-height and passing the left end of the small overlap.

Hundreds and Thousands   20m   HVS 5a   (1989)
Start at the slabby wall just up and left of Molehill directly below three curving overlaps and a small tree on a heather ledge. Climb up to the tree, pass the second overlap to the right and go through the widest part of the third overlap.

The Mica Boot Route   20m   HVS 5a   (1988)
Climb the clean rock on the left side of the middle slab *via* a small tree on a heather ledge at half-height. Belay just below the top. Escapable.

Just left again is a small, steep, slabby buttress.

Flab Route   10m   VS 4c   (1988)
Climb the slabby nose of the buttress passing a flake at half-height.

An area of scattered buttresses lie to the left.

Splinters   15m   VS 4c   (1988)
Follow the obvious diagonal crack, traverse below a heather block to the right edge of the buttress and finish up this.

FLOATING BUTTRESS

This small but impressive buttress lies at the far left end of the lower tier.

Stonefingers   15m   E1 5b *   (1988)
A fine but poorly protected slab climb on the left face of the buttress. Pull right onto the slab from a long boulder and follow the pockets to the top.

The Ascent of Yan   15m   E4 5c *
This route lies on the left side of the front face. Climb the slab to a quartz scoop, then move right to a flake (RP runners). Move back left to another flake and finish through a break in the overhangs.

MIDDLE TIER

This is up and left of Sub-Station Crag, and is best approached from there. Most prominent is the impressive Roof Buttress.

CRESCENT BUTTRESS

This small buttress is up and right of Roof Buttress and is identified by a crescent-shaped roof (hidden from below) and the quartz streak of the following route:

Quartz-vein Arete   15m   HVS 5b   (1988)
Follow the quartz right of the right-hand arete, then continue directly to the top.

Saturn V   10m   E2 5c   (1993)
Climb the crack forming the right side of the crescent roof.

ROOF BUTTRESS

This impressive buttress is unfortunately disappointing at close quarters.

Disney Tour   15m   E2 5c *   (1988)
The left-hand buttress has a shallow groove on its left side, guarded by a bulge. Gain the groove, traverse awkwardly right into the right-facing corner line and follow it to a block below the roof. Pull left to a ledge and go up the wall to finish.

Hum   10m   VS 4c *   (1988)
Climb the bulge and groove direct.

NEB BUTTRESS

This is above and left of Roof Buttress, and can be identified by a central blunt arete with a wide slab on its left.

Follow On   15m   HVS 5a   (1988)
Climb grooves and slabs right of the blunt arete.

Anywhere   15m   HVS 4c   (1988)
Start at the lowest rocks, traverse left into a mossy groove and follow this until it is possible to pull onto the wide slab on the right. Finish up this.

   Left of Roof Buttress are a number of large boulders.

Autumn Arete   15m   HVS 4c **   (1988)
A hidden gem which takes the fine arete above the boulders. It is committing at the grade.

   Up and left of Autumn Arete is a shallow gully with a slabby wall on its right.

Hidden Slab   15m   VS 4b   (1988)
Start just right of a small tree and climb the wall direct to the top.

VIADUCT CRAG   *(Map Ref 322 107)*

This small crag lies on the hillside west of the railway viaduct just beyond Loch Sloy Power Station on the banks of Loch Lomond. Take a small path under the viaduct, gain an old track and follow this to its highest point. Go up the hill for about 10 minutes until a 15m wall appears on the right. There are two routes.

Pale Wall   15m   HVS 5a   (1988)
Start about 2 metres right of a shallow corner at the central depression, climb up and slightly right to gain an overlap. Move left slightly before pulling over and going up to the top. Boulder belay well back.

Beyond the Pale   15m   E1 5b   (1988)
Start about 5 metres right of a holly tree and climb up to a thin flake leading to the overlap. Pull over and go up the slab to a boulder belay.

ARROCHAR CAVES   *(Map Ref 300 064)*

These interesting caves and fissures can be found on the west side of Glen Loin, about 200m up the hillside, surrounded by conifers. Some of the caves take a little finding, with the best descending some 30m to an underground lake. A happy weekend can be spent dossing and exploring, and they are good for a wet day alternative (see Borthwick's *Always a Little Further*, chapter 4, for some social commentary). One route has been recorded, although like many such routes in this area, it may have been climbed before if only to escape from the 'polis'.

   To reach the caves, walk along the forestry track from Succoth, pass a cottage and at a pylon take to a path going diagonally up the hillside.

The Vice   50m   Hard Severe   (1972)
From the foot of the largest cave a thin vertical chimney can be seen. It is completely waterproof.
1. 10m   Climb the overhanging wall on big holds on the right side of the cave to belay beneath a roof.
2. 20m   Bridge up and out and squeeze past the crux chockstone to belay in a recess.
3. 10m   Continue by back and foot to a thread runner, then move horizontally to a ledge on the left with a bolt belay.
4. 10m   Squeeze past the eyehole and wriggle horizontally to finish.

A'CHROIS

849m   (Map Ref 289 077)

A popular peak in times gone by, A'Chrois is largely neglected by the climbers of today. Considering the disturbing similarity between a good day on The Cobbler and Sauchiehall Street on a Bank Holiday Monday, this will be seen by some as a strong recommendation. However, A'Chrois is of real interest only in winter when some lower grade routes will be found. It is a good place to learn winter skills perhaps, although the low altitude and south-facing aspect mean that care should be taken with the snow, and good conditions are quite rare. The peak is easily seen above the Loch Lomondside road as you approach Tarbet. Under snow and especially in spring, Chrois Gully and the large terrace splitting it stand out like a cross — hence the peak's name.

Approach as for Creag Tharsuinn to the dam on the Allt Sugach, then continue above the forest until below the face (1hr 40mins). The crags are split by Chrois Gully, the deep gully in the centre.

Easy Gully   90m   II
The gully left of South Buttress gives one small pitch, which can be passed on the right (Grade I).

South Buttress   105m   II
The buttress left of Chrois Gully can be climbed by a choice of routes, of which the steepest overlooks Chrois Gully.

Chrois Gully   90m   II
Two or three short pitches may be enjoyed in the obvious central gully. However, it can bank out to Grade I.

Central Buttress   90m   Difficult   (1895)
This is the buttress right of Chrois Gully. Raeburn wrote: 'a steep and interesting little climb. A grass-covered chimney near the foot was found to be the most difficult portion. A good deal of time was spent in trying to force the "Absolute Arete" near the the top, but eventually an escape was found to the left by a narrow overhung grass ledge.'
Winter: 90m   III
Probably more fun.

Pinnacle Gully   75m   II   (1948)
The gully right of Central Buttress often has a pitch low down.

Pinnacle Buttress   75m   Difficult   (1905)
This is the buttress right of Pinnacle Gully. Near the top is the Chrois Pinnacle, connected to the cliffs by a narrow neck.
Winter: 75m   III
Follow the summer line (or should it be the other way round).

North Gully   75m   I   (1902)
The wide snow gully at the right end of the crag gives an easy climb.

CREAG THARSUINN

770m   (Map Ref 276 073)

A considerable amount of steep rock and vegetation greets climbers visiting Coire Sugach in summer and winter. Development in the corrie reflects changes in attitude to climbing in Scotland: early ascents of lower grade summer rock routes and winter gullies have developed to higher grade rock routes on the small steep mica-schist faces, and winter ascents of the early rock routes.

In summer the corrie contains some excellent routes and is well worth a visit, lacking the crowds that besiege The Cobbler, while being as accessible and having a southerly aspect. In winter the low altitude and sunny aspect mean that, like parts of The Cobbler, the best conditions will be found in the depth of winter when the freezing level is low and the sky is overcast.

The corrie lies on the north-east ridge of Beinn Narnain. The fastest approach starts from the large carpark at the head of Loch Long and ascends the steep ramp as for The Cobbler. At the horizontal path go right to a dam and from there go up into the corrie, keeping to the east of the stream (1hour 30 minutes).

SUGACH BUTTRESS

The large buttress on the left is defined on its left by the deep, hidden Anonymous Gully and on the right by a grassy ramp dividing it from the Upper Buttress. Sugach Buttress is split into three sections by Maclay's Gully, the right wall of which contains the best rock climbing in the corrie, and the steep fault of McLaren's Chimney to its right.

1   Anonymous Gully   100m   IV,6 *   (1994)
This is the deep, hidden gully on the left side of Sugach Buttress.
1. 30m   Easy snow leads to a blockage.
2. 30m   Gain a ledge on the left and make an awkward traverse to the

gully edge. Go up a short groove on the gully edge until an exposed move right leads to the upper gully.
3. 40m   Climb easy snow to the top.

2   Route Sinister   200m   IV,4 *   (1986)
Start just left of the very lowest rocks and climb a heathery groove to the large upper terrace. Go left along the terrace and climb up and left on frozen turf and slabby rocks for two pitches to belay below a steep wall on the edge of Anonymous Gully (old ring peg). Gain the hanging slab above, move up and right, and continue to belay at the next gully. Move left and climb the gully to a terrace and easier ground.

3   Metatarsal   130m   IV,5 *   (1989)
Start on the large upper terrace midway between Route Sinister and Garrick's Route, below a prominent vegetated groove.
1. 50m   Gain the groove with difficulty, then continue more easily to the terrace above. Belay below the centre of the steep upper wall.
2. 30m   Climb the wall via a faint right-trending fault to easier ground.
3. 50m   Follow the knife-edge arete of Original Buttress Route to the top.

4   Garrick's Route   200m   Very Difficult   (1921)
Start about halfway along the lowest tier and climb slabby rocks and a grassy groove to the large upper terrace. Go left a little, passing a steep edge and climb a steep wall trending back right over rock steps and ledges to the rock nose below The Pulpit recess on the Original Buttress Route. Finish by that route.
Winter: 200m   III,4 **
Follow the summer line. The upper rock steps can be avoided or taken direct.

5   Pulpit Grooves   75m   VS 4c   (1980)
This route climbs the groove line in the frontal face of the buttress. Start on the large upper terrace at a corner in the toe of the buttress. Follow grooves to a steepening, from where an ascending left traverse leads to The Pulpit. Finish up the knife-edge arete of Original Buttress Route.

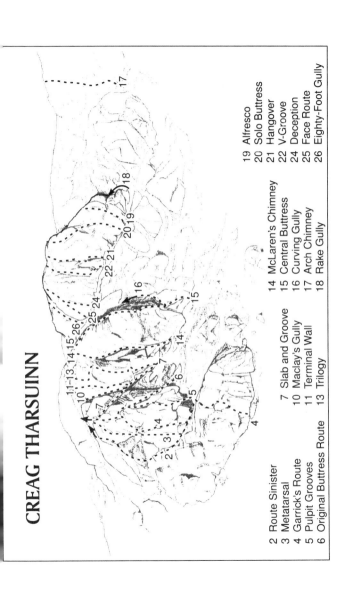

CREAG THARSUINN

2 Route Sinister
3 Metatarsal
4 Garrick's Route
5 Pulpit Grooves
6 Original Buttress Route

7 Slab and Groove
10 Maclay's Gully
11 Terminal Wall
13 Trilogy

14 McLaren's Chimney
15 Central Buttress
16 Curving Gully
17 Arch Chimney
18 Rake Gully

19 Alfresco
20 Solo Buttress
21 Hangover
22 V-Groove
24 Deception
25 Face Route
26 Eighty-Foot Gully

Winter: 155m   V,7 **   (1994)
Excellent climbing up a line approximating to the summer route. Start
on the large upper terrace at a groove right of the corner at the toe of
the buttress.
1. 45m   Climb the groove and pull out left onto the right end of a
terrace. Move up to the central of three possible lines. Head for a small
bush beckoning from the easy ground above, then follow the
prominent groove over a steepening to below another steepening.
2. 30m   Continue up the groove to gain the right side of The Pulpit.
3. 35m   Just left of the edge and above the belay is a short steep
groove. Climb it and follow easier ground up the blunt crest to the knife-
edge arete of Original Buttress Route. Finish up this.

6   Original Buttress Route   75m   Difficult   (1901)
Start above and right of the large upper terrace, at scree below
Maclay's Gully. Ledges and leftward traverses lead to a steep nose
more than halfway up the buttress. Climb a crack right of the nose to a
recess, The Pulpit. Above, climb easy slabs to the knife-edge arete,
which overlooks the Great Slab on the right and leads to the neck of the
buttress. Variations of up to Very Difficult are possible, including a
direct ascent of the nose beneath The Pulpit.
Winter: 100m   III *
Follow the summer route.

7   Slab and Groove   50m   Very Difficult   (1947)
This route climbs the curving corner formed where The Great Slab
meets the steep rib left of Maclay's Gully. From Maclay's Gully traverse
left to the corner which leads directly to the top, joining the knife-edge
arete of the Original Buttress Route.
Winter: 50m   III
Follow the summer line.

8   Tremolo   70m   E1 *   (1977)
A good route on the steep wall above The Great Slab. Start as for Slab
and Groove.
1. 25m   Climb halfway up Slab and Groove to a belay.
2. 30m 5b   Traverse the large flake right, then follow a thin crack up
right. Climb a crack over a hard bulge, moving up and left to belay on a
ledge.
3. 15m 4c   Move right, step off the left end of the flake and climb a
difficult wall to finish just left of The Tingler.

9   The Tingler   55m   VS **   (1974)
A good route taking the sharp arete left of Maclay's Gully. Start as for Slab and Groove.
1. 5m   Climb Slab and Groove to belay at an oblique crack left of the true edge.
2. 40m 4c   Climb the crack to a flake runner, continue straight up a steep wall on the left to a thin grass ledge, then move right to an edge which leads to a large grass ledge and belay.
3. 10m 4c   Climb the wide crack above the belay, swing left round the edge (the same point can be gained by a direct ascent of the front face, 5a), and climb straight up *via* a flake with a long reach near the top. A monster bolt belay lurks behind the edge.

10   Maclay's Gully   60m   III *   (1965)
This gully slants up and left through Sugach Buttress. Easy snow leads to a steep start with perhaps a 3m ice pitch and a possible short steepening at half-height. It is a traditional Very Difficult in summer.

11   Terminal Wall   60m   VS **   (1975)
The immaculate second pitch of this excellent route, high on the right wall of Maclay's Gully, offers bold and exposed climbing; one of the finest pitches at the grade in the Arrochar area. The route is high in the grade. Follow easy ground to below the gully proper and belay on the right wall opposite a grassy corner.
1. 10m 4a   Climb grassy corners to a niche under the large roof; better belays can be found on the left wall.
2. 35m 4c   Continue up the wall to a groove with flakes, leave this on the left and climb to a crack and groove left of the second overhang. Traverse hard left from the bottom of the crack, crux, to gain the main crack line which leads past a sentry box and over small bulges to a small ledge high on the face. Traversing left too early pushes the grade up to HVS.
3. 15m 4b   Climb the crack to finish.

12   Terminator   70m   VI,6 ***   (1991)
A fine ice climb, but it is slow to come into condition.
1. 50m   Climb the corner of Terminal Wall *via* iced slabs and bulges to a gangway below the steep upper wall.
2. 20m   Climb a crack in the centre of the wall for 5m to a ledge. Traverse 3m left, then go straight up a groove above and move right into a niche. Step right just below the top to finish.

13   Trilogy   60m   HVS **   (1976)
A fine climb with a sustained first pitch up the vertical wall down and
right of Terminal Wall, immediately left of the wet fault of McLaren's
Chimney. Start centrally beneath the undercut bulge crossing the face.
1. 30m 5a   Climb the wall to a bulge, traverse right and climb the
bulge using high holds to gain a juniper ledge. Climb the crack on the
left to enter a groove on the right leading to an overhung recess, then
move right to a grass ledge.
2. 15m 4b   Return left and climb the vertical wall on good holds to a
belay on the right.
3. 15m 4a   Go down and left to finish up a prominent crack.

14   McLaren's Chimney   60m   IV,5 **   (1965)
The chimney right of the vertical wall is slow to build up, but when in
condition it gives an excellent technical climb. There are four sustained
pitches, with the final chimney often being coated with verglas. It is
Very Difficult in summer and usually wet.
Variation start: 60m   IV   (1991)
Climb the right-hand icefall.

15   Central Buttress   150m   IV   (1974)
The buttress defined by McLaren's Chimney and Curving Gully. Start
well up and right of the lowest part of the buttress, at a steep line of
grooves. Follow grooves to below a steep wall, break out left onto the
crest passing a flake with difficulty, and continue to belay below a steep
wall. Traverse right to the edge, climb a chimney and continue more
easily to the top.

16   Curving Gully   105m   II   (1902)
The curving scoop right of Central Buttress has a choice of starts, the
best being *via* a small ice pitch 10m right of the gully mouth. Follow the
main branch of the gully on the left, continue up a steep groove and
finish on the right (Grade II) or left (Grade III).

UPPER BUTTRESS

This is separated from Sugach Buttress by the diagonal grassy ramp
of The Rake. The buttress is smaller than its lower neighbour. The
routes are described from right to left as approached from the corrie.

The first route takes a steep rocky chimney line on the back wall of the corrie, well to the right of the main buttress.

17   Arch Chimney   65m   Very Difficult   (1960)
Start by ascending a shallow gully slanting right from the small buttress at the very bottom of The Rake. The route is mostly hidden from the approach and was wrongly located on the diagram in the previous edition.
1. 30m   Follow the steep rocky chimney to an overhang. Skirt this on the left wall and pass a boulder to gain the large horizontal terrace.
2. 35m   Short pitches lead to a pillar forming an arch against the left wall, which is passed *en route* to the final chimney.

18   Rake Gully   120m   III **   (1976)
A pleasant and interesting route up the shallow gully and chimney bordering the Upper Buttress on its right. From The Rake follow a shallow gully to an ice pitch and ascend this by its right wall to enter a small amphitheatre. Climb a fine, steep, icy chimney to easier ground and the top. It is crumbling and wet in summer.

19   Alfresco   60m   Severe   (1959)
Start at the lowest part of the Upper Buttress, left of Rake Chimney. From The Rake climb the centre of the face on small holds for 30m, then traverse right to a heather ledge and belay. Traverse back left and finish directly up the centre of the wall.

20   Solo Buttress   75m   Very Difficult   (1953)
Start at a crack a little way up and left of the toe of the buttress. Follow the crack to within 5m of a bulge and traverse right to a vegetated groove which leads to some grass below the rock tier above. Make a descending left traverse to the foot of this upper tier and follow a wide-bottomed gully, keeping to the right branch. At the shelf, traverse right to the end, then go up left around a block onto the face of the buttress. Cross the face *via* a ledge and climb a short wall, then move left to finish up a gully.
Winter: 75m   III   (1986)
A rather poor route and low in the grade. Start at the leftmost groove on the buttress, left of the summer start. Follow the groove past a bulge to the foot of the wide-bottomed gully. Climb this, then follow the shelf

until it ends just short of a snowfield. From the snowfield climb up left over steepening steps to the top.

21   Hangover   55m   Severe   (1960)
This follows the large recessed corner, well seen from below, which leads to a bay high on the cliff. Scramble up a grass scoop left of and above the broken rocks of Solo Buttress.
1. 35m   From the apex of the grass scoop, climb to overhanging rocks and avoid them by an awkward left traverse to an out-sloping ledge. Climb a short wall to gain a groove which leads to a semi-detached block which can be passed on the right. Ascend a smooth bulge above and continue up a groove to a flake belay.
2. 20m   Make a short traverse right to the foot of the grooved wall, climbing on small holds to a final overhanging corner, and finish at a rock finger visible from the start.

22   V-Groove   60m   Very Difficult   (1958)
Left of the corner of Hangover is an obvious recessed gully line. Left of this a dirty chimney starts with a fan of vegetation on a steep slab. Start below and right of the dirty chimney. Climb up to a sloping ledge and traverse left to below a steep arete. Move awkwardly into a steep groove which leads to a ledge. Climb the groove mainly on the left wall to the top.
Winter: 70m   IV   (1976)
Start left of the summer route, directly below the chimney, where thin ice masks a slabby wall.
1. 40m   Climb the wall to enter the chimney and follow it as far as the final bulge at 25m, where rotten ice forced the first ascent team to make an exposed traverse across the left wall to a stance on the buttress.
2. 30m   Climb grooves and short walls overlooking the otherwise easy finish of V-Groove to a belay just below the top.

23   V-Groove Direct   60m   IV,5   (1994)
Start 5 metres left of the original winter start, below an obvious right-slanting corner.
1. 25m   A crack in the right edge of the slabby wall leads to a hard move onto the arete and a small niche. A short ramp above leads to a large ledge, then take the right edge of the slab to a large block belay.
2. 35m   Traverse right to the original route and climb the final bulge and the shallow chimney above.

24   Deception   40m   Severe   (1958)
This is the very narrow chimney left of V-Groove. Start up the initial steep chimney, then move onto the left edge of the upper chimney to finish up Face Route.
Winter: 60m   III   (1980)
Climb the chimney direct.

25   Face Route   35m   Very Difficult *   (1949)
This climb takes an exposed edge of rock right of Eighty-Foot Gully and left of the chimney of Deception. Start up the face, climbing the undercut rock before going up and right to the edge which leads directly to the top.

26   Eighty-Foot Gully   35m   III   (1902)
The gully line at the top left of the upper cliff. It is an unpleasant Difficult in summer.

A variety of other gullies and small crags scattered around the corrie to the right of Arch Chimney give pleasant entertainment.

BEINN IME

1011m   (Map Ref 255 085)

Beinn Ime's rather dull and tedious western slopes reveal little of the impressively large crag overlooking Coiregrogain. Like many other crags in the area, the routes on Beinn Ime were first ascended in summer. However, it is in winter that this large and rather vegetated east-facing buttress is now most appreciated. The relatively high altitude supports several good routes throughout the season. Having said that, the buttress catches some sun, and verglas and ice-filled cracks are often in evidence. Considerable care should be taken on the approach from the Bealach a'Mhaim as winter westerlies build large cornices above the traverse line and some massive collapses and avalanches have been observed in warm weather and late season.

The quickest access is from the A83 in Glen Croe. From the car-park at the bridge at Map Ref 241 060 follow the path north-east alongside the burn to a dam. Go straight up the backwall of the corrie to the Bealach a'Mhaim. Move onto the East Face and, with an eye to any cornice or avalanche danger, make a level traverse along the line of least resistance with some descent and ascent to arrive below Easy Gully. Fan Gully Buttress is up on the right.

Above and left of Easy Gully, various icefalls on the rim of the corrie give good sport at about Grade III/IV.

1   Easy Gully   250m   II
Start below and left of Fan Gully Buttress. After a steep lower section, the gully spreads out, offering a choice of finishes on snow. After a good early season freeze, the lower section gives a IV,4 * on ice and turf.

FAN GULLY BUTTRESS

The impressive central buttress is flanked on the left by the deep Hanging Groove and on the right by Airy Ridge. Ben's Fault takes the obvious curving chimney left of centre.

2   Hanging Groove   165m   IV   (1976)
Up and left of the lowest rocks, a small gully-snow slope leads to a steep corner (which may be banked out). This is the left-hand start to Ben's Fault.
1. 45m   Climb the corner to the base of the groove.
2. 45m   Follow the hanging groove on its left-bounding rib to gain the crest of the rib.
3 and 4. 75m   The rib leads directly to the top *via* some awkward walls.

3   Ma Fault   120m   III   (1985)
This route is 12 metres left of and parallel to Ben's Fault. On the left-hand side of the buttress is a deep recess. Climb the recess and grooves, passing left of a cave at 60m. Gain the buttress, and the top in a further 60m.

4   Ben's Fault   185m   IV,5 **   (1963)
A traditional winter mountaineering route of the character building variety, following the obvious deep fault in the left centre of the buttress. Snow and a good freeze will bring the route into condition. The route is possible early in the season, although the grade may be closer to V,6. In summer the route is a vegetated Difficult. Start directly below the line of the fault.
1. 50m   A short corner and crack in the lower wall (possibly banked out) lead to the fault. Climb this to a belay.
2. 40m   Continue to a cave, step left and follow the fault right to below a chimney.

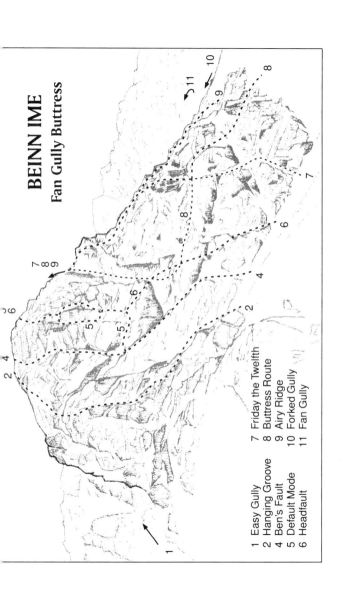

BEINN IME
Fan Gully Buttress

1 Easy Gully
2 Hanging Groove
4 Ben's Fault
5 Default Mode
6 Headfault
7 Friday the Twelfth
8 Buttress Route
9 Airy Ridge
10 Forked Gully
11 Fan Gully

3. 20m   Squirm up the chimney and the one after to belay at a chockstone where the fault becomes a continuous vertical slot.

4. 25m   Enter the slot and burrow past a wedged Damoclean flake (possibly banked out) to belay where the fault opens out below the final rock obstacle.

5. 50m   Bridge the open groove above and continue to a cave from where an exit left on turf leads to easier ground.

5   Default Mode   170m   V,6 *   (1995)

Interesting climbing with a varied crux pitch up the left-hand of the two obvious vertical lines on the upper buttress right of Ben's Fault. Start as for Ben's Fault.

1. 50m   Climb the first pitch of Ben's Fault.

2. 30m   Follow Ben's Fault for 15m, then break out right onto the slabby buttress and belay in the right-hand of two turfy cracks.

3. 20m   Climb the crack and groove to a ledge below the headwall.

4. 30m   Move up and left into the left-hand groove and climb this for 15m to where it overhangs. Traverse 5m right along a turfy break and step into the right-hand groove. Climb this to a good stance.

5. 40m   Short walls and grooves lead to the crest.

6   Headfault   185m   VII,7 *   (1995)

A big route with steep and serious climbing on pitch three up the right-hand vertical line on the upper buttress. Start beneath a shallow corner right of the start of Ben's Fault.

1. 50m   Climb the corner and its easier middle section, then continue over another steepening to easier ground and belay at a snow bay.

2. 50m   Step left and gain a snowy fault slanting up right. Move up and out of the fault, around a small rock wall to a line of turf slanting left up the wall above. Move right to belay just right of the right-hand fault.

3. 45m   Step left and climb the fault to a shallow niche. Move up and across right to a ledge below a wide flake crack. Climb the crack and continue with sustained interest to a good stance.

4. 40m   Short walls and grooves lead to the crest.

7   Friday the Twelfth   130m   IV,5 *   (1995)

This route climbs the prominent short chimney in the lower section of the wall right of Ben's Fault, then continues up the rambling buttress

An early ascent of The Nook on the North Peak of The Cobbler

(Climber, Dougal Haston)

above, right of the obvious right-slanting ramp line (Buttress Route) below the upper buttress. Start below the chimney just left of a small recess at the lowest part of the buttress. Climb the wall directly to the prominent chimney, then climb it to a belay under a groove at the top right of the terrace. The groove gives strenuous climbing to a second terrace, then go up and left to a thread on the left below an undercut corner. The corner leads to easy ground.

8   Buttress Route   120m   III *   (1976)
A pleasant route which wanders through interesting mountain scenery. Start up and right of the lowest rocks and zigzag up ledges to gain the horizontal terrace which leads left to the enjoyable right-trending ramp line below the upper buttress. A long chimney leads to the top. The climb is a vegetated Difficult in summer.

9   Airy Ridge   120m   III   (1990)
A poor route up the far right edge of Fan Gully Buttress. The route is Very Difficult in summer. Start up and right of the lowest rocks.
1. 50m   Climb mixed ground up snowy grooves to a snow patch.
2. 20m   From the right-hand end of the patch climb the left-hand of two grooves to a large ledge.
3. 50m   Go right, then finish up the arete left of the final rock mass.

10   Forked Gully   150m   II *
This is the narrow gully bounding Fan Gully Buttress on the right. A 20m ice pitch leads to snow with a choice of two finishes on snow above.

11   Fan Gully   90m   III   (1935)
The obvious wide gully up and right of Fan Gully Buttress. Easy snow leads to the narrowing, with a 5m pitch and a cave, normally climbed on the right wall. It is also possible to traverse into the left corner, then move right avoiding a bulge. Alternatively, avoid the pitch by finishing up the steep chimney on the right.

The main east face of Beinn Ime forms one side of a spur running north-east down the mountain. The following route lies on the steep north-west facing crag which forms the opposite side of the spur, and is best approached by making an ascent of the south ridge. From the col

Club Crack on the North Peak of The Cobbler

at Map Ref 260 084, descend northwards, west of the obvious hillock, into a subsidiary corrie.

The Lost Highway   100m   III,4   (1996)
Start from the base of the crag at an obvious bay leading to two chockstones and a deep narrow chimney. This aspect is hidden from the col.
1.   Climb a steep turf groove to a through-route at the first chockstone. A slab on the right leads to a short steep corner right of the second chockstone. Climb this to a large ledge and belay.
2.   Avoid the deep chimney by hard moves above the belay to get into a scoop, then go up a blocky wall to a ledge. Traverse the ledge to the left, then go up and back right *via* difficult turfy walls.
3.   A short section of easy ground leads to the top of the hummock.

BEINN NARNAIN

926m   (Map Ref 272 066)

A number of small crags can be found on the flanks of this peak, whose Munro status means you are unlikely to be alone on the summit. However the crags are not particularly popular with climbers, possibly due to the greater selection of better quality and easily accessible routes next door on The Cobbler. Still, a visit is well worthwhile, perhaps combined with a route in Coire Sugach, Creag Tharsuinn, or an ascent of Beinn Ime.
    Cruach nam Miseag is best approached up the Allt Sugach as for Creag Tharsuinn. Yawning Crag is best approached from the Narnain Boulders on The Cobbler path. Spearhead Ridge can be approached up the craggy south-east ridge or *via* Yawning Crag.

CRUACH NAM MISEAG   (Map Ref 278 064)

This crag lies on the south-east spur of Beinn Narnain, facing north-east over the Allt Sugach towards Creag Tharsuinn and at about the same altitude as Coire Sugach. It is worth exploring if the sun is rapidly stripping the crags of Coire Sugach.

Philosopher's Gully   200m   II   (1993)
The central and most obvious gully gives good early season sport with ample belays and protection. Easier climbing should be expected under greater snow and ice cover.

Hume's Buttress   200m   III,4   (1994)
This route climbs grooves and chimneys on the right side of the
buttress right of Philosopher's Gully. Start at a short chockstone-
capped gully at the lowest rocks. Climb the gully to the chockstone and
go right under this to a large terrace. Avoid the chimney at the back by a
10m traverse right, then follow a turfy ramp left to a cave. Avoid the
groove above the cave by traversing right and go up a turfy ramp
leftwards to return to the groove which leads to a chimney and a steep
terrace. Climb the wall and easier mixed ground to finish.

YAWNING CRAG   (Map Ref 273 064)

This south-east facing crag lies in the corrie due south of Beinn
Narnain's summit, above the Buttermilk Burn approach to The Cobbler
and the Narnain Boulders. A deep chimney splits the crag which has a
gully on the left.

Muckle Mou'   35m   Very Difficult   (1959)
This is the obvious deep chimney. Start in the back of the chimney on a
sunken floor and follow boulders to the back of the outer chimney.
Climb the wall to a spike and traverse up and left a short distance.
Continue in the inner chimney to belay at jammed blocks. Climb up and
out, going through an obvious passage to some boulders, and finish
on the right wall.

Lip Route   20m   Very Difficult   (1959)
Climb the left edge of Muckle Mou'.

Cicatrice   35m   Difficult   (1959)
Start 6m below and right of Muckle Mou'. Climb to a ledge and a block
belay, then climb a short wall to a cave and a good stance. Finish up a
crack above.

SPEARHEAD RIDGE   (Map Ref 274 066)

Although there is much rock scattered about Beinn Narnain, the most
extensive crags lie about 30m from the top, where the summit plateau
meets the south-east ridge. The sunny, open aspect means the mica-
schist dries quite quickly. The rock is quite fissured and variation is
possible.

Restricted Crack   30m   Moderate   (1935)
About 2 metres left of the most obvious deep chimney is a crack.
Follow its outer edges to the top by pleasant climbing.

Engine Room Crack   30m   Difficult *
A subterranean route in the deep crack right of Restricted Crack. Near
the top of Restricted Crack is a hole in the ground. Descend through
this to reach a level floor. Daylight can be seen above, and this marks
the top of Spearhead Ridge. Struggle up to the light.

Jamblock Chimney   45m   Very Difficult *   (1898)
The deep chimney leading to the top of the Spearhead gives a variety
of technical moves. Climb the chimney to a cave. In the roof above is a
small manhole which gives a strenuous or impossible exit depending
on girth.

No Highway   20m   Severe   (1961)
Near Spearhead Chimney is a small gully. Go across the left wall and
round the edge and follow the wall above on small holds, keeping left
until the top of Spearhead Ridge is reached.

Southern Comfort   20m   Severe   (1976)
To the left of Spearhead Chimney is a vertical wall split by shallow
cracks. Climb a steep crack left of the edge to a small ledge. Continue
up cracks and a groove to finish.

Spearhead Chimney   12m   Difficult
A few metres left of the arete is a groove. Climb the right wall to the top
of the ridge.

Spearhead Arete   30m   Difficult **   (1894)
The classic arete at the right end of the south face is climbable almost
anywhere on good rock and with fine open situations.

The following routes are on the Secondary Spearhead, a smaller
replica of the main crag, when viewed from the south-east ridge.

North-East Corner   12m   Difficult
A steep little climb by a corner and crack.

South-East Corner   10m   Severe
Climb directly up the south side near the edge.

The Twilight Zone   70m   III   (1994)
This route climbs a slab on the right-hand side of Spearhead Ridge,
clearly seen from the Allt Sugach. Start from the lowest point of the
slab. Move up from a ledge just below the top and bypass the
overhangs on the left.

GLEN CROE
(Map Ref 256 044)

A number of steep mica-schist crags are scattered on the east side of
Glen Croe, offering roadside climbing in a pleasant and sunny location.
Considering their closeness to Glasgow and easy access, the crags
appear much less popular now than they were at the time of the last
guide (1989). However, the outdoor pursuit abseilers have been busy
and the trough around Middle Crag deepens with the years. Many
routes have peg runners, but because of the closeness of the crags to
the road and the presence of non-climbers (and the thieving
abseilers), many are not in place. This is a pity, because some of the
routes (like Pockets of Excellence) are well worth doing if the pegs are
in place.

Park at the large lay-by below The Brack, at Map Ref 258 042 on
the west side of the A83 in Glen Croe. The crags can be seen in profile
straight ahead on the ridge to the right. Cross the road and follow the
old road through a gate. Continue until a rough path leads off right past
small walls to the Middle Crag, which is the most prominent. The Upper
Crag is a further 10 minutes up the hillside.

LOWER CRAG

This piece of rock faces the old road. It has a few short problems.
Cluer's Clue (5c) starts from the crag's lowest point and climbs the
blunt arete, then its right wall. **Shirley** (5a) takes the crack left of the
narrow roof, and **Under Arrest** (5a) climbs around the roof.

APPROACH WALLS

Various problems have been done on the micro wall left of the approach. **The Smee Merchant** (5a) takes left-trending scoops, just left of the wide crack. **The Handrail Effect** (5b) follows left-trending pockets right of the wide crack. There is another 5c problem up a line right of The Handrail Effect. **The Pocket Poseur** (5a) takes a line of pockets up the centre of the wall.

MIDDLE CRAG

The first real crag has some interesting routes, although the easier ones are short and generally badly protected. The crag gets much use from outdoor groups and is easily identified by an inordinate amount of path erosion. The protection pegs are unlikely to be in place.

1   Good Day Sunshine   8m   VS 4b
Climb the left-trending ramp and wall at the left end of the crag.

2   Rita   10m   VS 4c
The wall to the right.

3   Michelle   10m   HVS 4c
A left-trending line below and right of Rita, followed by the wall above.

Alabasta   10m   E2 5c *
The impressive wall left of the crack of Lady Madonna.

4   Lady Madonna   15m   5a *
The steep crack in the arete gives a well protected route.

5   Polythene Pam   15m   HVS 5a *
Fine but unprotected pockets lead up the wall right of Lady Madonna.

6   Doris   15m   VS 4b *
Climb the blunt arete with some hard unprotected moves out right onto the upper slab.

7   Dear Prudence   15m   HVS 5a
The bulging wall left of Student's Route.

GLEN CROE
Middle Crag

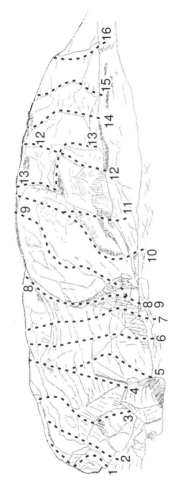

1 Good Day Sunshine
2 Rita
3 Michelle
4 Lady Madonna

5 Polythene Pam
6 Doris
7 Dear Prudence
8 Student's Route

9 Pockets of Excellence
10 Roadman's Crack
11 The Cost of Living
12 P.C.31

13 Lucy in the Sky
14 Martha
15 Molly
16 Desmond

8   Student's Route   15m   Severe 4a *
The polished curving crack can be well protected, although it's a fiddle to place.

9   Pockets of Excellence   20m   E4 6a **   (1985)
Excellent climbing. Right of Student's Route a line of small pockets lead to the base of a shallow right-slanting crack, peg. From its top, make some hard moves to gain a large inset pocket, peg runner above. Move directly up to gain a line of large pockets leading right to finish.

10   Roadman's Crack   20m   HVS 5a *
An obvious right-curving crack leads to a poorly protected wall, passing a large dubious flake, to finish through a small break on the right.

11   The Cost of Living   20m   E2 6a *
Start at an obvious pocket in the large bulge just right of Roadman's Crack. Pull over the bulge, peg runner, and finish up Roadman's Crack.

12   P.C.31   15m   E1 5c
Climb the wall to the right, finishing right of the tree.

13   Lucy in the Sky   15m   E1 5b
Climb the steep crack, then traverse left along the ledge to finish behind the tree.

Some short easy routes have been done on the slabby walls to the right.

Cadbury's   7m   E1 5a*
This route climbs the obvious flake on the small crag immediately above Middle Crag.

UPPER CRAG

The prominent overhanging crag seen in profile from the lay-by contains a number of steep routes in the upper grades. In general the wall climbs are steep, strenuous and poorly protected; the cracks just steep and strenuous. Again, the peg runners are unlikely to be in place.

Zigzag   10m   Very Difficult
This is the crack in the micro slab bounding the crag on the left.

Outside Edge   10m   HVS 4c *   (1986)
A short but very sweet climb up the right edge of the slabby left wall of
the crag. The talented will find quite adequate protection.

1   All Heroes Die Young   20m   E3 6a *   (1986)
Right of the slab of Outside Edge is an impressively steep wall. This
route climbs the shallow grooves near its left edge, starting at a thin
crack. Follow this to a small ledge, peg runner, then go up a shallow
bulging runnel, passing a further peg and an *in situ* thread to a blind
rounded finish.

2   Marabou Stork Nightmares   15m   E6 6b *   (1995)
The impressive wall and arete to the right of All Heroes Die Young.
Place side runners in the base of the crack of that route (a low runner in
the block down and right and a second belayer will reduce the impact
on the rocky ledges from a fall from the crux). Traverse the arch-
shaped overlap and make hard moves out right to a jug. Climb past a
flake and continue up the arete. High side runners make the route
much less serious.

3   Ledgeislation   20m   E2 5c   (1986)
A cracked overhang bars entry to the base of the big corner. Cut free,
crank through the overhang into the corner, then follow the corner's left
edge without much protection to finish as for Crossover.

   The obvious, dark-coloured groove with a thread in it was climbed
as a variation to Ledgeislation, entering and leaving the groove by that
route.

4   The Hooded Groove   20m   E2 5c **
Overhangs give a strenuous but well protected entry to and exit from
the big corner. Cut free and crank through the first overhang, then
ramble up the corner to layback the crack through the upper overhang.

5   Crossover   25m   E1 5b *
An excellent climb, gaining the corner from the right and exiting it on
the left. Right of the base of the big corner, a ramp comes in from the
right. Traverse the ramp to make difficult moves into the steep groove
which leads left into the big corner. Climb the corner and traverse left to
the arete, either low down (no protection), or high up (beware of rope
drag).

6   The Edge of Insanity   20m   E4 5c **   (1987)

The upper right arete of the corner gives a short but spectacular route with spaced protection. Follow Crossover to the upper ledge in the corner. Swing out right, place runners in the flake, and move up to gain a small ledge. Traverse right until a long reach gains a good pocket (runner), then swing right to a large spike on the arete in a fine position. Finish up the easy slab.

7   Short Sharp Shock   25m   E4 6a **   (1986)

Steep and strenuous climbing up the left-hand of two impressive finger cracks. Awkward moves gain the crack, which offers positive fingerlocks to a rest just below the top. Pull over on good holds to a slabby crack.

8   Double Clutching   25m   E3 6a *   (1985)

The right-hand crack is just as steep but marginally less strenuous. A long stretch gains the crack which leads to a sharp pull onto a ledge. Finish easily up the slabby crack.

9   Prime Ape   15m   E3 6a   (1986)

Long arms are useful. Climb the short bulging wall right of Double Clutching, followed by much easy ground.

10   Fear   15m   HVS 5a   (1985)

A couple of steep well protected moves gain good hand holds, followed by a move up and much easy ground. If only they were all like this.

Quartzymodo   15m   E1 5c   (1989)

Climb the quartz wall right of Fear on undercuts. Move left into Fear or finish direct at 6a.

11   Breakdance   10m   E2 5c   (1986)

The short wall left of Cosmic Corner offers a crux at the top and an unappealing landing. Runners can be found in the corner.

Pegomaniac   10m   E3 5c   (1988)

Start at the bottom of Cosmic Corner and follow a traverse line left across Breakdance to an arete, then finish up the arete.

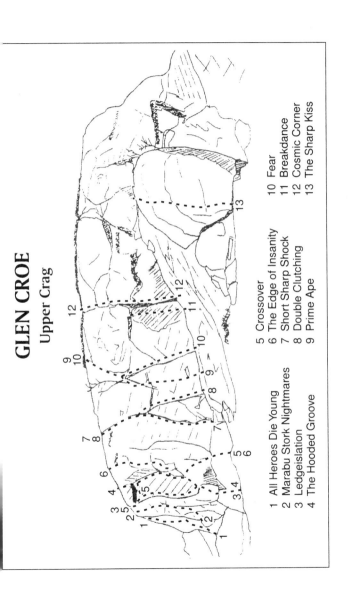

GLEN CROE
Upper Crag

1 All Heroes Die Young
2 Marabu Stork Nightmares
3 Ledgeislation
4 The Hooded Groove

5 Crossover
6 The Edge of Insanity
7 Short Sharp Shock
8 Double Clutching
9 Prime Ape

10 Fear
11 Breakdance
12 Cosmic Corner
13 The Sharp Kiss

Cosmic Corner   10m   VS 4b   (1985)
Climb the wide crack in the right-facing corner.

Down and right of the main crag is a large boulder with a steep front face and a prominent overhung right arete.

The Sharp Kiss   15m   E3 6a   (1987)
Steep and technical wall climbing up the left side of the front face. Start at the bottom left of the wall at a large flat boulder. Pull right and go up to a good horizontal break. Climb through the bulge above with difficulty to finish up an easy slab.

Litterbug   15m   E1 5b *   (1988)
Round the edge to the right of The Sharp Kiss is an overhanging wall. Start at the right end of this wall at an arete below a tree. Climb the wall keeping left of the arete, pull onto a steep slab and finish up and left. Belay well back. Once found, protection at the start is good.

Two routes with a common start have been climbed on the boulder down and left of the main crag.

Quartz Slab   10m   E2 5b   (1986)
Follow a line just left of the crack, pull on to the slab and continue directly.

Quartz Crack   10m   E2 5b   (1986)
The obvious crack leading out right.

INDEPENDENCE CRAG

This small crag lies at the same level and to the right of the top of Upper Crag. It is easily identified by a very steep left-facing corner in the centre.

New Position   15m   E2 5c **   (1986)
Strenuous but well protected climbing up the wildly overhanging finger crack splitting the crag, to the right of the prominent corner. High in the grade.

SO FAR AWAY BUTTRESS

The largest crag up and right of Upper Crag is split by a band of roofs with the diagonal break of Give us a Break running from right to left below them.

Aftershock   30m   E3 5c **   (1987)
An interesting route which improves with height. Start at the left edge of the buttress and climb directly to meet the break where it reaches the gully. Pull through the bulge above on sidepulls and continue to an obvious niche in the horizontal break. Follow the break rightwards for about 5m, then go directly up the slab past a poor tied-off peg. Belay some distance higher.

Give us a Break   30m   E1 5b   (1985)
Start below the right end of the diagonal break. Gain the break and follow it until it is possible to move into the gully and scramble to the top.

The Nitty-gritty Dirt Route   50m   E1   (1988)
A bold route on the series of slabs and walls with a tree at half-height, just left of the main buttress. Start directly below the tree.
1. 25m 5a   Ascend just left of the tree.
2. 25m 4c   Continue up slabs and belay well back.

Rough and Tumble   10m   E1 5b   (1988)
Left of the previous route is an area of dripping overhangs. Climb a rough rib to their left, keeping right of a heather bay.

GREAT SLAB

This is the large slab up and right of So Far Away Buttress.

Lapland   25m   E1 5a*   (1988)
A series of overlapping slabs at the left end of the slab provides the line. Start on top of a heather-capped block above and left of a rowan tree. Climb up to the right end of the first overlap, traverse left above the overlap to gain a slab and cross the next overlap where the slab above forms a bulge. Finish up a shallow corner.

The Ladder   25m   VS 4b   (1987)
Climb the slab directly, just left of a heathery gully.

Fearless   30m   HVS 4c *   (1987)
Very bold climbing up the centre of the main slab, moving right to finish.

Rock Sculpture   30m   E3 5c *   (1989)
Start at the right end of the slab, at a heathery flake crack. Climb up to gain a horizontal crack left of an overhang, continue on small holds (RP3 in a thin diagonal crack), then trend right to a foot ledge. Continue more easily to a peg belay.

The Incredible Hulk   15m   E5 6a
This route is included for completeness, although a number of climbers have expressed doubt about its first ascent. Round the left side of the main slab is an overhanging wall with a thin crack starting at half-height. Climb the wall and crack.

VIZ BUTTRESS

High on the hillside, up and left of all the other crags, is a buttress with a large triangular roof.

Bollocks   20m   E3 6a *   (1992)
Climb the hanging crack, flake and groove at the left end of the crag.

THE COBBLER

884m (Map Ref 259 058)

In an age where height increasingly appears to be a major criterion for a mountain's worth, The Cobbler stands as a proud example that small can be beautiful. The neighbouring Beinn Ime and Beinn Narnain may be among the chosen 277 Munros, but The Cobbler provides much more interest, both from the climbing and scenic points of view. Its North and South Peaks are two of the most distinctive mountain silhouettes in Scotland, and its highest point, the Central Peak, is one of an exclusive club of Scottish summits that can only be ascended by real rock climbing.

In general the rock climbs here are quite serious for their grade. The mica-schist can be alternatively smooth and slabby, then steep and pocketed, covered in a fine patina of tough, grey lichen, interspersed with luscious vegetation. As would be expected for this rock, protection ranges from bombproof through fiddly to frequently laughable and sometimes non-existent. But, with a confident approach there are some joyous experiences on offer at every grade.

Once scorned as a winter climbing joke, The Cobbler's meteoric rise to its worthy position as one of the finest mixed climbing venues in the Southern Highlands has taken a mere eight years. The mountain now contains a fine selection of quality routes from grade III to VIII, many of which can be combined to produce more than 100m of technical climbing. With a technical grade of 9 already achieved, the mountain's future as a winter mixed climbing venue is assured.

However, the low altitude and aspect means that hoar strips readily and climbers should make a particular effort to avoid climbing classic rock routes in poor winter conditions where crampons and axes may seriously damage the soft rock.

The slopes surrounding The Cobbler may be short, but they are steep and have been known to avalanche. The usual caution should be exercised, especially when descending straight from the ridge.

Access

Park at the large car park beside the A83 at the head of Loch Long. A path leads up through the forest to join a high horizontal path which leads south-west to the Allt a'Bhalachain and a dam. It is also possible to reach this point directly from the road bridge above the Torpedo Station and pier on Loch Long. Follow a path alongside the burn, past the Narnain Boulders and across the burn. Ascend the corrie below the South Face of North Peak to arrive at the col between the North and Centre Peaks. This takes about 2 hours.

A popular winter ascent which avoids the frequent deep snow in the corrie starts in Glen Croe at the small lay-by by the bridge over the burn falling from the Bealach a'Mhaim between The Cobbler and Beinn Ime. Follow the path on the north side of the burn to below a dam. Cross the burn, then climb a spur to a fence and stile and follow the steep spur above to arrive at the col between the North and Centre peaks; 1hr 30mins.

SOUTH PEAK

The two facets of this peak, whose summit can only be obtained by climbing, offer quite different styles of route and mountain atmosphere. The open, sunny South Face is generally quite clean and slabby and contains some of the best and most serious rock climbs on the mountain. By comparison, the North Face is dark, vegetated and gloomy and although it contains some good rock climbs, it is most popular in winter when it is frequently in condition, and routes like North Wall Groove, Gibber Crack and Deadman's Groove provide classic outings.

Routes on this peak are described from left to right in an anti-clockwise direction, starting from the col between South Peak and Centre Peak.

NORTH-WEST FACE

This is the small face overlooking the col. The vegetated left-hand side is taken by **Bell's Route** (Difficult, 1895), with its **Sloping Ledge Variation** (Very Difficult, 1895) and **Rutherford's Variation** (Very Difficult, 1927). All three are classics of their kind and are best avoided. Descent is down Original Route, polished but well protected, or by a 25m abseil from the block at the top of Original Route, overlooking the col between South Peak and Centre Peak.

Naismith's Route   15m   Difficult   (1898)
Climb direct from the col, finishing as for Original Route.

Original Route   15m   Moderate   (1894)
A short, exciting but polished route with excellent protection. A rope is recommended as a slip while descending would result in a swift and terminal descent of the South Face. From the col a steep step on the right gains a worn path which traverses out over the South Face. A short distance along, an easy cracked ramp, much scarred by nails, sweat and crampons, slants back left to a grass ledge and a block, frequently used for an abseil descent. A dirty blocky wall leads back right to the final smooth and awkward crack in a slab.

North-West Crack   15m   VS 4c   (1898)
Gain the path from the col as for Original Route. On the left, at the end of the worn path is a repulsively slimy green crack. Amazing – even for the predilections of the day.

Cupid's Groove   15m   VS 4c   (1952)
Gain the path from the col as for Original Route. From the very end of the path move round the corner onto the South Face and climb the shallow groove, past *in situ* ironmongery to a small ledge on the right and the top.

SOUTH FACE

This steep slabby wall overlooks Glen Croe and contains some of the best and cleanest rock on The Cobbler. It receives a considerable amount of sunshine and offers tremendous, but often quite serious rock routes. Descent is by traversing terraces right and descending the vegetated South-East Face.

   The left-hand side of the wall is flanked by the obvious deep fault of Porcupine Wall which slants up and left.

1   **Porcupine Wall**   45m   Severe   (1951)
A pointless route which starts 5 metres left of a frequently sopping overhanging corner sprouting an old peg (the original aided start).
1. 10m   Climb right across the wall to a belay above the crack.
2. 35m   Traverse right a short distance, then ascend to some shelves on the left. Climb a short wall on the left and continue up the overhanging groove to the summit. Scramble over the top and descend Original Route, polished but well protected, or abseil from the block near the top of Original Route, overlooking the col between South Peak and Centre Peak (25m).

2 Dicer's Groove   40m   E2 *   (1956)
A rather traditional Scottish mountain experience, but no less a route
for a' that! Start just down and right of Porcupine Wall at an obvious
right-slanting crack, the first feature on the wall.
1. 30m 5b   Follow the heathery handrail crack to a blocky, mossy
recess. Move down and left to a quartz block at the base of the groove
and follow this, exiting left or right at the top to easier ground and a
belay.
2. 10m   Easy ground leads to the terrace.

3 Ethereal   45m   E6 **   (1995)
Bold climbing up the left side of the compact scooped wall immediately
right of Dicer's Groove.
1. 30m 6b   From a flake at the base of the wall, climb up and right,
then go back left to a large pocket; Friend 3. Move up left to a shake out
and various nuts down left in a slot. Climb the wall with difficulty to the
top of the ramp and follow flakes, then move right to a belay.
2. 15m 4a   Occasional rock leads to the terrace.

4 Sleeping Gas   45m   E6 *   (1995)
A serious route up the centre of the compact scooped wall. Great
climbing, but not a great line.
1. 30m 6b   Climb Ethereal to the pocket and move out right to place a
good nut, then return. Move up to a skyhook placement, then go right,
then up and leftwards past two poor pegs (there is a rest down and
right before first peg, which is hard to clip). Continue direct to reach
good runners and the Ethereal belay.
2. 15m 4a   Easier ground leads to the terrace.

5 Glueless Groove   45m   E2 5b * (1957)
Good climbing, but not over-endowed with protection and a bit mossy
at the top. Right of the compact scooped wall a series of cracked ramp-
like grooves curve up from the ground towards the prominent left-
facing corner of Ithuriel's Wall. Start below a small patch of heather at
the base of a grassy crack. Climb the cracked groove to a ledge at 35m.
Continue up the mossy wall, trending left for 5m to some quartz
patches, then go up to a large ledge. Climb the overhanging groove
above to the top, passing a layback flake.

THE COBBLER
South Face of South Peak

1 Porcupine Wall
2 Dicer's Groove
3 Ethereal
4 Sleeping Gas
5 Glueless Groove

6 Ithuriel's Wall
7 Gladiator's Groove Direct
8 Geb
10 Osiris
11 Horus

6   Ithuriel's Wall   45m   E2 **   (1952)
A superb corner combining increasingly tenuous climbing with diminishing protection. The cleanest rock is fortuitously reserved for the hardest moves. Start at easy broken grooves below and left of the prominent left-facing corner.
1. 10m 4a   Climb the grooves to a block belay on the broad ledge below the corner.
2. 25m 5b   Follow the fine corner past bulges to the large ledge on Gladiator's Groove. Belay on wires in the corner on the right.
3. 10m 4c   Climb the arete on the right of the groove to the top.

7   Gladiator's Groove Direct   65m   E1 ***   (1951/52)
A Cobbler classic which takes the left edge of the impressive quartz-banded slab and the right-facing corner above. Much of the route is straightforward for the grade, but the two hard cruxes are characterised by poor protection and a confident approach is essential. Start at steep rock below the left end of the broad quartz band, at a grassy triangular recess.
1. 35m 5a   Awkward, strenuous and unprotected moves up the overhanging wall lead to the quartz. Continue up the steep slab to a ledge, then traverse delicately right to the large block. Continue up past a peg and flake to belay on the broad ledge below the corner.
2. 20m 5b   The corner gives enjoyable climbing until a step left and an awkward move gain a disturbingly overhanging groove which can only be protected through effort, care and cunning. A difficult and committing udge up and left usually gains the ledge. Belay on wires in the corner on the right.
3. 10m 4c   Climb the corner, to finish as for Ithuriel's Wall at the terrace.

8   Geb   40m   E4 6a **   (1995)
A left to right traverse of the slab right of Gladiator's Groove Direct, starting up that route. Climb the overhanging wall to the quartz band and traverse it rightwards past two peg runners. Climb the vague crack of Osiris, but continue right to finish up the right side of the block.

9   Ra   65m   E4 **   (1995)
This direct line up the left side of the slab is quite bold and runout, despite all the pegs! Start down and right of Gladiator's Groove Direct at a shallow groove.

1.35m 6a   Climb up past a peg onto a sloping ledge. Step left and go up to a small ledge above; skyhooks just above the peg and out on the right. Climb past three peg runners to the rising traverse on Gladiator's Groove Direct. Arrange protection (in a thin crack out left and a block on the right), ascend the wall to the terrace and belay under the corner of Gladiator's Groove.

2.30m 5c   Follow the corner, but where Gladiator's goes left onto the ledge, continue up a vague crack and easier ground to the terrace.

10   Osiris   30m   E4 6a ***   (1988)
The original route on the slab gives brilliant climbing with a steep, strenuous and technical crux, followed by a bold and delicate slab of excellent rock. High in the grade. Start at the lowest point of the slab to the right of a boulder, at an obvious cleaned ledge. Climb to ledges (peg runner), then go out leftwards under the overlap to an inset slab. Pull over the overlap to a peg and climb direct to an *in situ* thread runner, then straight up to a small overlap and a runner in a slot. Move left to large pockets, then go straight up to the quartz band and a peg runner. Climb up slightly right until below the prominent block on the arete and finish up its left side.

11   Horus   40m   E6 6b **   (1991)
A direct and sustained line up the wall right of Osiris, offering technical climbing and marginal protection. Start as for Osiris. Climb to the first peg and move up and right over the bulge (difficult to clip tied-off peg and Rock 1 above) to reach good quartz holds. Continue up past a small overlap to gain a good hanging flake and excellent protection. Continue directly to the base of a diagonal crack and move slightly left (crux; HB3 and Chouinard Stopper 3 on sides) to a prominent sidepull (RP3 in triangular niche). Continue up on improving holds to pull out right to easier ground and reach a belay further back on a ledge.

SOUTH-EAST FACE

This is the narrow face looking down to Loch Long. The South-East Ridge bounds it on the right.

   Descend by reversing the grassy South-East Ridge, care needed, or scramble over the summit and descend Original Route, polished but well protected, or abseil from the block near the top of Original Route, overlooking the col between South Peak and Centre Peak (25m).

12   Ardgartan Arete   55m   VS **   (1948)
This enjoyable, bold, route follows the prominent arete formed by the South and South-East Faces. Start about 15m up from the toe of the buttress where an obvious shallow groove slants up left to join the arete.

1. 30m 4a/b   Follow the groove with little protection over a bulge at 5m, then continue up grooves in the arete to belay at the end of the terrace which slants up below the corners of Gladiator's Groove and Ithuriel's Wall.

2. 10m 4a   Climb the wall above, then continue up cracks to belay on the left at a block on the arete.

3. 15m 4a   Follow the crack in the wall above to finish on the terrace. This is the descent terrace used by climbs on the South Face. The wall can also be climbed on the left, overlooking the South Face.

13   Ardgartan Wall   65m   VS *   (1937)
An impressive route for the day, but largely superseded by Ardgartan Arete. Start as for Ardgartan Arete.

1. 30m 4a/b   Follow Ardgartan Arete to belay at the terrace which runs below the corners of Gladiator's Groove and Ithuriel's Wall. The wall right of the initial groove can be climbed leftwards to the arete on small holds and at an easier grade, but with no more protection.

2. 25m 4a   Keeping to the right of the cracks of Ardgartan Arete, climb the wall above to a ledge, then go up a second wall, bearing right at 8m, then move left to quartz holds and the terrace. The South Face descent goes right from here; instead traverse left to below an overhang split by a wide crack.

3. 10m   Climb the steep wall right of the overhang to finish.

14   Pygmy Wall   70m   III,5 *   (1995)
Quite a bold first pitch, followed by a technical second pitch. The route is a vegetated Severe in summer (1951). Start to the right of the shallow groove of Ardgartan Wall, at a corner abutting the lower right end of the slabby wall.

1. 50m   Climb the corner to where it opens out, then climb up and left over turfy ledges, iced slabs and a steepening to the terrace used as a descent from the South Face rock climbs. Move left to below a right-facing corner and the prominent overhang split by a wide crack.

2. 20m   Climb the corner to pass the overhang on the left. The short overhanging corner above is used to gain a prominent projecting block on the right wall (crux). Corners then lead to easy ground. An alternate

finish climbs the groove in the wall right of the overhang at an easier technical grade.

15   South-East Ridge   105m   Moderate   (1889)
Start at the foot of the ridge forming the right side of the face and follow the line of least resistance on rock, vegetation and much exposure.
Winter: 105m   II/III *
A more satisfying experience. The route taken can be varied to suit the grade required.

Traverse of South and Centre Peaks   200m   III **
A superb mountaineering traverse through impressive scenery which requires some care. Ascend the South-East Ridge of South Peak, reverse Original Route or abseil to the col (see the introduction to the South-East Face), climb The Arete to the summit of Centre Peak and reverse Doorway Route.

NORTH-EAST FACE

This face, also known as the Corrie Face, is divided into three sections by two distinct vegetated ledges: Grassy Traverse, which begins midway up the right-hand side of the face, slants up left to the South-East Ridge and effectively divides the whole face in two; and North Wall Traverse which begins about 30m above the ground, slants up and right and further divides the right-hand section. The first two routes described are on a small buttress separated from the main face by a short deep gully.
    Descent is by reversing the grassy South-East Ridge, care needed, or by scrambling over the summit and descending Original Route, polished but well protected, or by abseiling from the block near the top of Original Route, above the col between South and Centre Peaks (25m).

16   Jughandle   105m   Very Difficult   (1933)
Some 20m down and right from South-East Ridge is an obvious corner with a deep crack. Follow the crack for 25m and continue up and right to cross the top of a prominent short gully. Climb an obvious chimney and continue directly to grass ledges. Follow easy vegetated ground up and right to a wide shelf, followed by two short walls to the summit.
Winter: 105m   IV,5
A good expedition, although the initial groove presents the only real interest.

17   Bow Crack   30m   Hard Severe **   (1952)
Well protected climbing up the crack in the wall right of Jughandle and
left of the short gully.
1. 15m 4b   Follow the crack for 5m, then cross the bulge on the left to
a small ledge. Go left for 5m to a belay on Jughandle.
2. 15m   Finish up and right as for Jughandle to grass ledges.
Variation: 20m   HVS 5a   (1995)
Start as for Bow Crack, but hand traverse left at a lower level along the
obvious crack for 6m to the arete. Step off a small grass ledge and
move up to the belay.

Right of Bow Crack is a short deep gully (unclimbed), and right
again an impressive crack.

18   S-Crack   40m   VS 4c **   (1948)
A superb sustained pitch which takes the clean curving crack in the
wall right of the short gully. Climb the crack over two bulges to finish on
a ledge. Walk off left to grassy ledges.
Winter: 50m   V,7 *   (1994)
A steep but well protected climb.

19   Aeon   45m   Severe   (1952)
A poor route. About 45 metres right of S-Crack is a big grassy groove
topped by an overhang.
1. 30m   Climb the groove, passing the overhang on the right to a
ledge and belay.
2. 15m   Traverse right for 5m, ascend the arete for 6m, then climb the
crack on the left to the Grassy Terrace.
Variation: 40m   Severe   (1952)
Just as poor. From the top of pitch 1 of the original route traverse left for
7m under an overhang, then climb the steep shallow chimney to a
belay (10m). Climb the groove on the right for 10m, then go up the
arete on the right to the top (30m).

20   Aeonoclast   70m   VI,6 **   (1995)
A fine winter route with a bit of everything. Start as for Aeon.
1. 15m   The groove leads to a belay in a corner below an overhang.
2. 25m   Climb the corner to a good spike, traverse left and climb a
steep turfy crack in the wall (poor protection) followed by the steep
shallow chimney splitting the second overhang. Belay on the left.

THE COBBLER
North Face of South Peak

16 Jughandle
17 Bow Crack
18 S–Crack
19 Aeon
20 Aeonoclast
21 Sesame Groove Direct
22 Grassy Traverse
23 Southern Freeze
24 Ruskoline
25 Deadman's Groove
25a Winter Variation

26 Grossen Zinnen
27 McLean's Folly
28 North Wall Groove
28a North Wall Groove Direct Start
29 North Wall Traverse
30 Viva Glasvegas
31 Gibber Crack
32 Slack's Route
33 Nimlin's Direct Route

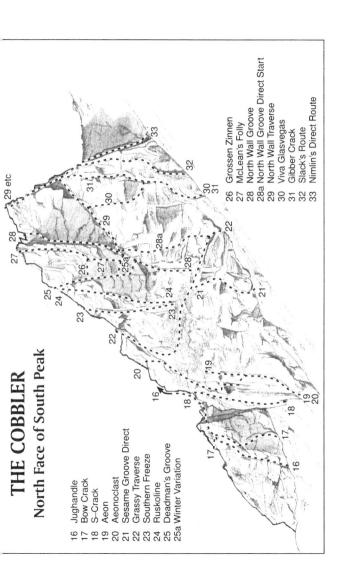

3. 30m   Move up and left with difficulty to climb a thin crack in the slabby wall in a superb position. Finish up walls and turf, keeping to the left edge of the finishing groove of Grassy Traverse.

Up and right from the big groove of Aeon, steep vegetated walls lead to the prominent corner of Gibber Crack. Below and left of the corner a steep broken fault gains the right-hand end of the terrace of Grassy Traverse. The following route climbs a wide flake crack in the wall, about 20m below the start of the Grassy Traverse.

21   Sesame Groove Direct   30m   IV,6   (1993)
Climb the flake crack until a short difficult traverse leads to a turfy left-trending line which joins Grassy Traverse. The grade reduces to III if the initial slab is banked out. The route can be used to extend any of the winter routes starting up Sesame Groove. Severe in summer (1955).

22   Grassy Traverse   60m   III *   (1962)
A very scenic route in winter, although care should be taken in avalanche conditions, and a vegetated and exposed Moderate (1898) in summer. Start at the right end of the terrace. A steep broken fault leads left past the base of a steep corner splitting the upper tier (Sesame Groove). Follow the wide terrace and finish up a rocky groove to the South-East Ridge. Ascend or descend that route.

The following two rock climbs ascend the prominent arete of the upper buttress above the Grassy Traverse terrace. They can be approached *via* Grassy Traverse, either from the right by traversing beyond the obvious corner (Sesame Groove), or from the left by ascending South-East Ridge to the col and descending the rocky groove on the right to gain the left end of the Grassy Traverse.

23   Southern Freeze   60m   E2   (1981)
Scramble up grass to a shallow groove with an undercut left wall, just left of Ruskoline (the obvious groove in the arete). Like Ruskoline, a good clean would make this a much more enjoyable route.
1. 30m 5b   Climb the shallow groove for about 5m to gain an obvious crack. Climb the crack and a short groove, then step right and go over a bulge in a corner, which leads to a roof. Belay on a foot ledge on the left.
2. 30m 4b   Traverse back right across the corner to gain an obvious groove which leads to a belay at the top of Deadman's Groove

24   Ruskoline   80m   E5 *   (1980)

With a good scrub, the groove in the overhanging arete left of Deadman's Groove could be one of the best E5s in the area – but not in its present state. Scramble up grass to belay below the groove.

1. 40m 6a   Climb to a ledge, traverse left, then go back right to enter a groove. Climb the groove past a dubious block to reach a steeper groove which provides increasing difficulty. Traverse right into an overhanging groove (poor Friend placements in pockets on the left) and climb this. Go over a bulge, gain a crack and follow it to a small foot ledge and belay.

2. 40m 5a   Step right, climb a groove, pull left over a bulge and finish up the rib.

In summer and winter, Grassy Traverse gives access to the following six routes. They all begin up the open groove which is the first pitch of North Wall Traverse and was later christened Sesame Groove. In winter these routes can be extended by starting up Sesame Groove Direct (see above).

25   Deadman's Groove   90m   VS 4c *   (1948)

A steep pitch up the obvious groove on the right side of the overhanging arete. It requires several days to dry. Start at the foot of Grassy Traverse.

1. 10m   Traverse left to below the open groove.

2. 40m   Sesame Groove. Climb the groove to an overhanging wall and traverse right on a small shelf to reach a hollow block. Climb steep turfy walls to a thread belay at the right end of a small roof.

3. 20m   Traverse easily left to an obvious crack and follow it over two bulges (dubious flakes) to a small ledge.

4. 20m   Enter the groove on the left and climb it to the ridge.

Winter: 90m   VII,7 ***   (1990)

A good covering of snow, combined with a short cold snap turn this into a classic winter prospect, which gives a fine technical route. Start as for the summer route and follow it to the top of pitch 2.

3. 20m   The summer line moves left here, instead, go up for 3m, then traverse left into the groove and move up to a belay at the foot of the upper groove.

4. 20m   Follow the groove to easy ground.

5. 50m   Move down leftwards, then go up easily to the top.

26 Grossen Zinnen 85m Severe (1952)
This route climbs the rib right of Deadman's Groove, before moving left
to join that route. Start at the foot of Grassy Traverse.
1 and 2. 50m Follow Deadman's Groove pitches 1 and 2.
3. 15m Traverse left and gain the open rib and climb it for 6m to an
overhung niche below the groove of McLean's Folly; peg belay.
4. 20m Swing right onto the arete and follow good holds to a ledge
directly below McLean's Folly. Traverse left along a ledge to gain
Deadman's Groove and finish up that.

27 McLean's Folly 85m E1 * (1968)
The obvious right-trending groove above Grossen Zinnen has seen
few ascents. Start at the foot of the Grassy Traverse.
1, 2 and 3. 65m Climb Grossen Zinnen to the end of its third pitch.
4. 20m 5b Swing onto the arete, climb to the ledge and follow the
steep groove above.

28 North Wall Groove 100m V,6 *** (1977)
A superb route climbing the big open groove. The exposed crux is both
delicate and strenuous, but reasonably well protected. A vegetated
Severe in summer (1945). Start at the foot of Grassy Traverse.
1. 10m Climb up and left to the base of the corner (Sesame Groove).
2. 50m Climb Sesame Groove to a choice of exits to the right (high is
intimidating, low is technical) and a possible belay at a hollow block
(20m). Climb steep turfy walls to enter the groove which leads to a
large flake crack below the upper groove.
3. 35m Continue up the groove until delicate moves right across a
thin slab gain clumps of turf in an exposed position. Move up to a belay.
4. 5m Continue steeply to finish.
Direct Start: 50m IV,6 (1995)
This variation climbs the slabby wall right of Sesame Groove. Start at
the foot of Grassy Traverse. Climb up and left a few metres until it is
possible to pull over the bulge and gain turf on the slabby wall. Turf and
a crack on the left lead left past a steepening to easier ground and the
flake crack belay on North Wall Groove.

29 North Wall Traverse 140m IV,5 ** (1961)
The upper right-slanting grassy traverse gives a good mountaineering
route with excellent positions. The second pitch (Sesame Groove) is
the crux. Warthogs are useful for the frozen turf on pitch three. A
vegetated Difficult in summer (1940). Start at the foot of Grassy
Traverse.

1 and 2. 60m   Follow North Wall Groove for two pitches to belay at the large flake.
3. 40m   Traverse up and right across turf and snowy slabs to a belay below a blocky arete (the final pitch of Nimlin's Direct Route, and a line followed by many winter routes hereabouts).
4. 40m   Right of the arete, short cracks, corners and large ledges lead to the top.
Original Finish: 40m   III   (1961)
From the belay, traverse ledges rightwards, then go up a right-slanting crack to arrive at the block at the top of Original Route. A good escape route in an impressive position.

Right of the start of Grassy Traverse, and below the upper terrace climbed by North Wall Traverse, an area of slabby turfy rock leads up and right to the prominent corner of Gibber Crack. Further right and higher up the slope is a short deep chimney at the base of a blunt arete, taken in its lower section by Slack's Route and higher up by Nimlin's Direct Route.

30   Viva Glasvegas   110m   VIII,7 *   (1996)
A serious, technical route on compact rock with poor protection. Start below the prominent corner of Gibber Crack.
1. 10m   Climb easily up the snowy groove (Gibber Crack) to a belay on the right.
2. 30m   From the base of the corner of Gibber Crack, follow the thin crack diagonally left across the wall to a turf ledge (drive-ins for protection). Climb the wall and make a rockover move up right to reach holds leading to a thin hanging corner. Follow this to a belay.
3. 30m   Climb up and step left, then out round a short corner to reach North Wall Traverse. Follow this to below the final arete.
4. 40m   Finish up the arete or out right as for North Wall Traverse.

31   Gibber Crack   110m   VS   (1989)
The prominent corner offers a good central pitch.
1. 10m   Climb the grassy groove to a ledge on the right.
2. 20m 5a   Climb the corner until a crack can be gained on the right wall. Follow the steepening crack until it is possible to traverse right and go up into a short corner. Belay above at a crack on the left.
3. 40m   Follow easy ground above to a chimney-crack, then continue up the wall on the right and ascend more easy ground to a belay below the final arete of Nimlin's Direct Route.

4. 40m Keeping right of the arete, short cracks, corners and large ledges lead to the top.
Winter: 110m VI,7 ** (1990)
Follow the summer line. The second pitch gives sustained and technical climbing, quite bold at first but with excellent protection once the crack is gained. The traverse right below the block at the top of the crack is very delicate.

32 Slack's Route 105m Hard Severe * (1947)
This route climbs the lower section of the arete formed by the North-East and North-West faces to join Nimlin's Direct Route higher up. Start below the arete forming the left side of the short deep chimney.
1. 20m Climb the arete to a ledge and block belay.
2. 15m 4b Go up and right across a steep wall on small holds and make an awkward move round an edge. Continue up and left with difficulty to a stance and belay.
3. 30m Follow a series of parallel cracks straight above to a belay below the final arete of Nimlin's Direct Route.
4. 40m Follow Nimlin's Direct Route to the summit.

33 Nimlin's Direct Route 75m Very Difficult * (1933)
Good situations, but a lack of traffic means the rock is loose and a bit dirty. Start up and right of the short deep chimney, near the left edge of the North-West Face.
1. 35m Small holds lead up and left across the wall to the arete. Follow the arete and easy ground to belay below the final arete.
2. 40m To the right of the arete, cracks, corners and ledges gain the summit.
Variation Start: 25m
Start about 30m up from the chimney and follow a large sloping ledge leading out left to the arete. Follow this and easy ground to belay below the final arete. The wall above the traverse has been climbed at Severe.
Winter: 65m IV,5 (1995)
Follow the summer route *via* the Variation Start.

At Map Ref 256 054, at approximately 600m altitude on the south-west flank of The Cobbler and overlooking Glen Croe, is a curious pinnacle with one route. It is best approached by descending south-west from Centre Peak. Head down towards the junction of two forest roads which can be seen across Glen Croe below The Brack. When an area of flat ground is reached, turn left to find the pinnacle.

The Lost Pinnacle   20m   VS 4b *   (1989)
Start at a narrow cave and gain a ledge by an awkward right traverse across a slab. Continue up an arete, keeping on its right side.

CENTRE PEAK

The highest of The Cobbler's three peaks is a rather sprawling affair. Its pleasant south ridge (The Arete) leads to a impressive rocky pinnacle forming the summit. Further right, the more extensive east face overlooks the main corrie and is a rambling mass of grass and rock cut through by a number of gullies. Closer to the North Peak, this turns into the more impressive Centre Peak Buttress.

    Descent from the summit pinnacle is by reversing Doorway Route.

34   **The Arete**   60m   Difficult **   (1889)
The south ridge of Centre Peak provides a pleasant continuation to the South-East Ridge of South Peak. Begin at the col between the South and Centre Peaks, climb a 15m crack and follow the arete to the summit with good situations and rapidly polishing holds.
Winter: 60m   III *
Follow the summer route. Easier variations exist to the right of the harder sections. Descend Doorway Route with care.

35   **MacGregor's Ledge**   15m   Very Difficult   (1895)
A short strenuous problem up the north side of the summit pinnacle, made more interesting by the possibility of impending doom below. Start just left of Doorway Route and make a difficult mantelshelf onto a ledge. Go left to the south 'doorway', then continue to the top.

36   **Doorway Route**   15m   Moderate **
The north face of the summit pinnacle is cut through by a 'doorway' in the rock. Squeeze through this to the south side and follow an exposed ledge from where a high step gains the top. Return by going out through the in door.
Winter: 15m   II
Care should be taken to adequately protect the second when reversing back to the col.

CENTRE PEAK BUTTRESS

The north-east flank of Centre Peak contains a large broken buttress, whose steep northern aspect faces North Peak and overlooks the confined gully that drops from the col dividing the Centre and North Peaks. The routes are described from right to left as approached descending the gully from the col.

37   Chimney Route   70m   V,7 **   (1994)
Good climbing with a short but technical crux in the obvious corner system above and right of the cave-like recess about 25m down the gully. The route is shaded from the stripping action of the sun. Start right of the recess where turfy ledges can be reached from the gully. Very Difficult in summer (1947).
1. 10m   Follow turf up and left to belay at the base of the first corner.
2. 20m   Climb the short technical corner to a large ledge. The corner above gives easier climbing to another ledge.
3. 15m   Ascend to a higher grass ledge, traverse it right, then step down to belay below a chimney.
4. 25m   Climb the chimney and walls above, taking a large jutting block on the left.

38   Lobby Dosser   90m   HVS   (1980)
Probably unrepeated. Start below the cave-like recess about 40m down the gully. Climb up to the main overhanging face and go up right of a small buttress. Swing out right onto the face and climb a crack to a belay. Climb the two cracks and corners above to belay at a large block. Climb directly above, keeping left of a hollow to climb an overhang, then traverse left and go up a groove to finish.

39   Cave Route   130m   III,4 **
Good scenery and a sensationally exposed last pitch. Descend the gully past an obvious snow traverse leading right, to a ramp-like groove near the lowest part of the buttress. The route is Difficult in summer (1898).
1. 40m   Deep snow in the gully allows direct access to the groove which leads to the base of a deep gully. If the gully is insufficiently banked out, the snow traverse higher up is easier (30m).
2 and 3. 65m   Follow the narrow gully to exit on the right at the top. A steeper section at 25m gains the open groove above and a belay in a cave.
4. 25m   Traverse delicately right round a bulge to regain the chimney and follow it to a second cave. A window at the top offers an exit (the slimmer's exit), but most will avoid it by an awkward exit right to finish up the chimney.

THE COBBLER

South Peak   Centre Peak   Centre Peak Buttress   North Peak

15 South-East Ridge
22 Grassy Traverse
29 North Wall Traverse
31 Gibber Crack
34 The Arete
37 Chimney Route

39 Cave Route
40 Drugs are for Mugs
41 Centre Gully
GG Great Gully
Ch G Chockstone Gully
A Sugar Walls

40   Drugs are for Mugs   100m   V,6   (1996)
Start below a steep turfy groove about 10m up and right from the toe of
the buttress.
1. 40m   Gain the groove and quit it for the left rib after 5m. Climb up
until it is poossible to move right into a steep corner crack formed by a
large pinnacle. Climb this and the groove above to reach easy ground
and a belay on the right-facing wall.
2 and 3. 60m   The climbing is now much easier. Climb the small
buttress above by a short crack on its left side past a chockstone. This
leads to easy snow and the top slabby buttress; climb this by a system
of pleasant turfy grooves to the right of a vague chimney line.

41   Centre Gully   70m   II
This steep narrow gully lies at the left end of Centre Peak Buttress and
gives a pleasant route whose grade can range from I to III, depending
on conditions. There is sometimes a cornice.

Left of Centre Gully, the open slopes and short gullies leading to the
summit pinnacle of the Centre Peak give easy winter opportunities.

NORTH PEAK

SOUTH FACE

A wide selection of quality climbs and lots of sunshine are the only
similarities between the climbing on this peak and the slabby South
Face of South Peak.
    This South Face is neatly divided into two contrasting tiers by a
grass terrace. The upper shorter tier presents two wildly overhanging
noses of compact mica-schist which are undoubtedly the most
impressive mountain features in the Southern Highlands. Weaving
their way through this steep ground are some classic routes from
Severe to E8.
    In contrast, the larger lower tier is more broken and vegetated and
offers routes of a more traditional mountaineering nature. Over the
past few years the South Face has seen a considerable amount of
activity in winter. However, anyone contemplating winter ascents must
ensure conditions are good. Find the South Face on a cold, overcast
day after stormy weather and the routes are comparable with the best

mixed climbing anywhere in Scotland. The slightest glimmer of sun and the face will strip before your eyes.

The routes are described from left to right, starting from the col.

1   Overhanging Recess   10m   Severe   (1948)
To quote the 1989 guide: "The route is probably technically Severe, but it started out as a Difficult in the 1954 guide and the authors would feel really humbled if it were upgraded again." The current authors apparently felt similarly, but the editor has no such scruples. One suggestion for this edition was 5a! Start at the extreme left end of the terrace, just under the ridge. Climb the damp, right-slanting groove in the wall, with a bulge above.

2   Spainkiller   15m   E1 5b   (1988)
This route climbs the wall left of Chimney Arete. Start up sloping ledges, then follow the thin left-slanting crack. Traverse right and finish up a thin crack.

3   Chimney Arete   25m   VS 4b **   (1947)
The arete left of the obvious corner-chimney gives a fine route with minimal protection until mid-height. Previously graded Severe! Climb the arete, with one difficult move onto a flat hold to avoid a bulge at mid-height.

4   Right-Angled Chimney   30m   Difficult **   (1994)
Climb the obvious big open chimney to pass the roof *via* sloping polished holds on the slabby left wall.
Winter: 30m   IV,5   (1994)
A good route, if a bit short. Optimum conditions are essential as there is little turf and the route is already showing signs of severe crampon scratching.

5   Cat Crawl   40m   VS **   (1936)
Start immediately right of Right-angled Chimney, below an obvious fault running up and right into a grassy groove.
1. 20m 4b   Gain the fault, traverse right and climb the groove above to belay on a spike below the bulge and the upper crack.
2. 20m 4b   Bridge over the bulge, then traverse left across the lip of the overhang to a crack. Continue to the top, or traverse back right into the upper crack of Direct Direct.

6 Direct Direct 30m HVS * (1948)

An overhanging technical start leads to a steep off-width. Right of Right-angled Chimney and opposite a large boulder is a recess with a bulging left rib.

1. 20m 5a Climb the crack in the bulging rib to a good hold. Continue up into the turfy groove and follow it to the spike belay of Cat Crawl below the bulge.

2. 10m 4b Bridge over the bulge and follow up the steep off-width crack to finish.

Winter: VII,9 * (1995)

The most technical winter route on the mountain gives a big tick, however acceptable conditions for a valid ascent are rare. A strenuous start leads to a desperate move to gain the turfy groove above, which is bold but relatively straightforward. The off-width crack on the top pitch requires large Friends or Hexes and is very tenuous.

7 Wild at Heart 60m E6 *** (1993)

An exposed top pitch up the impressive flying arete forming the left edge of the overhanging wall above the traverse on Punster's Crack. Start as for Direct Direct.

1. 25m 5c Follow Direct Direct to a point level with a roof on the right at 12m. Arrange protection, step down 3m, then ascend diagonally right across the wall to better holds. Continue to the roof and follow this rightwards to the block belay on Punster's Crack.

2. 35m 6b Follow Wild Country to the ledge. Committing moves left off the ledge, with a long reach to the first peg, lead to difficult reachy moves going slightly leftwards past a number of pegs to good finishing holds near the arete.

8 Wild Country 50m E6 *** (1979)

The original route on this wildly overhanging wall gives bold and powerful climbing. Despite repeats it still awaits an on sight ascent. Start in the recess of Direct Direct.

1. 20m 5c Climb the strenuous overhanging crack on the right, then go up to the block belay on Punster's Crack.

2. 30m 6b Climb leftwards up the wall, then continue up the quartz-blotched wall to a ledge (runners in a thin crack on the right). Ascend overhung ledges rightwards and where they peter out, step up and then right to a good hold at the foot of a thin overhanging crack. Climb the crack (Friend 1½ at the top) heading for a small but good sidepull on the left, before reaching a recess below the top. Good flake belay well back.

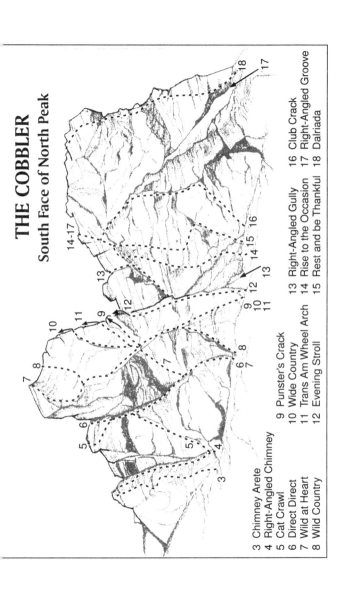

THE COBBLER
South Face of North Peak

3 Chimney Arete
4 Right-Angled Chimney
5 Cat Crawl
6 Direct Direct
7 Wild at Heart
8 Wild Country

9 Punster's Crack
10 Wide Country
11 Trans Am Wheel Arch
12 Evening Stroll

13 Right-Angled Gully
14 Rise to the Occasion
15 Rest and be Thankful

16 Club Crack
17 Right-Angled Groove
18 Dalriada

9   Punster's Crack   45m   Severe ***   (1949)
An excellent route taking the easiest line through some impressive
scenery. Start below a slabby wall leading to a short corner which is
right of the recess of Direct Direct and just left of a deep chimney to the
left of Right-Angled Gully.
1. 20m 4a   Climb the wall and corner, then continue up and left to a
large block belay below the overhanging wall.
2. 15m 4a   Traverse up and right, passing below the wide crack taken
by Wide Country, to an obvious gap. Bridge the gap and continue more
easily to a belay at the right end of the ledge beside Right-Angled Gully.
3. 10m 4a   Step left and follow cracks up the slabby wall in a fine
position. Good flake belay well back.
Winter: 45m   VII,8   (1993)
An impressive technical achievement. Follow the summer route , the
crux being the top slab.

10   Wide Country   50m   E5 6b ***   (1994)
The striking off-width in the headwall above Punster's Crack gives a
memorable experience; tape and large camming devices de rigeur.
The first pitch of Punster's Crack leads to the off-width. Climb this with
increasing difficulty to a semi-rest in a niche. From its top, swing right in
a spectacular position to finish up the easier slab. Good flake belay
well back.

11   Trans Am Wheel Arch Nostrils   40m   E4 6a *   (1994)
The shallow groove right of Wide Country. Start up the first corner of
Punster's Crack, then go straight up the wide crack to just before the
step around on the second pitch on Punster's Crack. Step right and
boldly climb the innocuous-looking overhanging shallow groove in the
headwall to a difficult pull over onto the upper slab of Punster's Crack.
Finish up the left-hand edge of the slab as for Evening Stroll.

12   Evening Stroll   40m   E2   (1979)
Serious and a bit contrived, this route follows the curving right edge of
the buttress. Start at the arete immediately left of Right-Angled Gully.
1. 20m 5c   Climb the arete, then step right into the gully (runner).
Return to the arete and climb it on fragile holds to a stance and good
belays in a horizontal crack.
2. 20m 4c   Follow Punster's Crack up and left to a crack, then take the
line of the left-curving overlap, finishing up the left-hand edge of the
slab. Good flake belay well back.

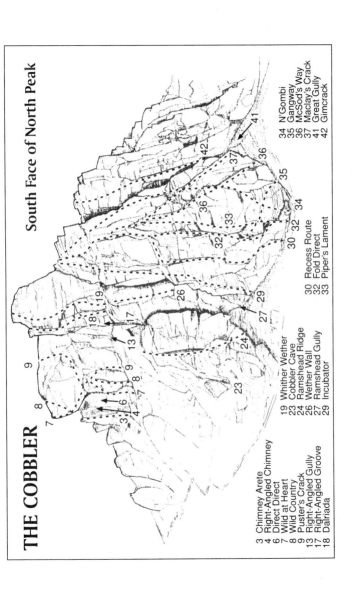

THE COBBLER

South Face of North Peak

3 Chimney Arete
4 Right-Angled Chimney
6 Direct Direct
7 Wild at Heart
8 Wild Country
9 Puster's Crack
13 Right-Angled Gully
17 Right-Angled Groove
18 Dalriada

19 Whither Wether
23 Cobbler Cave
24 Ramshead Ridge
26 Wether Wall
27 Ramshead Gully
29 Incubator

30 Recess Route
32 Fold Direct
33 Piper's Lament

34 N'Gombi
35 Gangway
36 McSod's Way
37 Maclay's Crack
41 Great Gully
42 Gimcrack

To the right of the wildly overhanging wall is the large open corner of Right-Angled Gully. Right of that is an impressive steep wall with a prominent groove to the left of centre. Left of the groove is a thin crack, Rise to the Occasion, while the groove and upper wall are taken by Rest and Be Thankful. The prominent jagged crack right of the groove is Club Crack, while Dalriada climbs the edge of the prow forming the wall's right arete.

13   Right-Angled Gully   35m   Very Difficult *   (1896)
Pleasant climbing, although the holds are becoming increasingly polished. The second pitch requires a forceful approach!
1. 30m   Climb the corner on slabby holds to where it narrows and steepens. Gain the terrace on the right and traverse it to belay at a short undercut corner.
2. 5m   Finish up the corner.
Direct Finish: 10m   Severe   (1930)
Instead of traversing right to the terrace, climb straight up the V-shaped groove above.
Winter: IV,5 *   (1896)
The start is steeper than it looks and the finishing corner is amusing with axe and crampons! Both this and the Direct Finish are best combined with Ramshead Ridge on the lower tier.
Direct Finish Winter: V,6 *   (1990)
An excellent pitch of back and footing up the V-shaped groove.

14   Rise to the Occasion   30m   E5 6a *   (1989)
Climb the thin crack in the wall right of Right-Angled Gully to exit with difficulty onto the wall above. Continue directly *via* breaks, passing through a bulge and continue to the top.

15   Rest and be Thankful   45m   E5 ***   (1980)
A classic Cobbler wall climb. Start at the foot of the obvious groove, often wet at the top, in the left-hand side of the wall.
1. 35m 6a   Follow the groove to its top, traverse left then step down and left to good holds. Traverse about 3 metres left, go up to a good foothold, then move up and right to a horizontal break. Continue up and left to a ledge. Climb the wall, then move easily right to a thread belay.
2. 10m 4c   Climb the wall above at its highest point.
Variation: E5 6b   (1987)
Climb diagonally up and left from the top of the initial groove.

16 Club Crack   40m   E2 ***   (1957)
Sustained, strenuous and technical with fiddly protection; only the
fittest will gain membership. Start below and left of the steep crack
springing from the cave. A direct start is also possible through the roof
above the cave at 5b.
1. 35m 5c   Traverse awkwardly right to gain the crack and climb it
past a wilting rusty peg and a good spike runner disturbingly far out
right. A difficult move where the crack closes brings better holds,
protection and respite. A final steep wall leads to the terrace.
2. 10m 4c   Climb the wall behind at its highest point.

   The next three routes start from a higher grass ledge on the right,
gained by overcoming a short steep step. It can also be gained by
squeezing through a fissure in the cave below Club Crack.

17 Right-Angled Groove   50m   VS *   (1934)
The slabby open corner gives a pleasant exposed climb. Moonlight
Arete, described later, starts on the lower tier and finishes up the left
edge of the corner.
1. 40m 4c   Follow the crack in the corner over an awkward bulge and
continue until a delicate traverse left at about 30m leads to easier
ground and a belay on the terrace as for Right-Angled Gully.
2. 5m   Finish up the corner.
Winter: 35m   V,7 *   (1996)
Good climbing, although rarely in acceptable condition. Ramshead
Ridge and Ramshead Gully on the lower tier offer excellent starts.

18 Dalriada   40m   E8 6c ***   (1995)
An awe-inspiring line up the superb jutting prow right of Right-
Angled Groove. It is sustained and technical with a powerful crux.
The route was redpointed, so the E8 grade is speculative until an on
sight ascent takes place. Start as for Right-Angled Groove. Climb
the groove for 3m to a ledge, then climb the flake crack above to two
peg runners. Move right round the arete and go up to a superb
thread. Climb straight up the thin finger crack and the arete past a
poor peg to a good rest under the roof. Very hard moves out left and
up lead to the prominent diagonal crack and a line of incut jugs
which lead past more pegs to the capping wall. Continue with
interest past two small finger pockets to pull out right to a ledge,
then move up to a belay.

The frontal face of the overhanging prow is **Baillie's Overhang,** A3 (1967). An on sight attempt to free climb it produced a route which goes out right on good holds from above the first roof, to join Whither Wether, at E2 5b (1989).

19   Whither Wether   45m   VS 4b ***   (1952)
One of the finest VS pitches in Scotland, this outstanding route takes a tremendous exposed line up the right side of the jutting prow, with a minimum of protection. It is best combined by starting up the excellent Wether Wall on the lower tier. Start on the grass ledge just right of Right-Angled Groove. Climb the steep wall up and right past an old bolt, then move round the edge on to the slabby wall. Climb the wall, keeping close to the left edge (crux) to gain the right side of a niche at 25m. Finish by going slightly right and up, or step left and climb the edge to the top.

The next three routes lie on the wall right of Whither Wether and overlooking the top of Ramshead Gully. They are normally climbed as a finish to Recess Route or adjacent climbs, but they can also be accessed from the grass ledge below Whither Wether, or by descending Ramshead Gully.

20   Grey Wall   35m   Hard Severe 4b *   (1952)
Good balancy climbing with a pronounced sense of exposure. Start about 10m down and left of the very top of Ramshead Gully. Climb up and slightly right for 10m, then go straight up the wall on small holds.

21   Telepathy Crack   25m   Severe   (1952)
Start near the top of Ramshead Gully on a grass ledge below an ill-defined crack, midway between Grey Wall and Ramshead Wall. Climb the crack and continue up the gradually easing wall.

22   Ramshead Wall   15m   Difficult   (1934)
This is the short wall with quartz at the top, right of the very top of Ramshead Gully.
Winter: 15m   III   (1995)
Follow the summer line.

Below these climbs is the generally more broken and vegetated lower tier. The tier is divided into two sections by the deep cleft of

Ramshead Gully. The first excursion starts at the base of the left-hand section, which is climbed by Ramshead Ridge.

23   Cobbler Cave   55m   Very Difficult   (1940)
A subterranean journey into the bowels of The Cobbler; headtorch, rope and troglodyte tendencies desirable. As an alternative to a railway on Cairn Gorm, the Highlands and Islands Enterprise Board have considered installing electric light and opening it as a show cave. Start at an opening in the ground at the left side of Ramshead Ridge, just off the approach path.
   Descend about 10m to the floor of a huge cave, from where a crawl inwards, then a sloping slab leads to a lower storey. (This can also be reached by an incline to the left). In the centre of the floor of this second storey, a vertical shaft drops to the basement from where there is no exit; try not to fall down it! Instead, follow a tortuous passage which winds inwards, narrows, then slopes down to a huge inner cavern. It is possible to ascend its far wall and continue a short distance to where the shaft narrows. The distance from the shaft inwards is about 45m.

24   Ramshead Ridge   45m   Difficult
This is the ill-defined ridge left of Ramshead Gully. Start at a rocky corner overlooking the grassy lower section of the gully on the right, and some distance above the very lowest rocks. Once on the ridge, various lines can be followed to the terrace.
Winter: 45m   IV,5 **   (1990)
An excellently positioned route which is short but good. Gain the ridge *via* a cave on the left and climb a wide crack up the crest to a steep corner. It is best combined by finishing up Right-Angled Gully or Groove.

   To the right is an obvious steep gully, Ramshead Gully. The following two climbs are on the left wall of the gully and start with a scramble up the easy initial section of the gully to where it steepens.

25   Moonlight Arete   80m   E2   (1980)
Necky climbing up the wall's left arete.
1. 40m 5c   Climb the obvious groove in the arete to finish on the grass ledge below Right-Angled Groove.
2. 40m 5a   Climb the left arete of that route. At one point some moves have to be made up the left wall.

26   Wether Wall   40m   VS 4c **   (1951)
A very good pitch, making a very fine excursion when combined with
Whither Wether. Step left onto the wall, move up and continue to an
obvious left-pointing flake. Pull over this and climb the groove above to
belay at the foot of Whither Wether.

27   Ramshead Gully   60m   IV,5 **
When in condition, the obvious gully right of Ramshead Ridge gives a
surprisingly good route. In summer it is Very Difficult (1936).

The following route climbs the obvious slanting crack in the wall right
of and overlooking Ramshead Gully. It can be gained by scrambling up
Ramshead Gully to the Halfway Terrace. This is the ledge that crosses
the face rightwards to below the upper chimney of Recess Route.

28   Echo Crack   40m   Hard Severe 4b   (1949)
Near the left end of Halfway Terrace is a right-angled corner with two
cracks. Climb the right-hand crack for 5m, then make awkward moves
left into a niche. Continue up and left almost into Ramshead Gully to a
point below a steep corner crack in the right wall. Pull up and follow the
crack to the top.

29   Incubator   80m   Hard Severe **   (1948)
Good climbing up the walls below and right of Ramshead Gully,
followed by the corner partially climbed by Echo Crack at the left end of
the Halfway Terrace. Start about 10 metres left of Recess Route.
1. 30m 4b   Follow a broken series of walls and ledges almost directly
to a belay below a steep wall.
2. 10m 4b   Step onto the wall and climb a crack through a bulge.
Continue up and left in a corner to the gain Halfway Terrace.
3. 40m 4b   At the left end of the Terrace is a right-angled corner with
two cracks. Climb the right-hand crack for 10m to a curious spike,
move right to grass ledges and finish by a short steep crack above.
Winter: 100m   VI,7 *   (1990)
Good climbing with a steep technical crux up the corner above the
Halfway Terrace. Start below the alternative winter start to Recess
Route, left of the cracked slab.
1. 50m   Gain the flake crack left of the top of the slab and follow it to
ledges below the bulging crack of the summer line. Move left up ledges
and make a stretchy pull over a short wall. Continue to the Halfway
Terrace.

2. 30m   Climb the obvious corner and move right as for the summer route. Go up a short way, then move around left and go up to a large ledge.
3. 25m   Finish up rightwards to easy ground.

30   Recess Route   85m   Severe **   (1935)
One of The Cobbler's best known climbs, Recess Route has a distinct mountaineering ambience and is deservedly popular. Some of the holds are very polished, and care should be taken in damp conditions. Start at the prominent cracked slab, just left of the large overhung recess of Fold Direct.
1. 20m   Climb the slab to where it steepens, then go up and right to climb a wide curving crack to a belay below a deep chimney.
2. 25m   Climb the chimney passing an overhang and continue by the deep chimney above to the Halfway Terrace.
3. 5m   Traverse easily right along the terrace to a belay.
4. 10m   From the right-hand end of the terrace step into and ascend the steep groove, The Fold (crux), utilising small holds on the left wall, and belay in a cave.
5. 25m   Climb round the overhang above on either side and finish by a final chimney.
Winter: V,6 ***
When in condition, this is one of the finest mixed routes at the grade in the Southern Highlands. If not banked out, the summer start is perhaps a technical grade harder. Alternatively, start up a short groove to the left.

31   Northern Heatwave   35m   HVS 4c *   (1989)
This route starts from the Halfway Terrace, between Incubator and The Fold pitch of Recess Route. Start left of The Fold at a shallow corner. Climb the corner to a niche, then continue up the rib on the right to a ledge. Finish up a short corner.

32   Fold Direct   85m   VS *   (1936)
About 10 metres right of Recess Route is a steep corner capped by a large overhang.
1. 25m 4b   Follow the corner to avoid the overhang on the left and continue to a ledge below a steep scooped chimney.
2. 15m 4c   Climb the scoop to the base of a chimney and belay.
3. 20m   Climb the chimney to the Halfway Terrace, then continue up the steep groove above, The Fold, utilising small holds on the left wall and belay in a cave.

4. 25m Climb round the overhang above on either side and finish by a final chimney.
Winter: 85m V,7 * (1990)
Left of the main corner of the summer line, a boulder problem start up a short steep recess-corner leads up and right to the base of the scooped chimney. Enter the scoop with difficulty and continue *via* the summer line.

33 Piper's Lament 80m E3 (1988)

A spooky route, low in the grade, but with a badly protected first pitch. Start as for Fold Direct.
1. 15m 5b Follow Fold Direct to below the overhang. Break out right into a shallow corner, climb this directly and pull onto the slab of Gangway and a belay.
2. 20m 5b Climb the crack above to below the large roof, traverse left and pull round its left end in a fine position. Continue above to belay at a quartz patch.
3. 45m 4b Climb the arete and short walls to the top.

34 N'Gombi 90m VS (1952)

A good first pitch, but the rest of the route fails to deliver. Start 5 metres right of the corner of Fold Direct at the foot of a shallow corner crack.
1. 25m 4c Climb the corner over a small bulge and continue up to a sloping ledge. Traverse right to below a small overhung corner and make a difficult move right to gain a good ledge on the arete.
2. 20m Continue round the corner, cross below a short chimney and exit right, then move up to join Maclay's Crack.
3. 45m Finish up Maclay's Crack left branch.
Direct Finish: VS
Above the initial corner is an obvious large niche. Traverse left from the ledge at the end of pitch 2 and climb the niche to a difficult exit.
Winter: 105m VI,8 * (1991)
Tenuous and technical.
1. 30m Follow the summer line to the ledge on the arete, then climb up and left to a corner and belay at a short chimney-niche.
2. 35m Move out right and go up a turfy wall to a large ledge. Climb an easy chimney (Maclay's Crack right branch) to a platform overlooking Great Gully.
3. 40m Move up left, then climb turfy ledges until it is possible to traverse left to easier ground.

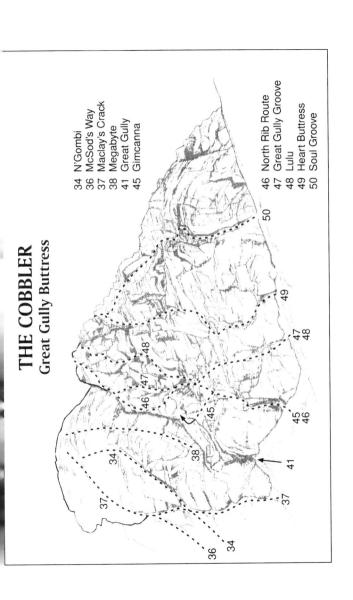

THE COBBLER
Great Gully Buttress

34 N'Gombi
36 McSod's Way
37 Maclay's Crack
38 Megabyte
41 Great Gully
45 Gimcanna

46 North Rib Route
47 Great Gully Groove
48 Lulu
49 Heart Buttress
50 Soul Groove

35   Gangway   90m   VS
An interesting pitch which leads into Fold Direct. Start about 10 metres right of N'Gombi at a large corner with a fine crack.
1. 30m 4b   Climb the crack to below where N'Gombi goes right, and traverse up and left along the sloping ledge. Make an awkward move round the edge to enter a grassy groove and follow it to below the chimney of Fold Direct. 2., 3 and 4. 60m   The remainder of the climb follows Fold Direct (see above).

36   McSod's Way   80m   IV,5 * (1991)
The turfy line parallel to and below Maclay's Crack. Start midway between that route and Gangway.
1. 20m   Turfy steps lead to the cave-like recess on N'Gombi. Pull out left onto ledge and move up to a belay.
2. 20m   Continue in the same line, moving left to a ledge on the arete. Move right into Maclay's Crack and go up to a small ledge overlooking Fold Direct.
3. 40m   A short right-angled corner leads to a wider ledge. Follow this for about 5m to finish up a shallow groove in the wall above.

37   Maclay's Crack   70m   III,4 **
An excellent route, and the best hereabouts at the grade. The recessed nature of the route means that it is often in condition. Start at an obvious turfy corner, just around right from Gangway and within the lower left reaches of Great Gully. In summer the route is Difficult (1895).
1. 20m   Climb the turfy corner.
2. 10m   Continue up the left branch to a small ledge overlooking Fold Direct.
3. 40m   A short right-angled corner leads to a wider ledge. Follow this for about 5m to finish up a shallow groove in the wall above.

The following three routes lie on the left wall of the deep gully, Great Gully. The wall is scrappy and unattractive in summer, but offers one excellent route in winter. Its sheltered position means it is less prone to stripping than other routes on the North Peak.

Opposite: Dalriada, North Peak of The Cobbler (Climber, Gary Latter)

Next Page: A Crack in the Clouds, North Peak of The Cobbler
(Climber, Paul Thorburn)

38   **Megabyte**   55m   VI,6 **   (1996)

Sustained and technical. Scramble up Great Gully to below twin cracks in the left wall.

1. 25m   Climb the crack line, initially well protected, to a bold section in the middle where the crack becomes incipient. Move up to a turfy crack, better gear and a belay on the terrace.

2. 30m   Climb the blunt arete directly above to the top.

39   **Great Gully Wall**   30m   Severe   (1976)

This and the following route climb the scrappy wall above the second chockstone in Great Gully. Start below Moss Crack near the top of the wall, by a pinnacle. Climb shelves, then go up a crack and a wall and traverse left to a cave (belay). Traverse right to finish.

40   **Moss Crack**   20m   Very Difficult   (1952)

Start at a grass ledge about 20m from the top of the gully. Climb a mossy groove, the overhang and an arete.

41   **Great Gully**   60m   II *

The obvious wide gully gives a pleasant route. Two rock steps form the main obstacles, although they can often bank out. In summer the route is a vegetated and scree-filled Moderate (1895).

GREAT GULLY BUTTRESS

This is the stepped and rather vegetated buttress flanking Great Gully on the right. The best rock climbing is on the wall overlooking Great Gully and the prominent rocky rib flanking it on the right, which gives the line of North Rib Route. A number of interesting winter lines have been added in recent years and the turfy shaded nature of the buttress means it retains snow well.

The first four routes take lines on the wall overlooking Great Gully. Start by scrambling up the gully to above the lower chockstone.

Previous page: North Rib on the North Peak of The Cobbler
(Climber, Rab Anderson)

Opposite: Megabyte on the North Peak of The Cobbler
(Climber, Robin McAllister)

42 Gimcrack 50m VS   (1952)
Start below the obvious V-corner in the right wall of Great Gully.
1. 30m 4c   Climb the wall on the left to a ledge below the corner, then
follow it to a good stance and belay.
2. 20m 4b   Go slightly up then left along a ledge for 5m to below a
steep crack. Climb the crack, going over a small overhang on the right.
Continue easily to the top.

43 The Mog 30m VS 4c *   (1986)
Some 2 metres right of Gimcrack is the bulging rib climbed by Spinal
Rib. This route climbs the ramp-gangway between the two routes,
leading to an overhang. Climb the overhang.

44 Spinal Rib 30m VS 4b **   (1952)
A steep, sustained and well protected route with amazing exposure.
Start below the undercut rib just right of Gimcrack. Pull up onto the rib
and climb it over several bulges to a resting spot under the final
overhang. Climb this to the right (strenuous) or the left (technical) to
join North Rib Route. Go a short way up to belay below a short wall.

45 Gimcanna 105m V,7 *   (1994)
Good climbing based on the summer line of Gimcrack. The second
pitch is technical and strenuous, but well protected. Start as for North
Rib Route, about 5 metres right of the base of Great Gully at a steep
shallow recess.
1. 35m   Climb the recess and the groove on the right to easy ground.
Move left into Great Gully and go up a short way to beneath the
obvious V-corner.
2. 30m   Climb the corner to a ledge, possible belay, then take the
bulging crack to a spacious ledge.
3. 40m   Continue straight up to a short groove at the back of a huge
block and finish up a shallow fault.

46 North Rib Route 90m Very Difficult **   (1935)
A traditional mountaineering route with good rock and situations up the
short steep walls on the rib bounding the right side of Great Gully. Start
about 5 metres right of the gully at a steep shallow recess. Gain the rib
and cross grass to belay in a corner. Surmount a block, then traverse
left for a few metres to the rib which leads to the top.

Winter: 90m V,7 ** (1994)
Good climbing with an awkward crux.
1. 15m Climb the recess and a groove on the right to easy ground and a ledge; belay on the right.
2. 35m Move up and left into a square-cut recess to gain the base of the obvious groove. Pull up the groove to stand on the block and traverse round left, then go up awkwardly to reach the edge overlooking Great Gully. Climb straight up to slabby ground and a belay.
3. 40m Move back right, climb a short step *via* a nose, then go right and follow a steep crack up the right side of the huge block to finish up a shallow fault.

47 Great Gully Groove 95m IV,6 * (1994)
This is the obvious groove immediately to the right of North Rib Route. Start some 10 metres right of that route, up and right of the lowest rocks.
1. 20m Climb a short step into a shallow bay and continue up and slightly left to belay as for North Rib Route.
2. 35m Enter the bay and climb the groove on the left. Near the top of the groove swing out left around a roof with a chockstone and continue up a crack to a ledge.
3. 40m Continue as for North Rib Route or move left and finish as for Gimcanna.

48 Lulu 95m IV,6 * (1994)
This route follows the groove just to the right of Great Gully Groove. The hard final pitch can be avoided by the short crack of North Rib Route, up and left from the belay. This reduces the grade, but maintains a standard consistent with the lower pitches. Start as for Great Gully Groove.
1. 20m Climb a short step into a shallow bay and continue up and slightly left to belay as for North Rib Route.
2. 35m Enter the bay above as for the previous two routes, then pull out right and climb a shallow groove to belay beneath a short corner.
3. 40m Climb the corner, swing out right beneath the capping block and gain the ledge. The crack on the left is taken by the other routes hereabouts. Instead, climb the blunt arete to the top.

49   Heart Buttress   100m   III *   (1987)
Start just right of Great Gully Groove and follow turf to a large ledge.
Frozen turf, short walls and grooves lead sinuously up, out right and up
to a final short gully. Exit out right to finish on a prow just right of Great
Gully.

50   Soul Groove   100m   III   (1991)
Just left of some large boulders on the right side of the buttress, a
prominent groove leads to easier ground. Climb the groove, then move
right up easy ground to a further groove. Climb this and a short wall,
then continue up easy ground on the left to finish right of the final
chimney of Heart Buttress.

CHOCKSTONE BUTTRESS

Directly below Great Gully is an extensive buttress split through by the
line of Chockstone Gully. Leave the last steep section of the approach
path at about one-third height and traverse easy ledges going right
and up for about 200m.

Chockstone Gully   100m   II   (1983)
Two or three pitches lead to an impressive arch formed by a giant
chockstone. Exit by a narrow squeeze on the left or *via* a thin slab on
the right to finish below Great Gully. This route gives a good scramble
through interesting rock scenery when combined with Great Gully. It is
entertaining, but the low altitude means it isn't always in condition.

A Crack in the Clouds   20m   E3 6a ***   (1995)
A tremendous route up the prominent crack line in the north-facing wall
of Chockstone Gully; not to be missed. Approach from above by cutting
down diagonally left, then back right. Belay on a slab behind the route.
From cleaned ledges, gain the niche left of the crack *via* a large roof.
Pull into the crack and follow it with difficulty to the top. Belay well back.

NORTH BUTTRESS

Directly north of North Peak lies a steep buttress split by a large crack
and groove system (unclimbed!). This route lies below and to the left.
Approach by going over North Peak and descending the gully, North
Gully, on the right.

North Winds   30m   E3 6a *   (1995)
Start at a flake below the left edge of the buttress, climb a shallow
groove to a small overlap, step right and climb a wall to good breaks.
Move left to the arete and finish easily above.

North Gully   50m   I
The narrow gully flanking North Buttress on the right provides pleasant
climbing.

In winter the large rambling buttress right of North Gully readily
comes into condition and contains some entertaining routes, most of
which have interchangeable pitches.

THE SUGAR WALLS

About halfway up the approach path below the South Face of the North
Peak is a steep section of scrambling in an ill-defined gully. The first
route described below lies on the leftmost of two slabby walls just
before this steep rocky scramble.

Gearless   20m   Severe *   (1992)
Start a couple of metres left of the central green gully. Climb the slab
direct past a quartz flake at half-height.

Overlooking and to the right of the steep rocky scramble is a pale
wall with a prominent arete and corner.

Straight Flush   15m   E2 5b **   (1987)
Climb the arete by its right flank. There is little protection in the upper
section.

Lumpy Custard   15m   E1 5b **   (1995)
Climb the centre of the wall, starting below a small flake and finishing
at a small notch.

Comical Corner   25m   Severe *   (1987)
Climb the obvious corner to the right of the quartz-blocked wall. Exit
left.

THE BRACK

787m   (Map Ref 245 031)

Massive, dank and sun-starved, the Upper Buttress of the Brack is the antithesis of The Cobbler's sunny South Peak, which faces it across Glen Croe. And yet, in Edge of Extinction, The Brack contains one of the finest hard mountain Extremes in Scotland. During the summer months this impressive arete of compact mica-schist is spectacularly profiled by the morning sun. Of the rest of the crag, only the left-hand section receives much sun. Not surprisingly, seepage, vegetation and tough, north face lichen mean The Brack is not a popular climbing venue. However, for those with a traditional and adventurous frame of mind, seeking routes with atmosphere by the bucket load and willing to play the waiting game, The Brack will provide a memorable experience. In winter the crag comes into its own, although its lowly altitude means that as in summer, routes have to be grabbed when the opportunity arises. Great Central Groove is certainly one of the best Grade V routes in the Arrochar area, with a big mountain feel.

Park at the large lay-by below The Brack, at Map Ref 258 042 on the west side of the A83 in Glen Croe. Follow the road north, cross the bridge over the river, climb over the crash barrier on the left and ascend through new forestry to the track. Turn right and continue to a hairpin bend. About 140 metres after the hairpin the track crosses a burn falling from the corrie left of the cliffs. A cairn and a white pole mark the start of a well worn path on the left side of the burn. Allow about an hour to reach the crags.

To descend from the top of the climbs, take the open gully left of the Upper Tier, cutting left (facing out) below the second rock bluff at the terrace between the Upper and Lower Tier.

LOWER TIER

This is marked at its south-east end by a split pinnacle clearly seen from the road. Right of that is a small broken crag with the larger, vegetated Inglis Clark Buttress below and right again. The low altitude means good winter conditions are rare. The routes are decribed from right to left as they are approached from below.

INGLIS CLARK BUTTRESS

This large vegetated buttress is identified by the clean cone of rock towards its left end, taken by Lilliput.

1 Hell's Teeth 150m III,3 * (1986)
Start in the first bay right of the lowest rocks. Climb mixed ground, passing a chimney on the right, then go up and left to a large block. Go behind the block to the left, then thread through interesting walls to the top.

2 The Abyss 180m IV,4 * (1986)
Start at a prominent solitary tree above the lowest rocks. Go up and right to the foot of a corner; flake belay up and right on a ledge. Climb the corner to a difficult exit, then continue more easily to belay on the open slope. Continue up and left to belay below a short wall just before the left edge of this section of buttress. Go back right a short way, gain a ledge above and climb to a corner which steepens and leads over a seemingly bottomless cavern. Bridge up a chimney to belay on the right. Climb a short steep ramp, go right, then go up and back left to a ledge and the steep wall above.

3 The Plunge 130m IV,5 * (1987)
This route starts up and left at a short steep gully flanking a large cone of clean rock on the right. The steep initial section can be climbed directly, or avoided in two pitches by traversing right and moving back left above an overhanging wall. An awkward short wall and two easy but scenic pitches in the gully lead to steep ice in a corner. The ice pitch can be avoided by a wall about 8 metres further right (V,5). Follow the right fork to finish on the terrace dividing the Upper and Lower Tiers.

The Deep Start: 110m IV * (1996)
Climb the deep chimney and corner left of the cone of clean rock and right of the Inglis Clark Arete to join the original route at the awkward short wall.

4 Lilliput 50m VS (1976)
The obvious cone of rock gives a pleasant route up the best and cleanest rock hereabouts. The cone is split by a wide vertical crack; start right of this.
1. 30m 4c   Climb up to a small overlap, go diagonally left to the fault, then climb up and left to a small ledge. Traverse right to a grass ramp and a poor stance.
2. 20m   Climb the groove above, move right to a grass ledge and finish up the right-hand arete.

Left of Lilliput lies The Deep Start to The Plunge, and left of that a vegetated ridge with a large pointed boulder below its base.

5   Inglis Clark Arete   120m   Moderate   (1895)
The vegetated ridge is taken by The Brack's earliest recorded route. Start up a crack right of a steep rib, then follow short walls and ledges on the ridge.
Winter: 120m   III *   (1973)
A much more enjoyable outing, especially if followed by January Buttress on the Upper Tier. Follow the crack and the line of least resistance up the ridge.

To the left of the ridge is a wide gully. The next buttress lies on the skyline, up the gully and well to the left.

6   Four Step Ridge   45m   Very Difficult *   (1947)
Either of the two obvious chimneys leads to an awkward chimney groove. Climb a crack to the left of a steep crack, or use the nose to gain a heathery corner and continue up the steep fold above.

7   Bobcrack   15m   Difficult   (1947)
To the left is a small buttress. Climb a chimney for 6m, then go straight up the crack on small holds.

The split pinnacle seen from the road is now easily identified on the left.

8   Gimcrack   15m   Moderate **   (1947)
The pinnacle is split by a crack. Climb the longer, right-hand side on excellent holds. Variation is possible.

9   Edge Route   15m   Moderate   (1947)
Pleasant climbing on good holds up the left edge.

UPPER TIER

The impressive rock buttresses on this tier are dominated by the large open corner of Great Central Groove in the centre, flanked on the left by the blunt arete of Edge of Extinction and on the right by the deep curving Elephant Gully. The routes are described from right to left, as approached from below.

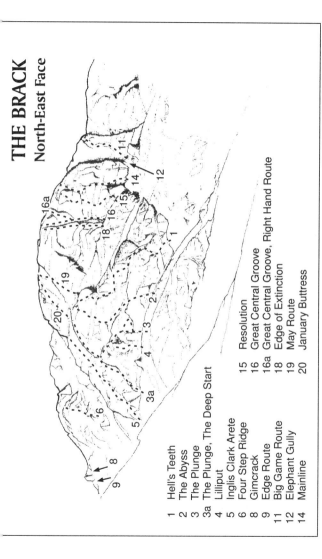

THE BRACK
North-East Face

1 Hell's Teeth
2 The Abyss
3 The Plunge
3a The Plunge, The Deep Start
4 Lilliput
5 Inglis Clark Arete
6 Four Step Ridge
8 Gimcrack
9 Edge Route
11 Big Game Route
12 Elephant Gully
14 Mainline

15 Resolution
16 Great Central Groove
16a Great Central Groove, Right Hand Route
18 Edge of Extinction
19 May Route
20 January Buttress

10   Small Fry   100m   III   (1995)

Start right and below Big Game Route. Climb gully to a chockstone and pass this with difficulty to reach a 5 metre slab and the easier gully above. The crux can be avoided to the right at Grade II.

11   Big Game Route   120m   III   (1979)

The shallow gully to the right of Elephant Gully.
1. 15m   Climb easily to a stance.
2. 30m   A short steep ice pitch on the right leads to easier ground and the foot of a steep slab.
3. 20m   Climb the slab and traverse left to a chockstone belay.
4. 55m   Easy climbing to the top.

12   Elephant Gully   90m   IV *   (1906)

The obvious deep gully in whose confines a herd of elephants could graze — hence the name. Avoid the first cave on the right. The giant chockstone is reached from the left by traversing up onto a platform, from which a delicate step right leads into a scoop and so to the top of the boulder. Either traverse left for 5 metres and climb a bulge, or go straight up and swing round the rib on the left to gain the same point. Continue until a traverse left leads back to the gully bed. Easier climbing leads to the final tunnel and an exit. If this is blocked, a strenuous exit may be found halfway up, going through a skylight. The climb is Difficult in summer, but not recommended.

13   Sideline   45m   A3   (1968)

The obvious overhanging crack in the right edge of the steep wall left of Elephant Gully has been climbed using 30 pegs. Traverse left under the roof for 10m, go up to the second roof, move back right, then go straight up to gain the crack. Follow this over a bulge into the final groove and a large ledge. Walk off right.

14   Mainline   125m   E2   (1968)

Aside from the first pitch, this is a pretty horrible-looking route up the vegetated line flanking the steep wall on the left of Elephant Gully. Start at the obvious line of cracks and flakes.
1. 20m 5a   The strenuous crack leads to a ledge.
2. 15m 5a   Follow the short green crack and groove to below an overhang. Traverse left to ascend the rib before stepping left to a grass ledge.

THE BRACK

North-East Face, Upper Tier

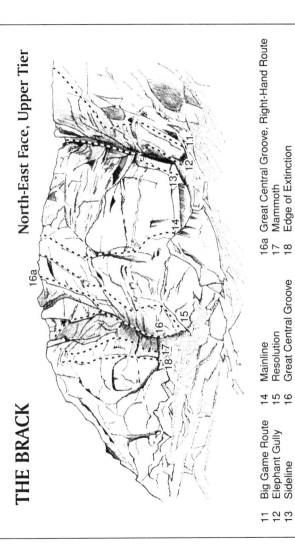

11 Big Game Route
12 Elephant Gully
13 Sideline

14 Mainline
15 Resolution
16 Great Central Groove

16a Great Central Groove, Right-Hand Route
17 Mammoth
18 Edge of Extinction

3. 20m 5b   Climb the thin crack in the overhanging corner, then move left to a ledge. A short wall leads to a higher ledge.

4. 35m   Go left into the groove and climb over a bulge. Take a long step left to a ledge and follow awkward walls and slabs to a large grass ledge.

5. 25m   Follow the oblique tapering fault right to a good finishing hold, then easy grass leads to the final wall.

6. 10m   Climb the wall on the right.

15   Resolution   125m   VI,7 ***   (1997)
One of the best routes in Arrochar, this climb takes the impressive turfy slab/wall right of Great Central Groove, exiting *via* a technical groove and slab system right of Right-Hand Route. A good selection of pegs and warthogs is desirable. The third pitch would be easier with more ice. Start at the bottom right-hand toe of the wall.

1. 35m   Climb up to an obvious line trending up and right, then go back left into the centre of the wall. Climb a short rock step into a vaguely defined scoop and belay at the right-hand side of the ledge.

2. 40m   Gain the ledge above the belay, traverse right, then go back left above the belay until about 10 metres left of it. Climb straight up the wall (bold) and continue to a good belay below an overlap and the upper groove.

3. 30m   From the right-hand side of the ledge above the overlap, climb an awkward hanging corner to enter the upper groove. Climb this to the overhang, descend slightly across the slab on the right, then go up its thinly iced right-hand margin (crux). Belay at the top of the continuation groove below an overlap.

4. 20m   Exit from the groove *via* its right wall to gain a large shelf. Climb the chimney-groove above to finish.

16   Great Central Groove   100m   HVS   (1958)
The central corner gives a very traditional route. Start below the chimney crack at the base of the corner.

1. 15m 4b   Grassy ledges lead to the steep chimney. At its top, exit right to a large ledge.

2. 25m 4b   Follow the slabby crack above, cross an overlap and continue up the vegetated corner. Pass a block on the right to reach a recess.

3. 20m 4a   Climb the chimney on the right, then go back left into the main corner line.

4. 15m   The open corner leads to a recess with thread runners.

5. 25m 5a   The steep corner above leads over bulges to a rocky platform. The wide groove above leads to the gallery and the top.
Winter: 100m   V,6 ***   (1968)
A superb varied route with a steep crux and a big mountain feel. The initial chimney can be avoided when the slabs on the right are well iced. The top pitch requires a good build-up of ice and good conditions are infrequent.

16a   Right-Hand Route   90m   V,6 ***   (1977)
Bold climbing up the obvious right-slanting ramp above and right of the lower corner. Follow Great Central Groove for about two pitches until thinly iced ledges lead out right to the base of the icy ramp and a peg on the left. Continue up the ramp to the top.

17   Mammoth   80m   E3 *   (1967)
A fine line up the right-hand of two obvious cracks in the wall left of Great Central Groove. Alas, the wall gets little sun and is often wet. Even when dry, some greasiness and dirt are inevitable. Start at the bottom of the obvious flack crack at the base of the arete of Edge of Extinction, about 6 metres left of Great Central Groove.
1. 15m 5c   Climb a small recess at the start of the crack. Exit right to a ledge and follow a deep crack to a ledge.
2. 15m 5c   Go straight up to an overhanging crack which leads with difficulty to a recess. Cross a short slab and go over the split overhang to a ledge.
3. 35m 5b   Go up and right to a grass ledge, then climb easily to a higher ledge at 10m. Follow the long curving crack to a cave.
4. 15m 5a   From the cave a crack line leads to grass, then climb a short corner to the gallery.

18   Edge of Extinction   90m   E6 ***   (1980)
A serious route, technical with poor protection, up the obvious arete left of the big corner. "The definitive mountain route of its grade in Scotland." The route receives few ascents, so it can become quite lichenous; it is graded for an on sight uncleaned ascent.
1. 45m 6a   Climb the recess and the crack above to a ledge at 12m. Move onto the wall just right of the arete (poor peg runner), climb diagonally right to a flake and climb the steep wall above on small holds to a ledge below the prominent hanging corner. Climb the corner (peg runner), and exit left at the top to ledges on the arete. Step down and left to peg and nut belays.

2. 45m 6a   Follow the right-hand side of the arete for 6m to a small ledge, then climb a ramp left of the arete until it merges into a steep wall (poor peg runner and a hand-placed peg in the pocket above). Climb the wall trending left to a ledge, then go up to good holds which lead back to the arete at 25m. Climb the overlap above on its right, then step back left to the arete and continue easily to the top.

The following two routes lie at the left end of the terrace dividing the Upper and Lower Tier. They can be approached along the terrace or perhaps more directly by ascending the wide gully which starts left of the Inglis Clark Arete on the Lower Tier, until it is possible to traverse right below the second of two rocky bluffs.

19   May Route   90m   III,3   (1976)
The buttress right of January Buttress is separated from it by a small gully. Start at a short corner and follow grooves and short walls until a rock band forces a short left traverse to finish up a gully. The climb is a vegetated Difficult in summer.

20   January Buttress   90m   III,3   (1976)
The small crag at the left end of the terrace is a natural continuation to the Inglis Clark Arete. Gain and climb a sloping groove on the right flank of the buttress, to finish easily up the gully on the right, or more directly by an icefall on the left wall.

BEN DONICH

847m   (Map Ref 219 043)

The north corrie of Ben Donich contains a number of small but steep crags of mica-schist which remain largely hidden until the Rest and Be Thankful. Perhaps for this reason coupled with their northerly aspect and slowness to dry, the crags have never been popular in summer and some scope remains for new routes. The corrie receives the evening sun. A belay needs to be fixed on the grassy slopes above some of the routes and a metal stake may be found in the howff below the crag.

A similar lack of attention has been evident in winter, despite having one of the harder mixed routes in the Arrochar area and, in a good winter, a number of still unclimbed ice lines.

There are five obvious crags, numbered one to five from left to right. The first and the fifth are detached from the other three, which are divided by short gullies giving generally easy winter routes.

Turn off the A83 onto the B828 at the Rest and be Thankful. After a very short distance park on the left at a forestry track with a gate. Follow the track and take the left fork downhill and round a right-hand bend where a vague, wet path marked with white posts leads up through the forest to a stile and the ridge. Follow the ridge to the crags. An interesting feature of the ground hereabouts is several deep fissures which penetrate deep into the heart of the mountain. Don't fall down one!

NUMBER ONE CRAG

The crag furthest left and just below the ridge is easily identified by the steep grooves of the following routes.

Deja Vu   35m   VS *   (1980)
This route climbs the left-bounding fault of the prominent overhanging prow. Start from a grassy recess.
1. 10m 4b   Climb the left wall, move left under a bulge and go up to a grass ledge and belay.
2. 25m 5a   Meander up the left wall to enter and climb a hanging V-groove to top.

Voulez Vous   35m   VS *   (1981)
This route takes the right-bounding fault of the prow.
1. 20m 4b   Follow the first pitch of Deja Vu, then move right and climb an awkward bottomless crack to a commodious bay.
2. 15m 4c   The steep sparsely protected off-width leads to the top.

NUMBER THREE CRAG

Number Two Crag is tiny and has no routes. A gully separates it from Number Three Crag. The main face of this crag is very steep.

Flakewalk   60m   VI,8 ***   (1990)
A superb route taking a natural line up a very steep piece of rock on the left side of the buttress, finishing at an obvious perched boulder on the top. The first ascent was only accomplished after a number of attempts. The route was graded Severe in summer, but VS 5a is probably more likely. A fault runs across the main face, from bottom right to top left.
1. 20m   Gain the thin fault just left of where it reaches the ground and climb to a small niche.

2. 10m   Climb the bulging off-width and move left to an excellent overhung niche.

3. 10m   Climb the strenuous overhanging off-width flake (1 outsize hexentric for aid, but climbed without by one member of the first ascent party) and exit left onto a good ledge.

4. 20m   Continue straight up *via* a flake, and climb the ice smear to finish just left of a perched skyline boulder.

Skywalk   45m   E1 **   (1981)
A serious climb near the left end of the main face, drying more quickly than neighbouring routes. Start at a short black groove under a knobbly grey wall.

1. 20m 5a   Climb a groove to ledges and take a thin wall on the right to a bay (poor peg runner). Climb a bulge on the left and a wall which leads to the overhung recess of Flakewalk.

2. 25m 5b   Gain a high right traverse under the roof and follow a good flake. Stand on the flake, step left (bolt runner in situ) and pull over a strenuous bulge to a small ledge. The way is barred by a roof; traverse left across a deceptively delicate wall to finish just right of the perched boulder.

Simple Visions   55m   HVS *   (1981)
A steep route taking the wall right of the bulging crack line and starting about 10m left of Flakewalk at a deep vertical fault. It requires a dry period of weather.

1. 15m 4a   Climb the fault to ledges and move up left to a better ledge.

2. 20m 5a   Traverse right across a knobbly wall to a thin crack. Climb the crack to a right-trending mossy ramp which leads to an airy belay on top of a perched block.

3. 20m 5b   Move up, traverse left and climb a steep wall to a good flake. Climb the diagonal corner above and go through the roof to finish. Belay well up the slope.

NUMBER FIVE CRAG

Number Four Crag also has no routes on it. Number Five Crag lies down and below the other crags.

Night on the Tiles   35m   E1 5b *   (1995)
This route is low in the grade, but it is only just adequately protected. Scramble up to start at a slab just left of a right-facing corner. There is an obvious rectangular overhang at two-thirds height with a smaller

overhang below and right. Climb delicately right to the right-hand overhang and surmount it at its left end, or more easily by traversing right to a mossy corner. A rising traverse left leads to a niche to the right of the rectangular overhang. Move left over this on good holds, then go up steeply to ledges.

D.J.   40m   E1 5b   (1995)
This follows the corner system which is the first feature right of the main face where the crag lies back into a series of broken buttresses. Start by a small cave below the corner system which begins as a grassy groove above a steep gully. Climb the groove and gain the corner by its slabby right wall. Continue more steeply until an escape may be made onto a ledge on the left, crux. Finish up the corner at a more amenable grade, past a block.

BEINN AN LOCHAIN

901m   (Map Ref 218 080)

This fine mountain stands in a commanding position above Loch Restil, and forms the apex of the high ground dividing Glen Croe from Glen Kinglas. Known principally as a winter climbing venue, the North Face with its impressive Monolith and the walls of Kinglas Crag have recently received the wire brush of the rock climber to produce a number of easily accessible, high quality routes in the upper grades. However, due to the sunless north-facing nature of the crags, and the stubborn lichen on the mica-schist, it is likely that the mountain will remain more popular with climbers in the winter.

The mountain just misses Munro status, but the North Face is just below the summit and routes like the classic Monolith Grooves come into condition quite fast.

For routes on the North Face and Kinglas Crag, the quickest approach is to park at the lay-by beyond Loch Restil, and close to the North-East Ridge, as the road begins to descend to Glen Kinglas. Cross the burn and gain the ridge which leads past Kinglas Crag to the north face. The east face is accessed easily from Loch Restil, and Slabby Crag can be reached through forestry from the bridge at Map Ref 221 063 in Gleann Mor.

In descent from the summit, go down the North-East Ridge which is very exposed in places and particular care should be taken in icy conditions or poor visibility. It is also possible to descend the South Ridge and East Face well to the south of Loch Restil.

EAST FACE

A number of climbs have been made on the extensive and ill-defined face overlooking Loch Restil, however the lack of obvious lines and the infinite variation possible makes many routes difficult to locate precisely. The face is cut from left to right by a Grade I shelf.

Frog   200m   III   (1991)
This route follows the obvious ice cascade immediately right of a small gully near the initial narrowing of the diagonal shelf. Climb the cascade direct in two obvious pitches to an easier-angled curving gully leading up right to join Toad above a wide ice slab. Cross Toad and continue up the steepening shallow gully just right of the narrow ice-capped slab above. Continue to the upper slopes of the north-east ridge.

Toad   400m   III   (1983)
Start directly below the summit, right of the lowest rocks of the buttress below and to the right of the right-slanting shelf. A very narrow 30m ice gully widens above. A further pitch and snow leads to the Grade I shelf. Go left along the shelf to easy-angled ice which leads to a large V-shaped icefall. Turn this on the left *via* a cave pitch, and climb mixed ground to the summit.

Bufo   250m   III   (1986)
Start to the right and higher up than Toad, in a right-trending snow gully at a corner below a large obvious ice slab. Climb the steep ice slab to the left of the corner and the wall above in two pitches to easy snow slopes. Follow slopes for 100m, trending right and passing occasional ice steps, to reach the upper buttress. A short steep icefall leads to mixed ground and the north-east ridge.

Twin Caves Gully   90m   III   (1976)
This narrow gully lies at the north end of the face above the lochan. Snow and ice lead to either a through-route (rather artificial), then into a cave, or the right wall of the gully. A second cave can be passed on the right to finish.

Whiteout Gully   60m   II   (1977)
At the top right of this face is a line of cliffs split by a narrow gully. Climb the gully with a 12m ice pitch near top. This is a less tedious way of gaining the ridge crest.

KINGLAS CRAG

This small north-facing crag forms a step in the North-East Ridge and is the first to be reached when ascending towards the main crags of the North Face. A couple of excellent routes have been done in summer, but the face gets no sun and seepage can be a problem. In a cold winter a number of icefalls form on the crag, however their low altitude means they are not often in condition. The left side of the crag is snowy and cut by two obvious grooves, while the right-hand side is rocky and much steeper.

The Palantir   90m   III   (1987)
Poor climbing up the left-hand groove.

Galadriel's Mirror   70m   III   (1986)
Climb the right-hand groove.

Bakerloo Line   85m   V,6   (1996)
Start about 30 metres left of the arete of AWOL in Thailand. The upper left-hand ramp line is flanked on the left by an overhanging wall which terminates in a distinctive beak of rock.
1. 30m   A steep start leads to the awkward turfy ramp. Follow this past various short steps to where it narrows to a funnel. Climb this to a belay in a shallow recess.
2. 35m   Climb up until it is possible to traverse right to a short icefall which gains the continuation of the turfy ramp. Skirt the beak on the right and climb the groove on the left to a belay near its top.
3. 20m   Move left and climb short walls to a good belay well back.

AWOL in Thailand   45m   E4 5c **   (1996)
This is the obvious impressive arete on the left-hand side of the first steep buttress. Start up a shallow blocky groove 5 metres left of the arete, then move right onto the arete. Climb it on its left-hand side with increasing difficulty to a sloping ledge, then climb the scoop on the right to a huge block. Descend by abseil from an *in situ* thread.
Direct Start: **Julian Can't Cope**   E6 6b *   (1996)
Climb the undercut arete from the left (a small skyhook runner was used on the first ascent), passing a low peg runner.

Swimming with the Tide   60m   E5 ***   (1996)
Excellent, sustained climbing. About 20 metres right of the arete is a line of short corners. Right again and high up is a prominent left-

slanting crack taken by this route. Start slightly up and right of a fallen flake buried in the grass.

1. 15m 5b   A serious pitch. Take a left-trending line up the slab and go over a steepening to make thin moves left under a bulge. Friend belays on a heather ledge.

2. 45m 6a   Pull into the undercut slim groove to gain and follow the left-trending wavey break. Climb the wall left of a thin crack, then move right to finish up the prominent left-slanting crack line. Easier ground leads to a stake well back.

Tonton Macout   65m   IV,4 **   (1986)
An exposed and serious route up the obvious left-slanting ramp of ice that bisects the steep right-hand side of the first buttress.

1. 20m   Bulging ice gives access to the obvious groove below the ramp. Follow the groove to a belay.

2. 45m   Climb the ramp, then steep ground leads to the top.

Appoggiatura   50m   E6 6b **   (1996)
Technically sustained climbing with improving protection. Right of the last route the crag drops to a lower level, then turns a corner past two vegetated chimney lines and an impressive wall to an open recess with the stumpy pinnacle. This route climbs the wall left of the chimney lines. Gain a rounded spike 3m up, move up to twin pockets, then follow holds up and right to a bulge. Move delicately left and step up to clip an *in situ* thread. Continue up past twin breaks to follow a right-trending line just right of a scoop to gain a juggy pocket and protection, then go up and back left to gain a thin crack which leads with difficulty to a turf ledge. The short wall on the left, the slimey groove above or the shelves out right lead to a belay well back on the grass slope above.

Benylin   55m   IV,5 *   (1984)
A short but enjoyable route up the square-cut recessed chimney-groove right of and behind the pinnacle.

NORTH FACE

This open corrie lies further up the North-East Ridge and is dominated by the impressively steep two-tiered buttress of The Monolith on the right. The first three routes lie on the small buttress on the North-East Ridge itself, about 120m below the summit.

1   Saxifrage Gully   75m   III   (1974)
Right of the first rocks is a gully, narrowing to a chimney crack. In
summer the route is a loose and vegetated Moderate.

2   The Edge of Darkness   70m   IV,6 **   (1987)
A technical but well protected route in a good position. Start at the
obvious right-slanting ramp in the buttress immediately right of
Saxifrage Gully.
1. 10m   A short slab leads to a belay below the ramp.
2. 25m   Follow the ramp until forced right at the top by a steep wall.
Technical moves past a peg runner lead right, around the edge of the
buttress, until it is possible to climb up and right into a corner and belay.
3. 35m   Continue up the corner, go over a small bulge and into a
grassy hollow. Follow the steep corner on the left, exiting right below
the top.

3   The Back Alley   60m   III   (1986)
Above and right of the last route and almost directly below the summit
is an undercut buttress with a prominent left-facing corner. Traverse
right along a narrow shelf below the undercut base and surmount an
awkward bulge to enter the corner. Follow the corner to a belay under
the headwall, then pull out left onto the north-east ridge.

To the right is an open snow slope, steeper at the top and scattered
with rocks. A number of variations are possible, especially under heavy
snow cover.

4   Central Gully   100m   II
This is the open gully just right of the summit rocks. There may be a
small step in lean conditions. The gully leads to a point immediately
west of the summit.

5   Promenade Gully   150m   II   (1977)
Pleasant climbing up the face and vague gully between Central Gully
and The Monolith. Start about 30 metres left of the buttress and climb
directly past a narrowing in the gully to below a steep cave (there is a
prominent pinnacle high on the left). Go left and round a wall to climb
the shelf parallel to the main gully. Climb past a narrowing, then go
right to rejoin the main gully. Continue to a fan-shaped exit, which may
be heavily corniced.

The Monolith is the impressive two-tiered buttress which dominates Beinn an Lochain's North Face.

6 Purple Blaze 120m V,6 ** (1994/97)
An excellent and varied route with an atmospheric top pitch up the overhanging corners and hanging slab right of the top pitch of Monolith Grooves. Start as for Monolith Grooves.
1. 20m A shallow gully-groove leads to good rock belays.
2. 50m Some 10 metres left of the gully of Monolith Grooves is a narrow steep chimney with an overhanging chockstone. Climb the chimney with difficulty, then traverse right under steep rock for 6m. Follow the grooves above to the terrace and traverse right to belay below a fault leading to a steep corner on the broken arete of the upper buttress.
3. 50m Gain the corner with difficulty and climb it to a grass ledge. Traverse the hanging ledge to the left and pull awkwardly round to the left to reach the base of the slab. Continue to a snowy recess from where a thin crack fortuitously leads to the upper grass ledge. Traverse this up and right with poor protection and increasing exposure to finish on the very edge of the buttress.

7 Monolith Grooves 130m IV,5 *** (1977)
A tremendous mountaineering route with a variety of pitches in exciting situations and a fine crux at the top. The route is climbable in most conditions, providing the turf is well frozen, and deserves greater popularity. Start below the impressive hidden cleft on the left side of The Monolith.
1. 20m A shallow gully-groove leads to good rock belays on the left.
2. 30m Traverse right into the cleft and follow it until a steeper section leads to a superb cave.
3. 10m Move delicately right onto the exposed arete and commit yourself to the groove above. Belay on the snowy ledge, The Table.
4. 30m At the top left edge of The Table is a large block. Traverse left below it and follow a line of exposed turf ledges up and left, above the cleft of pitch 2. Belay below a short chimney in the upper wall.
5. 40m Climb the constricted chimney (the more snow at the start the easier), then follow easier ground to a ledge. The open groove on the right leads *via* hanging turf and icy walls to a short snow ramp.

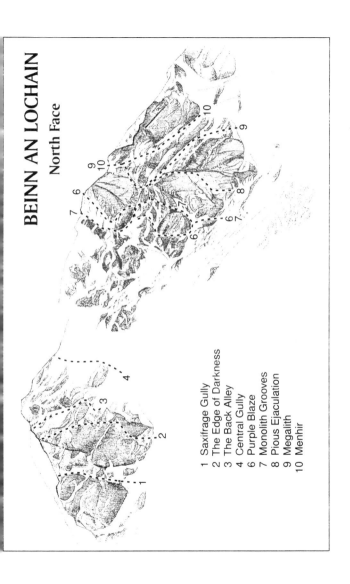

BEINN AN LOCHAIN
North Face

1 Saxifrage Gully
2 The Edge of Darkness
3 The Back Alley
4 Central Gully
6 Purple Blaze
7 Monolith Grooves
8 Pious Ejaculation
9 Megalith
10 Menhir

The Monolith's lower rock buttress has an obvious vegetated crack line high on the left side which descends to a large patch of white lichen. Below and right of this are two steep corner grooves leading to two ramp lines slanting left to right across the face on the right-hand side of the buttress. The following route gains the right-hand corner and follows the less distinct lower ramp-crack line.

8   Pious Ejaculation   70m   E4 **   (1996)
Exciting climbing with bags of 'North Face' atmosphere. On the first ascent both ropes jammed near the top and the leader was forced to untie, resulting in the 'pious utterance'.
1. 45m 6a   Start up a crack and pull into the right-hand groove. Move up this to where it curves left, then pull right onto the wall and move up into the right-slanting crack. Follow this steeply until it is possible to swing round on to the frontal face of the buttress. Move up then swing back left to belay in a recess with nuts and an old peg.
2. 25m 4c   Move back right and go up to easy ground and a block belay well back.

9   Megalith   110m   IV,4 *   (1993)
A good companion to Monolith Grooves. Start at the first groove immediately right of the lowest point of The Monolith's lower rock buttress.
1. 45m   Climb a steep icefall on the right of the groove (or, in thinner conditions, the groove), and continue directly to gain and follow a narrow left-trending chimney. Directly above this, climb a short hard corner to a ledge and belay. Both the initial icefall and the hard corner can be avoided, which reduces the climb to an easy Grade III.
2. 15m   Traverse easily left to the left edge of The Table.
3. 50m   Beneath the upper section of The Monolith is a right-trending flake system. Gain the left end of this, then follow it easily right to snow slopes and go over an ice bulge to the top.

10   Menhir   60m   II   (1995)
A poor route up the vegetated, slabby face right of Megalith. Start 30m up and right of Megalith.
1. 30m   Climb up and left heading for a large pinnacle block with a short chimney on its right-hand side. Poor belay on top of the block.
2. 30m   Continue left to join Megalith at the short icy step.

SLABBY CRAG

This steep but rather poor crag is a prominent feature on the south flank of Beinn an Lochain, overlooking Gleann Mor and the Lochgoilhead road. Park at the bridge at Map Ref 221 063 and bash up through the forestry.

Edge　40m　VS 4c　(1980)
The crag is split into two unequal parts by an obvious chimney. Start at a shallow groove 6 metres to the left of the chimney. Climb the groove for about 5m, then move right and go up to a flake. Climb up, then move right below bulging rock to the chimney edge. Climb a grassy crack to a ledge, then go straight up the edge to a large block belay.

Sidewalk　30m　Severe　(1980)
Start at an open heathery corner about 13 metres left of the chimney. Climb the slabby wall to a ledge, then move left and go up a wall to a heather ledge. Slabby rock and broken ground lead to the top.

Point Counter Point　40m　HVS 5b　(1980)
Start 5 metres left of the obvious vegetated crack in the main face. Climb the centre of the slabby wall to a heather ledge. Continue up the mossy wall and vegetated rock steps to belay on an iron stake a short distance back.

BINNEIN AN FHIDHLEIR
811m　(Map Ref 215 107)

The crags of Creag Coire an Creagach overlook Glen Kinglas, on the flanks of an unnamed 817m peak which lies about 2km east of the 811m peak named Binnein an Fhidhleir. A variety of interesting routes exist, mostly in the lower and middle grades. The crag reaches a maximum of 80m on the Central Wall, but this is deceptive as the bottom half is a mixture of rock and heather. The slabby right-hand side of the main crag, and a variety of other outcrops in the corrie, give routes of about 25m. Generally, the mica-schist is of excellent quality, being quite clean and compact. However, protection is often at a premium, although this gives many of the routes a level of excitement which belies their grades!

A south-easterly aspect means that the rock dries fast and the location provides extensive and unusual views of popular mountains, while revealing the Arrochar Alps in all their glory.

Park at Butterbridge, at the base of the North-East Ridge of Beinn an Lochain. Cross the road, climb over a locked gate, turn immediately left and go through another gate. Follow the fence steeply up the hillside, then a burn slanting right to cross the shoulder. The corrie and the crags are immediately ahead (allow 1 hour).

SUMMIT BUTTRESS

When viewed from the base of the corrie, this crag lies below and to the right of the unnamed 817m peak and is the largest rather rambling crag on this section of the hillside. On its left, a long grassy gully descends from the ridge to the corrie; to the left of that is the buttress taken by Fiddler's Slab and left again is a small crag with a prominent quartz patch.

Jig and Reel   45m   VS   (1996)
Bold slab climbing. Start at the foot of the slabby, rambling crag below two overhangs.
1. 25m 4c   The centre of the slab leads to the left of the right-hand and lower overhang. Traverse right to gain the top, then go up and left to a heather terrace.
2. 20m 4c   The pocketed wall above leads to an overlap. Pull over left on good holds and finish up a crack on the left.

Fiddler's Slab   40m   Severe **   (1996)
A route for lovers of minimally protected slabs – probably best soloed. Left of the grassy gully is a buttress with a prominent perched flake at 10m and a grassy groove and clean slab to its left.
1. 20m   Climb the slab to a grass ledge but no belay.
2. 20m   Climb the slab above to the top and good nut belays.

SKYLINE BUTTRESS

In the centre of the corrie a boulder-scree slope rises to two steep slabby crags below the summit ridge. A vegetated vertical fault separates the crags, of which the left-hand is easily identified by a prominent horizontal streak of quartz. The first route is on the left-hand crag, and the remainder are on the right-hand crag.

Mark's Arete 35m Severe (1996)
Start at the left end of the left-hand crag and climb the arete right of a deep slabby corner with an overlap at 10m.

Luss Crack 25m E1 5b ** (1990)
Delicate but never desperate climbing with adequate protection, although the gear is a little sparse higher up. Right of the arete the slabby wall is split by a clean thin crack leading to a small overlap near the top. Climb the crack until it runs out and continue in the same line before trending left to the arete, just below the overlap. Traverse right for 3 metres and carefully pull up, avoiding a loose block.

Paganini 25m VS 4c* (1996)
An exciting route with a poorly protected crux through the overhang. Some 2 metres right of Luss Crack, and in the centre of the crag, is an obvious crack line. Climb the crack to cross the overhang centrally.

AQUILA BUTTRESS

Below and right of Skyline Buttress is a crag shaped like an inverted triangle with a prominent wide corner crack capped by a roof in the centre (Aquila) and moss streaked slabs on the right.

Aquila 20m HVS 5a * (1996)
Wild laybacking on undercuts round the roof adds excitement to this route up the prominent wide corner crack. Finish up the chimney.

Schistophrenia 20m VS 4c (1996)
Start 3 metres left of the foot of the buttress, below an undercut arete. Pull right through overhangs and climb the slab just right of the arete.

Lacklustre 30m Hard Severe 4b (1996)
From the foot of the buttress a large V-groove leads to a left-slanting crack through moss-streaked slabs.

Schistosomiasis 20m VS 4b * (1996)
Good but poorly protected climbing up the clean slab on the right of the buttress. Up and right of the V-groove of Lacklustre, two niches form an M-shape. Start in the left-hand niche and pull left to gain the slab or, more easily, start further left and make a rising traverse to this point. Climb the slab, taking the small overlap direct.

HABILIS BUTTRESS

This small scrappy crag lies well below and about 180 metres right of Skyline Buttress above some small lochans on the right edge of the corrie. It is easily recognised by a ramp and blunt right-slanting arete.

Erectus   30m   Severe   (1987)
1. 20m   The smooth slab to the left of the ramp leads to a ledge and belay.
2. 10m   Climb the wall above.

Habilis   20m   Severe   (1987)
The prominent arete right of the ramp leads to a ledge and belay.

CENTRAL WALL

From the approach corrie, the main crag can be seen in profile on the right and lies about 130 metres to the right of Habilis Buttress. It is easily recognised by the impressive clean corner of Horn of Plenty. The chockstone-filled Africa Gully flanks the crag on the left, while the narrower slot of Abyssinia Chimney is on the right.

1   Africa Gully   60m   III   (1990)
The chockstone gives the only difficulty, although the route may be harder if the snow is lean. A dangerous Difficult in summer.

2   Horn of Plenty   40m   VS 4c *   (1977)
Fine climbing up the impressive corner on the left edge of the Central Wall. Scramble up Africa Gully to belay below the wall blocking access to the corner. Gain and climb the corner before traversing left to a small ledge at the left edge of the overhang. Move up with a long reach for a crucial horn of rock and finish up the slab above.

3   Hamite   75m   HVS **   (1996)
An exciting airy experience up the right arete of the impressive corner. Start 5 metres left of Serengeti below a clean slab with a short right-facing corner in its centre. Although neither pitch is technically too difficult, protection is spaced and a confident approach is essential.

1. 40m 4c   Scramble up to the base of the slab and a possible belay above and left of the corner. Climb the corner to an awkward exit left. Climb the unprotected wall above, easier to the left, until a traverse right leads to heather. Scramble up and left to a small wall below the corner.
2. 35m 4c   Gain the corner, move right onto the arete and climb it with little protection to a large Friend below the steep section near the top.

4   Serengeti   80m   VS   (1987)
Start at an obvious narrow pillar of compact pink schist at the lowest point of the Central Wall.
1. 35m 4b   Climb the pillar to a groove on the left, then scramble up heather to a ramp splitting the wall below a large pale slab.
2. 20m 4a   Follow the steep ramp to belay in a niche below a corner.
3. 25m 4b   Climb the corner, move round a flake at the top, then go up *via* a ledge to a groove and wall.

5   Witch Doctor   80m   VS   (1990)
This route makes the most of the rock right of Serengeti, with the second pitch climbing the obvious clean wall streaked with horizontal quartz.
1. 35m   Mossy slabs lead up and right to a belay below the quartz-streaked wall.
2. 35m 4b   Climb the wall on fine incuts, first up and right to a ledge, then up and left. Continue by the grassy corner beyond to belay below a chockstone.
3. 10m   Finish by a choice of routes.

To the right is a steep wall of about 30m, capped with overhangs and presently unclimbed. Right again is the obvious slot of Abyssinia Chimney.

6   Abyssinia Chimney   30m   III,4 *   (1990)
The narrow chimney gives an interesting back and foot exercise. Very Difficult in summer.

To the right of Abyssinia Chimney is a small buttress with grassy slopes on either side. The following route climbs the right-hand side of the buttress.

7   Safari   55m   Very Difficult   (1996)
Start about 30m up the grassy slope where the crag steepens at a
horizontal quartz band and below a patch of quartz. Poor climbing and
poorer protection!
1. 20m   Step left onto the buttress and climb a vague groove to a
grass shoulder and large boulder.
2. 35m   Cross the grass to the wall behind and follow the cleanest
line, trending slightly left to a pinnacle-shaped boulder on the skyline.

RIGHT WALL

Further right again, this slabby wall is split into two by a turf ledge.

8   Africanus   30m   VS 4b *   (1991)
Start at the undercut arete at the left end of the buttress and climb a
slabby wall to a ledge and block, finishing straight up.

9   Amin's Can-Can   30m   Very Difficult   (1976)
From the left end of the wall, traverse to ledges, step right and go up a
groove to a ledge. Follow the 12m chimney groove on the left past a
chockstone.

10   Two-Step   40m   Severe   (1977)
A good top pitch spoilt by a dirty and vegetated lower pitch. On the left
side of the wall is a vegetated fault, running up and right.
1. 15m   Follow the fault to the ledge and go right to beneath the
central cracks in the upper wall above, obvious from below.
2. 25m   Climb directly up the cracks past a small niche.

11   Nostromo   25m   E1 5b **   (1990)
Bold and sustained climbing up the clean slab between Two-Step and
Heart of Darkness. Gain the slab by following any of the existing routes
to the ledge.

12   Heart of Darkness   40m   Hard Severe **   (1987)
Excellent climbing and protection. Just right of the start of Two-Step is
a cleaner crack.
1. 15m 4a   Climb the clean crack, trending slightly right, to gain the
ledge and a belay below the crack in the upper wall, left of the more
prominent cracks of Two-Step.
2. 25m 4b   Follow the crack, move right to a further crack (not obvious
from below) and finish up this.

BINNEIN AN FHIDHLEIR

Creag Coire an Creagach

1 Africa Gully
2 Horn of Plenty
3 Hamite
4 Serengeti
6 Abyssinia Chimney

7 Safari
10 Two-Step
11 Nostromo
12 Heart of Darkness
13 Harmony

14 Roots
15 Victoria Falls
16 Origins
17 Slightly Silly Arete
18 Amindergroove

13   Harmony   40m   VS *   (1990)
Good climbing, starting 5 metres right of the initial crack of Heart of
Darkness.
1. 15m 4b   Climb the clean slabby wall, exiting right to the ledge.
2. 25m 4b   Continue up the slab, to the right of the Two-Step cracks.

To the right, the lower wall has been climbed through the faint
overlap at VS 4b. Right of this are three short cracks and right again is
a leaning two-stepped buttress.

14   Roots   30m   Very Difficult   (1987)
1. 20m   The left-hand crack is wide and vegetated.
2. 10m   Finish up the short wall above.

15   Victoria Falls   30m   Severe   (1987)
1. 20m   The middle crack leads to a niche and small roof.
2. 10m   Climb the short wall above.

16   Origins   30m   Very Difficult *   (1987)
1. 20m   Climb the shallow right-hand V-groove.
2. 10m   Finish up the short wall above.

17   Slightly Silly Arete   30m   Hard Severe 4b   (1990)
This route folows the hanging slabby edge of the two-stepped buttress.

Below the left end of the Right Wall is a smaller wall with a small tree
at its base.

18   Amindergroove   25m   Hard Severe 4b *   (1977)
Start left of the tree and right of a thin crack. Climb the slab directly to
join a shallow groove near the top. Finish straight up. The short tier
above can be climbed to the broad ledge at Severe.

To the right of the main crags lies a broad couloir. The following route
climbs the buttress immediately right of this.

OK Buttress   60m   IV   (1994)
Start at the bottom of the continuous rock.
1. 15m   Climb the stepped face on the right to belay on a terrace.
2. 45m   Quit the terrace on the right for a slab and finish up the crest
of the buttress.

The Bridge of Orchy Hills

The mountains described under this heading are to be found on a line passing approximately from north to south through Bridge of Orchy. Stob Ghabhar, to the north of Loch Tulla, has several routes, including the venerable Upper Couloir, a classic gully.

The bulk of the routes however are to be found just east of Loch Tulla, on the superb Bridge of Orchy Range stretching from Beinn a'Chreachain in the north to Beinn Dorain in the south. Across Auch Gleann to the south is Beinn a'Chaisteil, while some little way down Glen Orchy itself is the ice climbing in Coire Daimh of Beinn Udlaidh. Much of the climbing has a comparatively recent history but already includes several routes destined to become modern classics. Several of the most recent routes, especially those on Beinn Dorain, are of a very high standard. The climbing is described from north to south, beginning with Stob Ghabhar, and finishing with Beinn Udlaidh.

STOB GHABHAR

1087m   (Map Ref 230 455)

Leave the A82 at Bridge of Orchy and follow the A8005 round Loch Tulla to Victoria Bridge (parking just before the bridge). Take the footpath from Forest Lodge west along the Linne nam Beathach as far as the tiny corrugated metal hut belonging to Glasgow University M.C.(Clashgour, distinct from the farm at Clashgour further west). At the hut (which was the local school in the past) turn up to follow the good stalker's path north along the Allt Toaig. This leads in about 5km from Forest Lodge to the col between Stob Ghabhar and Stob a'Choire Odhair.

Now contour west over rough ground, rising gently to enter the small north-east corrie of Stob Ghabhar, with the cliffs and the Upper Couloir ahead. Avoid a lower tier of easy rock on the left and go up and right to the upper buttress. The final section of the approach is avalanche-prone and accordingly careful recognition of the prevailing conditions should be made before making the traverse towards the routes. (6km, 2h 30m).

To descend from the summit follow the south-east ridge, descending to reach easy ground west of the Allt Toaig. Cross this to regain the approach track. If the burn is in spate, continue along its bank to gain the track from Clashgour Farm. The small crag right of the

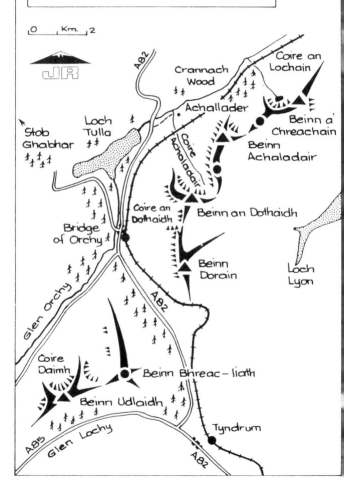

THE BRIDGE of ORCHY HILLS

0 Km. 2

JR

A82

Crannach Wood

Coire an Lochain

Achallader

Beinn a' Chreachain

Coire Achaladair

Beinn Achaladair

Stob Ghabhar

Loch Tulla

Coire an Dothaidh

Beinn an Dothaidh

Bridge of Orchy

Beinn Dorain

Loch Lyon

Glen Orchy

A82

Coire Daimh

Beinn Bhreac-liath

Beinn Udlaidh

Tyndrum

A85

Glen Lochy

A82

waterfall seen from the approach path provides several short routes at about Very Difficult to Severe (not described).

The routes on the summit crags are described from left to right.

Hircine Rib   130m   VI,7 *   (1989)
A natural mixed winter line following the buttress immediately left of the Upper Couloir. The rock is friendlier than it appears from below, and with a conventional modern rack of gear good protection can be found. Excellent, technical climbing – high in the grade. Start just right of the lowest rocks below a left-slanting groove system.
1. 10m   Gain the groove by climbing a steep wall (bold) to a snowy ledge.
2. 20m   Climb the groove, stepping left after a vertical section to gain an icy runnel which leads to a belay on the right arete.
3. 25m   Above is a steep friable rib bounded on the left by a slabby groove. Climb the groove to half-height, then traverse delicately left across the slab to reach a snow ledge on the left arete. Continue up and right up the vertical continuation corner to reach an exposed stance above.
4. 75m   Follow the groove above for 5m before stepping left onto easier ground which leads to the plateau.
Summer: Severe   (1961)
Start at the lowest rocks, just right of centre. The rock is of unusual form and appears to slope down awkwardly.

Upper Couloir   90m   II **   (1897)
Normally a straightforward snow gully, with one ice pitch in the middle of perhaps 10m in height and 70 degrees angle. In very lean conditions there may be an impassable chockstone pitch. The route should be considered as only part of a good day out, to avoid a potential feeling of anti-climax! The summit often has a strong wind blowing.

Capricorn   60m   Difficult *   (1982)
The right-bounding rib of the Upper Couloir. Climb the rib, keeping to the edge overlooking the couloir until the rib narrows. Continue up a knife-edge arete with fine situations to reach a tiny pinnacle at 60m. Some 30m above is the summit.

Upper Couloir Keyhole   90m   III *   (1952)
A short distance right of the Upper Couloir, a narrow deep-cut gully rises from the left corner of a rock-bay. This is just right of Capricorn, which is joined higher up. Climb steep snow and the icy chimney above to a thread belay (35m). Steep snow then leads to an ice arete and finish as for Capricorn.

Short scrambles may be found on the north face of the north-east spur of Stob Ghabhar, approached from below *via* the lochan, or by a right traverse from below the Upper Couloir.

BEINN A' CHREACHAIN
1081m   (Map Ref 373 441)

COIRE AN LOCHAIN

Access to the climbs in this corrie begins at Achallader Farm, 5½km north-north-east of Bridge of Orchy and 1½km along the track from the A82 at the north-east end of Loch Tulla. The estate owner, Mr Fleming of Glen Etive, has very kindly provided car parking at the historical old keep next to the farm. (A pleasant character named Black Duncan won this land by fraud and built a keep here in the mid-16th century to keep out the legal owners.) Maintain good relations by observing the customary good manners. Continue past the farm on foot along the track parallel to the Water of Tulla. Where the track crosses the Tulla *via* a ford, strike diagonally up towards the railway line and Crannach Wood, a beautiful pocket of the ancient Caledonian Forest. A short way into the wood cross the line *via* a footbridge and climb the hillside diagonally to enter Coire an Lochain (6km, 2 hours).

Three buttresses back the north-facing Coire an Lochain: the large, left-hand buttress is sprawling and indistinct; the central buttress, lying above Lochan a' Chreachain, is more defined, with mixed ground leading to a central snow gully high on the buttress. The right-hand buttress is smaller though steeper, with an obvious ice ramp in its upper half and an occasional impressive 30m hanging icicle (unclimbed to date) lower down. The buttresses are separated by easy snow gullies. Only four routes have been recorded; more may be found at around Grade II/III, particularly on the left-hand buttress.

Leucocyte Buttress   210m   III *   (1986)
This route climbs the central buttress, above the lochan. Start at an
icefall right of centre. In icier conditions an alternative start may be
found up a ramp beginning further left. Climb the icefall, trending left to
easy rocks left of the upper central gully. The rocks then lead to an
elegant finish on the buttress crest, left of the central gully (which may
be corniced).

A Bit on the Side   85m   II   (1994)
Start well up the wide gully between the central and right-hand
buttresses where a steep rock spur juts from the flank of the latter, i.e.
on the right side of the gully looking up, well above the rock island.
Climb a runnel running on the right side of this rock spur with a
steepening, then gain a wide snow ramp. Climb the ramp and the short
snowfield above to the ridge.

Brittle Ramp   160m   IV   (1987)
This route is on the right-hand buttress. Start about halfway up the
easy gully between the central and right-hand buttresses, at a rock
island. Climb the left flank of the buttress by grooves to gain an
obvious ice ramp. Follow the ramp and broken ground above to the
top.

Soft Option   265m   III   (1991)
A route on the front face of Coire an Lochain's right-hand (westerly)
buttress. Start at the first snow bay to the left of the bay below the
imposing icicle.
1. 40m   Ascend a ramp trending left until steep but turfy ground can
be climbed to belay at dubious jammed flakes at the right-hand end of
a short ledge.
2. 25m   Move left to the end of the ledge, go up a groove, then move
back right to belay.
3 and 4. 95m   Move right and ascend a snowfield in 2 long pitches
aiming for an ice groove breaking through a short rock band.
5. 35m   Climb the groove and snow above.
6. 40m   Easier ground runs off to the right. Instead, ascend an ice
flow on the right flank of the upper buttress to belay at a small cave.
7. 30m   Climb steep ice on the left, then go over the final rocks to
easier ground.

MEALL BUIDHE

977m   (Map Ref 359 439)

NORTH-WEST CORRIE

The approach starts as for Beinn a'Chreachain, from the car park at Achallader Farm. Turn up the hillside before Crannach Wood to enter the corrie (4km, 90 minutes) The cliffs lie to the north of the col between Beinn Achaladair and Meall Buidhe. There is a main central buttress, bounded on the left by a deep and (from the approach) partially hidden gully (Forked Gully). To the left of Forked Gully, the buttress wall is broken by several shallow scoops, then gradually merges into the hillside. The main buttress decreases in height rightwards towards the col. Below and right of the main buttress is a small steep buttress. The routes are described from left to right.

Several routes have names leading from a strange story. In March 1925, three young men set off to climb Beinn Achaladair. It was cold and frosty with hard snow. One of the trio went ahead and became separated from the party. The other two searched until dusk but gave up and descended. For several days parties searched the hill, with no luck, then mysterious letters postmarked Peterhead began to arrive, telling of a supernatural voice giving information. In all five letters were received, including a rough sketch map. One of the letters indicated that he would be found at a height of 3060ft. He was, some three weeks following his disappearance. Having no crampons, he probably slipped on hard snow or ice, and failed to brake with his axe. The letter writer was eventually traced as being a Norman MacDiarmid, who seemed to have possessed a gift of writing messages backwards. Now if only weather forecasting were included ...

1   Eldritch   125m   II   (1995)
Start 40 metres left of the start of Forked Gully. Climb a shallow groove to easing ground.

2   Rock Scar Groove   125m   III   (1984)
Start 30 metres left of the start of Forked Gully. The groove becomes more defined with height and gives two ice pitches leading to a final short snow slope.

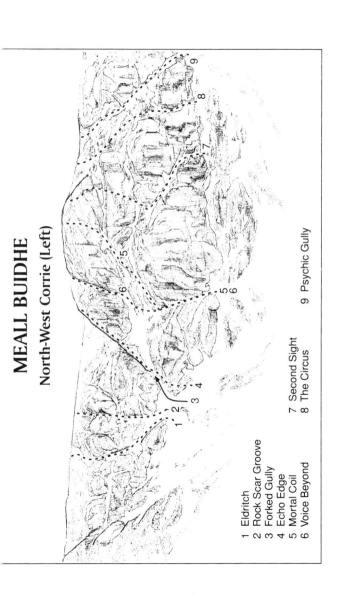

MEALL BUIDHE

North-West Corrie (Left)

1 Eldritch
2 Rock Scar Groove
3 Forked Gully
4 Echo Edge
5 Mortal Coil
6 Voice Beyond

7 Second Sight
8 The Circus

9 Psychic Gully

3   Forked Gully   105m   II *   (1984)
Easy snow leads to a fork at two-thirds height. The left fork is normally easier, on uncomplicated snow. The right fork narrows to give about 20m of steep climbing with possible cornice problems.

The following five routes climb the main buttress.

4   Echo Edge   135m   III **   (1987)
Climb the edge formed by the right-hand retaining wall of Forked Gully and the main buttress on the right. Good in the middle.

5   Mortal Coil   170m   II   (1984)
Start at the base of an obvious diagonal gully to the right of Forked Gully. Climb the gully past an easy-angled ice pitch to just before a large snowfield. Take the right-slanting snow ramp to steepening ground. Climb directly up steep, exposed, though broken ground to gain the plateau.

6   Voice Beyond   155m   IV   (1988)
Climb the diagonal gully of Mortal Coil, but instead of moving right, climb the snowfield directly to gain a bay in the face above. Climb the fine steep 25m ice pitch followed by broken ground above.

7   Second Sight   170m   III   (1984)
Near the centre of the main buttress is an obvious wide left-slanting snow ramp. Climb a steep ice pitch to gain the ramp and follow this to its end below a steep groove. Traverse 10 metres hard right, then take the line of least resistance up mixed ground above.

8   The Circus   160m   IV   (1977)
This is the icefall about 30 metres right of Mortal Coil, and bounding the right-hand side of the steepest part of the crag.
1. 45m   Climb the icefall to a ledge.
2. 45m   Climb an ice chimney to the snow slopes above.
3 and 4. 70m   Climb up and left by walls and grooves to the top.

9   Psychic Gully   150m   III   (1984)
This diagonal gully bounds the right side of the steepest part of the main buttress, and starts at the base of the snow shelf dividing the

MEALL BUIDHE
North-West Corrie (Right)

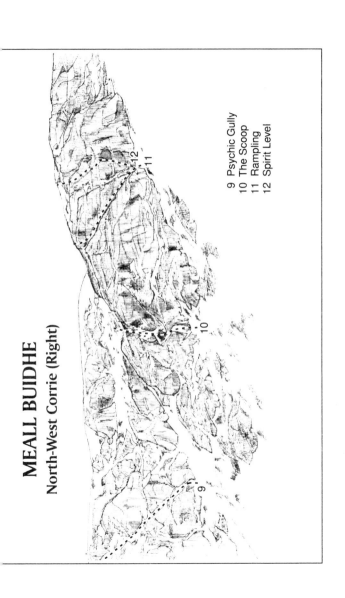

9 Psychic Gully
10 The Scoop
11 Rampling
12 Spirit Level

main buttress from the steep right-hand lower buttress. It may be hidden from the approach. A short ice pitch gives access to the gully. Its upper reaches contain a double ice pitch and a short awkward finishing corner on the right.

The following three routes climb the steep lower buttress right of the main buttress.

10   The Scoop   55m   III   (1984)
Climb the ice-filled scoop near the left end of the buttress directly.

11   Rampling   80m   II   (1987)
In the centre of the lower buttress a faint ramp line goes up and left (just left of a discontinuous ice fall). It provides an exposed snow climb.

12   Spirit Level   90m   III   (1987)
Start as for Rampling. Climb up and right to a bay below a roofed corner. Move left and climb a steep groove and the continuation above to a left-trending ramp. Climb this to the top.

BEINN ACHALADAIR

1039m   (Map Ref 345 434)

The routes are in the north-eastern corrie of this hill. Approach as for Meall Buidhe, from Achallader Farm (4km, 90 minutes). A low line of north-facing crags extends westwards in the corrie. The most obvious feature is a rock rib, low down near the eastern end, with a distinctive, clean, cracked left-hand retaining wall.

Medium Groove   150m   II *   (1987)
About 30 metres left of the obvious rock rib is a thin groove, widening into a gully above. Climb the groove directly, with two chockstoned narrowings. (It is easier if these are banked out).

Manifestation   160m   III *   (1987)
Immediately left of the rock rib is a slabby corner. Climb this to steepening rock, move slightly left, climb up, then back right. Climb a steep groove, in line with the lower corner, to gain more broken ground and so to the top.

Redemption   140m   II   (1988)
Start just right of the lowest rocks, well right of Manifestation, and climb a short steep corner to a hidden groove. Higher up the groove a ramp leads left onto easy snow and so to the top.

Near the west end of the crags, just before a little col, is a steep tower-like buttress, taken by the following route:

Premonition   65m   IV **   (1988)
Climb the tower-like buttress by a central line and follow the snow arete to finish. Sustained.

Apprehension   65m   IV *   (1988)
This climb follows the open icy corner formed by the left flank of the tower and the slabby face on the left. Frequently the finish is corniced.

The scenic north-east corrie of Beinn Achaladair contains several wedge-shaped buttresses and easy snow gullies, including an impressive narrow gully below the summit. About 100 metres south-east of the summit are two parallel broad gullies. Difficulties in these gullies should be confined to possible cornices only, while snow conditions of course should be checked for avalanche potential.

BEINN AN DOTHAIDH

1002m   (Map Ref 332 408)

The summit is the central of three tops, which is 500 metres to the east of, and 6m higher than, the West top. The latter is nearest to the north-east cliffs. Climbing on this fine hill is in two corries, the North-East and the South-West, gained from Achallader Farm and Bridge of Orchy Station respectively. The North-East Corrie gives more reliable conditions but requires a snow build-up, there being little ice, while some climbs in the South-West Corrie are fed by springs and come into condition with a good freeze. The cliffs in the North-East Corrie, though partly visible from the road over the Blackmount, are mostly hidden by the North Ridge, perhaps explaining their late development. They provide an excellent alternative to Glen Coe and indeed with a shorter drive from the central belt and easier access, their popularity sees climbing teams from the north of England visiting them for the day.

NORTH-EAST CORRIE

Access to the climbs in this corrie begins at Achallader Farm car park. Walk round the barn opposite the house and through the gate beyond to reach the moor. Continue above the farm and cross the railway by a bridge. Follow the west bank of the Allt Coire Achaladair for about an hour, then head diagonally right to pass under the end of the north ridge, aiming for a cone-shaped hillock as a target. Enter the subsidiary corrie under the cliffs (4km, 90 minutes). Either strike up into the corrie just right of the hillock (steeper), or continue on a bit and head up left of the hillock. To the left of the corrie entrance are several easy gullies on the north face, overlooking Coire Daingean (pronounced 'tingin', as in 'tingin in the rain'). The obvious wide gully above and just inside the subsidiary corrie is the West Gully, a useful landmark in misty conditions. In very icy conditions a short steep icefall has been climbed on the terminating wall of the ridge right of the hillock.

Most of the climbing, and certainly all of the steeper and more technical routes, are to be found in the right-hand subsidiary corrie. The two large buttresses here are North Buttress on the left and the West Buttresses further right, these two separated by West Gully. Further east, and leading to the plateau close to the col between the summit and the West Top, are several easy snow gullies.

The routes are described from left to right, starting with the snow gullies. Descent following a climb may be effected by West Gully, given safe snow, though it is often corniced, or more reliably by continuing west behind the cliff edge and dropping down to the flat section of the North Ridge. An easy descent then leads into the subsidiary corrie, but avoid descending too soon and beware of avalanche danger.

1   East Gully   250m   I
Straightforward snow leads to a possible cornice exit. On the left of the gully a well-defined ridge provides an alternative easy route of ascent.

2   Emel Ridge   200m   II   (1978)
Climb the ridge between the eastern and central gullies directly to the summit.

3   Zigzag Gully   250m   I   (1894)
This gully lies just left of Central Gully, and gives a straightforward ascent on snow and some easy rocks.

4   Central Gully   250m   I   (1894)
The easy snow gully immediately left of North Buttress has a possible cornice finish.

The following routes are approached from the floor of the fine little subsidiary corrie. The obvious gully is West Gully. About one-third of the way up this a steeper gully breaks up on the left (Taxus). The buttress left of West Gully is somewhat indeterminate, and is climbed by four lines. The lower section of the buttress is marked by a large icicle fringe which forms just left of centre, and a square-shaped snow bay which lies at the bottom left-hand side.

5   Jobseeker's Allowance   125m   IV,6   (1996)
This is a good and varied line threading the overhangs on the left-hand side of the buttress via an obvious chimney-groove line. Start on the left side of the large snow bay some 20 metres left of Femme Fatale.
1. 15m   Climb the shallow right-facing groove to a small recess below a bulge.
2. 30m   Climb the bulge above (crux) and exit left just below the start of the main overhang to reach a narrow terrace. Traverse about 10 metres left along the terrace to reach a deep and narrow chimney.
3. 35m   Climb the awkward chimney and continue up the steep groove, exiting rightwards to easier ground.
4. 45m   Follow the line of least resistance to easy ground.

6   Femme Fatale   120m   IV,4 **   (1995)
This excellent sustained route follows a direct line straight up the obvious line in the centre of the buttress, just right of the icicle fringe. It is steeper than it appears from below.
1. 30m   Belay at the top right-hand corner of the square-shaped snow bay, directly below the first steep chimney. Enter and climb the corner on steep but good turf, then continue directly and up the corner to climb a short overhanging corner (crux) to a small ledge and belay.
2. 40m   Continue up the next series of corners, which may be heavily iced, to reach a small snow field. Above is an obvious corkscrew-shaped chimney. Climb this and belay 5m further on.
3. 50m   Continue up and left to reach easy ground and a choice of finishes. Either continue up the buttress above to join up with Taxus near the summit or, conditions allowing, traverse left and down to join one of the easier gullies and so descend to the corrie floor.

7 Circean 145m IV,5 ** (1995)

An excellent, harder companion route to Femme Fatale. Below and right of the square-shaped snow bay the buttress descends in a series of easier-angled slabs. Belay at the start of the slabs, at the lowest point of the buttress and below an obvious corner 10 metres right of Femme Fatale.

1. 25m Climb the slabs, difficult if thinly iced, trending left to a belay below the corner.

2. 35m Enter the corner above (strenuous). Continue up the steep right-trending corner for 30m (sustained), until it ends at a small ledge. Above and left is a small cave with a good belay.

3 and 4. 85m Just to the left is an undercut blocky wall. Climb over this with difficulty (exposed) to enter the small snowfield and continue up the corkscrew chimney as for Femme Fatale.

8 Spring Fever 115m III,4 (1996)

Start at the lowest point of the buttress as for Circean.

1. 25m Climb straight up by the line of least resistance to a belay below and just to the right of a distinctive wide slot.

2. 30m Climb through the wide slot, then follow a right-trending groove to belay on a ledge steeply overlooking the snow slope that runs up into Taxus.

3. 40m Ascend slabby vegetated ground to reach a small snowfield. Move up and right to belay at a wall just left of a bay.

4. 20m Move right into the bay, then climb a short steep scoop to reach snow above. An easy left traverse at this point allows a descent or alternatively carry on climbing *via* broken ground for several hundred metres to reach the summit ridge.

9 Journey to the East 260m III * (1987)

This climb takes a ramp line on the left wall of Taxus. Start 50m below and left of Taxus. Climb the ramp roughly parallel to Taxus until below a steep rock corner. Traverse right to join Taxus above its ice pitches. Immediately above, a wide snow ramp breaks back left. Follow the ramp, then zigzag up, trending left to the top of the buttress and a junction with Taxus at the snow ridge. Finish up Taxus.

10 Taxus 240m III *** (1969)

The classic middle grade climb on the mountain takes a gully line branching left out of West Gully. Difficulties on the original line are confined to the initial steep section of one or two pitches, which can be of ice or steep snow. Above this, snow leads to a bifurcation. Climb the left branch to a snow ridge and follow this until an easy leftward traverse leads to a narrow gully. Climb this to the summit. It is prone to avalanche in poor conditions.

10a   The Icefall Finish   90m   IV,4 ***   (1976)
The length given is for the variation pitches only. This direct finish to Taxus starts at the bifurcation of that route and climbs the prominent icefall above to reach the summit *via* an obvious recess.

11   The Beechgrove Garden   210m   III   (1978)
This route follows the vegetated buttress just right of Taxus, starting from West Gully 15m above Taxus. To the right again is the obvious ramp taken by The Upper Circle. Climb up and left onto the buttress crest. Follow a line left of the crest to join a small gully common with The Upper Circle. The gully leads back right to a saddle and a choice of finishes.

12   The Upper Circle   200m   III **   (1981)
On the left wall of West Gully, and beyond the start of Taxus, is a prominent ramp, protected by a steep wall. Gain the ramp by a short hard corner, then follow the ramp in three pitches, going right at the top of the third pitch to gain a platform. To avoid a short vertical wall, traverse down and left round a corner into a small gully which leads back right to a saddle. Finish by a choice of lines.

13   The Goatherd   90m   IV   (1994)
Start very high up West Gully, beneath its final snowfield fan. The route climbs the last buttress on the left, below a snow ridge. Start at the gully on the left of the buttress and meander up the buttress, taking the easiest line *via* icefalls for 60m to finish up an easy snow ridge.

14   West Gully   300m   I   (1894)
The uncomplicated snow gully cutting up between the North and West Buttresses goes through good scenery, but as usual beware of avalanche risk.

The rocks lying right of West Gully are divided by fault lines into (from left to right) the North-West, West, and Far West Buttresses. All the routes bar the first two start from a sloping terrace gained from the small corrie under the buttresses, easier from the right. The rock is a compact schist, and protection on the buttress routes is sometimes provided by drive-in screws in frozen turf. From the normal approach *via* the Allt Coire Achaladair, the most obvious line apart from the West Gully is the gully of Haar, starting up the left corner of a square-cut recess dividing the two left-hand buttresses. The routes are described from left to right.

NORTH-WEST BUTTRESS

15   Stairway to Heaven   135m   III *   (1982)
Climb the left edge of North-West Buttress by walls and ramps, leaving West Gully where Taxus starts. There are two rocky steps, with one good pitch at half-height on the second step. This is a useful climb in poor conditions with good views of optimistic teams being avalanched in Taxus.

16   The Skraeling   270m   IV,5 **   (1976)
A good climb following a natural line up the buttress left of Haar. A Skraeling, for the curious, is not the sound made by a bottoming drive-in, it's the name the Vikings applied to the North American Indians, the ones who were such a hassle that the Vikings eventually left.
1 and 2. 80m   Start up rocks right of the foot of West Gully and climb easily to gain the broad terrace below the main buttress. Alternatively gain the terrace from the right *via* the corrie and traverse left to gain the same point. Belay under an obvious roof.
3. 40m   On the buttress, left of Haar, is an obvious corner. From the belay move down and left for 10m, then follow turf up the wall to gain the left edge of the main corner. Belay 20m up the corner under a small roof.
4. 25m   Climb the upper section of the corner (crux, good protection), moving left below the roof to gain the upper grooves.
5. etc 125m   Several easier pitches in the upper grooves lead to the plateau.

The prominent buttress edge left of Haar has been climbed, with the crux being a fierce overhanging corner at mid-height (**Pedant's Corner** V,7 1996). No further details are available.

Ménage à Trois, North-East Corrie of Beinn an Dothaidh
                                        (Climber, Jonathan Baird)

17   Haar   135m   III *   (1972)
This is the gully dividing the North-West and West Buttresses. Start on
the terrace below the cliff, below a square-cut recess. A short ice pitch
leads up into the left corner of the recess (belay). On the right is the
crux ice pitch leading to the gully proper. Above, normally
straightforward snow leads to the top.

18   Valhalla   150m   IV,5   (1984)
This route tackles a steep icefall starting approximately 10 metres right
of Haar, i.e. the right-hand corner of the square-cut recess. The icefall
is very variable and may not exist in some seasons. There have been
several recent ascents of this route, which has been closely observed
by many parties, all waiting for the ice column to form fully and reach
the ground. This ascent is the earliest known and is yet another
deplorable case of belated recording. If it's worth climbing, report it
promptly!
1. 50m   Climb the icefall and belay on the right in the narrow gully
above.
2. 50m   Trend right and climb steep rock and ice bulges to belay at the
foot of the summit snow cone.
3. 50m   Climb the snow cone to the summit.

WEST BUTTRESS

19   Stormbringer   150m   III *   (1977)
The steep buttress right of Haar. Start on the terrace below the corner
of Valhalla. Gain a ledge on the right, make a difficult step up, then go
up and right to belay in a corner. Continue directly by a shallow scoop
and mixed climbing.
Direct Start: 50m   V,6   (1996)
Good steep climbing following the true line of the Stormbringer fault.
Start midway between Haar and the fault line of West Buttress Direct
Start, below a vertical right-facing corner.
1. 25m   Climb the corner and pull over a bulge to a good ledge.
2. 25m   Continue over an impending block to enter the lower section
of the main Stormbringer corner. Follow this for 20m to where the
original route comes in from the left.

  Above the terrace under the main face is an undercut wall. On its
right is a tapering shelf, starting about halfway between Haar and the

Quartzvein Scoop, Beinn Udlaidh (Climbers, Mick Fowler and Chris Watts)

next gully right, Cirrus. The shelf is taken by West Buttress, while the undercut wall is taken by the Direct Start, described first.

20   West Buttress, Direct Start   45m   V,6   (1996)
The undercut wall bypassed by the initial ramp of West Buttress is cut by a prominent overhanging chimney. Climb this, stepping out right then back left to avoid an awkward section. Bridge past a roof at 25m to gain an easier deep continuation chimney and the original route above. A good pitch. Continuing in the fault line throughout when following the original line results in a fine logical route.

21   West Buttress   120m   III *   (1976)
The original line on the West Buttress gives a good turf climb, requiring a minimum of snow in a good freeze. It was first climbed in summer by 1935, giving a vegetatious climb (Ghyll Buttress, Very Difficult). Start from the terrace below the main cliff. Above an undercut section will be seen a series of chimney grooves. Gain this system from the right using a tapering shelf, starting about halfway between Haar and Cirrus. After the initial left traverse, zigzag up using the grooves and go over one steepening to gain easier ground above.

22   Slow March   195m   IV   (1976)
A rather circuitous route. Start at the right edge of West Buttress, some 6 metres left of the obvious deep cleft taken by Cirrus. Climb up and left to a belay in a snow bay. Go up and right beneath an overhanging corner, then follow a left-slanting ramp to a wide triangular corner and belay. Step down and traverse horizontally left for 15 metres to an ice groove, follow the groove for 30m, then an easy traverse left leads to pleasant snow and ice grooves. Climb these to finish.

23   Splitting the Difference   180m   IV,6   (1989)
This is a direct variation on Slow March, with a hard and technical crux. Climb straight up to the foot of the overhanging triangular corner; belay. Climb the corner direct by wide bridging (crux; ice is useful) to ledges and a belay. Follow the steep but straightforward groove system above, just left of the barrel-fronted buttress, over several bulges to the top.

24   Pas de Deux   165m   V,6 **   (1986)
This neo-classic route weaves an intriguing way up the steep ground left of Cirrus. Start below and left of the foot of Cirrus at a short open groove which leads to an obvious left-trending ramp.

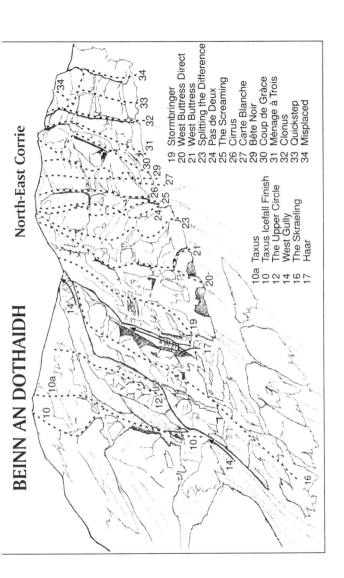

BEINN AN DOTHAIDH

North-East Corrie

10a Taxus
10   Taxus Icefall Finish
12   The Upper Circle
14   West Gully
16   The Skraeling
17   Haar

19   Stormbringer
20   West Buttress Direct
21   West Buttress
23   Splitting the Difference
24   Pas de Deux
25   The Screaming
26   Cirrus
27   Carte Blanche
29   Bête Noir
30   Coup de Grâce
31   Ménage à Trois
32   Clonus
33   Quickstep
34   Misplaced

1. 35m   Climb the ramp with increasing difficulty to gain a good ledge (optional belay on a loose flake at 30m), then move back right to belay beneath a short open corner. It is possible to take a slightly harder and more direct variation for the final part of this pitch.
2. 50m   Climb the technical corner on tufts and edges to easier ground. Remembering to place a runner for the second, traverse a ledge rightwards until it narrows, then go up a short wall to gain a right-trending zigzag line leading to a thread belay overlooking Cirrus. This is below and right of a striking tower of clean rock, well seen from below.
3. 30m   Climb the left side of slot, past an icicle fringe, to spacious ledges below the overhanging face of the tower. Climb the short but steep corner on the right of the tower, exiting steeply rightwards to reach easy ground.
4. 50m   A snow ramp trends left above and leads to the top.

25   The Screaming   135m   VIII,8 **   (1996)
A very steep mixed route taking the front face of the barrel-shaped buttress of Pas de Deux. The route is sustained throughout, but the highlight is the compelling crack line in the final tower. A monstrous hexentric is required to protect the final section. Start at the foot of Cirrus, below an undercut ramp, 15m up and right of Pas de Deux.
1. 25m   Climb into a niche, then edge out left to below a short overhanging wall. Climb this to a ramp which leads to a horizontal ledge. Move right along this for 5m to a thread belay on a large block. A steep pitch.
2. 40m   Climb the wall directly above the belay to a horizontal break (junction with Pas de Deux). Step right to gain a left-slanting chimney-groove and follow this to a good ledge. Step left to a fine steep corner. Climb this to below the final tower, then move right to the spacious ledge of Pas de Deux.
3. 20m   The front face of the tower is split by a prominent crack. Gain a niche from the right and continue up the crack above. At its top, move right to a second niche, then pull through the overhanging slot to the top. This pitch overhangs continuously and is very strenuous both to climb and to stop to place gear; 3 axe rests were taken on the first ascent. A free ascent has been made with a runner in place where the crack widens.
4. 50m   Continue up the straightforward upper buttress to the top.

26 Cirrus   110m   IV,4 **   (1974)

This is the obvious deep gully-cleft dividing the West and Far West Buttresses. There will normally be a steep 10m ice pitch at about mid-height and several other short pitches. Early in the season it can be desperate.

27 Carte Blanche   120m   IV,5 *   (1989)

This varied line climbs the great slab between Cirrus and Far West Buttress, then takes a steep chimney-groove system above. Start at the foot of Cirrus.

1. 45m   A slightly rising fault line runs out right across the slab. Follow this fault for about 10m until it is possible to break back leftwards to reach the base of a short, inverted, two-stepped groove. Climb the first part of the groove, then step right on a ledge. Move slightly right, go up, traverse back left (delicate), then climb directly to a snowfield.

2. 20m   Climb the snowfield to a steep chimney-groove system in the upper face; belay on the left.

3. 40m   Climb the chimney-groove with a difficult finish onto easier ground.

4. 15m   Ascend snow to finish.

28 Far West Buttress   135m   III   (1977)

The buttress right of Cirrus. Start just right of the foot of Cirrus, as for Carte Blanche. Go up and right by a ramp to a chimney, climb this to a belay. Go slightly left and back right by a ramp to a ledge. Go right 15 metres to a groove which leads to the top. In poor conditions it is possible to avoid the upper section by traversing across Cirrus to reach the easy ramps above the top of the barrel-shaped buttress.

29 Bête Noire   130m   V,7   (1996)

A direct line between Cirrus and Carte Blanche, with a spectacular and unlikely finish through the headwall. Start directly below the left-facing groove which cuts through the great slab of Carte Blanche.

1. 15m   Scramble up easy ground to the base of the slab.

2. 50m   Climb up directly on thin and spaced turf to reach the foot of the groove. Climb the lower section (common with Carte Blanche), and continue up the upper groove to a roof. Pull round this on the right and continue directly up the snowfield above. Belay below the steep headwall about 10 metres left of the upper chimney of Carte Blanche.

3. 25m   Pull onto the ledge above, step left, then move right onto a ramp. Climb this up and right, then move across a hidden turfy break across the overhanging wall on the left to a steep exit. A good pitch.

4. 40m   Finish up easy ground to the top.

Can't, Won't, Shan't (25m VII,6 1996) is a very difficult and bold slab climb right of Carte Blanche, starting after scrambling up Far West Buttress for 30m to a small ledge where Far West Buttress steps down and moves 15 metres right. Climb straight up the slab heading for the 'frog's eyes' of turf, then regain the line of Far West Buttress. Protection is in the form of tied-off drive-ins and a hand hook.

30   Coup de Grâce   120m   V,7 *   (1993)
This good technical mixed route takes the bulging groove line to the left of the prominent right-facing corner of Menage a Trois. Start directly below the groove.

1. 40m   Climb a short wall and continue up turf and snow to a belay at the top of the first chimney of Far West Buttress.

2. 20m   Climb the crack above, pull round the bulge, and move up a turfy depression to belay below the second bulge.

3. 20m   Make a difficult series of moves up the smooth vertical wall above, step right onto the arete and bridge up the impending corner. A fine pitch.

4. 40m   Traverse left for 10m to the foot of a right-slanting turfy ramp. Follow this to the top.

31   Ménage à Trois   105m   V,6 **   (1987)
About 12 metres to the left of Clonus is a steep parallel corner, facing right at mid-height on the face. Start below the steep corner.

1. 25m   Climb a steep wall to a snow bay.

2. 45m   Climb a steep awkward wall, then move right up a ramp leading into the base of the corner. The corner gives excellent, sustained but well protected climbing with a hard section near the top. Break out right just below the top to belay on a wide ledge.

3. 35m   Step right and follow the groove above to the top.

Variation Finish: 40m   V,5   (1996)
A way of extending the interest. From the belay at the end of pitch 3, step back left to climb the true finish of the groove steeply. From the large ledge above, step left to the foot of a steep crack. Climb this to exit leftwards steeply but on good turf.

32 Clonus 115m IV ** (1976)
This is the right-facing corner about 30 metres right of Cirrus.
1. 35m Climb the corner and iced slabs to a good stance and belay above a small slot.
2. 40m Climb slabs to an overhanging barrier pitch in a corner; peg runner *in situ*. Climb the difficult groove right of the corner for 5m, gain a ledge and traverse left across the top of the corner to easy snow. A rising right traverse leads back into the corner and a belay. Escape is possible below the crux *via* a snow shelf which leads to the right.
3. 40m Continue up the corner, now almost a gully, to the top.

33 Quickstep 90m III,3 (1987)
Start 20 metres right of Clonus. Climb faint snow grooves bounding the right side of steep rock to a short barrier. Climb this, then traverse a wide ledge left below a vertical rock wall to join Clonus. Either break back right by a short ramp, or finish up Clonus. Contrived.

34 Misplaced 135m III,4 (1995)
1. 35m Climb broken stepped rock bounding the right side of Far West Buttress to a belay below a steep wall.
2. 15m Traverse right to a steep corner-chimney breaching the wall and climb this; crux.
3. 45m A rising traverse left leads back into the corner and a belay above Clonus.
4. 40m Finish up the corner-gully to the top.

Finally, the short gully at the right end of this cliff provides a pleasant and straightforward ascent of at most Grade II.

COIRE AN DOTHAIDH

This is the west-facing corrie above Bridge of Orchy, which provides a convenient starting point. With the exception of one good rock climb, the corrie is of winter interest only. Car parking is available at the railway station above the A82. From the carpark walk through the tunnel under the line and go through a gate to the open hillside. Head left towards the Allt Coire an Dothaidh and follow the path parallel to the burn to enter the corrie. On the left or north wall is a prominent gully, directly ahead is the vegetatious Creag Coire an Dothaidh, while on the right or south wall of the corrie is the steep Creag an Socach. For the latter crag it is best to follow the path to where it crosses the burn, then head up and right. For Creag Coire an Dothaidh continue over the burn, climb a short steep section of the path, then go left on a terrace to reach the crag. (2km, 1 hour).

The routes in the corrie are described clockwise, starting with the gully on the north flank.

Highway to Hell   300m   III/IV   (1982)
The obvious deep gully on the left of the corrie requires a good freeze for a sufficient ice build up. The gully is escapable in the middle section and finishes up a 20m icefall.

CREAG COIRE AN DOTHAIDH
(Map Ref 325 403)

This is the vegetatious crag facing west down to Bridge of Orchy. It is well seen from the window of the Bridge of Orchy Hotel bar, preferably after a good ascent. Some of the climbs are fed by springs and require a good freeze of at least several days' duration to come into condition. Two obvious lines are Salamander Gully on the left, crowned with an icefall high up, and the series of icefalls on the right taken by Fahrenheit 451, which requires about a week of cold weather. Preferably avoid the cliff on clear days, when the ice may thaw in the sun, with risk of falling ice, particularly on Fahrenheit 451. The rock is a compact schist, with most protection in the form of drive-ins into frozen turf.

Coire an Dothaidh translates as the corrie of the burning, hence several route names have tried to fit in with this. Most are obvious, though not all readers may be aware of the classic SF novella *Fahrenheit 451* (the temperature at which paper spontaneously combusts. It was also the length of the route, in Imperial feet.)

To descend from the climbs, go right and down to the col between Beinn an Dothaidh and Beinn Dorain. The routes are described from left to right.

1   The Firebird   170m   III,3   (1985)
Near the left end of the cliff is the starting gully of Salamander. Start about 30m up and left of Salamander, at an icefall. Climb the icefall, then go up an easy-angled scoop to below a rock buttress. Thread through the buttress, finishing *via* a right-slanting ramp seen from the approach.

A shorter gully on the left provides a Grade II/III

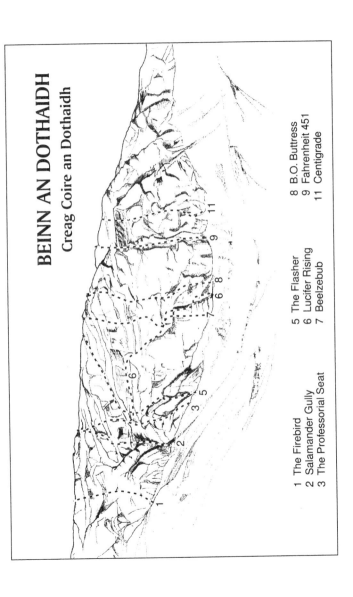

BEINN AN DOTHAIDH
Creag Coire an Dothaidh

1 The Firebird
2 Salamander Gully
3 The Professorial Seat

5 The Flasher
6 Lucifer Rising
7 Beelzebub

8 B.O. Buttress
9 Fahrenheit 451
11 Centigrade

2 Salamander Gully 150m III ** (1976)

Near the left end of the cliff will be seen a shallow gully leading to an icefall, very obvious from the approach if formed. This gives a scenic and enjoyable route, which should be in condition after 3-4 days' good freeze. Climb the gully to the icefall, which is crossed by a ledge. Escape leftwards is possible below the icefall by following an easy continuation of the gully. The easiest line up the ice takes a groove on the left leading to a right traverse across the icefall and a belay below a bulging icefall. Climb the icefall, moving up and left, then climb an icy slab to a small ice pitch and so to the plateau.

3 The Professorial Seat 180m IV * (1981)

Down and right from Salamander Gully is a slabby corner starting above an old iron fence post and to the left of an obvious rock slab.

1. 45m Climb the corner, with a hard groove at 30m, to belay in a bay.

2. 20m Continue up the corner *via* its slabby left wall, exiting right at the top. Follow a groove above to a snowfield, go rightwards up this, then move back left across an obvious ice ramp to finish as for Salamander Gully. The Professor's second winter route!

4 The Flasher Slab 60m Hard Severe (1989)

The clean slab and wall left of The Flasher provides a good summer climb.

1. 40m Climb an obvious line up the slab.

2. 20m Continue over an awkward overlap, climbed on its left (crux). Descend down and left, using the lower section of Salamander Gully.

5 The Flasher 165m III,3 * (1982)

Immediately right of the slabby corner taken by The Professorial Seat, a shallow gully goes up, then bends left to a short icy corner. Climb the gully and corner, finishing rightwards by the easy ramp high on the face. An alternative start takes the next corner to the right on steep frozen turf.

6 Lucifer Rising 150m IV,5 (1988)

This mixed route climbs the steep central face of the buttress, starting at the lowest rocks. Some 20 metres right is the left-sloping first pitch of B.O. Buttress. Good, intricate but rather illogical route-finding.

1. 30m Climb to a peg belay below a small roof on the left wall of a shallow scoop.

2. 25m   Go down 3m and traverse a small ledge to the left (exposed). Now climb directly up a steep rib *via* shallow corners and small turf ledges to a peg belay on the wall (sustained).

3 and 4. 95m   Traverse left and climb a short deep chimney to belay above. The next pitch breaks through the roofs above at their left end. Either climb slabs (if sufficiently iced), or move hard left along an exposed ledge to belay, then go back up and right to gain the same point at the left end of the roofs, with a belay above and right on an easier-angled terrace crossing the face. The final, easier tier of rock lies above, and offers a choice of finishes up grooves and corners.

7   Beelzebub   170m   VI,6 *   (1994)

A direct line up the crest of the buttress in the centre of the crag between Lucifer Rising and B.O. Buttress. Start at the lowest rocks, 5 metres left of the first pitch of Lucifer Rising, and directly below a prominent smooth red wall 50m above.

1. 50m   Pull over a small roof and continue directly up the centre of the buttress following a series of turfy grooves. The climbing is thin at times and the protection is spaced. The left traverse and downward step of Lucifer Rising are crossed after 25m. Belay at the foot of the prominent red wall.

2. 50m   The easiest route through the steep slabs above the stance will depend on the amount of ice present. On the first ascent, a broad snow ledge was followed leftwards for 10 metres to below a 10m high corner which lies 5 metres right of the short chimney of Lucifer Rising. From the foot of the corner (poor peg runners), a right-slanting ramp leads to easier ground above the belay. Continue up and left to a short right-facing corner. Climb this and belay on the snowfield above.

3. 40m   Go left and up snow and ice to belay below a prominent roof.

4. 30m   Climb the ice step on the left, then follow icy grooves leading up and right to the top.

8   B.O. Buttress   165m   III,3 *   (1976)

This climb lies just right of the centre of the buttress, bypassing steep rock walls in the lower part by short traverses. The climbing is mainly on frozen turf and rock. Start just right of the middle of crag at a broad scoop right of ill-defined rocks. Above is a prominent red wall. The route has a big face atmosphere at an easy grade.

1. 30m   Climb mixed ground up and left to belay at foot of the red wall.

2. 40m   Traverse right, climb a short corner, then go up and left to a ledge below a short wall.

3. 35m   Go right to the end of the ledge, then work back left and go up to a belay.

4 and 5. 60m   Continue directly to the top.

9   Fahrenheit 451   135m   IV,4 ***   (1976)
Near the right end of the face a prominent icefall builds up, requiring at least a week of good freeze. An initial gully leads to ice walls, corners, short traverses, and huge sheets of water ice. When in condition it is an immensely enjoyable route giving continuous ice climbing.

10   Right Guard   150m   III,3 *   (1982)
Start up and right of Fahrenheit 451. Climb the buttress for one pitch, then go left across Fahrenheit 451 and take the easiest line to the top.

11   Centigrade   105m   III,3 *   (1983)
Start below a large protruding rock 15 metres right of Fahrenheit 451. A pleasant, varied route.

1. 45m   Climb diagonally right under the wall for 20m to an ice groove, then climb this to a belay above.

2. 45m   Climb the ramp above, move left on ice, then go up and right to belay at the foot of a scoop.

3. 15m   Climb directly out of the scoop.

Summer: 105m   Severe *   (1989)
Follow the approximate line of the winter route, taking in short entertaining walls of reasonably good rock.

BEINN DORAIN

1076m   (Map Ref 326 378)

The awesome regular flanks of this popular hillwalking mountain are broken at their northern end by a crag which is a mixed winter climbers' delight.

CREAG AN SOCACH   (Map Ref 323 397)

This is the steep crag forming the south wall of Coire an Dothaidh, seen in profile from Bridge of Orchy. It has only recently been developed in winter and contains several steep mixed routes of a high technical standard. Too much snow can be a disadvantage, and there is usually limited ice. The rock is a compact schist and protection is sometimes difficult to arrange.

The routes are described from left to right. Descend by going hard left, then follow the burn down into main corrie. It is possible in good visibility to take significant short cuts when descending, but in the dark or in thick weather it is best to aim for the path inevitably created by the hillwalkers, to avoid falling over the crags.

1   False Rumour Gully   60m   IV,4 *   (1988)
The short steep chimney at the left end of the crag gives one long ice pitch and two short ones leading to easy snow. It is rarely complete.

2   Days of Future Past   120m   IV,5 *   (1994)
This route climbs the slabby area of rock where the vertical left flanking wall of the crag gives way to the main face. It shares a common start with The Glass Bead Game and finishes at the same place as Kick Start, but otherwise stays well left of these routes for its entire length.
1. 35m   Climb a short slabby groove, then move left up an obvious fault line for about 10m to a little recess with an ancient peg. Traverse horizontally left to the base of a wide shallow scoop. Ascend this to a horizontal snow ledge, then traverse back right to belay about 4 metres left of an obvious groove.
2. 25m   A tricky move right leads into the groove, then climb straight up to a narrow exit under a big hanging icicle. Move up right on a snow ledge to belay.
3. 45m   Traverse horizontally left, with one awkward step, to a snow bay. Move back right up a snow ramp to belay at a small rock recess.
4. 15m   Move right, then go straight up to finish.

3   The Glass Bead Game   120m   V,6 **   (1987)
A wide ledge runs out right from below the chimney at the left end of the crag. Start where the ledge curves round the toe of the buttress. The ledge continues on round and up for another 10 to 15 metres.
1. 30m   Climb the short corner, pull out left and go up a groove to a small niche (old peg). Step left round an exposed edge, then go up and left to a ledge and block belay.
2. 30m   Step onto the slabby wall directly above the block, then make a rising traverse right aiming for small spike right of a steep wall. Gain the slab above the spike and belay above (sustained and technical).
3. 30m   Go hard right passing a corner to gain a ramp. Follow this to a short overhanging chimney. Climb the chimney over a roof and continue to a belay above.
4. 30m   Easy ground leads to the top.

4   Kick Start   120m   IV,4 *   (1980)
At the lowest point of the cliff a curving chimney-groove leads to a horizontal ledge cutting across the cliff at half-height. Start about 10 metres right of The Glass Bead Game, below vegetatious slabs. Climb up and right to enter the chimney-groove. Follow this to gain the ledge and traverse left along this to a groove (crossing The Glass Bead Game) which leads onto a rock ramp and the top.

5   The Prophet   120m   VI,7 **   (1991)
A direct line between Kick Start and Scorpion. Start just left of the 'conspicuous rib' on the first pitch of Scorpion.
1. 30m   Climb a snowy groove, exiting right to gain a snow bay below an obvious open corner. Belay on a large block on the right.
2. 30m   Climb the open corner until forced out onto the slabby left wall. Very thin climbing leads to easier ground. Ascend directly to gain a snow ledge with a jammed flake thread belay.
3. 35m   Step left for 2 metres, then ascend to an overhang. Cross the overhang moving right (clipped axe for aid). Go up to a second small overhang, make a long step left, then move up to a snow ramp. Move right up the ramp for a few metres to take a poor belay.
4. 25m   Continue to near the top of the ramp, then climb a slabby scoop (hard start), trending slightly left to finish.

6   Scorpion   105m   HVS **   (1976)
A good climb on good, compact rock. In the centre of the face are waterworn slabs. Start at the short conspicuous rib on the left.
1. 20m 4a   Climb the rib to a good stance on a small grass ledge; there is a good belay low down on the right.
2. 40m 5a   Climb the steep slab on the right for 25m, with an awkward finish onto a grass ledge (no protection). Follow the ledge leftwards to the foot of a corner crack.
3. 15m 4c   Climb the corner crack with a very awkward left exit at the top.
4. 30m 4a   Move up to a higher ledge, traverse slightly rightwards, then climb clean slabs to the top.

7   The Sting   120m   V,6 **   (1991)
Between Scorpion and The Promised Land lies an area of dark clean bulging rock low down on the face. A narrow rock ramp cuts across its right flank. Start at a fan of slabs below the clean bulging rock.

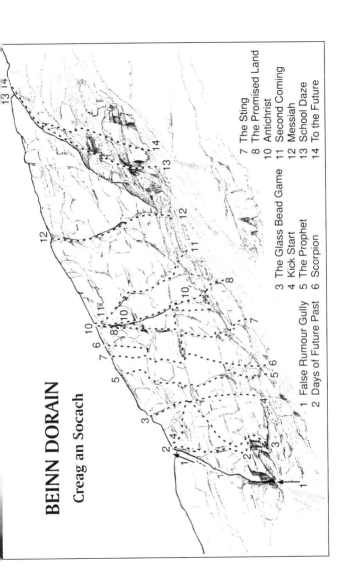

BEINN DORAIN
Creag an Socach

1 False Rumour Gully
2 Days of Future Past
3 The Glass Bead Game
4 Kick Start
5 The Prophet
6 Scorpion
7 The Sting
8 The Promised Land
10 Antichrist
11 Second Coming
12 Messiah
13 School Daze
14 To the Future

1. 30m   Move up, then left across slabs to a block with a horizontal crack. Take a snow ramp trending right until it is possible to climb up to gain a small rock bay at the base of the above-mentioned rock ramp.
2. 25m   Ascend the rock ramp, then climb directly up steep ground to belay at the right end of the central snow ledge.
3. 10m   Cross to the left end of the snow ledge to belay below the slim corner of Scorpion.
4. 15m   Climb the superb corner crack to its top (large hexentrics give useful protection), then make an interesting move left to a ledge and belay.
5. 40m   Climb to the base of a vague wide rock rib. Move slightly left, surmount a short difficult wall, then trend right up steepening ground to the top. A groove on the right of the vague rock rib would give an alternative and longer final pitch.

8   The Promised Land   120m   VI,6 **   (1987)
Start about 20m down from Second Coming, well right of Scorpion.
1. 45m   Move up to a snow ledge, then traverse left to its termination at flakes. Ascend very steep rock, then move right into a snow bay below a groove (flake runner). Traverse hard left for 8m, then go up to a large snow ledge and belay below an ice scoop (The corner of Scorpion is on the left).
2. 35m   Climb the ice scoop, exiting right by a short awkward wall, then move up to below an ice chimney.
3. 40m   Climb the left wall of the chimney on poor thin ice to gain an ice groove, then continue directly to the top by a second ice groove (common to Second Coming).

9   Deliverance   120m   VI,6   (1995)
This is a direct variation to the middle section of The Promised Land, which may overlap with Antichrist to some extent. Climb the steep turf wall, then instead of traversing left, climb the chimney followed by a left-trending open groove, then make a steep step left and move up to belay at the foot of the upper icefall. No further details are available.

10   Antichrist   120m   VI,7 **   (1992)
A good mixed route taking the groove system and wall between Promised Land and Second Coming. The final pitch might not be possible if heavily rimed, but it should be possible to escape into The Promised Land.

1.15m   Start 20 metres left of Second Coming and climb easily to the rake.

2. 25m   Climb the awkward wall 5 metres right of the flakes of Promised Land and enter the groove. Follow this to a good stance.

3. 40m   Continue up the fault line, trending left to an overhang. Climb this, then traverse right on to the lip of the overhanging wall on the right. Move up in a spectacularly exposed position to reach the terrace 5m up and right of the ice chimney of Promised Land.

4. 20m   The route continues up the impending wall above. Start on the right arete, then move left to reach a hairline crack. A series of steep moves on widely spaced tufts (not visible from below) lead to a ledge. Protection is in the form of a poor knife-blade peg in a crack on the right.

5. 20m   Continue to the top *via* the final ice groove of Second Coming.

11   Second Coming   95m   III,4 **   (1978)

High in the centre of the cliff is an obvious curving ramp line which forms the demarcation between the very steep clean wall on the right and the more slabby vegetated face on the left. A steep turfy groove drops from the ramp but does not reach the base of the crag.

1. 50m   Start to the right of the turfy groove and ascend steepening broken ground to a ledge (old peg). Hand traverse a sharp flake leftwards to gain ledges which lead to the groove. Climb this to belay in corner below steep ice.

2. 45m   Climb the ice or a little chimney on the left, traverse left along a snow ramp, then go up an icy groove to the top.

12   Messiah   85m   VII,7 ***   (1988)

The face right of Second Coming is intimidatingly steep and ledgeless. The only apparent breach is an open corner low down, which leads to a thin groove. A sustained, technical route, one of the finest lines in the Southern Highlands.

1. 30m   Climb the corner to a niche below overhanging rock. Move up and hand traverse hard left to below a groove. Gain this and go up to a small ledge.

2. 10m   Climb a short corner, then move directly up to the base of a vertical ice-filled groove. Linking the first two pitches would cause serious rope drag.

3. 45m   Climb the groove into the continuation gully above and climb this to the top.

13   School Daze   150m   II,3   (1980)

On the right of the main cliff is a buttress of more broken ground, inclined at an easier angle. Climb a difficult pitch at the junction of the main cliff and the subsidiary buttress. Thereafter follow a snow ramp onto a snowfield which leads into the finishing gully.

14   To the Future   130m   IV,5   (1995)

Start at the extreme right-hand end of the main crags, about 50m below the terminal buttress and below an obvious icefall. This route shares its last 5m with School Daze.

1. 35m   Climb the sustained and poorly protected icefall directly to a block belay.

2. 50m   An easy snow slope leads directly to the buttress above.

3. 45m   Climb the buttress *via* easy mixed ground on the left.

BEINN A' CHAISTEIL

883m   (Map Ref 346 370)

The routes on this hill face across Auch Gleann to Beinn Dorain. The access road to Auch Farm is private and cars must be left at the A82 turn-off, 5km north of Tyndrum (Map Ref 317 354). Continue on foot past the farm, go under the viaduct and up the Auch Gleann until opposite an experimental forestry plot on the left. The routes will now be seen high on the right, with rock faces and a central prominent icefall.

Benoovi Five   75m   III   (1983)

At the far left-hand of the main crag is a deep gully. Go further left to a small corrie. High up is an obvious icefall. Climb the gully to the icefall, ascend this to gain a small amphitheatre and finish direct.

Jimmy Dewar's Icefall   210m   IV *   (1982)

This is the central icefall.

1. 35m   Climb ice direct to a belay.

2. 45m   Continue directly to another belay.

3. 45m   Go left into the gully and climb it to yet another belay.

4 and 5. 85m   Continue up the gully to the headwall, climb this and continue to top.

Valkyrie   215m   IV   (1983)

Immediately right of Jimmy Dewar's Icefall is a deep-set gully. Climb the gully; there are at least four nice wee ice pitches.

Berkshire Hunt   240m   IV   (1983)

This chimney-buttress climb lies just left of the first icefall as you walk up the terrace after the obvious main gully.

1. 45m   Climb a chimney to a belay at a cave.
2. 30m   Traverse left over the cave, then move diagonally right.
3. 45m   Follow buttresses and icefalls, trending right.
4. 30m   Climb up right to a large wall.
5. 45m   Climb into an amphitheatre to belay below the final icefall.
6. 45m   Finish up the icefall.

BEINN UDLAIDH
840m(Map Ref 274 330)

Leave the A82 1km south of Bridge of Orchy and take the B8074 down Glen Orchy for 5km to where the Allt Daimh joins the Orchy. In heavy snowfall the Glen Orchy road may not be cleared quickly. Slightly further on is the entrance to Glen Orchy Farm. There is limited parking on the verge at the start of the path up the north-east side of the Allt Daimh. Because of forestry work, the walking on this path may may be very uncomfortable. The cliffs are 2½km from the road; allow 1 hour.

COIRE DAIMH

This north-facing, crescent-shaped corrie is backed by two lines of cliff; a lower, 30m tier of quartzite, and an upper tier of schist. The flat otherwise uninteresting summit slopes of Beinn Udlaidh collect sufficient precipitation to feed a series of springs which flow over the cliff edge. In a good freeze these build up impressive ice flows fairly quickly, giving routes of up to 90m in length. The climbs may come into and go out of condition from about mid-November onwards. Between the harder icefall lines are several more amenable snow and ice gullies.

Prominent landmarks on entering the corrie are the left- and right-sloping Central and West Gullies, lying in the middle of the cliffs on either side of the wide, V-shaped Central Buttress. West Gully is hidden from below but is indicated by its right-bounding ridge. The next prominent gully left of Central Gully is Sunshine Gully, appearing from below as a left-slanting ramp. Left again is Ramshead Gully, on the right flank of a square-cut recess. On the left flank of this buttress is the South Gully of the Black Wall, left of which stretches the ice-draped Black Wall. The section of cliff right of West Gully, the West Wall, is marked high up by the prominent wide icefall of Organ Pipe Wall.

Further right, on the final stretch of cliff, is the very steep ice column taken by The Smirk. The routes are described from left to right.

**1 Zigzag Gully 90m II ** (1970)
This gully starts at the leftmost edge of the corrie. It may include one ice-pitch of 30m in the centre. From the top of this traverse left into a shallow gully which leads to the top.

2 Junior's Joke 90m II (1979)
A poor route, following a corner up the buttress right of Zigzag, finishing by a traverse to gain the long final corner of that route. The true finish beckons in a good winter.

**3 Ice Crew 90m III,3 ** (1980)
A parallel route left of Quartzvein Scoop, finishing up a steep scoop.

4 Quartzvein Scoop 90m IV,4 * (1979)
The line of icy grooves immediately left of the Black Wall gives an excellent route amongst impressive scenery. There is one steep section up an ice flow.

5 Captain Hook 75m VI,6 * (1980)
Climb the funnel-shaped icefall on the Black Wall trending right, about 90m left of The Croc. The exit may be corniced and there may be unstable snow.

6 Cut-throat 75m VI,6 * (1980)
Directly between The Croc and Captain Hook is an obvious icicle. Climb the lower icefall, then go up the icicle to the top. The icicle is seldom in condition and it may require a free pull-up.

**7 The Croc 75m V,5 ** (1979)
This route takes the icefall on the right section of the Black Wall, *via* a rib. Climb the ice streak in two pitches. If the ice does not reach the ground, it can be gained by a traverse from Cut-throat.

**8 Peter Pan Direct 85m V,5 ** (1982)
At the left of the upper cliff are two obvious icefalls. This route climbs the right-hand fall. Start at its foot and climb directly to the top. The original route included some traversing. It is in condition more readily than the neighbouring routes.

BEINN UDLAIDH
Coire Daimh – East Sector

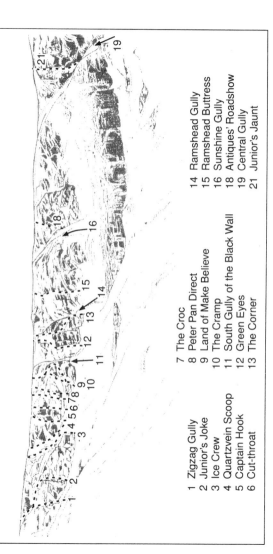

1 Zigzag Gully
2 Junior's Joke
3 Ice Crew
4 Quartzvein Scoop
5 Captain Hook
6 Cut-throat

7 The Croc
8 Peter Pan Direct
9 Land of Make Believe
10 The Cramp
11 South Gully of the Black Wall
12 Green Eyes
13 The Corner

14 Ramshead Gully
15 Ramshead Buttress
16 Sunshine Gully
18 Antiques' Roadshow
19 Central Gully
21 Junior's Jaunt

9   Land of Make Believe   90m   II *   (1979)
Start below and right of Peter Pan Direct. Climb up, trending right to a belay. Continue right to a small gully, then go up and left to belay at the top of the gully. Traverse hard right to a block, step up and continue directly to the top. An easy route through impressive scenery.

10   The Cramp   120m   IV,4 *   (1977)
Left of The South Gully of the Black Wall is a buttress often masked in ice. This route finds a jinking way up the buttress. Start to the left of the lowest rocks. Climb the first 35m of the icefall to a belay up on the right. Traverse right for 15 metres to a ledge overlooking the gully, then climb a short wall to a belay. Climb to a vertical rock wall, gain a ledge (peg runner) and go left to belay on a pedestal. Follow the obvious ice chute and continue rightwards to a corniced finish.

11   South Gully of The Black Wall   120m   IV,4 **   (1969)
The gully right of the ice-draped Black Wall gives a good route which can often carry a large cornice. A narrow chimney leads to easy ground, then a steep icefall which can be taken direct.

12   Green Eyes   120m   IV,4 *   (1979)
On the bottom of the buttress left of Ramshead Gully there is a very steep wall with an icy corner at its left margin. Gain and climb the corner, then follow a depression up and right. The lower section is good.

13   The Corner   105m   IV,4 *   (1987)
This route takes the buttress left of Ramshead Gully. Start up the gully, then traverse left onto the buttress to below an obvious 10m corner Climb the corner (crux), then continue up the ridge above to the top.

14   Ramshead Gully   120m   III *   (1976)
Easy climbing leads to a narrow chimney with an overhanging chockstone (crux). The gully then widens. Finish up a steep pitch, exiting right onto slabs.

15   Ramshead Buttress   120m   IV,4   (1980)
The broad rambling buttress between Ramshead and Sunshine Gullies carries a good deal of ice. Climb the icefall to the right-hand side of an easier slope at half-height. Finish up and right.

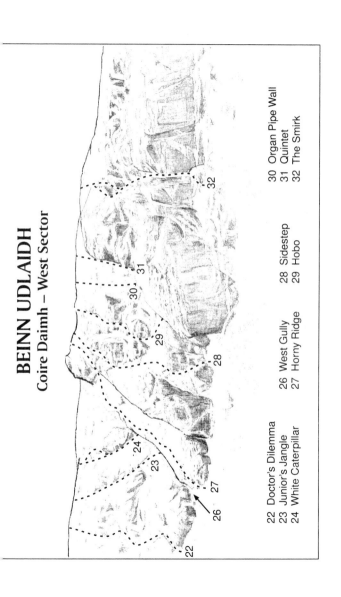

BEINN UDLAIDH
Coire Daimh – West Sector

22 Doctor's Dilemma
23 Junior's Jangle
24 White Caterpillar

26 West Gully
27 Horny Ridge

28 Sidestep
29 Hobo

30 Organ Pipe Wall
31 Quintet
32 The Smirk

16 Sunshine Gully   90m   III,3 ***   (1970)
This gully lies midway between Central Gully and South Gully of the
Black Wall. From the entrance to the corrie it looks like a left-slanting
ramp. The gully can contain much ice and gives an interesting climb.

17 Suspended Animation   90m   IV,4   (1992)
This route takes the line of icefalls to the right of the previous route
Start from a large shelf right of Sunshine Gully. Climb a vertical icefall
directly to an ice-screw belay at the foot of a steep iced slab. Climb the
slab to a sloping platform, then continue up the icefall to easier ground
Traverse left to belay behind a rock toadstool overlooking Sunshine
Gully. Return to the original line and climb directly to the top.

18 Antiques' Roadshow   100m   III,3   (1986)
The buttress between Sunshine Gully and Central Gully. Start at the
foot of Sunshine Gully, climb an iced corner, then go up steepish mixed
ground and snow up and right to the top.

Just left of the entrance to Central Gully, on the lower quartzite crag
there are two short chimneys. These have been climbed in summer
the left-hand chimney gives a 30m Very Difficult, while the right-hand
chimney is short and easy. Summer ascents have probably also been
made of Quartzvein Scoop, Ramshead Gully and the South Gully of
the Black Wall.

19 Central Gully   180m   II   (1968)
This is the left-slanting gully in the centre of the corrie. There may be
four pitches, the second one being the hardest. It banks out later in the
season.

CENTRAL BUTTRESS

20 Taking the Bait   80m   V,5 *   (1994)
Start on the right hand side of Central Gully, about 25m up the gully.
1. 30m   Climb an obvious 20m wall or ice sheet, continue through a
niche, then move left to belay.
2. 50m   Traverse back right and into a big cave, then step left and
climb the icicle. Break through the cornice where possible.

21 Junior's Jaunt   80m   IV,5 **   (1979)
This route climbs the obvious icefall starting 45m up the right side of
Central Gully. Although short, it has two good, technically hard pitches

1. 40m   Step right onto a steep iced slab and climb to its top at 30m. Traverse left to belays.
2. 40m   Traverse back right and follow the steep icefall direct to a cave. Trend right to the top.

22   Doctor's Dilemma   180m   IV,4 **   (1978)
A very good route taking the obvious wide central line of icefalls running the height of the buttress.

23   Junior's Jangle   90m   IV,4 *   (1979)
Climb a line of corners right of centre on the buttress starting just inside West Gully.

24   White Caterpillar   105m   III,3 *   (1978)
Start halfway up West Gully and break left up a wide ice ramp until a short gully leads right to another left-trending ramp, which leads to the top. A more direct line avoiding the short gully is Grade IV,4.

25   Hot Keks   95m   IV,5   (1996)
This route lies between White Caterpillar and West Gully.
1. 50m   Climb steep ice on the left to a diagonal traverse up and right to reach a vague rib.
2. 45m   Make a long traverse right and finish up a two-stepped ice fall.

26   West Gully   180m   III **
The obvious right-slanting gully can contain two enjoyable pitches, both short, leading to an easy-angled groove and finish. It can partially bank out.

THE WEST WALL

27   Horny Ridge   180m   I   (1972)
Climb the right edge of West Gully.

28   Sidestep   180m   III,3   (1979)
To the right of West Gully the buttress front leads round into a deep chimney leading up easily to below an obvious icefall. Climb the buttress left of the deep chimney to a snowfield, then go left up easier ground to the top. A better route would be to link the lower buttress with the turfy fault of Hobo.

Access to the next three routes is *via* the easy deep-cut chimney, hidden from the approach.

29   Hobo   165m   III,3   (1979)
From the bay below the icefall move out left to climb a wide turfy fault.

30   Organ Pipe Wall   75m   V,5 **   (1979)
This route climbs the obvious icefall high up on the cliff to the right of West Gully. Climb the icefall directly, *via* a groove and the wall up the middle.

31   Quintet   120m   IV,4   (1980)
Climb the right-hand side of the icefall.

32   The Smirk   90m   V,5 ***   (1979)
This is the very steep and obvious chimney-gully towards the right-hand side of the West Wall. The left fork can be climbed, but a more direct finish is also possible. It is a superb climb but slow to come into condition.

COIRE GHAMHNAIN

This is the north-east corrie of Beinn Udlaidh, probably best gained by crossing the north spur of Beinn Udlaidh, then contouring in. There are two routes to date:

Hyde and Seek   50m   IV,4   (1991)
This climb takes the most obvious steep icefall at the top right-hand corner of the corrie. Follow the ice out of a small cave on the right to a belay on top of a pinnacle. Finish up and rightwards.

Tinkerbell   70m   III,3   (1994)
Climb the stepped stream at the extreme right of the corrie above a dry stane dyke.

Other Hills and Crags in the Southern Highlands

One of the fascinating aspects of this area is the uncountable number of crags, gullies and other features of interest to the climber. Many are mica-schist outcrops, providing short sporty routes. Some, as with Ben Lui and Beinn Cruachan, have longer winter climbs which are well worth a visit and often provide a quiet day on the hill. Some of the unrecorded crags would probably find their way into a guidebook had they been in a busier, more populated area. That there is a sufficiency of good climbing present allows these unrecorded crags to preserve a sense of exploration lost elsewhere. In time the better ones may be found in a future edition, but in the meantime we hope that the current sense of balance prevails, permitting that elusive feeling of exploratory excitement so crucial to the development of each generation of climbers.

This section is described roughly from north to south.

BEN LUI
1130m   (Map Ref 266 263)

The north-east face of Ben Lui, and its bounding ridges, provide several easy and scenic winter climbs in Coire Gaothaich, well seen from the A82 just south of Tyndrum. Access to the corrie is by two routes. The longer starts from Dalrigh (Map Ref 343 292) or at Tyndrum Lower Station, with both starts taking a private road which join 1km east of Cononish Farm. A mountain bike would be a useful tool. Follow the private road leading to Cononish Farm (Map Ref 302 285), continue west to the track end at the Allt an Rund; the corrie is directly ahead (about 8.5km; allow 2½ hours to get into the corrie from the car).

The shorter route begins from Glen Lochy. Start at a car park off the A85 road near the foot of the Eas Daimh (Map Ref 239 279). If the Lochy is in spate, cross at a bridge about 1km downstream. Follow a path on the north side of the Eas Daimh to the end of the forest. Continue to cross the col on the north side of Ben Lui, traverse upwards below the Ciochan Beinn Laoigh, continue under the lower end of the rocky north-east ridge of Stob Garbh and so enter Coire Gaothaich (about 4.5km).

The routes are described from left to right.

East Ridge   Easy
An easy scramble taking the left-bounding ridge of the corrie.

South Gully   I
A broad snow gully with several finishes. The left-hand and direct finishes gain the South Ridge, the right-hand finish ends on the upper part of the South Rib.

South Rib   II
The difficulties are confined to the lower section. This route is a safer alternative to the gullies in avalanche conditions.

South-Central Gully   I
The ill-defined gully immediately right of South Rib.

Central Gully   180m   I   (1891)
This popular route is the classic winter route in the corrie. Normally it is uncomplicated snow with a choice of finishes to the summit ridge. It opens up after about 100m below the final slopes, and there may be a cornice, but it should always be possible to outflank it.

Upper Snowfield   I
The snowfield up and right of Central Gully is open to much variation. Finish at the north-west top by a narrow gully, or on the north-east ridge a short distance below the top.

North Rib   I
This is the ill-defined buttress adjoining the north-east ridge.

Descent to the Cononish approach from the summit is *via* the north top and down the north-north-east ridge (Stob Garbh) until an easy descent can be made into the corrie. For Glen Lochy, descend *via* the south-west ridge to the bealach at the head of the Fionn Choire and go down this to gain the wood and path leading to the Eas Daimh.

BEINN CHUIRN

877m   (Map Ref 289 284)

Eas Anie   150m   IV,4 **
This is the waterfall on the east flank of Beinn Chuirn, above Cononish Farm. The start is only a few hundred metres from the gold mine workings, so it counts almost as a roadside crag (although you're not

allowed to drive there!). It comes into condition fairly readily, and provides an excellent ice climb with a lower introductory gully followed by a splendid ice wall. This provides two long pitches with ice-screw protection. There is also a right-hand finish up the gully (Grade III).

Alchemist's Wall   160m   V,5   (1986)
This route climbs the mixed face on the left side of Eas Anie. Start below a large icicle, at the left-hand side of a roof, at half-height on the face. Climb steep ice trending right to an ice ribbon at the right-hand side of the roof. Climb the ice ribbon and bulging slabs above to reach easy snow and a possible cornice finish.

BEINN DUBH
701m   (Map Ref 261 290)

This hill is the western spur of Beinn Chuirn. There are three long gullies on the steep northern face, overlooking Glenlochy crossing.

Quartz Gully   150m   Easy   (1973)
This is the left-hand gully. In winter there is one ice pitch.

Sickle Gully   300m   III   (1969)
The central gully is narrow and Nevis-like. The gully walls rise 15 to 50 metres on either side. The crux on the first ascent was a 20m pitch near the top, where the gully narrows. In thin conditions there will be more pitches, including one of over 45m.
Summer: 300m   Very Difficult   (1971)
There are four main waterfall pitches. The first (45m) can be turned on the left by broken rock. Begin the second on the right of the fall, then pass through it to gain an exposed left traverse from the top of the fall into the main gully. This is followed by a long easy stretch, leading eventually to a 60m quartz rib studded with beautiful crystals and some rare rose quartz. Above this a steep white quartz wall leads to an overhung pitch. Climb this on steep loose rock to a cave with a difficult exit. Finally, climb an awkward chockstone pitch by very steep turf.

Amethyst Gully   210m   Very Difficult   (1973)
The right-hand gully contains a triple chimney low down. Walking then leads to further short pitches, including one with quartz crystals. The exit is steep and is taken on the left by a flake. In winter the route is Grade III.

BEN CRUACHAN

1126m   (Map Ref 069 305)

This fine hill throws down four corries to the north, all of which contain headwalls providing climbing. Like many interesting hills, it lies close to the main east-west fold of the map, leading to engrossing struggles in bad weather map reading. The traverse of the main ridge is a fine route, as described in the SMC guide *The Central Highlands.*

Most of the climbing on the main Cruachan chain is best approached from the south *via* the Cruachan Reservoir. Start from the road several km west of Dalmally in the Pass of Brander at the Cruachan Power Station (Map Ref 078 268). The early bird might find one or two roadside spots to park, with parking in the Visitor Centre discouraged or closed. From the Power Station, walk east along the road for about 100 metres, then scramble under the left-hand arch of the railway bridge which goes over the Falls of Cruachan burn and climb steeply up the path on the west side of the burn. Once on the open boggy ground above the trees, it is possible to cross the burn and strike uphill to the right to join the access road to the dam. From the dam there are a variety of options depending on the chosen crag. Note that the climbs are on the opposite side of the main ridge, so good visibility or prior experience is necessary to locate the climbs.

MEALL NAN EACH

874m   (Map Ref 055 317)

This is the subsidiary hill to the west of the main Cruachan chain, and it is best approached directly from the A85 up the Allt Gruiniche starting from Map Ref 037 294. A short descent from the col separating Meall nan Each from Stob Dearg and a traverse leads to the crag on the north-east face. The main cliff, some 100m in height, is dominated by a band of overlaps at two-thirds height. Right of this, beyond the edge of the main cliff and hidden from the approach, the crag falls back into easier-angled gullies and ribs before ending at a deeply recessed gully (a possible descent route, Grade I). There are two routes:

Epona Gully   90m   II   (1996)
This is the open gully just to the right of the main cliff. At the final impasse, exits are possible either to the left or the right.

White Horse Grooves   120m   III   (1996)
This route gives mixed climbing following a right-slanting line up the
lower section of the main cliff to the edge overlooking Epona Gully.
Start at the lowest rocks.
1. 45m   Zigzag up and right *via* a turfy slab to belay in a fault line.
2. 35m   Pass a thin spike by a groove on the left, then traverse right
under corners to a notch on the buttress edge; belay above.
3. 40m   Move up, then step right into Epona Gully, finishing directly.

STOB DEARG

1104m   (Map Ref 062 307)

This shapely peak is the western extremity of the main Cruachan
ridge. Its north-east face, bounded on one side by the north ridge, has
an extent of granite slabs, on which two winter routes and a variation
have been recorded. The best approach is from the col between Stob
Dearg and the main summit of Ben Cruachan, which is most enjoyably
approached by following the track leading west across the hillside from
below the dam and taking a good path which goes up Coire Dearg to a
col at the foot of the south ridge of the main summit. A pleasant
scramble up the ridge leads to the top. Turn west along the main ridge
to reach the col, then a short easy descent leads to the foot of the face.

Original Route   150m   III   (1970)
Start at the bottom left-hand corner of the slabs, make a rising traverse
to the right, then continue straight up. The angle eases after two
pitches and snow leads to the top.
Direct Start: 60m   III   (1976)
This variation climbs the icefall which rises from the left-hand side of
the snowfield below the face, and leads to the foot of the gully of
Original Route.

Central Grooves   260m   IV   (1978)
This climb follows the prominent groove line in the centre of the face,
rising above a short steep corner at the top of a steep snowfield. In lean
conditions the snowfield may be found to be icy grooves up granite
slabs.
1, 2 and 3. 95m   Climb the groove to the right-hand side of a small
central bay.
4. 45m   Climb the 7m slab corner at the top of the bay, move left into a

recess, exit on the right and continue more easily to a recess.
5. 35m   Traverse horizontally left round an edge then go up leftwards.
6 and 7. 85m   Follow a short chimney crack to an easy groove and
finish up a short overhanging chimney to belay just below the summit.

DROCHAID GHLAS

1009m   (Map Ref 083 306)

There are five winter routes lying close together on the east face of the
north ridge of Drochaid Ghlas. The best approach is to take the track
on the west side of the Cruachan reservoir to its end, then go straight
up the steep hillside to reach the main ridge at the col between
Drochaid Ghlas and Stob Diamh (997m). Descend from a point about
a hundred metres east of the summit of Drochaid Ghlas, then contour
under the north side of the ridge. This can be quite tricky unless the
snow is good. Alternatively, from the summit of Drochaid Ghlas
descend the north ridge a little, then take the obvious easy gully
leading to slopes under the east face of the north ridge. The crag
should be avoided following heavy snowfall as the approach slopes
are avalanche-prone. The routes are described as approached from
the col. Jamie's Lum takes the central chimney-groove.

Stonethrower's Buttress   100m   III   (1990)
This slight route climbs the buttress to the left (east) of the obvious
easy gully. It was climbed in thaw during a mild winter and the name
has something to do with greenhouses. Start at the lowest rocks and
follow easy snow up a small gully in the centre of the buttress. At the
first steepening, step right into the continuation deeper gully. Follow
this to a huge jammed block which is climbed by ice forming on its left
side. Easy snow then leads to the summit cairn.

Drumnadrochaid   85m   IV,4   (1994)
This route climbs the buttress just left of Jamie's Lum on the main face.
1. 45m   Climb the right-hand of the two parallel grooves trending left.
Move back right and go up the buttress crest, then trend leftwards to
belay below an open corner.
2. 40m   Climb the corner, exiting left past a spike to gain easier
ground and the top.

Eas Anie, Beinn Chuirn (Climber, Des Rubens)

Jamie's Lum   85m   IV,5 **   (1994)

A fine route which follows the central chimney groove. It requires icy conditions.

1. 25m   Climb a short ice pitch into a snow bay below the short chimney. Belay on the right of the chimney.

2. 50m   Continue up the chimney, well iced on the left wall, and climb the continuation groove above.

3. 10m   Finish up easy ground above.

Gaoth Mhor   110m   IV,4   (1994)

The buttress between Jamie's Lum and Into the Fire.

1. 40m   Start just right of Jamie's Lum and follow the vague crest by a steep turfy chimney to belay below a wall. Move 2m to the right and climb a short square-cut chimney and a groove to a block belay.

2. 35m   Move straight up to below a steep wall, then traverse 15 metres rightwards across ledges to belay close to Into the Fire.

3. 35m   Climb the fault line above which leads up and left past a large block (clearly seen on the skyline from the belay) to finish on the ridge crest.

Into the Fire   130m   IV,5 **   (1990)

This excellent climb takes a left-slanting line on the highest part of the face. It is a mixed route which is probably the first to come into condition on the crag, and it resulted from an escape from the compelling direct line, which presents a formidable and unclimbed challenge. Start 20 metres right of an obvious groove system, at a left-slanting ramp line beneath smooth steep slabs.

1. 35m   Follow the ramp over a few steep steps to a belay at the foot of a groove.

2. 25m   Climb the groove for 15m to a huge spike on the left. Swing down left round the arete to a commodious ledge.

3. 40m   Step left, climb the left wall of the corner groove for 5m, then swing right across the groove. Traverse right round the arete, then continue straight up to belay below a chimney.

4. 30m   Climb the chimney, then continue direct to the crest of the ridge.

Left-Hand Finish: IV,4   (1995)

Follow the original route to the top of pitch 2, then continue trending up and left to finish up a chimney-groove and the open fault to the top.

First ascent of Gaoth Mhor, East Face of Drochaid Ghlas
(Climber, Neil Marshall)

BEINN EUNAICH

989m   (Map Ref 135 327)

This hill is perhaps best known for its infamous Black Shoot, a wet slimy gully which was the target of many a hard team in the last years of the previous century. Amazing what they got up to, really. The victorious party, consisting of SMC stalwarts, vowed never to repeat the experience, but that of course should not deter the young bold climbers of today (older ones are, of course, far more sensible). Gardening implements and a wet suit might be advantageous, while lightweight ladders and grappling hooks could add considerably to the enjoyment. It is best approached *via* the track on the west of the River Strae. Keep left at the fork and reach some forest after 1km. From the northern rim of the forest a faint path follows the west bank of the main burn. In just over 30 minutes or so the Black Shoot may be seen steeply above to the left. The gradings are to a certain degree hypothetical.

The Black Shoot   90m   Severe   (1892)
The obvious deep fissure in the face of a steep rocky face contains mossy waterslides, a curious twisted chimney, and other classic features. An apparently easy wall above a chimney has foiled most parties, who to their dismay have to continue up the slimy chimney instead.
Winter: 90m   III   (1900)
It is perhaps a better route if deep-frozen; it would certainly be drier.

Beaver Buttress   120m   III   (1927)
This is the buttress immediately right of the Black Shoot, with another gully bounding it on the right. The modern grade is a guesstimate. The climbing is apparently varied, with several traverses and short steep corners.

Eager Beaver   150m   IV   (1986)
This route is on the buttress immediately left of the The Black Shoot. Further left the buttress merges into the hillside shortly before a long wide gully. Climb the centre of the buttress *via* a sickle-shaped groove-ramp for two pitches, then gain an obvious steep ice-smeared slabby groove. A long snow pitch above leads to the top of the buttress.

CREAG AN AONAIDH

(Map Ref 066 272)

Lumberjacks' Fall   140m   III   (1977)

This is the burn flowing from Lochan Cuaig above the shore of Loch Awe opposite the Cruachan Power Station. The best approach (other than by boat), is from Ballimore Farm to the lochside near Tervine, followed by a walk along the lochside. The route can be seen from the A85 in the Pass of Brander. It provides continuous ice and is good for a short day's outing.

BEN LAWERS

This area has seen sporadic interest by climbers since 1898, when Raeburn and friends began exploring here in winter. Access to the summits of Ben Lawers and the Tarmachans is easy from the Ben Lawers Centre (Map Ref 608 378) on the Lochan na Lairige road. This is a good starting point for some (but not all) of the climbing areas, as detailed later. The single track road is not gritted and it may be impassable by ordinary vehicles in wintry conditions.

The climbing is almost solely reliant on frozen turf on the buttresses, and sufficient snow in the gullies. Rock protection is hard to find, but this is more than compensated for by the ease of drive-in protection; carry four or five drive-in screws. Facing east or south-east for the main part, the crags begin to receive too much sun later in the season. December and January mark the high season, when it may be possible to enjoy several sporting routes on a good day when the higher cliffs are not yet in condition. The climbing is yet to mature in this area, and it may be that some routes have been climbed but not recorded.

The crags are described from north to south, beginning with the climbing above Lochan nan Cat.

LOCHAN NAN CAT

The wide corrie holding Lochan nan Cat and a variety of crags and gullies belongs jointly to Ben Lawers, An Stuc and Meall Garbh. The north ridge of Ben Lawers (1214m, Map Ref 636 414) drops over the spur of Creag an Fhithich (1047m) and down to a col (the Bealach Dubh, 942m), then rises to the peak of An Stuc (1118m). This latter top is pointed and steep-sided, particularly on its east side overlooking Lochan nan Cat. The entire east side of the ridge from Ben Lawers to An Stuc is steep and rocky.

The two main crags are the slabby Creag an Fhithich (Map Ref 640 421), which lies at the termination of a short spur jutting east from the north ridge of Ben Lawers, and the large but more broken Creag nan Cat (Map Ref 640 430) on the south-west flank of An Stuc. Both these crags lie at an altitude of over 800m and are turfy in nature. However, their easterly aspect tends to give the best climbing conditions from early to mid-winter.

The shortest approach is to follow the path up the Lawers Burn from Lawers village. Parking is a problem, although it is possible to park at the Hotel for a fee.

Cat Gully 120m I

This is the easy gully lying above Lochan nan Cat. There are no difficulties and it finishes close to the summit of An Stuc.

CREAG AN FHITHICH

Raven's Gully

This easy gully lies some 750 metres south of Cat Gully in the same corrie, and splits the north-east facing crag of Creag an Fhithich above Lochan nan Cat.

Felinity 125m III (1993)

Start well right of the centre of the crag where a low snow ledge runs out to the right. Follow the ledge for about 15m to below a shallow groove. Climb the turfy groove to reach an obvious small pinnacle on the right. Traverse right, then follow a ramp to reach an easy-angled tapering snowfield. Climb this to a pointed block, then go up a short section of mixed ground to the top.

Cool for Cats 125m VI,5 (1993)

The general line of this route can be identified by an obvious thin chimney just below mid-height near the centre of the crag. To the right of the lowest point of the crag are two well defined corners with a big block roof between them at 15m. Start further right at a vague open groove (co-linear with the aforementioned chimney).

1. 45m Climb the vague open groove which proves much harder than it looks (poor protection) to gain a better defined turfy groove. Follow this to belay about 5m below the thin chimney.

2. 25m Move right and climb an icy slab to a point under the right end of an overhang where protection can be arranged. Step right around

the edge to the base of a turf-filled crack (running roughly parallel to the thin chimney). Climb this to a tiny ledge below a band of small overhangs.
3. 25m   Step left and move up to good protection under a roof (this provides an alternative belay for pitch 2). Move left into a turfy groove and follow it to a ledge on the left.
4. 30m   Easy-angled snow leads to the top.

Cataract   85m   IV,4   (1994)
This is the obvious wide icefall, left of centre, just below a low band of roofs running out left.
1. 40m   Climb a short ice step, then move up to below the main icefall. Climb this to take a good but exposed rock belay on the left before the top of the steepest section.
2. 45m   Step right, then climb steep ice to a rock overlap. Move right into a groove. Climb this, then go up an easier-angled snow scoop to belay at a big block on the left.

Catalyst   95m   V,6   (1996)
Start at the lowest point of the crag at a slabby toe left of the open easy groove of Cataract.
1. 40m   Climb turfy, slabby rock to a warthog belay just below the top of a turfy ramp.
2. 15m   Move up, then climb a short bare slab to below the long band of overhangs. Move right, then pull up left to merely vertical rock (crux) to gain a niche.
3. 40m   Climb an ice bulge just above the belay to gain a shallow groove. Climb this and the gradually easing ground above to the top.

CREAG LOISGTE   (Map Ref 632 412)

This small crag lies on the south flank of the south-west ridge of Ben Lawers, and is well seen when approaching Ben Lawers from Beinn Ghlas. The best approach is from the Ben Lawers Centre carpark. The main feature is a narrow crested rib right of a snow bay, delineating the west side of the crag. At least two of the gullies below have been climbed since 1980 or earlier.

Balcony Rib   80m   III   (1992)
A delightful little route climbing the tower-like front face of the rib to gain the perfect knife-edged snow arete above.

Front Stalls Gully   70m   II   (1992)
The gully immediately right of Balcony Rib has one ice pitch.

Back Stalls Gully   70m   II   (1992)
The second gully to the right of Balcony Rib has one short pitch near the start which may bank out.

Aisle Gully   60m   III   (1992)
This gully is steeper and narrower than the previous two gullies, with a difficult constriction at half-height.

MEALL NAN TARMACHAN

1043m   (Map Ref 594 396)

CREAG AN LOCHAIN, ARROW BUTTRESS

This south-facing crag, situated just north-west of the Lochan na Lairige dam, is readily accessible from the Ben Lawers Centre carpark. It lies a few hundred metres from the dam and not far above it. At the left and highest end of the crag lies the distinctive Arrow Buttress, with the shallow Arrow Chimney on its left flank.

Arrow Chimney   150m   IV   (1898)
The chimney is crossed at about half-height by a ledge, above which it steepens. The first ascent party found several pitches, at least two requiring the full run-out of 60 feet.

Toxophily   220m   IV,4   (1988)
This recommended route takes a fairly direct line up the centre of the face. It was climbed under unfavourable conditions of partially consolidated snow.
1. 45m   Start just right of the toe of the buttress at a fence post. Ascend a steep groove, then climb its left edge to a narrow ledge. Move right to belay on an icicle.
2. 25m   Move back left, then trend leftwards until a short turfy wall can be climbed to a good belay under an overhang. Under good conditions the groove directly above the icicle may be climbable.
3. 40m   Climb up past a tree, then break back right across the face to belay on a short ramp.
4. 35m   Move right, then climb directly up a shallow groove to belay at rocks on the left.

5. 30m   Climb a tiny chimney and the steep ground above to a point below an overhang. Traverse right and move up to a ledge.

6. 45m   Continue further right until it is possible to break back left and climb up to belay on a large iron post.

The Dambusters   100m   III   (1986)

At the right-hand side of the south face (facing the dam) there is a very prominent right-sloping gully. This is the line of the route, which is steep and well protected.

Tote Gully   140m   III   (1987)

Right of centre on the east-facing crag above Lochan na Lairige is a wall with several ice smears below a snow basin. This route follows the icy gully on the left-hand side of the wall, in two pitches to the snowfields. A choice of routes leads easily to an easy cornice exit.

Turf Accountant   140m   III   (1989)

Left of Tote Gully is an obvious ice smear. About 10 metres left of this is a thin chimney-gully. Climb this, then the turfy buttress above to an easy cornice exit.

CAM CHREAG

Below the ridge joining the top of Meall Garbh and Meall nan Tarmachan, just south-west of the main sumit, lie the south-east facing crags of Cam Chreag. The easiest access is by following the track which contours in from the Lochan na Lairige road, leaving it after about 2km to strike up into the corrie. It is also possible, if the road is blocked by snow, to follow the water-pipe directly up above the power station, leaving the A827 and walking up the tracks of the funicular railway; brutally direct but fast walking. The moor above is heathery with fair going. At the small rounded hump of Meall Liath go north-west for Creag na Cailleach, or north for Cam Chreag. On a dark evening descent beware of the deeply-cut burn flowing down the corrie.

The full potential and layout of Cam Chreag is not realised until one is level with the crag. There are eleven winter routes. The cliffs are split into two main sections by the Grade I **Easy Gully** (a useful descent route). On the left-hand and larger section of cliff, Fan Buttress, another easy gully (**Fan Gully**, Grade I) slopes up and left. There are two easy gullies on the left of Fan Gully (**Chimney One** and **Chimney Two**, both Grade II). The right-hand section of cliffs is formed by three buttresses. The left-hand buttress, lying above Easy Gully, is indeterminate. The central, slender Lozenge Buttress is defined by two short, easy but attractive gullies which begin at the foot of the buttress, embracing both sides of the buttress to eventually gain a mutual snow terrace. A final tower of rock completes the buttress above. The right-hand buttress, Carlin's Buttress, provides several routes. A central recess, up and right of the lowest rocks, is a feature best seen from the east, as is a clean-cut corner on the right side of the crag. The routes are described from left to right.

FAN BUTTRESS

Maxwell's Hammer   140m   III   (1986)
1. 30m   Start just left of Fan Gully. Climb a short ice pitch to Fan Gully, then cross it to a snow bay below shallow groove.
2. 35m   Follow a groove *via* a steep ice pitch and a ramp to a belay on the left.
3. 40m   Steep snow covered rocks lead up and right.
4. 35m   Continue directly to the apex of crag *via* another ice pitch.

Turf Going   120m   III,3   (1997)
Starting at the foot of Fan Buttress, a ramp runs up and left above Fan Gully. Start at the foot of the ramp, about 10 metres left of an obvious corner formed by an overhanging left wall.
1. 40m   Climb the ramp and continue across the face to belay on the turfy edge.
2. 40m   Continue directly up the face to belay below the headwall.
3. 40m   Break through the headwall above and continue on easy ground to a belay above.

Knucklebuster Corner   80m   IV,4 *   (1997)
Start about 10 metres right of Turf Going, below an obvious corner with an overhanging left wall.
1. 40m   Climb the corner (crux), past several ice bosses and awkward moves, then follow easier ground above to a belay.
2. 40m   Climb turf to the headwall with a small ice column. Move awkwardly past this to easier ground and a belay above.

Mackay's Gully   100m   II *   (1902)
This lies to the right of Easy Gully and gives straightforward snow in normal conditions. It may have several small pitches in leaner conditions. It starts at the foot of Lozenge Buttress and runs up the left

side of the buttress to gain a snowfield below the final tower of the buttress. Finish by a choice of routes.

Lozenge Buttress   120m   III *   (1994)
This buttress is the central and highest part of the crag, and lies about due east of Meall Garbh at approximately Map Ref 581 384, and to the south of the Meall Garbh – Meall nan Tarmachan col. Its lozenge shape is readily identified by the two gullies that start nearly at the same point and curve upwards to embrace the rock face. Start underneath the overhanging rock at the lowest point of the buttress. Skirt the overhang on the left, traverse back right to above the belay and continue directly to the top. Warthogs in frozen turf were used for runners and belays.

Clark's Gully   100m   II   (1898)
This gives straightforward snow in normal conditions, with perhaps one short pitch. It starts at the foot of Lozenge Buttress and runs up the right side of the buttress to gain a snowfield below the final tower of the buttress. Finish by a choice of routes.

CARLIN'S BUTTRESS

This is the attractive buttress right of Lozenge Buttress. Descent is possible using the easy gully about 30 metres right of the buttress, which has one short pitch at a narrowing.

Spaewife   90m   IV,4 *   (1996)
1. 30m   Start at the foot of the buttress and climb easily up and right to belay below a wall overlooking the central recess of the buttress and below and right of a rock wall.
2. 30m   Move up and left on a series of turf steps to gain the foot of a two-stepped corner. Climb this (crux) and continue up to belay in a niche.
3. 30m   Continue up and left over a small bulge to finish on easier ground overlooking the finish of Clark's Gully. Belay further back.

Witch's Brew   80m   III,3 *   (1996)
Running up the centre of the buttress are two parallel lines of open grooves; this route follows the right-hand line.
1. 30m   Follow an open corner to a belay below an overhanging dry crack.
2. 50m   Make exposed moves right (crux), then continue directly up to finish up a fine steepening corner. There is a thread belay on the rock directly above the finish.

Beldame Buttress   90m   III,3   (1996)
The section of buttress right of the central recess lies back slightly and
provides varied climbing up ledges of turf.

CREAG NA CAILLICH
916m   (Map Ref 563 377)

From the south, the east face of this hill shows three well-defined
routes of ascent: a broad ledge crossing the face from left to right; a
wide chimney or gully running straight from top to bottom; and the
arete forming the right wall of the chimney. The main buttress on the
right is marked by a large wall of steep rock. There is a descent on the
right *via* open slopes just right of an easy gully (the top of the gully can
be icy). Approach as for Cam Chreag *via* the track countouring under
Coire Fionn Lairige, or more directly from Bridge of Lochay at the north
end of Killin, climbing north directly towards the crag.

Great Gully   150m   III   (1902)
The first ascent party found three short pitches below the traversing
ledge, with five steeper pitches above.

Great Gully Arete   150m   III   (1903)
This provides fairly steep ground but with sufficient ledges where
needed.

   The largest mass of rock forms a very steep face overlooking the
corrie. There is a wide gully right of this buttress, with possibly a short
pitch near the top. Above and left of the steep rock face is a mixed
buttress, taken fairly centrally by the following route:

Pensioner's Buttress   120m   IV,3 *   (1997)
1. 30m   Climb easy ground to belay on a block at the left end of the
terrace, left of the rock wall.
2. 30m   A straightforward-looking ramp runs up and right, above the
rock face. Instead, step down and left under a rock nose and continue
up the steepening corner (crux) to gain a narrow ledge girdling the
face. Pull out right and belay on the ledge.
3. 30m   Step out right and continue up to belay in a niche.
4. 30m   Continue up the buttress to the top of the face.

BEN LOMOND
974m   (Map Ref 367 029)

This well trodden mountain is the most southerly Munro. Being close to Glasgow and with super views of both Lowland and Highland areas, it is understandably a very popular ascent. Less popular though are the winter routes tucked away in its north-east corrie. Ben Lomond is in condition less often than other peaks further north, but it may offer a good day in an interesting position.

There are two main approaches. The most commonly used and probably the better route starts at Rowardennan, beginning at the car park a few hundred metres north of the hotel. From the east side of the car park, follow the trail through the forest to gain open slopes below the south ridge of the hill. Continue almost to the summit and descend a scree slope into the corrie from a little col before the top. The alternative route starts from the east and provides a more peaceful but roughly undulating route directly into the corrie. Leave the B829 road 9km north-west of Aberfoyle at Loch Dhu and follow the private road round the foot of this little loch and walk south-west through the forest over a low pass into Gleann Dubh. Continue up the glen to Comer Farm, then climb south-west alongside the burn issuing from the main corrie of Ben Lomond. Mountain bikes useful as far as the farm, with undulating going.

The summit of Ben Lomond stands above the northern buttress. Just left of the buttress is a scree slope, which provides the first of the approaches described above. Further left are the cliffs, which have three tiny tops with their respective buttresses below. Following a description of this corrie in the SMC guidebook of 1901 (published first in the SMC Journal) these buttresses are named A, B and C, from right to left. A Buttress is insignificant, and has another scree slope on its left. B Buttress, the middle top, is larger and steeper, and is bounded on the left by three narrow parallel gullies, separated by ribs. The third cliff, C Buttress, is the most interesting from a climbing point of view, being the largest and steepest. There is a prominent corner on this buttress towards the left, taken by Lomond Corner. Another landmark is a ledge sloping up from left to right, above which at about halfway rise two parallel lines. Several easy lines have been scrambled up on the lower left section of cliff, but these are not described. It may well be that some routes have earlier ascents than described here. Tough. It is fairly safe to state that all of the obvious easy gullies or buttresses had been climbed by 1895, with none being so difficult as to retain more than a passing note. The routes are described from right to left, as encountered on an approach from the summit ridge.

B BUTTRESS

Solo Buttress   100m   III   (1991)
Roughly centrally on the buttress, a snow ramp or shelf trends up rightwards to a recess under a rocky barrier. An easy snow gully above the barrier leads to the top.

Lomond Delight   85m   III   (1994)
Start about 100 metres right of Lomond Corner, beginning in a snow bay on the bottom left of B Buttress.
1. 45m   Go up a shallow groove for 8m, then turn right up a ramp to a small cave and belay.
2. 40m   Exit on the left up over a bulge, then follow steep snow and exit onto the ridge.

   Left of B Buttress are three parallel gullies, all about Grade I or II at most. A buttress route has been climbed above the left-hand gully (Grade III), taking the upper part of C Buttress.

C BUTTRESS

Lost in Snow   100m   III   (1990)
Climb the sloping shelf to reach the left-hand corner and follow this to the top.

Lomond Corner   100m   IV,5 **   (1994)
The obvious corner on the left of the buttress provides the hardest climb on the mountain. There are three pitches, the middle one being the crux.

Zigzag   145m   III,4   (1992)
This route follows a line on the largest area of cliff, finishing on the north-east spur. It is not known how it relates to the other routes hereabouts.
1. 30m   Follow an icy ramp to a line of grooves and a large ledge, belaying under an overhang near a detached flake.
2. 35m   Go left over the overhang into a broad easy scoop, then follow the groove diagonally leftwards to an overhanging corner. Climb

this using the right wall to a ledge on the left. Traverse 8 metres right to belay on a ledge to the right of a roof.

3. 35m   Climb the small steep arete directly above the belay, then follow a groove to a broken ledge beneath the very steep upper wall. Make a hard move diagonally left over the bulge to reach holds leading across the slabby wall to the base of a hanging corner.

4. 45m   Continue up the corner. At its top, move diagonally right to easier ground.

GLEN FALLOCH
GLEANN NAN CAORANN

Eas Ruaridh   60m   III   (1986)
Situated a hundred metres or so above Glenfalloch Farm is a large waterfall on the Dubh Eas burn which occasionally forms a fine icefall. It is well seen from the A82. Climb the icefall in two pitches.

BEN GLAS   (Map Ref 325 185)

Eagle Falls   III
This is the prominent waterfall behind the Inverarnan Hotel in Glen Falloch, above the head of Loch Lomond. Approach by leaving the road and walking over the bridge to Beinglas Farm, then take the path to the right as for the West Highland Way to bypass the farm. The climb is dangerously close to the hotel bar.

GLEN FYNE

Fyne Falls   70m   III   (1985)
This is the waterfall facing north-west directly above the bridge at Map Ref 228 159. The fall runs into a hydro collecting dam (not marked on the map). Reach the base of the fall across a frozen pool.

List of First Ascents

ARRAN

S 1889	Jul		Witch's Step	T.F.S.Campbell, W.R.Lister
S 1891			Summit Chimney	W.W.Naismith (solo)
S 1891	Sep		Gully D (Cir Mhor)	W.W.Naismith, G.Thomson
S 1891	Sep		Stoneshoot Ridge	W.W.Naismith, G.Thomson
S 1892	Aug		Gully B2 (Cir Mhor)	J.Bristow, F.P.Evers, W.Wickham-King
S 1892	30 Jan		A'Chir Ridge	T.F.S.Campbell, W.Douglas,J.H.Gibson, H.Fleming, R.A.Robertson and Dr Leith
S 1893	Sep		Western Stoneshoot	G.Thompson, W.W.Naismith
S 1894			Bow Window Cave	W.W.Naismith, W.Douglas
S 1894			Pinnacle Ridge	J.MacLay, W.W.Naismith
S 1894	Sep		Bell's Groove	J.H.Bell, E.W.Green

An impressive lead by the good Dr Bell.

S 1895	6 Jul		Gully 5 (Beinn Nuis)	Messrs. Boyd and Green
S 1895	7 Jul		B2C Rib	Messrs. J.H.Bell, Boyd, Green, Napier

Not a great route, but well ahead of its time for commitment and exposure. Variation A: D.Gilchrist, T.Wallace, Apr 1959.

S 1896			MacLay's Gully	J.MacLay, W.Douglas, W.W.Naismith
S 1896	Jul		1896 Route (Cioch na'Oighe)	W.P.Haskett-Smith, W.W.Naismith
S 1896	Jul		Naismith/Haskett-Smith Route	W.P.Haskett-Smith, W.W.Naismith
S 1896	Jul		Shelf Gully	W.P.Haskett-Smith, W.W.Naismith
S 1897			Gully 1 (Beinn Nuis)	W.Inglis Clark, H.Raeburn
S 1897			Gully 2 (Beinn Nuis)	W.Inglis Clark, H.Raeburn
S 1897			Green Gully	W.Inglis Clark, H.Raeburn
S 1901	Aug 18		Gully 3 (Nuis Chimney)	Messrs. Baker, L.J.Oppenheimer, Puttrell
W 1907			Gully 4 (Beinn Nuis)	H.MacRobert (solo)
S 1907			Gully 4 (A'Chir)	H.MacRobert (solo)
S 1907			Gully 8 (A'Chir)	H.McRobert (solo)
S 1907			The Chimney (Maol Donn)	H.MacRobert (solo)
S 1908	Jun		Crack Climb	H.MacRobert, W.A.Morrison
S 1911	Jul		Gully 3 (A'Chir)	A.Arthur, H.MacRobert
S 1920			Garrick's Route	J.A.Garrick, D.Biggart,
S 1933			Woolpack	E.W.Hodge and party
S 1933			Lower Left Chimney	E.W.Hodge and party
S 1935			South Ridge Original	J.A.Ramsay and party

An adventurous route for its date. Traverse variation: G.H.Townend and party, 1944.

S 1938	Apr		Easter Route	K.Barber, A.S.Pigott

The hardest of the pre World War II routes.

S 1938	18 Apr		Coxon's Route	G.S.Bower, L.S.Bower, A.S.Pigott
S 1941	23 Jul		Tarsuinn No. 2 Chimney	W.Carr, H.Grant, F.Grant, G.McKinley, C.McPherson, W.Russel, A.Slack
S 1941	Sep		South Ridge Direct	J.F.Hamilton, D.Paterson

A major line doing much to change opinion about the quality of Arran granite.

S 1942	Jun		Gully B1 (Cir Mhor)	G.C.Curtis, H.K.Moneypenny
S 1943	May 25		Pagoda Ridge	G.H.Townend, G.C.Curtis
S 1943	27 Jun		Sucker Slabs	G.C.Curtis, H.K.Moneypenny, G.H.Townend
S 1943	4 Jul		Boundary Ridge	G.C.Curtis, H.J.Dunster, H.K.Moneypenny, G.H.Townend

Pitch 5 Variation I: G.C.Curtis, Jul 1943.
Pitch 5 Variation II: G.M.Johnston, M.Palmer, Mr King, 1944.

S 1943	25 Jul	Caliban's Creep	G.C.Curtis, G.H.Townend
S 1943	25 Jul	Prospero's Peril	G.H.Townend, G.C.Curtis
S 1943	26 Jul	Prospero's Prelude	H.K.Moneypenny, G.C.Curtis
S 1943	12 Sep	Gaints Staircase	G.H.Townend, H.J.Dunster
S 1943	12 Sep	Imposter Crack	H.J.Dunster, G.H.Townend
S 1943	19 Sep	Slab and Flake Route	G.H.Townend, G.C.Curtis, H.F.Dunster
S 1943	26 Sep	Labyrinth	G.C.Curtis, H.K.Moneypenny

Direct Finish: J.C.MacLaurin, J.S.Orr, May 1951

S 1944	Mar	Broomstick Ridge	C.E.Willes-Johnson (solo)
S 1944	30 Apr	Hanging Gully	G.C.Curtis, R.K.Fraser, H.K.Moneypenny, G.H.Townend
S 1944	6 May	Midnight Ridge Direct	G.H.Townend, G.C.Curtis
S 1944	11 Jun	Gully 7 (A'Chir)	G.C.Curtis, G.H.Townend
S 1944	11 Jun	7-8 Buttress (A'Chir)	G.C.Curtis, G.H.Townend
S 1944	19 Jul	Twilight Slabs	G.C.Curtis, F.M.King
S 1944	20 Aug	Meadow Grooves	G.C.Curtis, H.K.Moneypenny, E.J.W.Morrison
S 1944	20 Aug	Meadow Slabs	G.C.Curtis, H.K.Moneypenny, E.J.W.Morrison
S 1944	3 Sep	Sou'wester Slabs	G.H.Townend, G.C.Curtis, M.J.H.Hawkins, H.Hore

A great find, paving the way for a splendid collection of routes on these marvellous slabs.

S 1944	17 Sep	Cubic Ridge	G.H.Townend, F.Foxcroft
S 1945	22 Apr	Hellfire Crack	G.C.Curtis, H.K.Moneypenny
S 1945	17 Jun	Portcullis	G.C.Curtis, H.K.Monneypenny, E.J.W.Morrison
S 1945	17 Jun	The Rift	G.C.Curtis, H.K.Moneypenny, E.J.W.Morrison
S 1945	5 Aug	Fourth Wall	G.H.Townend, H.K.Moneypenny

Variation: A: G.H.Townend, H.K.Moneypenny, Aug 1944.
Variation B: R.A.Hockey (solo), 6th Sep 1959.

S 1945	16 Aug	V Gully	G.H.Townend, H.K.Moneypenny, M.M.Carty, G.C.Curtis, F.M.King
S 1945	16 Aug	The Rampart	G.H.Townend, H.K.Moneypenny, G.C.Curtis, F.M.King, M.M.Carty
S 1945	Sep	Haakon's Highway	G.S.Johnstone and M.Johnstone
S 1945	Sep	15 Minute Ridge	G.S.Johnstone and M.Johnstone
S 1945	9 Sep	Avalanche Gully	G.C.Curtis, G.M.Johnson
S 1945	9 Sep	Cupboard and Stairs	G.C.Curtis, G.M.Johnson
S 1946		Lower East Chimney	G.H.Townend and party
S 1946		Verdant Gully	G.H.Townend (solo)
S 1946	Apr	Anvil Gully	G.C.Curtis, M.H.J.Hawkins, E.J.W.Morrison
S 1946	12 May	Keyhole Crack	E.B.Mendus, G.P.Pinder
S 1946	Aug	Sub Rosa Slabs	J.R.Jenkins, G.H.Townend
S 1946	Aug	Old East	J.R.Jenkins, G.H.Townend
S 1947	27 Mar	Ruddy Knuckles	P.W.Bedford, D.H.Haworth
S 1947	27 Mar	Brodick Chimney	P.W.Bedford, D.H.Haworth, P.Lockwood
S 1947	30 Mar	Birthday Chimney	P.W.Bedford, D.H.Haworth
S 1947	1 Apr	Tarsuinn No. 1 Chimney	D.H.Haworth
S 1947	4 Apr	Schist Buttress	G.C.Curtis, E.J.W.Morrison, G.H.Townend
S 1949		Left-Hand Route	E.W.Rudge and party
S 1949		Right-Hand Route	E.W.Rudge and party
S 1950	3 Aug	Lee Climb	V.J.Desmond, V.T.Dillon
S 1950	5 Aug	Aquila	V.J.Desmond, V.T.Dillon

S 1955	Aug	Evening Traverse	W.C.Harrison, J.M.Johnstone
S 1955	May	The Rosetta Stone	R. Smith (solo)
S 1957		Route 1 (South Slabs)	R.Sim, D.McKelvie
S 1957	Nov	The Sickle	J.H.Ashford, D.Burke
S 1958		West Gully	W.Skidmore (solo)
S 1958	Apr	Leaning Block Chimney	G.W.Hamilton, J.M.Johnstone, W.Wallace
S 1958	Aug	Minotaur	D.McKelvie, R.Sim
S 1958	Jun	Easter Route; Double Cracks Start	J.M.Johnstone, W.Wallace
S 1958	Jun	Pinnacle Gully Buttress	J.M.Johnstone, W,Wallace
S 1958	Jun	Zigzag	D.McKelvie, R.Sim
S 1958	May	First Pinnacle Chimney	J.M.Johnstone, E.Wrench
S 1958	22 Nov	November Chimney	J.W.Simpson, W.Wallace
S 1959	19 Apr	April Arete	J.W.Simpson, W.Wallace
S 1959	26 Sep	Slapstick Wall	R.Hutchison , J.Gardner, W.Gartshore

Variation 2 (pitch 1) and variation to pitch 2: G.E.Little, P.Linning 1st Apr 1983.

S 1960		The Big Slab	J.W.Simpson (solo)
S 1960		Stacach Gully	W.Wallace (solo)
S 1960	Aug	Diamond Slab	J.W.Simpson, W.Wallace, G.W.Hamilton
S 1960	6 Aug	Hammer	R.Sim, D.Cameron
S 1960	6 Aug	Anvil	D.McKelvie, R.Richardson

Recess Start: W.Skidmore, J.Crawford, J.Madden; 16th July, 1964.
Variation Finish: R.Richardson, J.Madden, 1965

S 1960	27 Jul	Angel's Pavement	G.Kilgour, N.MacNiven
S 1960	27 Jul	Fool's Causeway	G.Kilgour, N.MacNiven
S 1960	6 Jun	Routes 1 and 2 (Beinn Bharrain)	A.J.Maxfield, J.Peacock
S 1960	9 Jun	Tidemark	A.J.Maxfield, J.Peacock

The first clean route on Cioch na h-Oighe.

S 1961	May	Hangover Slabs	A.Cowmeadow, J.Stewart
S 1961	May	Afterthought	A.Cowmeadow, J.Stewart
S 1961	May	Nor-Easter Slabs	R.N.Campbell, N.MacNiven
S 1961	May	Rosa Pinnacle Girdle	R.N.Campbell, N.MacNiven
S 1961	24 Aug	Eastern Ridge	R.Brown, A.Howard
S 1961	2 Sep	Route 2 (South Slabs)	R.McCulloch, W.Wallace
S 1962	Apr	Left Edge (Caisteal Abhail)	G.W.Hamilton, W.Wallace
S 1962	Apr	Central Grooves	G.W.Hamilton, W.Wallace
S 1962	Aug 18	The Rake	W.Skidmore, R.T.Richardson

2 points of aid. Although messy, the first major line on the Meadow Face

S 1963	3 Aug	West Flank Route	W.Skidmore, R.Richardson, J.Crawford, J.Madden

As significant an ascent as Sou'wester Slabs, nineteen years earlier.

S 1962	18 Aug	Slant	P.McKenzie, N.Mcphie
S 1963	13 Sep	Blank	B.Kelly, A.McKeith
S 1964	1 Apr	Trundle	W.Bailey, R.White
S 1964	20 Jun	Guttersnipe	G.Anderson, A.McKeith
S 1964	21 Jun	Dogleg	J.R.Brumfitt, A.McKeith
S 1964	21 Jun	Pussyfoot	D.Bathgate, J.Renny
S 1965	Aug	Girdle (South Slabs)	W.Wallace, H.Stirling
S 1965	Aug	Slapstick Wall	H.Stirling, W.Wallace

Pitch 1, Variation 1: G.Szuca (solo), 27th May 1992.
Pitch 3 Variation: G.Szuca, C.Lampton, May 1993

S 1965	Aug	Carlin's Rib	H.Stirling, W.Wallace
S 1965	May	Ribbish	P.Brian, R.N.Campbell
S 1966		Donn Corner	A.J.Maxfield, A.Verity
S 1966		Spelunca	H.Donohoe, W.Skidmore

S 1966   The Cannon   A.J.Maxfield, R.Wilde
S 1966   Jun Oread   A.Corley, A.J.Maxfield, P.Verity
S 1966 18 Sep Brachistrochrone   M.Galbraith, A. McKeith (alt)
      Extensive aid was used. FFA: J.Perrin, Aug 1976
S 1966 19 Sep Pochmahone   M.Kelsey, A.McKeith
S 1966 19 Sep Polhode   M.Galbraith, G.Miller
S 1966 19 Sep Herpolhode (original)   M.Galbraith, G.Miller
S 1967 22 July Bogle   I.G.Rowe, I.Dundas (alt)
      Extensive aid was used. FFA: J.Perrin, Aug 1976 – '20 feet of ferocious fist jamming'.
S 1967   Jun First Footing   A.Alldred, W.Blake
S 1967   May Eilythia   A.J.Maxfield, R.Wilde
S 1967 25 May Klepht   A.J.Maxfield, R.Wilde
      Extensive aid was used on a very daunting line. Direct Variation: 16th Apr 1981,
      G.E.Little, C.Ritchie. The aid was reduced to 4 points. FFA: C. Macadam, A.Fraser,
      10th Aug 1981.
S 1967 23 Sep Staravation   R.N.Castro, S.M.Carruthers
S 1968   The Pitch   W.Skidmore, J.Gillespie
S 1968   Apr Minaret   J.R.Jackson, J.Park, J.M.Shaw
      Several points of aid were used.
S 1968   Aug Anticlimax   H.Stirling, W.Wallace
S 1968 30 Aug Galloway Slabs   A.J.Maxfield, D.F.Price
S 1968   Jul Keelhaul   H.Donohoe, E.McLelland
S 1968 20 Jul Mosque   I.Fulton, J.M.Shaw
S 1968 20 Jul Bluff   H.Donohoe, E.McLelland
      2 points of aid; a steep route hinting at other potential on Cir Mhor
S 1968   3 Jun Ardito   A.J.Maxfield, R.Wilde
S 1968   3 Jun Fuocco   A.J.Maxfield, D.F.Price, R.Wilde
S 1968   3 Jun Pompiere   A.J.Maxfield, R.Wilde
S 1968 28 Jun Pothole Slab   W.Skidmore, J.Gillespie
      A taste of things to come on the vast North-East Face of Cir Mhor.
S 1968   May Whit Fur   W.Wallace, H.Stirling
S 1968   May Whit Way   W.Wallace, H.Stirling
S 1968 18/19 May Silo   I.G.Rowe, A.J.Trees, M.Watson
      Extensive aid was used; the first (and last?) multi-day route on Arran?
S 1969   Apr Donjon   P.Brian, R.N.Campbell
S 1969   Aug Geison   A.J.Maxfield, M.Weedon
S 1969   Aug Entasis   A.J.Maxfield, R.Wilde
      Direct line: C.Macadam, G.Macadam, 1975.
S 1969 23 Aug Ziggurat   A.J.Maxfield, D.Overton, R.Wilde
S 1969 29 Aug Atreus   A.J.Maxfield, R.Wilde
S 1969 14 Jun The Curver   R.Carrington, I.Fulton (alt)
S 1969 15 Jun Insertion   R.Carrington, I.Fulton
      A bold climb, the first E3 on Arran.
S 1969   May Diagonal   W.Wallace, G.W.Hamilton, H.Stirling
S 1969 12 Sep Voodoo Chile   G.E.Little, J.Dykes
      8 points of aid, later reduced to 4 by G.E.Little and R.J.Little on the 15 Apr 1979. FFA:
      R.McAllister, M.Reed, 29 May 1993.
W 1970 15 Feb Gully 3 (Nuis Chimney)   W.Skidmore, J.Crawford
      The first modern winter route on Arran
S 1970 27 Jun Right On   I.G.Rowe, D.S.B.Wright
      Extensive aid was used; the route is probably unrepeated.
S 1971   Apr Hode On   S.Docherty, B.Dunn
S 1971 21 Aug The Blinder   W.Skidmore, J.Crawford
      Two points of aid; the subject of much competition (both real and imagined). FFA:
      J.Perrin, Aug 1976. Improved variation to Pitch 4: R.Stevenson, N.Stevenson, 31st
      May 1991.

S 1971	12 Jul	Sunshine Corner	W.Skidmore, D.Marshall, R.Richardson
S 1971	Jul	Mystic	K.V.Crocket, D.C.Forrest
S 1973	Jul	Stoic	W.Skidmore, J.Gillespie
S 1973	23 Mar	Airlift	B. Clarke, J.Mackenzie
S 1973	29 May	The Crack	I.W.Cranston, J.W.Earl, R.G.Hutchinson
S 1974	14 Apr	Intruder	J.Mackenzie, B.Clarke
S 1974	18 Aug	Chestnut Edge	J.Mackenzie, B.Clarke
S 1974	Jul	Introduction	E.M.Wallace, W.Wallace
S 1974	Jul	Encore	E. M.Wallace, W.Wallace
S 1975	Apr	Brobdingnag	I.F.Duckworth, J.Fraser, W.G.Smith

Four points of aid, consolidating on earlier efforts by Rowe and Geoff Cohen – a major line.

S 1975	7 Aug	Manners	K.Schwartz (solo)
S 1975	7 Jun	Slipway	W. Skidmore, J.Madden

(1 point of aid)

S 1975	24 May	The Eyrie	J.W.Earl, R.G.Hutchinson
S 1975	24 May	The Geordie	J.W.Earl, R.G.Hutchinson
S 1975	25 May	The Engie	J.W.Earl, R.G.Hutchinson
S 1977	5 Jul	Gazebo	W.Skidmore, A.Walker

Climbed in very dry conditions.

S 1977	14 Jul	Armadillo	W.Skidmore, R.Richardson

3 points of aid – a major line to the 'home team'. FFA and Direct Variation: C.Macadam, S.Steer, 29th May 1985.

S 1977	Jun	Na Ciste	W. McKerrow, D.Nichols, A.Nisbet, G.S.Strange
S 1977	27 May	Lower Right Chimney	N. McPherson, C.Moody
S 1978	3 Jun	Cairn's Cream Corner	C. Smith, I.McColl
S 1978	May	The Iron Fist	D.Dinwoodie, D.Renshaw (alt)
W 1979	3 Feb	Eastern Stoneshoot	D.McBrayne, C.Smith (alt)
W 1979	17 Feb	Gully B1 (Cir Mhor)	R.Gatehouse, C.Smith (alt)
W 1979	18 Feb	Gully C	R.Gatehouse, C.Smith (alt)

A significant winter ascent, the most obvious unclimbed line on the North-East Face

W 1979	27 Jan	Green Gully	C.Smith (solo)
S 1979	May	Dumperama	M.Elms, G.Rees
S 1979	26 May	Black Cave Pillar	R.J.Little, W.Skidmore, G.E.Little (alt)

Several earlier attempts had been repulsed.

S 1979	28 May	El Dee	T.McAulay, B.Swan
S 1979	3 Jun	Rhino	G.E.Little (solo)

2 points of aid -the start of an obsession! FFA: P.Whillance and party 1983. This ascent included the variation

S 1979	23 Jun	The Sword of Theseus	H.Henderson, D.MacDonald
S 1979	4 Jul	Pan's Pillar	W.Skidmore, R.Richardson
S 1980	26 May	Abraxas	G.E.Little, R.J.Little

12 points of aid (reduced to 9 on 24th Jul 1982 by G.E.Little and C. Ritchie). This ascent did more than perhaps any other to fuel the ethical debate and to attract Scotland's top activists to Arran. FFA: C.Macadam, S.Steer, 1st Jun 1985 (using the in situ gear and bolt belays). The second free ascent, dispensing with these, was by G.Latter and D.Cuthbertson two days later.

S 1981	4 Apr	Digitalis	G.E.Little, W.Skidmore

3 points of aid, including a tension traverse. FFA: P.Linning, C.Ritchie (alt) 24th Jul 1982 (via a bypass line on the right of the top pitch). FFA of the original line: G.Latter, A.Ramsey, 25th May 1991.

S 1981	18 Apr	Hedonist	G.E.Little, R.Little, C.Ritchie
S 1981	18 Apr	Changeling	G.E.Little, C.Ritchie
S 1981	19 Apr	Synagogue	J.Hosie, S.Kennedy

S	1981	19 Apr	The Perfect Fool	A.Nisbet, A.Robertson
S	1981	1 Aug	Skydiver	G.E.Little, C.Ritchie

4 points of aid—a major on sight ascent involving several falls. FFA and Direct Finish: C.McLean, A.Nisbet, 7th May 1984. The completion of a truly magnificent route.

W	1981	12 Dec	Gully B2 (Cir Mhor)	G.E.Little (solo)
W	1981	12 Dec	Pan's Pipe	G.E.Little (solo)

Cold weather and a cool head!

W	1981	18 Dec	Cascade	G.E.Little (solo)
S	1981	4 Jul	South Sou'wester Slabs	G.E.Little, C.Ritchie
S	1982	Jun	Extraction	P.Clarke, K.Martin
S	1982	19 Jun	Arctic Way	W.Hood, C.Moody (alt)

Variation: R.Carchrie, A.Walker, 26th Sep 1987

S	1982	9 May	Ulysses	G.E.Little, W.Skidmore

The first of a series hard routes on the pale left hand wall of Cuithe Mheadonach and Skidmore's last new route on the island.

W	1983	5 Feb	Maclay's Gully	S.Kennedy, C.MacLeod
W	1983	5 Feb	North-East Face Route	G.Harper, S.Kennedy, C.MacLeod, A.Nisbet
W	1983	6 Feb	Outrider	S.Kennedy, C.MacLeod
W	1983	7 Feb	Labyrinth	G.Harper, S.Kennedy, C.MacLean, A. Nisbet

A splendid route, bagged under the noses of the west coasters!

W	1983	7 Feb	Pinnacle Gully Buttress	G.Harper, A,Nisbet
W	1983	7 Feb	Shelf Gully	G.Harper, A.Nisbet
W	1983	8 Feb	Bypass Route	G.Harper, A.Nisbet
W	1983	8 Feb	Stoneshoot Buttress	G.Harper, A.Nisbet
S	1983	9 Jul	Pegasus	G.E.Little, R.J.Little
S	1983	29 May	Lawyer's Leap	B. Davidson, S.Kennedy, N.Morrison, A.Nisbet
W	1984	7 Apr	White Magic Groove	G.E.Little (solo)
S	1984	29 Apr	Achilles	G.E.Little (unseconded)

Two points of aid – Little is criticised for placing the first aid bolt on Arran (in place of the two rivets used on this ascent). Free variation: G.E.Little, K.Howett (alt) 6th Aug 1995. The most sought after aid elimination since Abraxas, giving very technical climbing in a splendid situation. Howett pulls out all the stops on the crux 6c moves.

W	1984	21 Jan	Gully 3 (A'Chir)	G.E.Little, A.Watson
W	1984	28 Jan	West Gully	G.Pryde, G.Rimmer, C.Smith
S	1984	May	One Eyed Jacks	C.Macadam, S.Steer
S	1984	5 May	True Grit	C. McLean, A.Nisbet
S	1985	20 Apr	Ribald	P.Brownsort, H.Irvine
W	1985	19 Jan	Pinnacle Ridge	G.E.Little, C.Smith (alt)

The first confirmed winter ascent

W	1985	19 Jan	V Gully	G.E.Little (solo)
W	1985	20 Jan	The Shelf	G.E.Little (solo)
W	1985	27 Jan	The Riddle	G.E.Little, C.Smith (alt)

A significant development on a neglected crag

W	1985	27 Jan	Imposter Crack	G.E.Little, A.Reid, C.Smith
S	1985	May	Absent Friends	B.Davidson (unseconded; 2 points of aid)
S	1985	May	Vanishing Point	C. MacAdam, S.Steer

A very bold lead.

S	1985	May	Beyond the Pale	C.Macadam, S.Steer

It is less so when dry!

S	1985	May	Electric Avenue	A.Atkinson, S.Bissel B.Davidson
S	1985	May	Fork Lightning	B.Davidson, A.Atkinson, S.Bissel
S	1985	May	Shock Treatment	B.Davidson, A.Atkinson, S.Bissel
S	1985	May	Hertz Crack	B.Davidson, A.Atkinson, S.Bissel

S 1985	May	Electric Chair	A.Atkinson, S.Bissel, B.Davidson
S 1985	May	First Shock	S.Bissel, A.Atkinson, B.Davidson
S 1985	May	Electro-Therapy	S.Bissel, A.Atkinson, B.Davidson
S 1985	5 Jun	Token Gesture	D. Cuthbertson, K.Howett (alt)

The first E5 on Arran granite.

W 1986	8 Feb	Once in a Lifetime	G.E.Little, D.Saddler (alt)

An oft-fancied line — an eight hour climb resulting in a descent in the dark and a very cold bivouac!

S 1986	Jun	Insertion Direct	M.Charlton, K.Howett (alt)

Bold as hell!

S 1986	7 Jun	West Point	M. Charlton, K.Howett (alt)
S 1986	Aug	Ohm	B.Davidson, A.Smith
S 1986	Aug	Electrocak	B.Davidson, A.Smith
S 1986	Aug	Wind Generator	B.Davidson, A.Smith
S 1986	Aug	Dodgy Tranformer	B.Davidson, A.Smith
S 1986	Aug	Repeater	B.Davidson, A.Smith
S 1986	Aug	Circuit Board	B.Davidson, A.Smith
S 1986	Aug	Quark Jive	A.Smith, C.Moody, N.Horn, B.Davidson
S 1986	Aug	Warp Drive	N.Horn, C.Moody, B.Davidson, A.Smith
S 1986	Aug	Are Friends Electric	B.Davidson, A.Smith
S 1986	Aug	How's Your Teslas	B.Davidson, A.Smith
S 1986	Aug	Electrickery	B.Davidson, A.Smith
S 1986	Aug	Giv'em Enough Volts	B.Davidson, A.Smith
S 1986	Aug	Short Circuit	B.Davidson, A.Smith
S 1986	Aug	Tellingbone	B.Davidson, A.Smith
S 1986	Aug	Do Androids Dream	B.Davidson, A.Smith
W 1986	22 Dec	Boundary Ridge	F. McKie (solo)
W 1987	10 Jan	Crack Climb	F.McKie, F.Thompson
W 1987	17 Jan	April Arete	G.E.Little, D.Saddler (alt)

Success came 94 years after the first attempt!

W 1987	14 Feb	Gully 7 (A'Chir)	F.McKie
W 1987	21 Feb	Gully 5 (Beinn Nuis)	P.Craig, A.Walker (alt)
S 1987	20 Jun	Sesame Street	F.McKie, F.Thomson
W 1988	23 Jan	Cubic Ridge	G.A.McEwan, A.Walker
W 1988	30 Jan	Broomstick Ridge	F.McKie, D.Tolmie
S 1988	21 May	The Rake Direct	G.A.McEwan, A.Walker (alt)
S 1988	1 Jun	Alternative Medicine	K.Sharples, R.Brown
S 1988	2 Jun	Endangered Species	N.Slater, R.Brown

The first E6 on Arran.

S 1988	2 Jun	The Groove of Distinction	K.Sharples (unseconded)
W 1989	25 Feb	The Ozone Layer	K.V.Crocket, A.Walker, R.Carchrie, G.A.McEwan
S 1989	7 May	Ne Parl Pas	W.Hood, I.Taylor, B.Williamson
S 1990	29 Sep	Stranger than Fiction	G.Szuca, A.Connolly

The first use of a bicycle spanner runner on Arran!

W 1991	2 Feb	When the Going Gets Turf	G.E.Little (solo)
W 1991	2 Feb	The Rift	G.E.Little (solo)
W 1991	2 Feb	Hellfire Crack	G.E.Little (solo)
S 1991	7 Jul	Gwynserthni	V.Ross, I.Roberts (alt)
S 1991	29 Jul	Accipiter	N.Kebel, G.McArthur
S 1992	27 May	Crystal	G.Szuca (solo)
S 1992	7 Oct	Grimly Fiendish	A.Fraser, S.Frigget

The name says it all!

S 1993	29 May	All Along the Watchtower	A.Fraser, R.McAllister
S 1993	29 May	Solpadeine	G.Borland, M.Sayers

S 1993   29 May   Tight Squeeze   M.Sayers, G.Borland
W 1994   15 Jan   Meadow Slabs   P.Hyde, G.Szuca
W 1994   10 Apr   Sou'wester Slabs   A.Forsyth, B.Goodlad, J.Turner
          A very controversial ascent of a classic, clean rock route
S 1994   27 July   Baron Samedi   A. Fraser, K.Douglas
S 1994   15 Oct   The Key   G.E.Little (solo)
S 1995   29 Apr   Fat Man's Dilemma   G.E.Little, D.Saddler
S 1995   22 July   Icarus   K.Howett, G.E.Little
          Very sustained climbing, bringing Cuithe Mheadonach well into the 1990s.
S 1995   4 Aug   Spirits Colliding   G.E.Little, C.Woodrow
S 1995   5 Aug   Blundecral   G.E.Little, K.Howett (alt)
          The last great problem on the Meadow Face? Blunderbuss Finish: A.Fraser,
          R.McAllister (alt) 31st Aug 1995. True Finish: R. McAllister, D. McGimpsey, 14 Aug
          1996. A bold and technical pitch.
S 1995   20 Aug   Blankist   G.E.Little, K.Howett
S 1995   20 Aug   Long Hot Summer   G.E.Little, K.Howett
S 1995   20 Sep   Gulliver's Travels   A, Fraser, R.McAllister (alt)
          A grand day out!
W 1995   28 Dec   Anvil Gully   G.E.Little (solo)
W 1995   28 Dec   Gully 1 (Beinn Nuis)   G.E.Little (solo)
W 1995   28 Dec   Gully 2 (Beinn Nuis)   G.E.Little (solo)
W 1995   29 Dec   The Strand   S. Kennedy, A. Nelson (alt)
          A pointer to the future?
W 1996   30 Mar   The Wayward Seaman   S.McFarlane, A.Reid
W 1996   30 Mar   Generation Gap   G.E.Little, S. Muir (alt)
          Only 27 years!
W 1996   30 Mar   Mixed Emotions   S.Muir, G.E.Little (alt)
W 1996   31 Mar   Un Petit Voyage   S.Muir, G.E.Little (alt)
W 1996   31 Mar   Western Stoneshoot,   G.E.Little, S.Muir
                  Right Fork, Right Branch
          A wonderfully traditional climb – how did the early pioneers miss it?
S 1996   4 May   Socket Slabs   G.E.Little, K. Howett
S 1996   4 May   Herpolhode – direct link G.E.Little, K. Howett
S 1996   6 May   Squids and Elephants   G.E.Little, K. Howett
          A wee gem, proving that excellent new routes exist in familar places.
S 1996   6 May   Flakes and Foreigners   G.E.Little, K.Howett (alt)
S 1996   12 July   The Brigand   G.E.Little, K.Howett (alt), L.Hughes
          The first E6 on Arran granite – very meaty.

KNAPDALE

S 1940s   Moby Dick   A.Small and party
S 1981   10 Jul   The Razor's Edge   G.E.Little (unseconded)
S 1982   5 Jun   America   G.E.Little, C.Ritchie
S 1982   5 Jun   Chamonix Crack   G.E.Little, C.Ritchie
S 1982   5 Jun   The Prow   G.E.Little, C.Ritchie
S 1982   6 Jun   The Trial   G.E.Little, C.Ritchie
S 1982   9 Oct   Baffin Crack   P.Linning, G.E.Little
S 1982   9 Oct   Badile Crack   G.E.Little, P.Linning
S 1982   .9 Oct   Trundle Crack   P.Linning, G.E.Little
S 1982   9 Oct   Crucifixion Crack   G.E.Little, P.Linning
S 1982   9 Oct   Pocket Wall   P.Linning, G.E.Little
S 1982   9 Oct   Eastern Groove   G.E.Little, P.Linning
S 1982   10 Oct   The Corner   G.E.Little, P.Linning
S 1982   10 Oct   Metamorphosis   G.E.Little, P.Linning
          One point of aid was used on the first ascent.

S 1985	25 May	Flakeaway	G.E.Little (solo)
S 1985	25 May	Steerpike	G.E.Little (solo)
S 1988	21 Feb	Maneater	D.Griffiths, C.Bell
S 1988	20 Jul	Temptation	D.Griffiths, I.Griffiths
S 1988	29 Jul	Crystal Vision	D.Griffiths (unseconded)
S 1988	Aug	Not Waving, But Drowning	M.McGowan, S. Lampard

Top roped practice prior to the first ascent.

S 1995	16 Sep	The Changeling	D.Griffiths, I.Griffiths

CARA

S 1990	15 Sep	Rubha Rib	G.E.Little, R.Reid
S 1990	16 Sep	Cara Corner	G.E.Little, R.Reid
S 1990	16 Sep	Thomas Traverse	R.Reid, G.E.Little
S 1995	13 May	Caraway	G.E.Little, K.Howett, C. Woodrow
S 1995	13 May	Caracontortion	K.Howett, G.E.Little (alt)
S 1995	13 May	Carapace	K.Howett, G.E.Little
S 1995	14 May	Carachameleon	G.E.Little, K. Howett

MULL OF KINTYRE

S 1992	1 Aug	Signal Stack	G.E.Little, W.Skidmore
S 1992	22 Aug	The Hoot	G.E.Little, R. Reid
S 1992	23 Aug	The Tablet	G.E.Little, R.Reid
S 1992	23 Aug	Rites of Passage	G.E.Little, R Reid, W.Skidmore
S 1992	19 Sept	Hornblower	R.Reid, G.E.Little (alt)
S 1992	19 Sept	Horatio	R.Reid, G.E.Little
S 1992	19 Sept	Close Hauled	R.Reid, W.Skidmore
S 1992	20 Sept	Straight Reaching	G.E.Little, R.Reid, W.Skidmore
S 1992	20 Sept	Campion Crack	R.Reid, W.Skidmore, G.E.Little
S 1993	10 Apr	Cresting the Wave	G.E.Little, E.Fraser, K.Howett
S 1993	10 Apr	Ripple Groove	K.Howett, E.Fraser, G.E.Little
S 1993	10 Apr	Brass in Pocket	G.E.Little, K.Howett, E Fraser
S 1993	10 Apr	Big Chief Skidding More	K.Howett, G.E.Little, E.Fraser, W.Skidmore
S 1993	10 Apr	The Prentender	K.Howett, G.E.Little
S 1993	10 Apr	Barking Rock Shrimp	K.Howett, G.E.Little
S 1993	10 Apr	Rusty but Still Working	K.Howett, G.E.Little
S 1993	11 Apr	Pulling Through	G.E.Little, K.Howett, E.Fraser
S 1993	11 Apr	Caulking Wall	G.E.Little, K.Howett
S 1993	11 Apr	Walking the Plank	K.Howett, G.E.Little
S 1993	11 Apr	Captain Pugwash	G.E.Little, K.Howett (alt)
S 1993	24 Apr	Plumbline	G.E.Little, K.Howett, W. Skidmore
S 1993	24 Apr	Coming up Smelling of Fish	K.Howett, G.E.Little
S 1993	24 Apr	Silver Darlings	K.Howett, G.E.Little (alt)
S 1993	25 Apr	Fault Flower Flake	G.E.Little, K.Howett
S 1993	25 Apr	Sea Thrift Wall	G.E.Little, K.Howett
S 1993	25 Apr	Arms Beat	K.Howett, G.E.Little
S 1993	8 May	Olive Oyl	W.Skidmore, W.Thomson
S 1993	8 May	Popeye	W.Skidmore, W.Thomson
S 1993	21 Aug	Amino Flacid	K.Howett, G.E.Little
S 1993	21 Aug	Bluto	G.E.Little, K.Howett
S 1993	21 Aug	The Dragon's Run	K.Howett, G.E.Little
S 1993	22 Aug	The Children of the Open Sea	G.E.Little, K.Howett
S 1993	22 Aug	Undertow	G.E.Little, K.Howett

S 1993	22 Aug	Man Overboard	K.Howett, G.E.Little
S 1993	18 Sept	Bella's Groove	G.E.Little, W.Skidmore
S 1994	1 Apr	Foolish Journey	K.Howett, A.Banks
S 1994	1 Apr	Grattons Gallore	K.Howett, S.Smith, A.Banks
S 1994	16 Apr	The Slice	G.E.Little, W.Skidmore
S 1994	16 Apr	Cakewalk	G.E.Little, M.Riley, W.Skidmore
S 1994	16 Apr	Hooded Groove	G.E.Little (solo)
S 1994	17 Apr	Guilty by Default	G.E.Little, W.Skidmore
S 1994	30 Apr	Crime and Punishment	G.E.Little, K.Howett
S 1994	30 Apr	Flak	W.Skidmore (solo)
S 1994	30 Apr	Back to Basics	G.E.Little, W.Skidmore
S 1994	30 Apr	Kissing the Gunner's Daughter	K.Howett, G.E.Little
S 1994	30 Apr	The Spinach Trail	K.Howett, G.E.Little
S 1994	1 May	Brain Dead	K.Howett (solo)
S 1994	1 May	Wall of the Winds	G.E.Little, K.Howett
S 1994	1 May	Coming Up for Air	K.Howett, G.E.Little (alt)
S 1994	21 May	Old Dog	W.Skidmore (solo)
S 1994	2 Sept	Black Crack	G.E.Little, W.Skidmore
S 1994	4 Sept	Cold Scuttle	K.Howett (unseconded)
S 1994	4 Sept	White Water Slab	A McPherson, N.Kempe
S 1994	4 Sept	White Water Arete	R.Reid, J.Finlay
S 1994	4 Sept	Honeysuckle Wall	G.E.Little, K.Howett, R.Reid
S 1995	14 Apr	Second Thoughts	K. Howett, G.E.Little
S 1995	14 Apr	The Christening	G.E.Little, C.Woodrow, K.Howett
S 1995	15 Apr	In the Lee	K.Howett, G.E.Little
S 1995	15 Apr	The Cleat	K.Howett, G.E.Little
S 1995	15 Apr	Bramble Crack	G.E.Little, C.Woodrow
S 1995	15 Apr	Hesitant Halibut	G.E.Little, K.Howett
S 1996	5 Apr	Canopy Crack	G. E.Little, W.Skidmore
S 1996	6 Apr	Lightning Crack	G.E.Little, M. Rutter, W.Skidmore
S 1996	6 Apr	Warming Up	G.E.Little, C. Woodrow
S 1996	7 Apr	Blood on the Cracks	G.E.Little (unseconded)
S 1996	7 Apr	Corvine Chimney	G.E.Little, C.Woodrow
S 1996	5 Jun	Stairway to Heaven	S.Muir, M.McIraith
S 1996	5 Jun	The Captain and the Kid	K.Howett, L.Hughes (alt)
S 1996	6 Jun	Black Beard	K.Howett, L.Hughes
S 1996	6 Jun	Slow Pup	M.McIraith, S.Muir
S 1996	6 Jun	Sixth Sense	S.Muir, K.Howett, L.Hughes, M.McIraith
S 1996	6 Jun	The Female of the Species	L.Hughes, K.Howett (alt)
S 1996	7 Jun	Realm of Senses	S.Muir, K.Howett, L.Hughes, M. McIraith
S 1996	7 Jun	Black Dog	S.Muir, M.McIraith
S 1996	7 Jun	Continuous Air Play	L.Hughes, K.Howett (alt)

ARROCHAR

LOCH SLOY CRAGS

Charge of the Light Brigade, Power to the People, Current Affair, Wired for Sound and Live Coverage were climbed by J.Divall and R.Cluer in Spring 1995.

S 1988	3 Nov	The Pylon Effect	I.Taylor, C.Moody
S 1988	3 Nov	White Meter	C.Moody, I.Taylor
S 1988	15 Sep	Hum	I.Taylor
S 1988	15 Sep	Disney Tour	I.Taylor, J.Nairn
S 1988	15 Sep	Anywhere	J.Nairn
S 1988	15 Oct	Follow On	I.Taylor, W.Hood

S 1988	15 Oct	Quartz-vein Arete	B.Williamson, C.Moody
S 1988	15 Oct	Silver Soles	I.Taylor, W.Hood
S 1988	15 Oct	Flab Route	W.Hood, I.Taylor
S 1988	30 Sep	Autumn Arete	I.Taylor
S 1988	30 Sep	Hidden Slab	I.Taylor
S 1988	30 Sep	The Mica Boot Route	I.Taylor
S 1988	30 Sep	Splinters	I.Taylor
S 1988	30 Sep	Stonefingers	I.Taylor
S 1989	27 May	Hundreds and Thousands	A.Caren, I.Taylor
S 1989	27 May	Molehill	I.Taylor, A.Caren
S 1992	Oct	The Ascent of Yan	I.Taylor, G.Stanworth
S 1993	31 Oct	Saturn V	C.Pettigrew, L.Collier

VIADUCT CRAG

S 1988	25 May	Beyond the Pale	C.Bell, D.Griffiths
S 1988	25 May	Pale Wall	D.Griffiths (solo)

A'CHROIS

S 1895	23 May	Central Buttress	F.S.Goggs, H.Raeburn
S 1905	Apr	Pinnacle Buttress	C.W.Walker, H.Walker, and the Inglis Clarks
W 1948	Jan	Pinnacle Gully	B.H.Humble, J.B.Nimlin

CREAG THARSUINN

S 1900	Apr	Maclay's Gully	J.Maclay, F.S.Goggs, Messrs Robertson, Nettleton, Marler
S 1901	2 May	80 Foot Gully	J.Maclay, R.E.Workman
S 1901	2 May	Rake Gully	J.Maclay, R.E.Workman
S 1901	23 Nov	Original Buttress Route	W.I.Clark, J.G.Inglis
W 1902	1 Jan	Curving Gully	J.Rennie, H.Raeburn, J.Maclay
W 1902	1 Jan	80 Foot Gully	J.Rennie, H.Raeburn, J.Maclay
S 1906	Jun	McLaren's Chimney	A.C.McLaren, S.G.Shadbolt, C.P.Shadbolt
S 1921	30 Apr	Garrick's Route	J.A.Garrick, D.Biggar
S 1947	Jun	Slab and Groove	J.B.Nimlin, D.Easson, B.H.Humble
S 1949	Sep	Face Route	J.B.Nimlin (solo)
S 1953	Jun	Solo Buttress	R.D.B.Stewart
S 1958	4 May	Deception	D.McKelvie, C.Whyte, A.Burns
S 1958	31 May	V-Groove	P.Mitchell, J.Morrison
S 1959	21 Jun	Alfresco	D.McKelvie, C.Whyte, H.Martin, A.Burns
S 1960	26 Jun	Hangover	P.Mitchell, J.Morrison
S 1960	18 Apr	Arch Chimney	P.Mitchell, J.R.Ewing
W 1965	30 Jan	Maclay's Gully	W.Skidmore, J.Crawford, J.Madden
W 1965	31 Jan	McLaren's Chimney	W.Skidmore, J.Crawford, J.Madden
		Variation start: M.Garthwaite, G.Szuca, 12th Jan, 1991.	
W 1974	15 Dec	Central Buttress	K.V.Crocket, I.Fulton
S 1974	23 Jun	The Tingler	J.Gillespie, W.Skidmore
S 1975	29 Jun	Terminal Wall	J.Johnson, W.Skidmore
W 1976	24 Jan	V-Groove	K.V.Crocket, I.Fulton
W 1976	31 Jan	Rake Gully	ACraig, J.R.Mackenzie
S 1976	8 Aug	Trilogy	D.Hodgson, W.Skidmore
S 1977	19 Jul	Tremolo	D.Dawson, W.Skidmore
S 1980		Pulpit Grooves	A.Walker, D.Walker
W 1980		Deception	A.Walker, D.Walker
W 1986	1 Feb	Solo Buttress	R.T.Richardson, A.Walker
W 1986	Dec	Route Sinister	C.Campbell, K.V.Crocket
W 1989	16 Dec	Metatarsal	R.Everett, S.Richardson (alts)

W 1991	13 Jan	Terminator	M.Garthwaite, G.Szuca
W 1994	8 Jan	Pulpit Grooves	R.Anderson, D.McCallum, R.Milne (alts)
W 1994	2 Jan	Anonymous Gully	I.Taylor, A.Robertson.
W 1994	23 Feb	V-Groove Direct	D.MacLardie, G.Szuca

BEINN NARNAIN

S 1894	May	Spearhead Arete	J.Maclay, W.W.Naismith
S 1898		Jamblock Chimney	J.Maclay, R.E.Workman
S 1935	May	Restricted Crack	T.Donaldson, J.R.Hewitt
S 1959	12 Sep	Cicatrice	P.Mitchell, J.R.Ewing
S 1959	12 Sep	Lip Route	P.Mitchell, J.R.Ewing
S 1959	12 Sep	Muckle Mou'	P.Mitchell, J.R.Ewing
S 1961	May	No Highway	I.C.Davies, J.Blair
S 1976	25 Jul	Southern Comfort	J.R.Mackenzie
W 1993	Mar	Philosopher's Gully	T.Archer, E.Ewing
W 1994	25 Nov	Hume's Buttress	T.Archer, E.Ewing
W 1994	14 Nov	The Twilight Zone	T.Archer, E.Ewing

BEINN IME

| W 1935 | Feb | Fan Gully | J.B.Nimlin, R.Peel |
| S 1946 | Nov | Ben's Fault | J.B.Nimlin, D.Easson |

Left-Hand Start: R.D.B.Stewart, S.Horn, A.Kidd, A.N.Other, Feb 1957.

S 1957	30 Jun	Airy Ridge	R.D.B.Stewart, R.R.Shaw
S 1958	Oct	Buttress Route	P.Mitchell, D.McLuckie
W 1963	2 Feb	Ben's Fault via	W.Skidmore, R.T.Richardson
		Left-Hand Start	
W 1976	5 Dec	Buttress Route	D.Jenkins, A.Pettit, C.Stead
W 1976	26 Dec	Hanging Groove	C.D.Grant, C.Stead
W 1984	27 Dec	Ma Fault	T.McAuley, D.Sanderson
W 1990	27 Jan	Airy Ridge	N.Kekus, S.Richardson
W 1995	12 Jan	Friday the Twelth	A.Ogilvie, E.Robertson
W 1995	21 Jan	Default Mode	S.Richardson, C.French (alts), T.Prentice
W 1995	29 Jan	Headfault	R.Anderson, R.Milne
W 1996	29 Dec	The Lost Highway	D.Campbell, A.Brightman

THE COBBLER

S 1889	Jul	The Arete	W.W.Naismith, G.Thomson
S 1889	Oct	South-East Ridge	G.Thomson and party
S 1894	May	Original Route	W.W.Naismith, G.Thomson
S 1895	25 May	Great Gully	J. Maclay, W.W.Naismith
S 1895	25 May	Maclay's Crack	J.Maclay, W.W.Naismith
S 1895	26 Sep	Bell's Route	J.H.Bell, H.C.Boyd, J.S.MacGregor.

Variation: J.S.MacGregor, J.H.Bell, H.C.Boyd, R.G.Napier, W.W.Naismith, on the same day. Rutherford's Variation: R.N.Rutherford, A.G.Hutchison, 1927.

S 1895	26 Sep	MacGregor's Ledge	J.S.MacGregor, J.H.Bell, H.C.Boyd,
			R.G.Napier, W.W.Naismith
S 1896	27 Sep	Right-Angled Gully	W.W.Naismith, J.S.MacGregor.

Direct finish: J.B.Nimlin, 1930 (solo).

| W 1896 | 31 Oct | Right-Angled Gully | H.Raeburn, W.Tough |

The team attempted the direct finish under snow conditions, but finished by the original route. Rock Climbs on the Cobbler by Nimlin, Humble and Williams (SMCJ vol 22, Nov 1940, p 15) records the route as having been climbed 'in part.' The Direct Finish is reputed to have been climbed in winter by H.Hamilton in the 1930s. The first recorded ascent of Direct Finish in winter: C.Cartwright, S.Richardson, 30 Dec 1990.

S 1898	3 Jul	Cave Route	H.Raeburn, J.Rennie
S 1898	3 Jul	Grassy Traverse	H.Raeburn, J.Rennie
S 1898	26 Sep	Naismith's Route	W.W.Naismith, J.Rennie
S 1898	26 Sep	North-West Crack	W.W.Naismith, J.Rennie
S 1933	Apr	Nimlin's Direct Route	J.B.Nimlin, A.Sanders
S 1933	Oct	Jughandle	J.B.Nimlin, A.Sanders
S 1934	Aug	Ramshead Wall	J.B.Nimlin, A.Sanders
S 1934		Right-Angled Groove	J.B.Nimlin
S 1935		North Rib Route	J.B.Nimlin, J.Fox
S 1935	May	Recess Route	J.B.Nimlin, J.Fox, R.Ewing

The Fold (the crux) was first climbed by Harold Raeburn in 1904, after a traverse in from Ramshead Gully via the Halfway Terrace. At least part of the route was climbed in winter pre-1938. See: B.Humble Cobbler Calling (SMCJ vol 21 Nov 1938, p 397) and Rock Climbs on the Cobbler by Nimlin, Humble and Williams (SMCJ vol 22, Nov 1940, p 15).

S 1936		Cat Crawl	A.Lavery, A.N.Other
S 1936	Jun	Fold Direct	J.B.Nimlin, D.Browning
S 1936		Ramshead Gully	J.Muir, A.Muir.

An ascent by J.B.Nimlin, A.Sanders and J.Hart in 1934 was 'disqualified' as a safety rope from above had protected the leader on a 5m section while he 'spring-cleaned'.

S 1937	Oct	Ardgartan Wall	J.B.Nimlin, J.Wynne, W.Neilson, R.Goldie
S 1940	May	North Wall Traverse	J.B.Nimlin, Miss J.Dryden, R.Peel

The first pitch has become known as Sesame Groove. Sesame Groove Direct Start: R.Barclay, J.Adams, Sept 1955. Sesame Groove Direct Start Winter: J.Turner, A.Ogilvie, 3 Mar 1993.

S 1940	22 Sep	Cobbler Cave	D.Beveridge, B.H.Humble
S 1945	Aug	North Wall Groove	W.Smith, C.Wilson
S 1947		Chimney Route	R.Smith, C.Downie
S 1947	Jun	Chimney Arete	J.Cunningham, I.Dingwall
S 1947		Slack's Route	A.Slack, G.Fraser
S 1948		Direct Direct	J.Cunningham

The upper crack was added by R.Muir and J.Wilson (date unknown).

S 1948		Incubator	J.Cunningham, I.Dingwall

The pitch below the halfway terrace was climbed by J.Cunningham, W.Smith and T.Paul.

S 1948	May	Deadman's Groove	J.Cunningham, W.Smith, S.Smith
S 1948	Jun	Ardgartan Arete	J.Cunningham
S 1948	Jun	S-Crack	J.Cunningham, W.Smith
S 1948		Recess	K.Copeland
S 1949	Aug	Echo Crack	J.Cunningham, C.Vigano
S 1949	Aug	Punster's Crack	J.Cunningham, W.Smith
S 1951	May	Porcupine Wall	H.MacInnes, J.Cunningham (aid)
S 1951	Aug	Gladiator's Groove	W.Smith, H.MacInnes

Direct start: W.Smith, R.Hope, Jun 1952

S 1951	Aug	Pygmy Wall	C.Vigano, J.Cullen, M.Noon
S 1951	Sep	Wether Wall	J.Cunningham, H.MacInnes
S 1952	Apr	Grossen Zinnen	H.MacInnes, R.Hope
S 1952	May	Aeon	J.Cullen, C.Vigano

Variation: J.Cullen, W.Smith, Aug 1952

S 1952	May	Cupid's Groove	J.Cunningham, H.MacInnes, W.Smith, H.Currie
S 1952	Jun	Bow Crack	W.Smith, W.Dobbie, R.Hope

Variation: G.Latter, P.McNally, 17 Apr 1995

S 1952	Aug	Ithuriel's Wall	H.MacInnes (aid)

FFA: J.Hutchison 1976

S 1952	Aug	N'Gombi	C.Vigano, C.White
S 1952	Aug	Telepathy Crack	W.Smith, T.Paul
S 1952	Aug	Whither Wether	H.MacInnes, W.Smith

Variation finish W.Smith, T.Paul, Aug 1952

S 1952		Grey Wall	W.Rowney, M.Noon
S 1952	Sep	Spinal Rib	P.Walsh
S 1952	Oct	Gimcrack	P.Walsh, J.Wilson, M.Noon
S 1952	Oct	Moss Crack	H.MacInnes, G.MacIntosh
S 1955		The Nook Direct	M.Noon, J.Cunningham, W.Smith,
			G.McIntosh, P.Walsh

Largely superseded by Wild Country and Wild at Heart.

S 1956	Sep	Dicer's Groove	E.Taylor, A.Crawford
S 1957		Club Crack	P.Walsh and party
S 1957	Jun	Glueless Groove	R. Smith
W 1961	Jan	North Wall Traverse	W.Skidmore, P.McKenzie

Skidmore starts to probe the winter potential the Southern Highlands.

W 1962	Jan	Grassy Traverse	R.Robb, P.McKenzie, W.Skidmore
S 1967		Baillie's Overhang	R.Baillie, J.Amatt (aid)

Climbed over two days. Free attempt route: G.Latter, M.McGowan, 21 Jun 1989

S 1968	Aug	McLean's Folly	R.Carrington, J.Gardiner
S 1976	25 Apr	Great Gully Wall	B.Clarke, A.Craig, J.R.Mackenzie
W 1977	16 Feb	North Wall Groove	N.Muir, A.Paul

A significant ascent of a classic, mixed route by two insatiable explorers. Direct start: T.Prentice, R.Anderson, C.French, Mar 1995.

S 1979	4 Jul	Wild Country	D.Cuthbertson, R.Kerr

Pitch 1 was climbed 5 Jul. An important breakthrough in standards. Cuthbertson initially attempted the route on sight, later cleaning it on abseil and pre-placing a runner.

S 1979	5 Jul	Evening Stroll	D.Cuthbertson, R.Kerr
S 1980	16 May	Ruskoline	D.Cuthbertson, K.Johnstone

Partly cleaned in the mistaken belief it would be 'about HVS, at the most maybe E2'!

S 1980	23 May	Moonlight Arete	D.Cuthbertson, K.Johnstone
S 1980	25 May	Rest and be Thankful	D.Cuthbertson, K.Johnstone

A classic mica schist wall climb. Attempted on sight, both climbers getting above, then reversing the crux. Climbed the next day after a 'quick clean'. Variation: P.Laughlan, May 1987

S 1980	13 Jun	Lobby Dosser	T.McAuley, N.Muir
S 1981	13 Sep	Southern Freeze	K.Johnstone, G.Pryde
W 1983	Dec	Chockstone Gully	K.V.Crocket, A.Walker
S 1886	13 Sep	The Mog	W.Hood, B.Williamson
W 1987	14 Feb	Heart Buttress	K.V.Crocket, T.Weir
S 1987	26 Jun	Comical Corner	I.Griffiths, D.Griffiths
S 1987	26 Jun	Straight Flush	D.Griffiths, I.Griffiths
S 1988	6 Apr	Osiris	D.Griffiths (unseconded)

A superb route on a surprisingly neglected piece of The Cobbler.

S 1988	18 Jun	Spainkiller	I.Taylor, A.Alexander, I.Ruiz
S 1988	19 Jun	Piper's Lament	T.Prentice, A.Kirk
S 1989	23 May	Northern Heatwave	I.Taylor, L.Thomas
S 1989	27 May	Gibber Crack	R.Carchrie, K.V.Crocket, D.Jenkins,
			G.A.McEwan, A.Walker
S 1989	15 Jun	The Lost Pinnacle	A.Caren, R.Turner, I.Taylor
S 1989		Rise to the Occasion	M.McGowan, G.Farquhar

The crack had been climbed previously by D.Griffiths.

W 1990	28 Jan	Deadman's Groove	R.Milne, R.Anderson (alt)

This ascent awakened climbers' eyes to The Cobbler's winter potential.

W 1990	3 Feb	Incubator	R. Anderson, T. Prentice (alt), C. Anderson
W 1990	25 Nov	Gibber Crack	R.Milne, R.Anderson

The start of earnest winter exploration.

W 1990	9 Dec	Fold Direct	R.Anderson, T.Prentice (alt)
W 1990	30 Dec	Ramshead Ridge	C.Cartwright, S.Richardson (alt)

Climbed in conjunction with the first winter ascent of Right-Angled Gully Direct.

W 1991	6 Jan	N'Gombi	R.Anderson, R.Milne (alt)

The first pitch took three hours to lead.

W 1991	6 Jan	Soul Groove	A.Fraser, J.Thomson, J.Blyth
S 1991	20 Jul	Horus	G.Latter

An attempt at the second ascent resulted in seven ripped runners and a 12m fall. The first of a new generation of hard rock climbs.

W 1991	17 Nov	McSod's Way	R.Anderson, R.Milne (alt)
S 1992	5 Jul	Gearless	G.Szuca, J.Craig
S 1993	3 Sep	Wild at Heart	G.Latter, B.Beer

(Pitch 1). Pitch 3 was added by G.Latter, T.Keenan, 27 Sep. On an earlier attempt a 12m ground fall on Pitch 1 needed the rescue team. Pitch 2 was redpointed with runners in place.

W 1993	24 Dec	Punster's Crack	A.Clarke, M.Garthwaite (alt)

An impressive, if controversial, technical ascent.

W 1994	2 Jan	Gimcanna	R.Anderson, R.Milne
W 1994	2 Jan	Chimney Route	T.Prentice, P.Beaumont

Attempted the day before. Two teams arrived independently at the carpark, with eyes on the same route.

W 1994	4 Jan	North Rib Route	R.Anderson, C.Anderson, D.McCallum, R.Milne

McCallum expressed surprise that mixed climbing could be so good.

W 1994	25 Feb	Right-Angled Chimney	B.Goodlad, A.Forsyth
W 1994	20 Mar	S-Crack	I.Taylor, C.Lyon
S 1994	20 Jul	Wide Country	R.Campbell, P.Thorburn

A much eyed line in a stunning position.

S 1994	20 Jul	Trans Am Wheel Arch Nostrils	M.Garthwaite, R.Campbell

A consolation route climbed on sight, after being beaten to the first ascent of Wide Country by 90 mins. The nostrils are believed to be Campbell's!

W 1994	27 Dec	Great Gully Groove	R.Anderson, R.Milne
W 1994	27 Dec	Lulu	R.Milne, R.Anderson
W 1995	4 Jan	Nimlin's Direct Route	T.Archer, O.Prodan
W 1995	12 Jan	Aeonoclast	C.Stewart, T.Prentice (alts)
W 1995	19 Jan	Pygmy Wall	R.McAllister, D.McGimpsey

Variation finish: T.Archer, E.Ewing, O.Prodan, P.Toniolo, 1995.

W 1995	24 Jan	Direct Direct	R.McAllister, D.McGimpsey

An excellent lead of a hard summer route.

W 1995	29 Jan	Ramshead Wall	S.Lampard, M.Reed
S 1995	Apr	Lumpy Custard	G.Latter, P.McNally

A quiet start to the best summer for a decade.

S 1995	1 May	Ra	G.Latter, P.Thorburn (alt)
S 1995	2 Jun	Geb	G.Latter, P.Thorburn
S 1995	5 Jun	North Winds	P.Thorburn, G.Latter
S 1995	21 Jun	Ethereal	P.Thorburn, R.Campbell
S 1995	16 Sep	A Crack in the Clouds	P.Thorburn, G.Latter

An obscure gem.

S 1995	17 Sep	Sleeping Gas	P.Thorburn, I.Pitcairn
S 1995	20 Sep	Dalriada	G.Latter

Attempted over seven days and finally redpointed. A stunning route in a stunning position.

W 1996   Viva Glasvegas   M.Garthwaite, A.Coish.
    A contender for the hardest winter route in the Southern Highlands.
W 1996 11 Feb Right-angled Groove   R.Anderson, R.Milne
W 1996   Feb Megabyte   R.McAllister, R.Milne, D.McGimpsey
W 1996 30 Dec Drugs are for Mugs   R.McAllister, D.McGimpsey

GLEN CROE
S 1985 17 Feb Cosmic Corner   G.Latter (solo)
S 1985 17 Feb Fear   G.Latter (solo)
S 1985 17 Feb Pockets of Excellence   G.Latter
    Buckets of Smee finish (as described): C.Gilchrist, G.Latter, 5 Aug 1985
S 1985 31 Jul Give us a Break   G.Latter, M.Fowler
S 1985   5 Aug Double Clutching   G.Latter, C.Gilchrist
S 1986   4 Oct Ledgeislation   D.Griffiths, C.Bell
S 1986 13 Apr Breakdance   D.Griffiths, C.Bell
S 1986 13 Apr The Cost of Living   D.Griffiths, C.Bell
S 1986   Jul Quartz Crack   R.Bruce, J.Christie
S 1986   Jul Quartz Slab   R.Bruce, J.Christie
S 1986   Jul Short Sharp Shock   R.Bruce (unseconded)
S 1986 12 Aug Outside Edge   D.Griffiths, C.Bell
S 1986 13 Sep All Heroes Die Young   D.Griffiths, C.Bell
S 1986 13 Sep Cadbury's   I.Griffiths, C.Bell
S 1986 14 Sep New Position   D.Griffiths, C.Bell
S 1986 23 Dec Prime Ape   D.Griffiths (unseconded)
S 1987 13 Apr The Edge of Insanity   D.Griffiths (unseconded)
    A bolt and a peg were used for runners. The bolt was removed on the second ascent
    by G.Latter, 7 June 1987.
S 1987   2 May Aftershock   D.Griffiths (unseconded)
S 1987 30 May Fearless   D.Griffiths (solo)
S 1987 30 May The Ladder   D.Griffiths (solo)
S 1987 13 Jul The Sharp Kiss   D.Griffiths (unseconded)
S 1988   4 Jul Pegomaniac   I.Taylor, C.Moody
S 1988   Jul Litterbug   I.Taylor, A.Caren
S 1988 16 Aug Lapland   I.Taylor, B.Williamson
S 1988   9 Sep The Nitty-gritty Dirt Route I.Taylor, J.Nairn
S 1988   9 Sep Rough and Tumble   J.Nairn, I.Taylor
S 1989   Apr Rock Sculpture   S.Robinson, K.Lawson
S 1989   Jun Quartzymodo   N.Brodie (solo)
S 1992   Bollocks   G.Latter, B.Longhurst
S 1995 19 Sep Marabou Stork Nightmares P.Thorburn (unseconded)

THE BRACK
S 1895   Jul Inglis Clark Arete   W.I.Clark, C.I.Clark, M.I.Clark
S 1906   Jun Elephant Gully   A.C.McLaren, S.G.Shadbolt, C.P.Shadbolt
S 1947   May Bobcrack   J.B.Nimlin, R.Peel
S 1947   May Four Step Ridge   J.B.Nimlin, R.Peel
S 1947   May Gimcrack   J.B.Nimlin, R.Peel
S 1947   May May Route   J.B.Nimlin, R.Peel
W 1953   Jan Elephant Gully   J.B.Nimlin, R.Grieve
S 1958 14 Jun Great Central Groove   P.Mitchell, J.Morrison
S 1967   Sep Mammoth   W.Skidmore, R.T.Richardson, J.Crawford
    Some aid was used. FFA: D.Mullin, A.Petit, 1978.

W	1968	Jan	Great Central Groove	W.Skidmore, R.T.Richardson

Some aid was used.

S	1968	Jul	Mainline	W.Skidmore, J.Crawford

At least 5 pegs for aid. FFA: I.Duckworth, A.Petit, 1976.

S	1968	Oct	Sideline	R.T.Richardson, W.Skidmore (A3)
W	1973	2 Dec	Inglis Clark Arete	T.Anderson, B.Clarke, C.Garthwaite, J.Mackenzie
S	1976	19 Sep	Lilliput	G.Skelton, A.Wilson
W	1976	31 Jan	May Route	K.V.Crocket, C.Stead
W	1976	31 Jan	January Buttress	K.V.Crocket, C.Stead
W	1977	24 Feb	Right-Hand Route	N.Muir, A.Paul
W	1979	14 Jan	Big Game Route	P.Bilsborough, I.Duckworth
S	1980	19 May	Edge of Extinction	P.Botterill, P.Whillance

A superb achievement – one of the finest mountain Extremes in Scotland.

W	1986	7 Feb	The Abyss	K.V.Crocket, A.Walker
W	1986	Jan	Hell's Teeth	K.V.Crocket, A.Walker
W	1987	10 Jan	The Plunge	K.V.Crocket, A.Walker

The Deep Start: D.Griffiths, I.Griffiths, 30 March 1996.

W	1995	21 Dec	Small Fry	K.Schwartz
W	1997	1 Jan	Resolution	R.McAllister, D.McGimpsey

BEN DONICH

S	1980	24 May	Deja Vu	G.E.Little, W.Skidmore
S	1980	Jun	Flakewalk	R.T.Richardson, W.Skidmore
S	1981	27 Jun	Voulez Vous	G.E.Little, C.Ritchie
S	1981	27 Jun	Simple Visions	G.E.Little, C.Ritchie
S	1981	16 Aug	Skywalk	G.E.Little, W.Skidmore
W	1990	31 Dec	Flakewalk	C.Cartwright, R.Everett, S.Richardson

A Hexcentric with modified wooden extensions was specially made to protect the crux and reluctantly used for aid. It was Richardson's fourth attempt at the route.

S	1995	31 Jul	Night on the Tiles	N.J,Smith, unseconded
S	1995	17 Aug	D.J.	I.Walker, A.Mayers, N.Smith

BEINN AN LOCHAIN

S	1952	Jul	Saxifrage Gully	J.B.Nimlin, B.H.Humble
W	1974	15 Dec	Saxifrage Gully	B.Clarke, J.R.Mackenzie
S	1976	3 Sep	Monolith Grooves	J.R.Mackenzie
W	1976	5 Dec	Twin Caves Gully	A.Craig, J.R.Mackenzie
W	1977	16 Jan	Monolith Grooves	B.Clarke, J.R.Mackenzie
W	1977	6 Feb	Promenade Gully	M.Asturz, J.R.Mackenzie
W	1977	20 Feb	Whiteout Gully	M.Astbury, J.R.Mackenzie (solo)
S	1980	24 Aug	Edge	G.E.Little
S	1980	12 Oct	Point Counter Point	G.E.Little
S	1980	12 Oct	Sidewalk	G.E.Little
W	1983	Feb	Toad	K.Schwartz, G.Moffat
W	1984	28 Jan	Benylin	W.Hood
W	1986	3 Jan	Galadriel's Mirror	H.Henderson, S.Kennedy, G.Ross
W	1986	3 Jan	The Back Alley	H.Henderson, S.Kennedy, R.G.Ross
W	1986	16 Feb	Bufo	T.Redfern, M.Leyland
W	1986	Winter	Tonton Macout	W.Hood, B.Williamson
W	1987	19 Jan	The Edge of Darkness	H.Henderson, S.Kennedy, M.Macdonald, R.G.Ross
W	1987	19 Jan	The Palantir	H.Henderson, S.Kennedy, M.Macdonald, R.G.Ross

W 1991	10 Feb	Frog	T.Redfern, K.Schwartz
W 1993	19 Jan	Megalith	A.Fraser, R.McAllister, D.McGimpsey, S.Mearns
W 1995	29 Jan	Menhir	S.Mearns, S.Archer
S 1996	20 Jun	AWOL in Thailand	J.Lines, P.Thorburn, R.Campbell

Direct Start (Julian Can't Cope): P.Thorburn, 21 Aug 1996.

S 1996	20 Jun	Swimming With The Tide	P.Thorburn, J.Lines
S 1996	20 Jun	Pious Ejaculation	R.Campbell, P.Thorburn
S 1996	7 Sep	Appoggiatura	R.Campbell, P.Thorburn
W 1996	29 Dec	Bakerloo Line	T.Prentice, R.Milne
W 1997	2 Jan	Purple Blaze	T.Prentice, R.Anderson, R.Milne

Pitches 1 and 2: T.Prentice, A.Fraser, D.McGimpsey; 10 Feb 1994

BINNEIN AN FHIDHLEIR

S 1976	Jul	Abyssinia Chimney	J.Mackenzie
S 1976	Jul	Africa Gully	J.Mackenzie
S 1976	Jul	Amin's Can-Can	J.Mackenzie
S 1977	Aug	Amindergroove	J.Mackenzie, C.Ogilvie
S 1977	Aug	Horn of Plenty	J.Mackenzie, C.Ogilvie
S 1977	Aug	Two-Step	C.Ogilvie, J.Mackenzie
S 1987	24 May	Heart of Darkness	K.V.Crocket, J.Divall, A.Walker
S 1987	24 May	Serengeti	K.V.Crocket, J.Divall, A.Walker
S 1987	21 Jun	Erectus	C.Campbell, K.V.Crocket, G.Jeffries
S 1987	21 Jun	Habilis	C.Campbell, K.V.Crocket, G.Jeffries
S 1987	21 Jun	Origins	C.Campbell, K.V.Crocket, G.Jeffries
S 1987	21 Jun	Roots	C.Campbell
S 1987	21 Jun	Victoria Falls	C.Campbell, K.V.Crocket, G.Jeffries
S 1989	13 May	Harmony	K.V.Crocket, J.M.Lackie (pitch 1)

Pitch 1 was added by R.Reid, I.Croften, 10 May 1991

W 1990	29 Dec	Africa Gully	S.Richardson, G.Muhlemann
W 1990	29 Dec	Abyssinia Chimney	G.Muhlemann, S.Richardson
S 1990	2 Jun	Nostromo	R.Reid, R.Webb
S 1990	17 Jun	Luss Crack	R.Reid, I.Davidson
S 1990	2 Aug	Witch-Doctor	K.V.Crocket, B.Dullea
S 1991	10 May	Slightly Silly Arete	R.Reid, I.Croften
S 1991		Africanus	K.V.Crocket, B.Dullea, D.Gardner
S 1994	1 Jan	OK Buttress	A.Ogilvie, J.Kavanaeh
S 1996	7 Apr	Safari	N.J.Smith, C.Bale
S 1996	11 Apr	Fiddler's Slab	N.J.Smith (solo)
S 1996	6 May	Schistosomiasis	N.Warnes, N.J.Smith
S 1996	6 May	Paganini	N.Smith, N.Warnes
S 1996	8 May	Hamite	N.J.Smith, D.Watkin, T.Prentice, C.Dunn
S 1996	12 May	Schistophrenia	N.Warnes, C.Bale
S 1996	14 May	Jig And Reel	N.J.Smith, M.Sandison
S 1996	14 May	Mark's Arete	M.Sandison, N.J.Smith
S 1996	14 May	Aquila	M.Sandison, N.J.Smith
S 1996	14 May	Lacklustre	N.J.Smith, M.Sandison

DUN LEACAINN

The dates of most of the first ascents are not known. Devil's Elbow, Excavator and The Rambler: F.Harper, M.A.Harper. Dominator: R.Baillie, P.Dyer (Direct Start P.Dyer, R.Baillie). Mutation: W.March, R.Baillie. Pluvial: R.Smith, W.Rowney (Direct Link: J.Amatt, R.Baillie).

| S 1991 | 24 Mar | Eliminator | G.Farquhar, C.Carolan |

BEINN MHOR

Gog, Magog, Thread the Needle, Ungodly and Winalot were climbed by R.Baillie in 1968. All other routes were added by K.Schwartz with various clients and partners.

CREAG LIATH

S 1962	Jun	Farewell	W.Skidmore, J.Crawford
S 1963	May	Stag	W.Skidmore, J.Crawford
S 1963	Jun	Severe Slab	W.Skidmore
S 1963	Jun	Apex Groove	W.Skidmore, J.Crawford
S 1963	Jun	Wedlock	W.Skidmore, J.Crawford, D.Golden, S.Fielding

Direct Start: K.Schwartz, K.Edgar, May 1994

S 1967		Fall Out	R.Baillie, W.March (Aid)
S 1974	Jun	H'eck	B.Clarke, J.R.Mackenzie
S 1974	Jun	Hand-Out Crack	B.Clarke, J.R.Mackenzie
S 1974	Jun	The Pod	B.Clarke, J.R.Mackenzie
S 1977		Heirat	K.Schwartz
S 1977	Jun	Ehe	R.Schwartz, K.Schwartz
S 1977	Jun	Canaille	J.Mount, K.Schwartz
S 1977	Sep	Bye Bye	J.Mount, K.Schwartz
S 1980		Fall Out Wall	A.Kellas and party
S 1980		Guides' Route	A.Kellas, I.Peter
S 1982	Apr	Pig Face	S.Kennedy, C.Moody
S 1982	May	Paranoia	W.Hood, C.Moody

Climbed after the rockfall by G.Latter, 20 Aug 1993.

S 1987	4 Oct	Aye-Up Youth	C.Moody, A.Smith
S 1987	19 Sep	Dawn Patrol	D.Griffiths (unseconded)

THE SOUTHERN HIGHLANDS

STOB GHABHAR

W 1897	May	The Upper Couloir, Stob Ghabhar	A.E.Maylard, Professor and Mrs Adamson, Miss Weiss.

Difficulties with long axes and even longer skirts.

W 1952	Mar	Upper Couloir Keyhole	C.L.Donaldson, G.J.F.Dutton
S 1961	May	Hircine Rib	P. Mitchell, J. Morrison, J.R.Ewing
S 1982	31 May	Capricorn	P Mitchell

Originally assumed to have been a winter ascent, due to the anomalous 'MacInnes' grade supplied.

W 1989	30 Dec	Hircine Rib	S.Richardson, G.Dudley

BEINN A' CHREACHAIN

W 1986	5 Apr	Leucocyte Buttress	K.V.Crocket, J.M.Lackie
W 1987	31 Jan	Brittle Ramp	G.E.Little, D.Saddler
W 1994	15 Jan	A Bit on the Side	G.E.Little
W 1991	3 Mar	Soft Option	A.Baker, G.E.Little

MEALL BUIDHE

W 1977	16 Jan	The Circus	C.D.Grant, C.Stead
W 1984	20 Feb	Rock Scar Groove, Forked Gully	G.E.Little
W 1984	22 Mar	The Scoop, Second Sight, Psychic Gully	G.E.Little

W 1984	29 Mar	Mortal Coil	G.E.Little
W 1987	12 Dec	Rampling, Spirit Level, Echo Edge	G.E.Little
W 1988	28 Feb	Voice Beyond	G.E.Little
W 1995		Eldritch	K.V.Crocket, B.Dullea

BEINN ACHALADAIR

| W 1987 | 12 Dec | Medium Groove, Manifestation | G.E.Little |
| W 1988 | 28 Feb | Redemption, Premonition, Apprehension | G.E.Little |

BEINN AN DOTHAIDH, NORTH-EAST CORRIE

W 1894	26 Mar	West Gully	Prof.W.Ramsay, W.Ramsay Jnr., F.Campbell, C.C.B.Moss
W 1894	27 Mar	ZigZag Gully	W.Ramsay, H.C.Boyd, G.Thomson
W 1894	27 Mar	Central Gully	W.Douglas, W.Naismith

The mountain faces an onslaught by climbers from an SMC Meet staying at Inveroran Inn. Bored, Norman Collie moves on to Ben Nevis and climbs Tower Ridge.

| S 1935 | | Ghyll Buttress | R.Peel |

Approximates to West Buttress, a turfy Very Difficult.

| W 1969 | 8 Mar | Taxus | A.W.Ewing, A.J.Trees |

The name probably derives from an article on the original ascents, when the SMC pioneers looked at this gully but decided it would have been too much of a tax on their time. Hard to believe that the corrie had been neglected for so long.

| W 1972 | 12 Mar | Haar | M.H.Moar, C.Walmsley |

After this incredible period of neglect, the first stirrings of the new winter revolution begins. Interestingly, it coincides with front-pointing. Not much step-cutting to be found on Beinn an Dothaidh.

| W 1974 | 24 Mar | Cirrus | J.Crawford, J.Gillespie, W.Skidmore |

The Greenock Team begin a period of good exploration with a classic but hard gully.

| W 1976 | 25 Jan | Taxus Icefall Finish | J.Crawford, D.Dawson, J.Madden, W.Skidmore |

A much better finish to Taxus.

| W 1976 | Feb | The Skraeling | I.Fulton, J.Hutchinson |

A good buttress route, the first of such on the North-East Face.

| W 1976 | 1 Feb | West Buttress | J.Crawford, D.Dawson, W.Skidmore |

The second buttress route on this face, possibly approximating to the summer route Ghyll Buttress. Direct Start: S.Richardson, R.Everett, 25th Feb 1996.

| W 1976 | 26 Dec | Clonus | D.Hodgson, W.Skidmore |

The thin gully line snatched by the Greenock Team, shaky muscles included.

| W 1976 | 28 Dec | Slow March | C.D.Grant, C.Stead |

An attempt at a direct buttress line was thwarted by a bulging wall.

| W 1977 | 3 Jan | Far West Buttress | C.D.Grant, C.Stead |
| W 1977 | 3 Jan | Stormbringer | K.V.Crocket, I.Fulton |

Direct Start: C.Cartwright, S.Richardson 24 Nov 1996.

| W 1978 | 24 Jan | The Beechgrove Garden | K.Schwartz |

A disgracefully late reporting of this route (1996) previously accorded to another team.

| W 1978 | 9 Feb | Emel Ridge | K.Schwartz |
| W 1981 | 10 Jan | The Upper Circle | S.Kennedy, N.Morrison, A.Nisbet |

A rare and early appearance by the Aberdonian Nisbet.

W 1982		Stairway to Heaven	D.Evans, A.Kay
W 1984	13 Jan	Valhalla	K.Schwartz, T.Groves

Another late recording, causing much disappointment amongst competing parties!

The second main wave of exploration opens with Graham Little.

W 1987	14 Feb	Menage a Trois	G.E.Little, D.Saddler, S.Visser

Direct Finish: R.Everett, A.Shand Feb 1996

W 1987	15 Feb	Journey to the East	G.E.Little
W 1987	15 Feb	Quickstep	G.E.Little
W 1986	17 Feb	Pas de Deux	G.E.Little, D.Saddler
W 1989	11 Mar	Carte Blanche	G.E.Little, L.MacDonald
W 1989	16 Mar	Splitting the Difference	C.S.Bonington and G.Little

Straightens out the kink in Slow March. Little declares the crag worked out. Now read on.

W 1993	28 Feb	Coup de Grace	A.Robertson, S.Richardson
W 1994	Jan	The Goatherd	K.J.Douglas, J.Dickson
W 1995	18 Feb	Femme Fatale	E.W.Brunskill, P.Greene, S.Archer
W 1995	16 Mar	Circean	E.W.Brunskill, P.Greene

Two good finds on the buttress left of Taxus.

W 1995	23 Dec	Misplaced	E.Kane, M.Boyle
W 1996	11 Feb	Bete Noire	S.Richardson, R.Everett

A hard 'warm-up' for The Screaming, climbing the impressive bulging wall right of Cirrus. Pitch 1 was climbed 27 Jan 1996 by S.Richardson, J.Currie.

W 1996	24 Feb	The Screaming	R.Everett, S.Richardson

Three axes rests were used on the final pitch. FFA (with a crucial *in situ* nut runner left by a previous party): M.Garthwaite, R.McAllister, Dec 1996.

W 1996	2 Mar	Spring Fever	G.E.Little, J.Lowther
W 1996	23 Nov	Jobseeker's Allowance	E.W.Brunskill, D.Crawford
W 1996	Dec	Pedant's Corner	A.Powell, R.Cross, S.Elworthy
W 1996	30 Dec	Can't, Won't, Shan't	M.Garthwaite, N.Gresham

CREAG COIRE AN DOTHAIDH

W 1976	25 Jan	Salamander Gully	K.V.Crocket, J.A.P.Hutchinson
W 1976	25 Jan	B.O.Buttress	C.J.Gilmore, C.D.Grant

Both sides of the hill receive a battering on the same day, with the Greenock Team in the NE Corrie. It would have been interesting to have met in the pub after, but it didn't happen!

W 1976	Feb	Fahrenheit 451	K.V.Crocket, I.Fulton

Noticed while climbing the previous month, the fine icefall was climbed *en route* to Taxus by the Icefall Finish, a possible 2nd ascent of the latter, finishing at sunset. The start of a good spell of weather and conditions.

W 1981	Jan	The Professorial Seat	Professor A.Morrison, N.Morrison

Neil Morrison name dropping again.

W 1982		Highway to Hell	A.Kay, J.Main

Right Branch: K.Schwartz, K.M.Edgar 3rd April 1996.

W 1982	22 Dec	The Flasher	N.Morrison
W 1982	22 Dec	Right Guard	N.Morrison, N.Claxton
W 1983	30 Jan	Centigrade	D.Baker, R.Howard

Summer ascent: J.Beaton, R.Carchrie, K.V.Crocket, A.Walker 15 Jul 1989

W 1985	16 Feb	The Firebird	K.V.Crocket, A.Walker
W 1985	16 Feb	Phoenix	K.V.Crocket, A.Walker

A series of easy and pleasant routes on the Coire an Dothaidh face.

W 1988	13 Mar	Lucifer Rising	K.V.Crocket, G.McEwan, A.Walker

The first of the harder buttress routes on this crag.

S 1989 29 Jun The Flasher Slab R.Reid and S.Richardson
  Probably climbed in 1936 by one T.Weir, who took the offer of half-price juvenile train tickets to climb two lines, including this and the line taken by B.O.Buttress. The fare, if you must know, was 2s 3d.
W 1994 16 Jan Beelzebub R.Everett, S.Richardson (AL)
  The hardest route on the crag.

BEINN DORAIN, CREAG AN SOCACH
S 1976 21 Aug Scorpion R.T.Richardson, A.Walker
  A surprisingly good line up the steep central slab.
W 1978 Second Coming I.Fulton, C.D.Grant
  The first winter route on this crag, though never properly recorded.
W 1980 21 Dec Kick Start N.Morrison, R.Stewart
W 1980 27 Dec School Daze D.Claxton, N.Morrison, R.Stewart
W 1987 29 Mar The Promised Land G.E.Little, D.Saddler
  Little takes the crag head-on and bags the first Grade VI. Direct variation (Deliverance): A.Powell, S.Elworthy 29 Jan 1995.
W 1987 13 Dec The Glass Bead Game R.Carchrie K.V.Crocket, R.Duncan, G.McEwan, A.Walker
  The line possibly approximates to a Very Difficult summer route climbed by D.Stewart in the 1950s.
W 1988 28 Jan Messiah G.E.Little, R.Reid
  The hardest route on the crag, involving some extremely thin mixed climbing.
W 1988 12 Feb False Rumour Gully G.E.Little, R.Reid
  Probably the first ascent, despite rumours.
W 1991 16 Jan The Prophet K.Howett, G.E.Little
W 1991 19 Jan The Sting K.Howett, G.E.Little (AL)
W 1992 15 Mar Antichrist R.Everett, S.Richardson (AL)
W 1994 13 Feb Days of Future Past G.E.Little, J.Lowther
W 1995 27 Dec To the Future C.Smith, S.Murray

BEINN UDLAIDH
W 1968 29 Dec Central Gully J.Buchanan, J.Forbes, G.Skelton
W 1969 30 Nov South Gully of The Black Wall R.McGowan, G.Skelton
W 1970 14 Nov Zigzag Gully A.Agnew, J.Jewel
W 1970 14 Nov Sunshine Gully E.Fowler, F.Jack, R.McGowan, G.Skelton
W 1972 Horny Ridge Ochils M.C.party
W 1976 4 Dec Ramshead Gully G.H.Caplan, I.D.Crofton
W 1977 16 Jan The Cramp I.Duckworth, G.Skelton
  'Geordie' Skelton suffers from cramp and is converted to wrist loops as he gracefully falls from his tools.
W 1978 Doctor's Dilemma I.Duckworth, M.Firth
  I'm sure it's mere coincidence, but the good Dr.Firth emigrates shortly afterwards to N.Z. The pace of exploration now speeds up as the secret gradually leaks, and coinciding with a good series of winters many good routes are done.
W 1978 30 Dec White Caterpillar G.Skelton, W.Woods
W 1979 Jan The Croc A.Barton, D.Evans, J.G.Fraser
W 1979 Quartzvein Scoop D.Evans, A.Gray, A.Shepherd
W 1979 27 Jan Sidestep N.Morrison, R.Stewart
  The young Neil Morrison begins poking around in the corrie.
W 1979 27 Jan Organ-Pipe Wall, The Smirk R.Duncan, J.G.Fraser
  The Smirk comes into condition after five lean years, as Duncan climbs both routes in one day. Good climbing, climaxing with an irritating smirk on Duncan's face.

W 1979	24 Feb	Junior's Jaunt	P.Bilsborough, I.Duckworth, N.Morrison, W.Woods
W 1979	20 Dec	Junior's Joke	N.Morrison, R.Stewart
W 1979	29 Dec	Land of Make Believe	N.Morrison, M.Orr
W 1979	29 Dec	Green Eyes	I.Duckworth, J.G.Fraser
W 1979	30 Dec	Junior's Jangle	J.G.Fraser, N.Morrison
W 1979		Hobo	I.Duckworth, G.Skelton
W 1980	Jan	Ramshead Buttress	I.Duckworth, J.G.Fraser
W 1980	Jan	Captain Hook	C.Calow, D.Cuthbertson

The first Grade V here by a young Cuthbertson.

| W 1980 | Jan | Quintet | I.Duckworth, J.G.Fraser, A.Pettit, W.Woods, R.Stewart |

Climbed on the Sunday after the above two routes.

| W 1980 | Jan | Cut-throat | R.Duncan, R.Young; C.Calow, D.Cuthbertson |

Also on the Sunday, with Duncan sneaking into the corrie early to poach the first ascent with Cubby's team fast on their heels.

| W 1980 | Feb | Ice Crew | I.Duckworth, N.Morrison |
| W 1982 | 1 Jan | Peter Pan Direct | D.Claxton, I.Duckworth, A.Kay, N.Morrison |

A more direct version of the earlier Peter Pan (climbed in 1979 by I.Duckworth and P.Bilsborough). These routes opened up the Black Wall, probably the show-piece of the corrie.

W 1986	Jan	Antiques' Roadshow	G.Allan, I.Taylor
W 1987	17 Jan	The Corner	H.Bennet, J.Bennet
W 1991	16 Feb	Hyde and Seek	S.Downie, G.Sczuca
W 1992	27 Dec	Suspended Animation	J.McLaughlin, J.Stevenson
W 1994	19 Feb	Taking the Bait	D.Musgrove, C.Ranner
W 1994	20 Feb	Tinkerbell	D.Musgrove, C.Ranner
W 1996	3 Apr	Hot Keks	K.Schwartz, K.M.Edgar

BEINN A' CHAISTEIL

W 1982	10 Jan	Jimmy Dewar's Icefall	T.McAuley, N.Muir
W 1983	20 Feb	Valkyrie, Berkshire Hunt	T.McAuley, D.Sanderson
W 1983	27 Mar	Benoovi Five	T.McAuley

BEINN DUBH

| W 1969 | Jan | Sickle Gully | R.Lambert, J.R.Mackenzie |

Climbed in summer conditions by A.Macdonald, J.R.Mackenzie 27 Nov 1971.

| S 1973 | 27 May | Amethyst Gully, Quartz Gully | J.R.Mackenzie |

BEN LUI AND BEINN CHUIRN

| W 1891 | Apr | Central Gully | W.W.Naismith, W.R.Lester, T.F.S.Campbell |

In descent. First ascent: A.E.Maylard, W.Brunskill, W.Douglas, J.Maclay Dec 1892.

| W 1986 | 22 Feb | Alchemist's Wall | S.Steer, M.Brydon, G.Lawton |

BEN CRUACHAN

| W 1970 | 11 Apr | Original Route | D.J.Bennet, E.I.Thompson |

Direct Start: C.J.Gilmore, C.D.Grant

W 1978	19 Feb	Central Grooves	I.Fulton, C.D.Grant
W 1990	24 Feb	Stonethrower's Buttress	S.Richardson, R.Everett (alts)
W 1990	4 Mar	Into the Fire	S.Richardson, R.Everett (alts)

Left-hand Finish: D.Ritchie, I.Stevenson 18th March 1995

| W 1994 | 15 Jan | Drumnadrochaid | D.Ritchie, D.Sinclair |
| W 1994 | 23 Jan | Gaoth Mhor | N.Marshall, D.Ritchie |

W 1994 13 Feb   Jamie's Lum   I.Blackwood, S.Kennedy, D.Ritchie
W 1996 24 Feb   Epona Gully   J.Andrew, A.P.Matthewson
W 1996 24 Feb   White Horse Grooves   J.Andrew, A.P.Matthewson

BEINN EUNAICH
S 1892 19 May   The Black Shoot   W.R.Lester, J.H.Gibson, W.W.Naismith,
                                               W.Douglas
     The fourth attempt by Lester to climb this herbivorous horror.
W 1900 30 Dec   The Black Shoot   H.Raeburn, A.M.MackayG.Sang
     Even Raeburn, who had made a summer ascent, reckoned it was better to climb the
     route in winter.
W 1927 31 Dec   Beaver Buttress   J.H.B.Bell, Corbett, Parry, Robinson
     Attracted by tales of vegetatious, slimy rock, the great Doktor Bell and team gnaw
     their way up the buttress.
W 1986 13 Feb   Eager Beaver   G.E.Little, D.Saddler

BEN LOMOND
W 1990   Lost in Snow   I.Taylor, J.Nairn
W 1991   Nov   Solo Buttress   E.Lynch, D.Gardner
W 1992   Zigzag   G.Dudley and party
W 1994 23 Jan   Lomond Delight   B.Swan, D.Ford, S.Donald
W 1994   Mar   Lomond Corner   I.Taylor, A.Robertson

BEN LAWERS AND THE TARMACHANS
W 1898 19 Feb   Arrow Chimney   H.Raeburn, H.G.S.Lawson
W 1898 30 Dec   Clark's Gully   J.G.Inglis, W.I.Clark
W 1902   6 Jan   Mackay's Gully   A.M.Mackay, S.A.Gillan, G.W.Young
     Yes. That Geoffrey Winthrop Young, making a rare appearance in Scotland.
W 1902   6 Jan   Great Gully, Creag na   A.M.Mackay, S.A.Gillan, G.W.Young
                 Caillich
     Partially climbed by Raeburn and Lawson in Feb 1898, being forced out left on the
     top section. The first ascent party climbed it as their second route of the day,
     finishing in good traditional style (i.e.darkness).
W 1903   4 Jan   Great Gully Arete   C.W.Walker, H.Walker, H.Raeburn
     An unstoppable team, with Raeburn making up for an earlier incomplete ascent of
     the gully.
W 1986 23 Feb   Maxwell's Hammer   R.Reid, D.Wastell
W 1986   2 Mar   The Dambusters   A.Fraser, G.Leslie
W 1987   Feb   Tote Gully   S.Steer, M.Bryden
W 1988   6 Feb   Toxophily   G.E.Little, D.Johnson
W 1989   Mar   Turf Accountant   M.Bryden, S.Steer
W 1992   4 Apr   Balcony Rib, Aisle Gully   G.E.Little
W 1992   4 Apr   Back and Front Stalls Gullies G.E.Little
     A standard G.E.Little approach to a crag. Some routes had been climbed earlier.
W 1993 14 Nov   Felinity   G.E.Little
W 1993 27 Nov   Cool for Cats   G.E.Little, C.Schaschke
W 1994 23 Jan   Lozenge Buttress   M.Shaw, A.Keith
W 1994 19 Mar   Cataract   C.Bonington, G.E.Little
W 1996   4 Feb   Catalyst   G.E.Little, K.Howett
W 1996 22 Dec   Witch's Brew   K.V.Cocket, R.T.Richardson
W 1996 28 Dec   Spaewife, Beldame Buttress   K.V.Crocket, R.T.Richardson
W 1997   3 Jan   Pensioner's Buttress   K.V.Crocket, I.H.M.Smart
W 1997   5 Jan   Turf Going, Knucklebuster   K.V.Crocket, B.Dullea
                 Corner

MISCELLANEOUS ROUTES

W 1977	16 Jan	Lumberjack's Fall	C.Blyth, V.Hammond, R.Wilson
S 1984	24 Aug	Three Steps to Heaven	J.Divall, R.Cluer, B.Smith
W 1985	19 Jan	Fyne Falls	W.Hood, R.Turner
W 1986		Eas Ruaridh	H.Henderson, G.Ross

Index of Routes

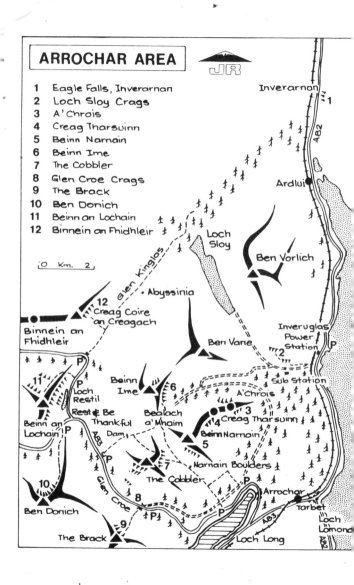

ARROCHAR AREA

1 Eagle Falls, Inverarnan
2 Loch Sloy Crags
3 A'Chrois
4 Creag Tharsuinn
5 Beinn Narnain
6 Beinn Ime
7 The Cobbler
8 Glen Croe Crags
9 The Brack
10 Ben Donich
11 Beinn an Lochain
12 Binnein an Fhidhleir

0 Km. 2

Inverarnan

A82

Ardlui

Glen Kinglos

Loch Sloy

Ben Vorlich

12
Creag Coire
an Creagach

Binnein an
Fhidhleir

Abyssinia

Ben Vane

Inveruglas
Power
Station

P

11
Loch
Restil

Beinn
Ime

6

Sub Station

A'Chrois

Beinn an
Lochain

Rest & Be
Thankful

Bealoch
a'Mhaim

4 Creag Tharsuinn

3

Dam

Beinn Narnain

5

Narnain Boulders

Glen Croe

7

The Cobbler

P

Arrochar

Tarbet

10

Ben Donich

8

P

A83

Loch
Lomond

9

The Brack

Loch Long